The Essentials of Adolescent Literacy

Integrating Evidence-Based Reading and Writing Instruction in Grades 5–12

by

Joan Sedita, M.Ed.

Baltimore • London • Sydney

Paul H. Brookes Publishing Co.
Post Office Box 10624
Baltimore, Maryland 21285-0624
USA
www.brookespublishing.com

Typeset by Absolute Service, Inc., Dover, Delaware.
Manufactured in the United States of America by Integrated Books International, Inc., Dulles, Virginia.

Library of Congress Cataloging-in-Publication Data

Names: Sedita, Joan, 1953- author
Title: The essentials of adolescent literacy: integrating evidence-based reading and writing instruction in grades 5–12 / by Joan Sedita, M.Ed.
Description: Baltimore: Paul H. Brookes Publishing Co., [2026] | Includes bibliographical references and index.
Identifiers: LCCN 2025043555 (print) | LCCN 2025043556 (ebook) | ISBN 9781681258898 paperback | ISBN 9781681258904 epub | ISBN 9781681258911 pdf
Subjects: LCSH: Reading comprehension | Literacy | Education, Secondary |BISAC: EDUCATION / General | LANGUAGE ARTS & DISCIPLINES / Literacy
Classification: LCC LB1050.45 .S43 2026 (print) | LCC LB1050.45 (ebook) |DDC 372.47—dc23/eng/20260127
LC record available at https://lccn.loc.gov/2025043555
LC ebook record available at https://lccn.loc.gov/2025043556

British Library Cataloguing in Publication data are available from the British Library.

2029 2028 2027 2026

10 9 8 7 6 5

Contents

About the Downloads

Purchasers of this book may download and/or print the teacher and student resources for educational use.

To access the materials that come with this book:

1. Go to the Brookes Download Hub: http://downloads.brookespublishing.com
2. Register to create an account (or log in with an existing account).
3. Click Redeem Code and enter the code found on the inside cover of this book.

Downloadable Material (also available at ends of relevant chapters):

Chapter 1
The Writing Rope *(Figure 1.3)*

Chapter 2
Levels of Adolescent Literacy Instruction *(Table 2.1)*

Chapter 3
Four-Square Template
Frayer Template
Two-Column Template
Word Knowledge Checklist *(Figure 3.4)*

Chapter 4
Examples of Text-Dependent Questions *(Figure 4.15)*
How to Write a Summary
Question Terms *(Figure 4.13)*
Summary Template *(Figure 4.11)*
Supporting Comprehension *(Figure 4.14)*
Two-Column Notes *(Figure 4.6)*

Chapter 5
Argument Writing Components *(Figure 5.2)*
Common Patterns of Organization *(Figure 5.3)*
Kernel Sentence Expansion *(Figure 5.9)*
Questions to Analyze Text Structure
Three Types of Text *(Figure 5.1)*
Transition Words and Phrases *(Figure 5.4)*

Chapter 6
Focus Areas for Using Mentor Text *(Table 6.2)*
Questions to Support Each Writing Process Stage

About the Author

Joan Sedita, M.Ed., has been in the literacy education field for more than 45 years. She began her career at the Landmark School in Massachusetts for students with reading and learning disabilities, where she worked from 1975 to 1998 as a teacher and administrator. Joan was Founder and Director of the Landmark College Preparation Program and the Landmark Outreach Training Program. While at the Landmark School, she also was a member of a team that conducted psychoeducational evaluations at Boston Children's Hospital. From 1998 to 2007, as Founder of Sedita Learning Strategies, Joan trained educators and consulted with schools and literacy organizations throughout the country. During this time, she was Lead Developer and Trainer for the Massachusetts Reading First initiative and Consultant to the state's Secondary Reading initiative. Joan also was a national author and trainer for *LETRS: Language Essentials for Teachers of Reading and Spelling,* published by Voyager Sopris Learning. She was a member of the Educational Testing Service Praxis National Reading Advisory Committee and a board member of Learning Disabilities Worldwide.

In 2007, Joan founded Keys to Literacy, a literacy professional learning company that develops, publishes, and delivers reading and writing professional development to educators across the country, as well as literacy planning and consulting services to districts and state departments of education. She continues to consult with school districts and state departments of education, presents at national and state literacy conferences, and develops content for literacy trainings, books, and online courses.

Joan developed *The Writing Rope®* framework in 2018 and has authored numerous books, book chapters, and articles related to literacy instruction. Her earlier books include *The Landmark Study Skills Guide* (1989), *Writing: A Road to Reading Comprehension* (2004), and three guides for the Kurzweil text-to-speech software to support reading and study skills: *Kurzweil 3000 Study Skills Guide* (1999), *Active Learning and Study Strategies* (2003), and *Guide to Effective Vocabulary Instruction* (2004). In 2022, Joan authored *The Writing Rope: A Framework for Explicit Writing Instruction in All Subjects* (Paul H. Brookes Publishing Co.). She has authored multiple professional development programs that include books, online courses, and training materials, including these titles published by Keys to Literacy: *Keys to Beginning Reading, Keys to Adolescent Literacy, The Key Comprehension Routine, The Key Vocabulary Routine, Keys to Content Writing,* and *Keys to Early Writing.*

Joan received her B.A. from Boston College and her M.Ed. in reading from Harvard University.

Foreword

In an ever-evolving world, literacy stands as a cornerstone of personal and academic success, particularly during the critical adolescent years. For example, the inability to read and gain meaning from text can have negative effects on students' course performance and, in turn, their ability to earn credits and graduate. Students who lack reading and writing proficiency by fourth grade are more likely than their proficient peers to drop out before completing high school. These consequences are correlated with negative outcomes in adulthood, including lower earnings and higher rates of physical and mental health problems. Thus, it is critical that we continue to address literacy as a high priority issue, even as students reach the secondary grades. However, it is important to recognize that the transition from childhood to adolescence is marked by profound changes, not just physically and emotionally, but also in the way young individuals engage with text and develop their literacy skills. Reaching our shared goal of literacy success for all adolescents is not an easy endeavor, but books like this one can help. *The Essentials of Adolescent Literacy* serves as a vital resource for educators, parents, and policymakers dedicated to fostering a culture of literacy that meets the diverse needs of adolescents. While educators and parents have many research-based resources to guide decision-making, there are few that provide the science of reading for students after Grade 4.

This book is rooted in the understanding that literacy is not merely about reading and writing; it encompasses critical thinking, comprehension, and the ability to communicate effectively across various platforms. Adolescents face unique challenges, including varying levels of motivation, engagement, and access to resources. As such, it is imperative that we equip them with the tools and strategies necessary to navigate these challenges and thrive in their academic journeys.

The insights and strategies presented in this book are drawn from extensive research and best practices in the field of literacy education providing a comprehensive framework that addresses the complexities of adolescent literacy. It is common for books at the secondary level to focus on reading *or* writing, despite our knowledge that reading and writing go hand in hand. Therefore, something that sets *The Essentials of Adolescent Literacy* apart is the emphasis throughout on the integration of reading and writing. Furthermore, you might hear people use the terms content-area and disciplinary literacy. What do these terms mean? What is the difference? This book addresses this issue with a review of content-area and disciplinary literacy, and the critical need to integrate content-area literacy into content-area instruction. This is crucial considering *all* students spend a majority of their instructional day in the content-area setting (e.g., science, history), including students with reading difficulties and disabilities. Accordingly, the book provides information on how to support adolescents with literacy difficulties in the general education classroom and how to provide data-driven reading intervention for students who require this type of support. Chapters emphasize the importance of culturally responsive teaching and provide essential information about understanding adolescent literacy within a framework of the significant role of motivation and engagement, including the integration of how collaborative grouping structures promote both engagement and shared learning. Recognizing that educators are increasingly aware of the powerful use of technology to meet the needs of adolescent learners, chapters also emphasize the importance of technology in the classroom. All of these features and more are represented in this book.

The Essentials of Adolescent Literacy serves as an essential, practical guide for fostering a robust literacy environment that not only enhances academic achievement but also empowers adolescents to become lifelong learners and informed citizens. With this book by our side, we are able to commit to nurturing the literacy skills of our youth, ensuring that they are well equipped to face the future with confidence and competence.

Sharon Vaughn, Ph.D., and Jade Wexler, Ph.D.

Acknowledgments

I began my career in education in 1975 as a summer tutor for teenagers with dyslexia and reading disabilities at the Landmark School in Massachusetts. One of my first students was Julie, a bright 14-year-old who could comprehend complex texts when they were read aloud but struggled to decode written words. She also had difficulty writing complete sentences. After 6 weeks of tutoring Julie for 2 hours each day, using explicit instruction to teach foundational reading and writing skills, her reading level improved from third to fifth grade. She was finally able to read books on her own and navigate practical texts such as restaurant menus and bus schedules. She even wrote a letter to her parents. Most important, after years of being told she would never learn to read, Julie's confidence soared. That experience sparked my lifelong passion for teaching literacy.

Over the decades I've spent in the literacy field, I have worked with students and the teachers who support them, kept up with evolving research, and developed teacher training courses for all grade levels. But my greatest passion remains helping adolescent learners—especially those who struggle with reading and writing.

This book represents the culmination of a 5-decade journey to improve literacy for all students, with a particular focus on those in Grades 5 through 12. I am deeply grateful to the many adolescent learners I had the privilege to teach—students who played a vital role in helping me develop effective approaches to teaching reading and writing instruction. I also extend my thanks to the thousands of educators who have offered insightful feedback on the professional development courses and books I have authored. My appreciation goes as well to the dedicated literacy consultants at Keys to Literacy, who have generously shared their expertise and insights since I founded the organization in 2007. Most of all, I am especially thankful to my husband, Joe DelGuidice, who introduced me to both teaching and Landmark School—an introduction that shaped the course of my professional life.

Introduction

Literacy skills are essential for success in school, in postsecondary education, in the workforce, and to communicate with others in our personal lives. However, many students leave the elementary grades without grade-level reading and writing skills. And there is no guarantee that those who have these skills will continue to develop the more challenging content and disciplinary literacy skills needed to read, write, and participate in discussion to learn in all subjects in middle and high school.

Furthermore, although significant school district and statewide initiatives were launched between 2015 and 2025 to address student literacy achievement, most of these initiatives have focused on beginning reading instruction in the elementary grades. Whereas there is a significant research base about effective literacy instruction for adolescents, including writing, minimal federal, state, and local initiatives have focused on Grades 5–12 in terms of funding, legislation, pre-service adolescent literacy courses in universities, and district- or school-based professional development.

This book was written for educators of students in Grades 5–12, including content teachers, intervention educators, and administrators who seek to provide effective literacy instruction in content classrooms as well as intervention settings. It includes evidence-based instructional suggestions for teaching vocabulary, comprehension, text structure, writing, discussion skills, and advanced word study to read unfamiliar multisyllabic words often encountered in different subject areas.

ABOUT THIS BOOK

The content of this book is organized as follows.

Section I: Introduction to Adolescent Literacy

This section provides background knowledge about how students acquire literacy skills across all grades and how adolescent literacy instruction for Grades 5–12 is different from elementary literacy instruction.

Chapter 1, "Literacy Basics," explains the Science of Reading and literacy frameworks including the Simple View of Reading (Gough & Tunmer, 1986), the Reading Rope (Scarborough, 2001), and The Writing Rope® (Sedita, 2019). The five components of reading are summarized, along with how the emphasis for teaching these components shifts as students move into Grade 5. Language components, principles of effective literacy instruction, and the importance of integrating reading and writing instruction for all grades are included.

Chapter 2, "What Is Adolescent Literacy?" explains why all teachers need to play a role in providing reading and writing instruction because literacy is the gatekeeper to learning in any subject. Research about effective adolescent literacy instruction is introduced, and the difference between content literacy and disciplinary literacy is explained along with the important role content teachers play.

Section II: Literacy Instruction

This section provides practical, evidence-based suggestions for teaching literacy skills in all subjects. The chapters are organized by literacy topics as follows.

Chapter 3, "Vocabulary Instruction," explains the role of academic vocabulary in reading comprehension and content learning and offers suggestions for previewing unfamiliar words, selecting and teaching targeted words in depth, planning activities to make connections among words, using text context and knowledge of word parts to determine word meanings, and fostering word consciousness.

Chapter 4, "Comprehension Instruction," describes factors that contribute to reading comprehension and instructional suggestions for text analysis and close reading, metacognition, and inferencing. Suggestions for teaching comprehension strategies are also offered, including using Top-Down Topic Webs and Two-Column Note graphic organizers, summarizing, and generating and answering questions.

Chapter 5, "Teaching Text Structure," explains the role that awareness of text structure plays in supporting reading comprehension and writing. Instructional suggestions are provided for several levels of text structure, including the three types of text (informational, argument, narrative), paragraph structure, patterns of organization, transition words and phrases, and complex sentences.

Chapter 6, "Writing Instruction," highlights the shift from learning to write in elementary grades to using writing to learn in Grades 5–12. The multiple writing skills and strategies needed for proficient writing are presented as part of The Writing Rope framework. The role of content teachers in developing student writing ability is stressed, and suggestions for using quick writes and responses to writing prompts based on content texts are offered. Suggestions for strategies to teach students that support the stages of the writing process (*Think, Plan, Write, Revise*) are also offered.

Chapter 7, "Supporting Learning Through Discussion," highlights the value of using discussion to support text comprehension and content learning. Suggestions for planning and facilitating different discussion formats are provided, including teacher and student "moves" that are part of the Accountable Talk framework.

Chapter 8, "Advanced Word Study and Fluency," provides an overview of phonics instruction and the advanced word study skills older students need to read and spell academic, multisyllabic words. Fluency is defined along with an explanation of how a lack of fluency contributes to reading difficulty for some older students.

Section III: Supporting Adolescents With Literacy Difficulties

This section focuses on supporting adolescents who have difficulty with literacy skills.

Chapter 9, "Adolescent Learners With Literacy Difficulties," explains the multiple reasons why some students struggle with reading and writing, including dyslexia and executive function deficits, and discusses how intervention needs to be based on individual student needs. The needs of older English learners related to developing literacy skills are addressed. Suggestions for evidence-based intervention instruction are provided that address writing, vocabulary, comprehension, phonics, and fluency as part of an MTSS (multi-tiered system of support) framework.

Chapter 10, "Data-Driven Reading Intervention," highlights the important role that assessment plays in informing intervention instruction decisions. The four types of assessment are explained (screening, diagnostic, progress monitoring, summative) and a secondary instruction model and secondary reading assessment plan are introduced. Suggestions for analyzing assessment data are also offered.

Questions for reflection are included at the end of each chapter, and an end-of-book piece titled, "Integrating Literacy Instruction in All Subjects," is designed to help content teachers incorporate the instructional practices into content teaching. In addition, many reproducible student and teacher resources included throughout the chapters may also be accessed through the Brookes Download Hub.

I

Introduction to Adolescent Literacy

1

Literacy Basics

It is important for educators who work with adolescent learners to understand how reading and writing ability develops across elementary and secondary grades. This chapter provides an overview of seminal research in literacy and the Science of Reading and how it can be used to better understand the instructional needs of both proficient readers and those who have weaknesses. Components of reading and language are introduced and explained, as well as general principles for effective instruction.

THE SCIENCE OF READING

The Science of Reading (SOR) refers to a comprehensive body of scientific knowledge and research from the fields of education, cognitive psychology, developmental psychology, and neuroscience that explains how individuals learn how to read and what are the best practices for reading instruction (Petscher et al., 2020; Seidenberg et al., 2020; The Reading League, n.d.). Research related to writing is also addressed in SOR. This research has been conducted over the last five decades across the world, and it is derived from thousands of studies conducted in multiple languages. Educators should keep in mind that SOR is not a curriculum, program, or a single component of literacy instruction such as phonics or comprehension.

Several frameworks that contribute to the understanding of the competencies and skills students need to develop to be proficient readers and writers are shared below: the Simple View of Reading (Gough & Tunmer, 1986), the Reading Rope (Scarborough, 2001), The Writing Rope (Sedita, 2019), and the five components of literacy instruction identified by the National Reading Panel (2000).

The Simple View of Reading

The Simple View of Reading (Gough & Tunmer, 1986), shown in Figure 1.1, proposes that reading comprehension cannot occur unless students are proficient with both word recognition skills and language comprehension. Automatic word recognition, also described as decoding, leads to fluent reading. Language comprehension includes having sufficient vocabulary knowledge and syntactic awareness (an understanding of English grammar) to comprehend while listening. If adolescent learners have not developed sufficient word recognition skills and language processes by Grade 5, they will most likely have difficulty making meaning while reading.

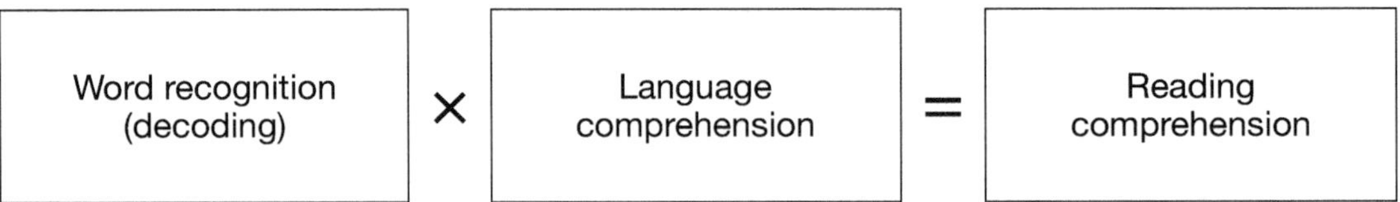

Figure 1.1. The Simple View of Reading. (Gough, P. B., & Tunmer, W. E. , Decoding, reading, and reading disability. *Remedial and Special Education, 7*[1], 6–10. Copyright © 1986 by Sage Publications. Reprinted by Permission of Sage Publications.)

Note that the Simple View is depicted as a formula where the two sides are not added together to predict reading comprehension. Rather, they are multiplied, with a total score of 1 predicting highly proficient reading comprehension, and a score of 0 meaning no comprehension ability. Each side has a maximum score of 1. Using the formula, if a student has strong word recognition skills (1) and strong language comprehension (1), it can be predicted that the student will have proficient reading comprehension. However, if a student has no word recognition skills (0) and strong language comprehension (1), the total score is 0, and it can be predicted that the student will not comprehend while reading.

Types of Readers: Four Quadrants

Using the Simple View as a framework, students can be grouped into four categories of readers (Cain, 2016; Catts et al., 2006) shown in the four quadrants in Figure 1.2: proficient readers, weak readers, readers with weak word recognition, and readers with weak comprehension.

Proficient Readers These students have strong word recognition and language comprehension. They typically have at or above grade-level reading ability. Content literacy instruction and regular reading of grade-level text are sufficient for these students to maintain proficient reading ability.

Weak Readers These are students who have difficulty with both word recognition and language comprehension. They typically benefit from supplemental instruction in phonics and advanced word study, fluency, vocabulary, and comprehension.

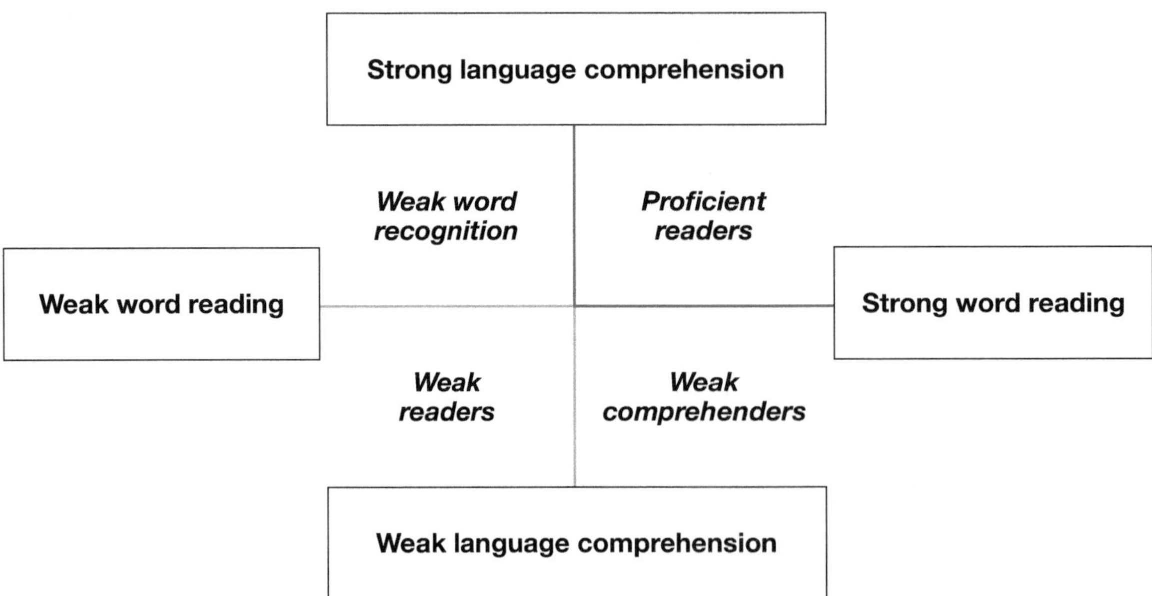

Figure 1.2. Four quadrants showing different categories of readers. (*Sources:* Cain, 2016; Catts et al., 2006.)

Readers With Weak Word Recognition These students have strong language comprehension but weak word recognition skills. Decoding difficulties interfere with their reading comprehension, which would otherwise be strong. These students benefit from supplemental instruction that focuses on phonics, advanced word study, and fluency. It is common for younger elementary students in this category to become weak readers if they do not receive intervention. Vocabulary and comprehension are affected over time because these students are not regularly reading grade-level text, which provides the exposure to academic vocabulary, complex sentences, and content knowledge that is important for reading in Grade 5 and beyond.

Weak Comprehenders These students have strong word recognition skills but weak language comprehension. They are sometimes called *word callers* because they can decode words but cannot make meaning from the words or sentences. They benefit from supplemental instruction focused on vocabulary and comprehension.

The Reading Rope

Scarborough (2001) developed a model of reading that depicts the multiple skills required to successfully read as strands in a rope. Scarborough's model groups four language comprehension components and three word recognition components into two sections listed below.

- Language Comprehension strands include Background Knowledge (facts, concepts, etc.), Vocabulary (breadth, precision, links, etc.), Language Structures (syntax, semantics, etc.), Verbal Reasoning (inference, metaphor, etc.), and Literacy Knowledge (print concepts, genres, etc.).
- Word Recognition strands include Phonological Awareness (syllables, phonemes, etc.), Decoding (alphabetical principle, spelling-sound correspondences), and Sight Recognition (of familiar words).

These seven components are represented as strands in a rope. As students become increasingly more strategic and automatic with the reading skills associated with these components, these strands become more tightly woven together, leading to proficient, fluent reading. When students have deficits in any of the strands, skilled reading is impeded.

The Writing Rope

The Writing Rope (Sedita, 2019) is an instructional framework for teaching writing across all grades. The framework, shown in Figure 1.3, identifies the following five components of writing skills and strategies that students must learn to become skilled writers, represented as strands in a rope:

- Critical Thinking: Generate ideas; gather information; apply the writing process.
- Syntax: Write sophisticated, elaborated sentences.
- Text Structure: Apply knowledge of paragraph and longer text structures; incorporate patterns of organization and related transitions.
- Writing Craft: Consider the task, audience, and purpose; incorporate writing craft techniques when writing.
- Transcription: Spell and handwrite or keyboard at an automatic level.

During the elementary grades, students must learn a significant number of skills, strategies, and techniques within each of the strands. As they move into Grade 5 and beyond, they integrate these skills to produce writing pieces that effectively convey what they want to communicate, much like weaving together strands in a rope.

A reproducible copy of The Writing Rope is included with the downloadable resources for this chapter. (See About the Downloads in the front of this book for directions on how to access the content on the Brookes Download Hub.)

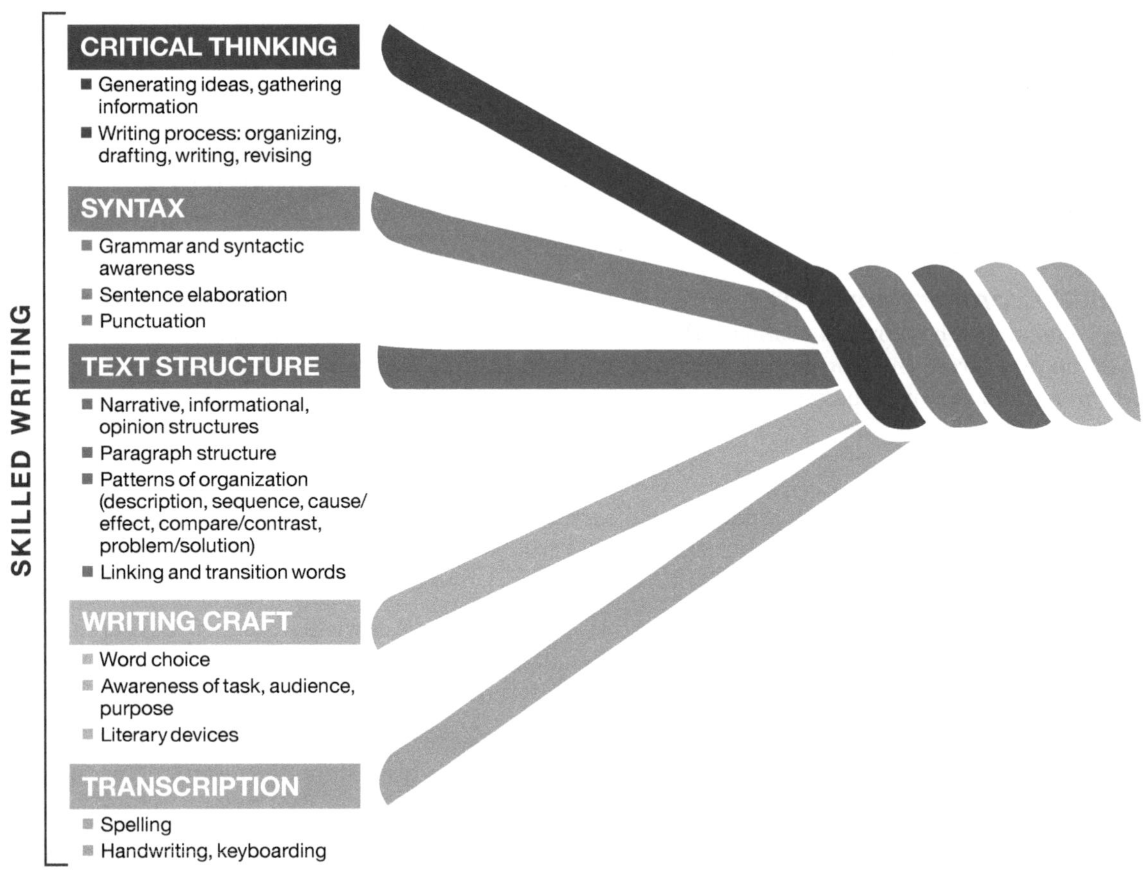

Figure 1.3. The Writing Rope®. *Full-color version available on the Brookes Download Hub.* (From *The Writing Rope®: The strands that are woven into skilled writing* [online article]. Keys to Literacy; reprinted by permission. © 2019 by Joan Sedita. All rights reserved.)

THE FIVE COMPONENTS OF READING

The National Reading Panel (2000) identified five components of reading instruction that are essential to learning to read, described in Figure 1.4. They are sometimes referred to as the five pillars of reading. *Phonemic awareness, phonics,* and *fluency* are associated with word-reading skills. *Vocabulary* and *comprehension* are associated with making meaning when reading.

As students progress from kindergarten through Grade 12, the focus for teaching the reading components changes. Instruction for the foundational skills of phonemic awareness and phonics is emphasized in the early grades, with phonics instruction shifting to advanced word study in Grades 4 and 5 as students learn to read and spell multisyllabic words derived from Latin and Greek. Students continue to develop text reading fluency across all elementary grades, with a benchmark goal of at least 150 words correct per minute (WCPM) after Grade 6. Vocabulary development and the ability to apply comprehension strategies to increasingly complex text should be a focus across all grades. Instruction in Grades 5–12 is organized into content literacy for vocabulary, comprehension, and writing to support learning that is taught in all subjects, and intervention instruction for adolescent struggling readers to fill in gaps they may have in any component of reading.

LANGUAGE COMPONENTS

When students learn a language, they are learning to navigate an existing set of conventions that are shared by other users of the language. There are seven English language components that contribute

The Five Components of Reading

- **Phonemic awareness** is the understanding that words are made up of separate sounds. To learn to read, students must understand how the sounds in words work, including the ability to separate and manipulate individual sounds in spoken words.
- **Phonics** refers to an understanding of the relationship between the letters of written language and the individual sounds of spoken language, also known as the alphabetic principle. It includes the use of letter combinations and patterns, syllable types, and word analysis skills to read and spell words.
- **Fluency** refers to the ability to read text accurately, quickly, and automatically, with proper expression (prosody) and understanding.
- **Vocabulary** refers to the ability to understand the meanings of words and how they are used in different contexts.
- **Reading comprehension** is the ability to derive meaning based on the information in the text in combination with the reader's own knowledge. Comprehension improves when students are metacognitive, aware of text structure, and use reading comprehension strategies.

Figure 1.4. The five components of reading. (*Source:* The National Reading Panel, 2000.)

to speaking, listening, reading, and writing: *phonology, orthography, morphology, semantics, syntax, discourse,* and *pragmatics,* defined as follows:

- *Phonology* is the sound system and includes awareness of speech sounds used in spoken English. Students must identify, segment, and blend sounds to read and spell words.
- *Orthography* is the spelling system. Students must learn sound-letter correspondences, common English spelling conventions and rules, and awareness of how morphology contributes to spelling.
- *Morphology* is the system of units of meaning in words. Recognition of prefixes, suffixes, and roots helps students read and spell multisyllabic words and determine the meaning of unfamiliar words.
- *Semantics* is knowledge of word meanings and relationships. Students must continually learn new words because vocabulary knowledge is highly related to reading comprehension and overall academic success.
- *Syntax* is the system of rules of English grammar and includes awareness of permissible word order in sentences. Students must develop syntactic awareness to support comprehension of long, complex sentences and to write high-quality, elaborated sentences.
- *Discourse* is the result of the ability to combine sentences to communicate ideas. Students need strong discourse ability to comprehend when reading and listening and to organize their writing pieces.
- *Pragmatics* is related to the social rules of language.

Note that phonology, orthography, and morphology are components of language that play an important role in learning foundational reading skills in elementary grades.

To deliver high-quality literacy instruction based in SOR, teachers also need a strong understanding of effective teaching principles, discussed in the next section.

PRINCIPLES OF EFFECTIVE TEACHING

Several teaching principles enable teachers to accommodate a wide variety of learning styles and student needs when teaching literacy skills:

1. Provide explicit, systematic instruction (Archer & Hughes, 2010).
2. Use a Gradual Release of Responsibility model (Pearson & Gallagher, 1983).
3. Provide models and use think-aloud.
4. Differentiate instruction and provide scaffolds.
5. Strive for automaticity through practice and review.

6. Provide data-driven instruction.
7. Provide culturally responsive literacy instruction.

These principles are referenced throughout this book. The sections that follow provide more information about each.

Provide Explicit, Systematic Instruction

As described by Archer and Hughes (2010), *explicit instruction* is a structured approach that guides students through the learning process by providing a clear explanation of a skill, modeling and demonstrating how it is applied using think-aloud, and providing time for guided practice with feedback. *Systematic instruction* refers to a planned and logical sequence of teaching, proceeding in small steps and checking for student understanding before moving to the next step. Teachers should follow a scope and sequence based on a logical order of reading and writing skills, progressing from basic to more complex. Effective explicit instruction teaches prerequisite skills needed to learn new skills.

Use a Gradual Release of Responsibility Model

This model (Pearson & Gallagher, 1983) gradually releases responsibility to students for independently using a skill or strategy. At the first instructional stage (I do it), the teacher presents a skill to students and uses modeling and think-aloud. At the second stage (We do it), students practice the skill as a whole group or in small groups. The teacher guides this practice and provides corrective feedback to students. At the last stage (You do it), students practice the skill independently. Students require different amounts of practice and degrees of support to reach independent use.

Provide Models and Use Think-Aloud

Teachers demonstrate how to perform a literacy task or skill, along with an explanation of what is being done, before expecting students to do it on their own. Modeling and thinking aloud lets students see and hear how to apply the skill or complete the task.

Differentiate Instruction and Provide Scaffolds

Differentiated instruction entails designing instruction to suit individual student needs rather than using a standardized approach to instruction that assumes all students will learn the same way. *Scaffolding* is a hallmark of differentiated instruction. Scaffolding is assistance offered by a teacher to support learning a skill that a student is initially unable to grasp independently, and then removing the assistance once the skill is learned. There are several types of scaffolds: teacher scaffolding, content scaffolding, task scaffolding, and material scaffolding.

Strive for Automaticity Through Practice and Review

When students learn a skill at an automatic (mastery) level, they have learned it so thoroughly they can use it with little or no conscious attention. Decoding and spelling skills, in particular, must become fluent and automatic to enable students to focus on comprehension while reading and composing while writing. Significant guided practice, repetition, and spiraling back to review previous skills are critical to achieving automaticity.

Provide Data-Driven Instruction

Teachers use formal and informal assessment data to inform instructional decisions. It is important to monitor progress on a frequent basis to determine which students are reaching benchmark goals for literacy skills and which students are not. Teachers use data to determine which skills need more explicit instruction and practice, how to group students for instruction, and which students may need supplemental intervention instruction beyond what is provided to all students.

Provide Culturally Responsive Literacy Instruction

Many classrooms include students who are racially, ethnically, culturally, and linguistically diverse. Culturally responsive teaching is a pedagogy that recognizes the importance of meeting students where they are culturally and linguistically. It puts students at the center of instruction that validates and affirms their identities, and it gives students from historically marginalized communities an equitable education experience. When culturally responsive educators validate and affirm students and bring them where they need to be academically, students are more likely to feel recognized, valued for their contributions, and eager to learn (Hollie, 2017). When teaching literacy skills, teachers should communicate high expectations for all students, use books that enable students to see themselves, and view linguistically and dialect differences positively.

INTEGRATING READING AND WRITING INSTRUCTION

There are significant benefits to teaching reading and writing in a connected way. They are built on the same foundation of oral language and share cognitive processes. Although reading is a receptive use of language and writing is a generative use, they are closely aligned and tap into similar knowledge, skills, and strategies. A number of instructional recommendations shared in this book can be used to support both reading and writing.

Too often, school curricula address reading and writing separately, taught in different lessons, but students benefit from instruction that integrates the two. Given the overlap in skills and strategies that support both reading comprehension and writing, teaching them together is more efficient and supports content learning.

Reading supports writing. When teachers help students analyze and attend to the features of text they are reading, it helps students write similar types of text. Reading supports knowledge of text structure, grammar, syntactic awareness, spelling, and use of literary devices.

Writing supports reading. Writing about text enhances reading abilities, including reading comprehension. Writers gain insight about reading by creating their own texts, leading to better comprehension of texts produced by others.

Steve Graham, writing research expert, notes the following about the value of integrating reading and writing (2020):

> Despite the many contributions of science to the study of literacy, I contend that the sciences of reading and writing are too narrowly focused on how to teach either reading or writing and not focused enough on how these two skills can be used to support each other. (p. S35).
>
> Although reading and writing can occur as a relatively solitary act, they can also be viewed as a collaborative act, in which students read and write together using print and digital tools. (p. S41)
>
> Available theory and evidence justify the use of writing and writing instruction as a means for improving students' reading and vice versa. (p. S42)

Teachers can integrate reading and writing instruction by using models of subject-area text and by using writing to learn. Connecting reading and writing this way also fulfills state content standards for English language arts.

Use Models of Subject-Area Text

An important way that students develop writing skills is to emulate others. Teachers can use mentor text (also called written exemplars) to show students what strong writing looks like in a subject area so they can imitate the style, language, and structure in their own writing (Sedita, 2023). For example:

- Teachers can closely read and analyze with students sentences from content classroom text, focusing on the way language is used, including the vocabulary and grammatical structure. This in turn helps students write longer, more complex sentences about that subject that include varied and precise vocabulary.
- Teachers can help students analyze the techniques and text structures employed by authors of discipline-specific text, such as a science lab report, a comparison of two primary sources in history, an example of personification or use of dialogue in a literary work, or a mathematical proof. Teachers can then help students apply similar techniques and text structures to their own content-specific writing.

Use Writing to Learn

Writing is an effective tool for enhancing students' learning of content material for all subject areas (Graham & Perin, 2007; Graham et al., 2015, 2020). This is because students engage in critical thinking as they use writing to communicate ideas and information, especially when that writing is based on sources. When students write about what they are reading and learning, they are *thinking on paper* (Sedita, 2020d). Writing helps them organize, clarify, and understand what they are reading. It also helps them engage with the information by extending their thinking and building relationships between the information and their background knowledge. Writing from sources includes writing assignments such as extended research reports, journal responses based on reactions to text, and written responses to prompts that require students to gather relevant information from one or more sources.

Research supports writing about text and other sources to develop comprehension and writing skills (Biancarosa & Snow, 2006; Graham & Hebert, 2010; Graham & Perin, 2007). Writing in various ways about text improves reading comprehension and learning better than reading alone, reading and rereading, or reading and discussing (Graham & Hebert, 2010). Research also finds that students' comprehension of science, social studies, and language arts texts improve when they write about what they read, including writing personal reactions, analyzing and interpreting the text, writing summaries and notes, and answering and creating questions about text in writing (Graham & Hebert, 2010; Graham et al., 2020).

Address State English Language Arts Standards

Common Core State Standards (National Governors Association Center for Best Practices & Council of Chief State School Officers [NGA/CCSSO], 2010) and similar literacy standards adopted by many states expect students to combine reading and writing for various purposes. Consider how reading and writing are integrated into the requirements for the following Common Core anchor standards (NGA/CCSSO, 2010).

- **Reading #1:** Read closely to determine what the text says explicitly and make logical inferences from it; cite specific textual evidence when writing or speaking and writing to support conclusions drawn from the text.
- **Reading #2:** Determine central ideas or themes of a text and analyze their development; summarize the key supporting ideas and details.
- **Reading #5:** Analyze the structure of texts, including how specific sentences, paragraph, and larger portions of the text relate to each other and the whole.
- **Writing #1:** Write opinions/arguments to support claims in an analysis of substantive topics or texts using valid reasoning and relevant and sufficient evidence.
- **Writing #2:** Write informative/explanatory texts to examine a topic and convey ideas and information clearly.

- **Writing #7:** Conduct short as well as more sustained research projects based on focused questions, demonstrating understanding of the subject under investigation.
- **Writing #8:** Gather relevant information from multiple print and digital sources, assess the credibility and accuracy of each source, and integrate the information while avoiding plagiarism.
- **Writing #9:** Draw evidence from literary or informational texts to support analysis, reflection, and research.

Social studies and science standards adopted by many states also require students to integrate reading and writing to support content learning. *The College, Career & Civic Life C3 Framework for Social Studies State Standards* (National Council for the Social Studies, 2017) described the role of social studies teachers in literacy instruction for secondary grades, and

> fully incorporates and extends the expectations for learning put forward in the Common Core Standards for ELA/Literacy . . . the authors of the C3 Framework view the literacy skills detailed in the CCSS as establishing a foundation for inquiry in social studies, and as such all CCSS Anchor Standards should be an indispensable part of any state's social studies standards (p. 20).

For science, the authors of the national *Next Generation Science Standards* (2013) explain that literacy skills are critical to building knowledge in science. They noted:

> Reading in science requires an appreciation of the norms and conventions of the discipline of science, including understanding the nature of evidence used, an attention to precision and detail, and the capacity to make and assess intricate arguments, synthesize complex information, and follow detailed procedures and accounts of events and concepts. Likewise, writing and presenting information orally are key means for students to assert and defend claims in science, demonstrate what they know about a concept, and convey what they have experienced, imagined, thought, and learned. (p. 1)

SUMMARY

This chapter introduces seminal research in literacy and the Science of Reading, focusing on several influential models: The Simple View of Reading (Gough & Tunmer, 1986), the Reading Rope (Scarborough, 2001), and The Writing Rope (Sedita, 2019). The chapter defines five components of reading identified by the National Reading Panel (2000) and seven components of language before presenting and explaining seven general principles for effective instruction. The benefits of integrating reading and writing instruction are addressed, including using subject-area text as models for writing and using writing to support learning.

REFLECTION QUESTIONS

1. Describe the Simple View of Reading and Scarborough's Reading Rope. What do they have in common?
2. Describe The Writing Rope framework. How is it similar to Scarborough's Reading Rope?
3. What are the five components of reading, and how does instruction for these components shift as students move across the grades?
4. Briefly explain each of the suggested teaching principles for teaching literacy skills.
5. What are some benefits to integrating reading and writing instruction, and how does writing support reading comprehension and content learning?

The Writing Rope

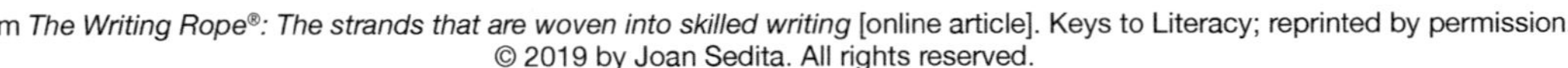

2

What Is Adolescent Literacy?

Literacy skills in the 21st century are more essential than ever for success in education, work, citizenship, and our personal lives. Unfortunately, far too many older students do not have the necessary reading and writing skills to succeed in postsecondary education or in the ever-increasing number of jobs that require strong literacy skills (Sedita, 2011).

The number of students with below-grade-level literacy skills is significant, based on National Assessment of Educational Progress (NAEP) assessments (U.S. Department of Education, 2012, 2025):

- *Reading:* The percentage of Grade 4 students in the nation who performed at or above the NAEP Proficient level was 31% in 2024, and for Grade 8 students it was 30%.
- *Writing:* The most recent NAEP writing scores from 2011 showed that only 27% of students in Grades 8 and 12 wrote at or above the NAEP Proficiency level.

Furthermore, reading difficulties in elementary grades can either persist in later grades or, in some cases, begin in later grades. Good early literacy instruction that results in grade-level reading ability at the end of Grade 3 is no guarantee that students will not have literacy difficulties later. Regardless of when difficulties start to appear, students who do not have grade-level reading and writing skills and cannot engage with and gain information from complex texts are at a disadvantage for academic achievement (Vaughn et al., 2022; Wanzek et al., 2013).

This chapter explains what is meant by *adolescent literacy* and how the research and instructional principles introduced in Chapter 1 apply to teaching adolescents. The chapter explores instructional concepts, practices, and challenges that are especially relevant for Grades 5–12, emphasizing the content literacy and disciplinary literacy that students are expected to develop in middle and high school.

ADOLESCENT LITERACY, DEFINED

The term *adolescent literacy* is used differently among experts in the literacy field. Some say it begins in Grade 4, based on the axiom that through Grade 3 students are learning to read, but beginning in Grade 4 they shift to reading to learn (Chall, 1983). Others use the term to describe literacy instruction that takes place in middle and high school grades, also referred to as *secondary literacy.* Most states have English language arts standards that are organized into an elementary band (kindergarten to Grade 5) and a secondary band (Grades 6–12) that includes a focus on literacy in the content areas. This book focuses on Grades 5–12.

Adolescent literacy encompasses the skills that must be taught to all students so they can meet increasingly challenging reading and writing demands, as well as supplemental intervention instruction for students who struggle with reading and writing. Teaching literacy skills to students in Grades 5–12 is not just the purview of English language arts teachers. Content teachers of all subjects play an important role in developing students' reading and writing ability.

Literacy: The Gatekeeper to Learning

Why do we need to continue teaching reading and writing after Grade 4? In many ways, literacy is the gatekeeper to learning in any subject. As students move from upper elementary through high school grades, the emphasis on independent learning increases. Students are expected to acquire, process, and remember information by reading, writing, and listening to teachers and peers, and by participating in discussions.

The report *Time to Act* (Carnegie Council on Advancing Adolescent Literacy, 2010, p. x) explored the issues of adolescent literacy and research, policy, and practice related to middle and high school students. The report explains:

> Middle and high school learners must learn from texts which, compared to those in earlier grades:
>
> - are significantly longer and more complex at the word, sentence and structural levels;
> - present greater conceptual challenges and obstacles to reading fluency;
> - contain more detailed graphic representations (as well as tables, charts and equations linked to text); and
> - demand a much greater ability to synthesize information.

Besides these challenges, many adolescents also need support with literacy difficulties.

Adolescents With Literacy Difficulties

One of the five recommendations in the research guide *Improving Adolescent Literacy: Effective Classroom and Intervention Practices* (Kamil et al., 2008) is to make available intensive and individualized interventions for struggling readers that can be provided by trained specialists. As the report notes, the purpose of this instruction is to accelerate literacy development so that students can make substantial progress toward catching up with their literacy skills. Reading difficulties range in terms of severity and the kinds of reading tasks affected. Intervention needs are different, with some students needing support for the foundational skills of phonics and fluency in addition to vocabulary and comprehension. Some students need instruction for basic writing skills such as sentence writing. Recommendations for intervention instruction are provided in Chapter 9, "Adolescent Learners With Literacy Difficulties."

Levels of Instruction

Adolescent literacy instruction must include content reading and writing skills and strategies in vocabulary and comprehension, as well as the specialized literacy skills that are unique to specific subject areas (i.e., disciplinary literacy). Teachers should provide this instruction to all students. In addition, intervention instruction for nonproficient readers and writers should target any skills that are not at grade level. For reading, this may include phonics and fluency instruction, and for writing, this may include teaching sentence and basic paragraph skills.

The chart in Table 2.1 organizes adolescent literacy instruction into three levels (Sedita, 2020c): *basic literacy, content literacy,* and *disciplinary literacy.* (A copy of this chart is included with the downloadable resources for this chapter.) In a multi-tiered system of support (MTSS), teachers of all subjects teach content literacy and disciplinary literacy skills. This is considered Tier 1 instruction. To address the needs of students who have difficulty with reading and writing, classroom teachers differentiate their instruction by providing accommodations, modifications, and scaffolds that ensure these students can access the same content knowledge as their peers who have proficient literacy skills.

In addition, educators provide Tier 2 supplemental or Tier 3 intensive intervention instruction for basic literacy skills to students who do not have proficient literacy skills. This instruction addresses students' individual areas of need and might focus on foundational skills (phonics, fluency), vocabulary, comprehension, and basic writing skills. This typically takes place in a pull-out setting because content teachers often do not have the time or experience to provide intervention instruction for basic skills.

Table 2.1. Levels of adolescent literacy instruction

<table>
<tr><th colspan="3">Levels of Adolescent Literacy Instruction</th></tr>
<tr><td>Disciplinary literacy</td><td>Advanced reading and writing to learn

specialized strategies unique to subject areas</td><td rowspan="2">Tier 1 Instruction

provides accommodations, modifications, and scaffolds that ensure struggling readers and writers can access the same content knowledge as their peers</td></tr>
<tr><td>Content literacy</td><td>Reading and writing to learn

vocabulary, comprehension, writing strategies used across all subjects</td></tr>
<tr><td>Basic literacy</td><td>Learning to read and write

intervention for basic skills, including phonics, fluency, vocabulary, comprehension, basic writing skills</td><td>Tiers 2 and 3 Instruction

remediate to develop basic skills</td></tr>
</table>

From Sedita, J. (2004b). *Middle and high school reading achievement: A school-wide approach*. Keys to Literacy; reprinted by permission.

Instruction Informed by Research

The art of how we teach is informed by shared, practical experience. However, similar to the medical profession, it is important for educators to consider research related to effective reading and writing instruction so their decisions are guided by more than their own personal theories about teaching literacy. There is a significant body of research that provides guidance about evidence-based literacy instruction for Grades 5–12.

The information and instructional recommendations in this book are informed by research, drawing from a number of individual research studies and reading and writing research guides based on meta-analyses of research. The findings from a meta-analysis are particularly helpful because they are based on consistent results from multiple studies. The following are seminal reports that offer evidence-based recommendations for teaching literacy to adolescents that are incorporated in this book:

- *Reading Next* (Biancarosa & Snow, 2006)
- *Improving Adolescent Literacy: Effective Classroom and Intervention Practices* (Kamil et al., 2008)
- *Teaching Secondary Students to Write Effectively* (Graham et al., 2016)

- *Writing to Read: Evidence for How Writing Can Improve Reading* (Graham & Hebert, 2010)

The remaining sections of this chapter explore in greater depth what core instruction should look like through elementary, middle, and high school, with an emphasis on content and disciplinary literacy instruction in Grades 5–12. Also addressed are the role of content teachers, suggestions for instruction and collaboration between teachers, and common challenges.

CORE LITERACY INSTRUCTION

Core literacy instruction refers to the curricula and programs that are used to teach reading and writing to all students to ensure they reach literacy levels that meet or exceed grade-level standards. It is described as Tier 1 instruction in an MTSS framework. Core instruction should address the instructional needs of the majority of students in a school. During core instruction, teachers differentiate their teaching and provide appropriate scaffolds to support the individual needs of students within the regular classroom.

Core Instruction: Kindergarten to Grade 4

In the primary grades, students are learning all five components of reading: phonemic awareness, phonics, fluency, vocabulary, and comprehension, with an emphasis on ensuring that students develop foundational skills for decoding by the end of Grade 3. In Grade 4, the focus of core instruction shifts to vocabulary and comprehension, along with instruction in advanced word study skills for multisyllabic words and continued growth in fluency skills. Across the elementary grades, core reading instruction is provided in English language arts blocks focused on teaching reading, with practice applying reading skills in other subjects such as social studies and science.

Core writing instruction in the primary grades focuses on using drawing to compose, learning to spell and write letters, sentence and paragraph writing, and learning the basic text structures for narrative, informational, and opinion writing. In Grade 4, students continue to develop sentence, paragraph, and text structure skills. They begin to develop skills, strategies, and techniques in the areas of writing craft and writing about text.

Differences for Grades 5–12

With the exception of instruction provided to older struggling readers, core reading instruction in Grades 5–12 focuses primarily on vocabulary, comprehension, and writing that is integrated across all subjects. Often these skills are applied to content-area text and practiced in combination. For example, a science teacher might preview vocabulary and use a prereading graphic organizer before students read a science text. During reading, the teacher may have students write notes, focusing on main ideas to support comprehension, and ask students to determine the meaning of new vocabulary based on the context. After reading, students might be asked to write a summary or generate and answer questions in writing, tasks that combine reading comprehension and writing strategies. As students move into the high school grades, content-area teachers begin to teach students how to apply content literacy skills to discipline-specific tasks.

Key Literacy Practices for Core Instruction

The Meadows Center (2016) developed a list of 10 key reading practices for middle and high schools with strong evidence of effectiveness from high-quality research, shown in Figure 2.1. Note that the list combines reading, writing, listening, and speaking. The recommendations in this list can be integrated into instruction in any subject area.

Core or Tier 1 literacy instruction in Grades 5–12 emphasizes teaching both content and disciplinary literacy. The sections that follow explore what each of these looks like in the classroom, including how they can be combined and how to approach content and disciplinary literacy with adolescents who lack proficiency in basic literacy skills.

Ten Key Practices for Middle and High School

All middle and high school students can become proficient readers across all content areas if, in all classes:

1. Students are explicitly taught the meanings of several new words every day and provided with opportunities to review words previously taught.
2. Students are taught and encouraged to apply word-learning practices (e.g., identifying prefixes, roots, and suffixes; context clues; synonyms) for new words encountered in texts.
3. Students' background knowledge is built through exposure to rich content in print and multimedia formats.
4. Students are taught to monitor their comprehension while reading a variety of texts by asking and answering questions, organizing text information with graphic organizers, generating main ideas and summaries, and discussing their developing understanding with the teacher and their peers.
5. Students have opportunities to work purposefully in collaborative formats with peers as they read, write, and talk about content area texts.
6. Students are taught to analyze an author's use of words, syntactical elements, and organization of ideas to establish the purpose of the text and convey its meaning.
7. Students read a variety of texts daily, compare and evaluate the texts, discuss them in relation to the specific discipline (e.g., history, science), and receive feedback on their responses.
8. Students are taught to cite textual evidence when writing, answering questions, and talking about different texts.
9. Student learning is monitored periodically to inform instructional decisions, such as collaborative group formation, lesson pacing, content for reviewing or reteaching, and supplemental intervention needs.
10. Students who are behind in reading are provided daily supplemental intervention, including instruction in reading and spelling unknown words.

Figure 2.1. Ten key practices for middle and high school. (From The Meadows Center [2016]. *10 key reading practices for all middle and high schools with strong evidence of effectiveness from high-quality research.* The University of Texas at Austin, The Meadows Center for Preventing Educational Risk.)

CONTENT LITERACY AND DISCIPLINARY LITERACY

As students advance into middle and high school grades, the required literacy skills are pushed further because each content area requires distinct reading and writing strategies. Students need to understand the language used in school texts that becomes increasingly complex and specialized. They benefit from explicit instruction and guided practice for vocabulary, comprehension, and writing skills and strategies in all subjects, often referred to as *content literacy* instruction. They also benefit from learning about the specialized literacy abilities that are specific and unique to each subject area, often referred to as *disciplinary literacy.*

What Is the Difference?

Content literacy instruction addresses skills, strategies, and routines that focus on reading, writing, discussion, word-learning skills, and language that can be used across subjects, sometimes referred to as *generic* skills and *study skills* (CEEDAR Center; Faggella-Luby et al., 2012; Shanahan, 2017; Shanahan & Shanahan, 2012). Research that has accumulated over decades has supported the use of general reading and writing strategies that are integrated into content classrooms (Brozo et al., 2013; Hwang et al., 2021; International Literacy Association, 2017; Sedita, 2024b).

Disciplinary literacy refers to how an expert in a discipline (i.e., science, history, mathematics, literature, and other subjects) uses specialized knowledge and abilities to read, write, think, and communicate (Goldman et al., 2016; Jetton & Shanahan, 2012; Shanahan & Shanahan, 2008, 2012). It encompasses the idea that students need to be taught highly specialized skills that differ from subject to subject, developed as *disciplinary habits of mind* (Fang, 2012). It presumes that reading and writing are specialized, unique, and vary across the disciplines, and different kinds of texts require different strategies (Schoenbach & Greenleaf, 2009; Shanahan, 2017). Disciplinary literacy is not just learning about a discipline; it is also about reading and writing the same way the historian, scientist, mathematician, or literary expert does. Also, the practices inherent in one content area are not generalizable to other content areas, or even within subjects of a single content area (Shanahan & Shanahan, 2008).

Disciplinary literacy moves beyond content literacy (common reading and writing strategies used across all content areas) and focuses on the unique aspects of specialized texts, forms of writing, and modes of inquiry that experts use in an academic discipline.

The International Literacy Association's literacy leadership brief *Content Area and Disciplinary Literacy* (2017) points out that content literacy and disciplinary literacy "are umbrella terms that describe two approaches to literacy instruction embedded within different subject areas or disciplines." The brief explains that with content literacy, teachers explicitly teach and model reading and writing processes that are common across disciplines and provide opportunities for students to practice them independently or in small groups. The brief identifies common content strategies in two categories (pp. 2–3):

- Interpreting texts: clarifying questions, reading headings and using text structure, summarizing, making predictions, and engaging in other comprehension or vocabulary strategies and word analysis strategies
- Composing and revising texts: organizing ideas in visual or graphical or written formats, applying stages of the writing process

Shanahan (2017) explains that general comprehension skills and study strategies are helpful teaching tools that can enhance student learning from text. He notes that content-area literacy aims to build students' reading and writing skills, whereas disciplinary literacy tries to get them to grasp the ways literacy is used to create, disseminate, and critique information in the various disciplines. Disciplinary literacy practices in some ways reframe general content literacy strategies for more advanced and specific purposes. Burke and Kennedy (2024, p. 642) explain:

> Disciplinary literacy provides a helpful way of thinking about how we can integrate our literacy instruction in a manner that serves our literacy aims while remaining true to the ways of thinking and inquiring that a scientist or artist might adopt.

Examples of Disciplinary Literacy

What is required for disciplinary literacy in different subjects? View the examples of discipline-specific focus areas, skills, and strategies in Figure 2.2 (Lent, 2017; Schoenbach & Greenleaf, 2009; Shanahan, 2015).

Discipline-Specific Focus Areas

- **History:** Experts in history interpret primary and secondary sources, corroborate sources, and use the past as a prelude to the future. They analyze historical documents, attending to bias and perspective, and evaluate the credibility of different sources of information. They also construct evidence-based accounts of probable historical events.
- **Mathematics:** Experts in mathematics decipher mathematical notation in the form of symbols and Greek alphabet letters that represent math concepts. They process abstract ideas, estimate, and generalize. They also understand specialized vocabulary, including words that have different meanings in mathematics than in everyday use (e.g., *plane, product, expression, operation, problem*).
- **Science:** Experts in science participate in scientific exploration and reasoning. They interpret data, charts, models, illustrations, and lab notes. They also conduct experiments and systematic observations, consider new hypotheses or evidence, and read and write scientific explanations.
- **English—Literary Works:** Experts in literary study read closely and examine texts in multiple genres. They recognize literary devices such as *hyperbole* and *personification*. They also look for metaphors, conflict, and other features of literature to interpret text. This includes interpreting the symbolism in poems, or how a poem's form contributes to its theme.

Figure 2.2. Discipline-specific focus areas. (*Sources:* Lent, 2017; Schoenbach & Greenleaf, 2009; Shanahan, 2015.)

Differences in Language and Text Structure

The text used in different content areas can vary greatly in terms of the language and vocabulary, sentence structure, and overall text structure, as shown in the different high school samples in Figure 2.3. An important part of teaching disciplinary literacy is making students aware of what is unique about a piece of content-area text and modeling how an expert in that discipline would go about reading that text.

Samples of Content-Area Text

History

Ming Dynasty: Chinese scholar-officials represented the backbone of the Chinese state and bureaucracy. Unlike Europe, China had no hereditary aristocracy, nor did its merchant class become politically significant as in some European countries. Deriving power and status from their education and high government office, scholar-officials became the most formidable check on the absolute power of the emperor. Scholar-officials gained their place in government by passing rigorous civil service examinations held at the prefecture, provincial and capital levels. Quotas ensured that each province could only send so many worthy candidates to the capital, ensuring no regional dominance in government. The prestige associated with being sent to the capital meant that families who could afford to do so would hire tutors to give their male children an advantage. Based mainly on Confucian texts, the examinations could last for several days. The grueling process of the exams, the writing of essays, the drafting of mock state papers and edicts, and commenting on Confucian texts, coupled with the meager passing rates, ensured that those who advanced would be adept public servants capable of administering the Chinese state.

(From Rankin, J. & Weise, C. [2022]. *World history since 1500: An open and free textbook* [p. 30]. East Tennessee State University. https://dc.etsu.edu/etsu-oer/13/ https://creativecommons.org/licenses/by/3.0/)

Mathematics

Solving Linear Equations—One-Step Equations

Objective: Solve one-step linear equations by balancing using inverse operations.

Solving linear equations is an important and fundamental skill in algebra. In algebra, we are often presented with a problem where the answer is known, but part of the problem is missing. This missing part of the problem is what we seek to find. An example of such a problem is shown below.

Example 1.

$4x + 16 = -4$

Notice the above problem has a missing part, or unknown, that is marked by *x*. If we are given that the solution to this equation is –5, it could be plugged into the equation, replacing *x* with –5. This is shown in Example 2.

Example 2.

$4(-5) + 16 = -4$	Multiply 4(-5)
$-20 + 16 = -4$	Add –20 + 16
$-4 = -4$	True!

Now the equation comes out to a true statement! Notice also that if another number, for example, 3, was plugged in, we would not get a true statement as seen in Example 3.

Example 3.

$4(3) + 16 = -4$	Multiply 4(3)
$12 + 16 = -4$	Add 12 + 16
$28 = -4$	False!

(From Wallace T. [2010]. *Beginning and intermediate algebra* [p. 28]. http://www.wallace.ccfaculty.org/book/Beginning_and_Intermediate_Algebra.pdf https://creativecommons.org/licenses/by/3.0/)

Science

How can we make antimalarial medicine faster?

A natural medicine against malaria is *artemisinin*. It comes from a plant named *Artemisia annua.* This plant takes a chemical, dihydroartemisinic acid (DHAA), and turns it into artemisinin. In this study, we wanted to find out which factors affect how fast artemisinin forms. Could heat, light, the amount of DHAA, or the chemical composition of DHAA hold the key?

Experiment:

We placed samples of DHAA under an infrared light, in a bath of hot oil, and under an ultraviolet (UV) light. The samples remained in their environments for 2.5 hours. We also put a sample of artemisinin under the UV lamp for 8 days to see how UV light can affect artemisinin. Then we measured the amount of artemisinin present in each sample using a nuclear magnetic resonance (NMR) spectrometer and a mass spectrometer.

Results:

The UV light sample showed a larger amount of artemisinin compared to the infrared and hot bath samples. But when artemisinin was left under light for 8 days, the amount of artemisinin started to decrease. Instead, we found a chemical that had all the atoms of artemisinin, but in a different arrangement that does not kill the parasite that causes malaria.

(From Varela, K., Arman, H. D., & Yoshimoto, F. K. [2021]. *Physical Science Journal for Teens* [p. 1]. https://www.sciencejournalforkids.org/wp-content/uploads/2021/09/artemisinin-2_article.pdf)

Figure 2.3. Samples of content-area text.

Literature
The Grapes of Wrath, John Steinbeck

The man took off his dark, stained hat and stood with a curious humility in front of the screen. "Could you see your way to sell us a loaf of bread, ma'am?"

Mae said, "This ain't a grocery store. We got bread to make san'widges."

"I know, ma'am." His humility was insistent. "We need bread and there ain't nothin' for quite a piece, they say."

"'F we sell bread we gonna run out." Mae's tone was faltering.

"We're hungry," the man said.

"Whyn't you buy a san'widge? We got nice san'widges, hamburgs."

"We'd sure admire to do that, ma'am. But we can't. We got to make a dime do all of us." And he said embarrassedly, "We ain't got but a little."

Mae said, "You can't get no loaf a bread for a dime. We only got fifteen-cent loafs."

From behind her Al growled, "God Almighty, Mae, give 'em bread."

"We'll run out 'fore the bread truck comes."

"Run out then, goddamn it," said Al. He looked sullenly down at the potato salad he was mixing.

Mae shrugged her plump shoulders and looked to the truck drivers to show them what she was up against.

She held the screen door open and the man came in, bringing a smell of sweat with him. The boys edged behind him and they went immediately to the candy case and stared in—not with craving or with hope or even with desire, but just with a kind of wonder that such things could be. They were alike in size and their faces were alike. One scratched his dusty ankle with the toenail of his other foot. The other whispered some soft message and then they straightened their arms so that their clenched fists in the overall pockets showed through the thin blue cloth.

(From Steinbeck, J. [1939]. *The grapes of wrath.* Viking Press.)

Figure 2.3. *(continued)*

Combining Content and Disciplinary Literacy Instruction

Most literacy experts suggest that it is best for content teachers to combine content literacy and disciplinary literacy; they are not mutually exclusive approaches. Content teachers play an important role in teaching students how general content literacy skills and strategies are used with the specific content and texts within their discipline. This is where content literacy and disciplinary literacy intersect. Students can practice common generic literacy strategies as they are introduced to discipline-specific frameworks and practices. This is especially the case in middle school grades where many students are still learning how to automatically decode multisyllabic words derived from Latin and Greek and increasing their overall fluency skills.

The guide *Reading in the Disciplines* (Lee & Spratley, 2010) suggests a combination of generic reading and discipline-specific reading strategies. Figure 2.4 outlines some examples.

Generic and Discipline-Specific Strategies

Generic Strategies	Discipline-Specific Strategies
• Set a purpose and goals prior to reading texts. • Make connections to prior knowledge about the topics in texts. • Make predictions about what will be in a text and check those predictions while reading. • Monitor comprehension while reading, recognize a lack of understanding, and employ fix-up strategies. • Generate questions before, during, and after reading to support comprehension. • Take notes about main ideas and supporting details. • Generate oral or written summaries of texts.	• Connect prior knowledge about the discipline-specific topics from previous texts to new texts. • Build specialized vocabulary unique to the discipline and related texts. • Learn to comprehend the unique language and grammatical structure of sentences in a particular discipline. • Use knowledge of text structures and genres that are unique to a particular discipline to support reading comprehension. • Map information provided in graphics, tables, charts, and other visuals unique to a particular discipline to explanations in the text. • Compare claims and ideas across texts. • Use norms for reasoning within the discipline to evaluate claims.

Figure 2.4. Generic and discipline-specific strategies.

Considering the Needs of Struggling Adolescents

Teaching disciplinary literacy is challenging. In addition to having limited comprehension strategies, students may lack experience reading lengthy expository text and lack sufficient subject-specific vocabulary or background knowledge about the topics in text. Some students who struggle with reading and writing may not have the ability to read the words on the page or write simple sentences. These students need intervention instruction for basic literacy skills in addition to content and disciplinary literacy instruction.

Some advocates of disciplinary literacy view content literacy as something significantly different from disciplinary literacy and think that content teachers should focus only on the latter. However, given the deep research base supporting the use of general content strategies for reading and writing across disciplines, a focus on just disciplinary instruction hinders discussion about how to blend both approaches to effectively teach students with varying degrees of literacy proficiency in content classrooms. This is especially the case for large numbers of adolescent students in today's schools who have not developed basic literacy skills, most of whom spend the majority of their time in regular classrooms (Brozo et al., 2013; Faggella-Luby et al., 2012), and for some English learners who have not developed sophisticated vocabulary and language skills.

Faggella-Luby and colleagues (2012) examined the research base related to discipline-specific strategies and struggling adolescent learners and concluded that there is insufficient research to support a focus on disciplinary literacy instruction over content literacy, especially for struggling learners. They suggest that content teachers should bear some responsibility for teaching general content strategies and make the following points:

> Although the rationality of developing discipline-specific strategies to improve depth of content area knowledge is clear, replacing general strategy instruction wholly with discipline-specific strategies in high schools at this time is not practical, grounded in a literature base, nor likely to meet the realistic needs of a majority of students. . . . it is unlikely that adolescents who struggle, who constitute a majority of students, will be able to master disciplinary literacy skills without the necessary prerequisite literacy building blocks that are embodied in general strategy instruction. (p. 81)

What level of student knowledge and disciplinary sophistication should educators expect across Grades 5 through 12? When is it reasonable to expect students to read and write like experts in the field? Do students need to master disciplinary literacy skills in all subjects? Currently there is insufficient research to provide definitive answers. Most likely the answers will vary based on the abilities and needs of individual students.

HOW CONTENT TEACHERS CAN INTEGRATE LITERACY

How will students learn content literacy and disciplinary literacy skills and strategies? Middle and high schools do not offer reading classes to most students, and the English language arts or English class is often focused on reading and writing related to literature. Therefore, the task of integrating literacy instruction into other content areas falls on content teachers.

Content teachers need to convey to students that learning in their subject area is not just about memorizing information in science and history or doing calculations in math. They should assign tasks that support this message and help students see the value of having proficient reading, writing, listening, and speaking skills to support learning in their areas of interest and to prepare them to succeed in post-secondary education, in their careers, and as productive citizens.

A common concern among secondary content teachers is that their primary responsibility is to teach subject-area content. Given the demands of grade-level curriculum requirements and limited class time, they often feel they lack the time to incorporate literacy instruction. However, rather than merely presenting content, teachers can help students develop a deeper understanding by equipping them with the skills to read, write, and discuss the content. When content teachers integrate literacy instruction into their subject teaching, they provide students with the tools to independently access and master the content.

Beginning in the middle grades, teachers should strive to adapt general reading practices into more discipline-specific variations. However, they do not have to wait until content literacy skills are fully developed to begin introducing students to disciplinary literacy practices. For example, they can teach and model for students how to review experimental data and write a lab report in science, how to determine the point of view of the author of a primary historical document, or how to determine the theme of a poem even if students have not mastered general content strategies such as note taking and summarizing. As students move into high school grades and encounter more sophisticated disciplinary texts, they need more support to learn discipline-specific strategies (Schoenbach & Greenleaf, 2009).

Literacy Practices for Each Subject

What are the literacy practices content teachers can share with students that are unique to each subject? Cynthia Shanahan (2015) suggests teaching students to use the disciplinary literacy practices shown in Figure 2.5.

Questions to Support Reading in the Disciplines

Different types of content-area text require different approaches to critical thinking. Students benefit from questions to support their comprehension of discipline-specific texts. View sets of questions for the four subjects in Figure 2.6 (CEEDAR Center, n.d.). Content teachers can share some or all of these questions for text that is used in the classroom.

Suggestions for Integrating Literacy

The following suggestions support the integration of literacy into content-instruction (Lee & Spratley, 2010; Regional Education Laboratory Northwest, 2024; Shanahan, 2017).

- Text should play a central role in subject instruction. Teachers should not avoid texts simply because they may be challenging to read. Reading and writing should be integral components of content instruction.
- Students need access to high-quality disciplinary texts that expose them to complex academic language. They should also read about various subjects and current events to expand their knowledge base.
- Content knowledge and literacy strategies should be taught in tandem.
- Teachers should incorporate both content literacy and discipline-specific reading strategies. Cross-disciplinary strategies help students comprehend different types of texts across content areas, whereas discipline-specific strategies address the unique demands of each subject.
- Instructional routines and supportive strategies should be implemented to foster students' self-efficacy, gradually shifting responsibility for thinking and making sense of texts from the teacher to the learner.
- Reading should be reinforced as a meaning-making process, with scaffolds provided to support comprehension.
- Classroom discussions should focus on how students interpret texts and apply what they learn to discipline-specific thinking tasks.
- Established routines can be used to create a culture of high expectations, helping students understand what they need to do, how to approach tasks, and why these practices are important.

Instructional Suggestions

The following suggestions support the integration of literacy into content-area instruction and are introduced in the next sections, and then they are explored in greater detail in other chapters of this book. These strategies can be used by teachers of any subject to support literacy development: providing explicit instruction using the Gradual Release of Responsibility model, previewing vocabulary and

Disciplinary Literacy Practices

Science

Scientists read proposals, lab reports, journal articles about experiments, and other documents. When scientists read to understand scientific information, they look for more than just surface understandings. When scientists read with a critical eye, the way they read descriptions of experiments or applications of science, they evaluate that information with scientific methods and accuracy in mind. At times they look for errors the way mathematicians do, and they expect information to be accurately and precisely described. Suggested practices:

- Transform prose to diagrams to equations, and vice versa.
- Write for different audiences and purposes.
- Learn science vocabulary.
- Take notes.
- Understand the language of science (how to interpret sentences or small pieces of text).

Mathematics

Mathematicians read and write journals, books, proofs, mathematical applications, and other documents. Mathematicians read carefully, evaluating the meaning of each word or symbol, and they apply logic to their reading. Suggested practices:

- Reread.
- Learn the names of variables before reading a formula.
- Read equations with appropriate directionality.
- Learn accurate definitions.
- Detect errors.
- Recognize distracting information.

History

Historical sources include documentaries, trade books, cartoons, photographs, paintings, artifacts, primary documents, maps, memoirs, audio and video recordings, newspaper articles, textbooks, and anything else that comes from the past or is an interpretation of the past. Historians have sophisticated ways of reading text. Suggested practices:

- Consider source and context.
- Corroborate.
- Analyze the relationships among events.
- Use interpretive frameworks (look at history through different lenses).
- Read multiple genres.
- Understand the language of history (how to interpret sentences or small pieces of text).
- Write history.

English

In the study of literature, texts usually consist of novels, short stories, and poetry. The study of literature requires learning the language of literary interpretation, an ability to see patterns within and across texts, and an understanding of the human experience. Suggested practices:

- Read different interpretations of the same text.
- Learn the structure of argument.
- Learn the language of literary criticism.
- Learn how to recognize themes.

Figure 2.5. Disciplinary literacy practices. (*Source:* Shanahan, 2015.)

developing background knowledge before reading, teaching comprehension strategies, incorporating discussion, and teaching close reading strategies.

Use Explicit Instruction and Gradual Release of Responsibility The goal of adolescent literacy instruction is to have students gradually develop content and disciplinary strategies through explicit instruction and guided practice. This is accomplished using the Gradual Release of Responsibility model (Pearson & Gallagher, 1983) introduced in Chapter 1, sometimes referred to as an *I do it,*

Questions to Support Reading

Science Questions

- What is the meaning of the prefixes, suffixes, and Latin or Greek roots of the vocabulary?
- What is the scientific meaning of the vocabulary?
- What is the meaning of the scientific signs and symbols?
- What are the relationships among concepts?
- What are the processes discussed?
- What are the facts I need to note?
- What is the interpretation of the graphs, charts, and formulas?
- What are the functions of the investigation?
- Have the conclusions been corroborated?
- How does this information transform our knowledge?

Mathematics Questions

- How is the information presented?
- Can I interpret the information?
- What is the specialized mathematics meaning of the vocabulary?
- Can I explain what the symbols mean, including the symbols from the Greek alphabet?
- What is the underlying logic of the theorem?
- What is the correct form of mathematical communication?
- How can I map mathematical representations against the explanations in the text?
- Where are the errors?

History Questions

Source Documents

- Who wrote this? What is the author's bias and purpose?
- When was it written?
- Who is the audience?

Contextualize the Document

- What is going on at this time?
- What were people thinking and doing?
- What did people believe?

Summarize the Document

- Who or what was this about?
- What is important about the who or what?

Corroborate/Cross-Check Documents

- Do the documents agree?
- Do they tell the same or different stories?
- Which document is more believable? Why?

English Questions

- What is the genre or text type?
- Is knowing about the author important for understanding this text?
- What is the author's purpose and point of view?
- What are the important elements of the text?
- What is the theme? Where in the text is the theme made evident?
- What is the literal meaning and the implied meaning in the text?

Figure 2.6. Questions to support reading. (Adapted from CEEDAR Center. [n.d.]. *Disciplinary literacy.* Professional development course offered by the University of Florida.)

We do it, You do it model. At the first instructional stage (I do it), the teacher presents and models how to use a reading or writing skill. At the second stage (We do it), students practice the skill as a whole group or in small groups. The teacher guides this practice and provides corrective feedback to students. At the last stage (You do it), students practice the skill independently.

Students need to be *apprenticed* and mentored (Moje, 2006; Shanahan, 2017), with some requiring more scaffolds than others, until they can eventually read, write, and communicate in an academic discipline. As apprentices, students need hands-on experience with the help of an insider (the teacher) who knows how to engage them in meaningful disciplinary inquiry and teach them to use texts and write about what they are learning, and students need time to practice.

Content teachers need to recognize their own invisible mental processes as they encounter challenging texts in their disciplines, and then bring students into a community of learners where the teacher's and students' thinking is made visible and available for discussion (Schoenbach & Greenleaf, 2009). Teachers need to model the cognitive processes they use to read and write about text and provide opportunities for students to discuss how they are using these strategies.

Preview Vocabulary and Provide Background Knowledge Research has determined that one's knowledge, including academic content knowledge and the cultural knowledge developed through day-to-day activities, affects one's reading comprehension. A student with more expertise in a subject covered in a text will comprehend better than a student who has minimal or no knowledge of the subject (Hwang & Duke, 2020; Willingham, 2017).

One of the reasons students have difficulty with subject-area text is that they lack background knowledge about the topics in the text and the academic vocabulary associated with those topics. Content teachers can do several things prior to reading a text that will support students, including previewing unfamiliar vocabulary, providing some background knowledge, sharing the big ideas, posing prereading questions, and using a prediction task (Sedita, 2024c). Instructional details for these suggestions are provided in Chapter 4, "Comprehension Instruction."

Teach Before, During, and After Comprehension Strategies Research has accumulated over decades that supports the use and integration of comprehension strategies into content classrooms. The CEEDAR Center at the University of Florida organizes universal strategies to support reading comprehension into a before, during, and after framework:

1. ***Before reading:*** Set a purpose for reading, preview the text, make predictions, make connections to prior knowledge, note text structure and genre, attend to the author and source information, and examine graphics (bold print, tables, graphs, pictures, charts).
2. ***During reading:*** Monitor comprehension, recognize barriers to comprehension, utilize fix-up strategies, define unknown vocabulary words, adjust reading rate, annotate text, form visual images, check accuracy of predictions, ask questions, make inferences, analyze graphics (tables, graphs, pictures, charts), determine important information, paraphrase chunks of text, reread text, and check whether the text makes sense.
3. ***After reading:*** Summarize the text, relate the text to prior knowledge, analyze the text, demonstrate understanding of the text, and evaluate the text.

Instructional suggestions for comprehension strategies are provided in Chapter 4.

Incorporate Discussion About Text One of the five recommendations in the research guide *Improving Adolescent Literacy: Effective Classroom and Intervention Practices* (Kamil et al., 2008) is for teachers to provide opportunities for students to engage in high-quality discussions of the meaning and interpretation of texts in various content areas as one important way to improve reading comprehension.

The report recommends these discussions occur in whole classroom groups or in small student groups under the general guidance of the teacher. To be particularly effective in promoting students' comprehension of complex text, these discussions can focus on building a deeper understanding of the author's meaning or critically analyzing, and perhaps challenging, the author's conclusions through reasoning or applying personal experiences and knowledge. In effective discussions, students have the opportunity to do the following:

- Have sustained exchanges with the teacher or other students
- Present and defend individual interpretations and points of view
- Use text content, background knowledge, and reasoning to support interpretations and conclusions
- Listen to the points of view and reasoned arguments of others participating in the discussions

Instructional details for discussion are provided in Chapter 7, "Supporting Learning Through Discussion."

Analyze Text and Teach Close Reading *Close reading* is something readers do to figure out a challenging text. It includes an intensive analysis of the text to determine what it says, how it says it, and what it means. Teachers should analyze text before assigning it to students to determine what about the text and the vocabulary is unique to their discipline and what parts might be particularly difficult for students. They can select parts of this text to model how it can be read critically for deep comprehension. This is part of close reading instruction. Instructional details for analyzing text and close reading are provided in Chapter 4.

Collaborate With Other Teachers

Teachers who teach the same subjects in a school or district can collaborate to identify the essential focus areas of disciplinary literacy in their subject area and determine the practical applications of both content and disciplinary literacy instruction. School and district literacy specialists can join in this collaboration to contribute literacy expertise, including how to apply generic reading strategies to content-specific text and writing tasks. Literacy experts can also work with disciplinary experts to develop instructional practices and routines for disciplinary literacy in each subject and determine how to provide scaffolds for students' wide spectrum of existing basic and content literacy skills.

Hwang and colleagues (2021, p. 7) suggest peer educators discuss the following questions that surround literacy:

- What is unique about your subject discipline in terms of reading, writing, speaking, and listening?
- How do members of this subject discipline use language on a daily basis?
- Are there any typical misconceptions held by students, for example, how to write an effective science report?
- Are there words and phrases used typically, or uniquely, in the subject discipline?

ADOLESCENT MOTIVATION AND ENGAGEMENT IN LITERACY

The report *What Content-Area Teachers Should Know About Adolescent Literacy* (National Institute for Literacy, 2007) addresses the role that motivation plays in developing successful adolescent readers and writers. The report notes, "An individual's goals, values, and beliefs regarding the topics, processes, and outcomes of reading affect students' motivation for reading. . . . Motivation also involves self-efficacy, or the belief that one is capable of success" (p. 34).

Motivation contributes to reading engagement, and engaged readers tend to enjoy reading and read more often. Motivated adolescent readers are self-determined (i.e., they feel they have control over their reading), they self-regulate (i.e., they recognize if they are on task and employ strategies to achieve their goal), and they are engaged. Multiple factors influence adolescents' motivation, including a change in their beliefs, values, and goals regarding school, and for struggling students, the effects of grading and grouping practices.

There is strong evidence that students' motivation and interest in reading school-related texts declines after they move from elementary to middle school, and this is particularly true for students who have difficulty learning to read (Ho & Guthrie, 2013; Kamil et al., 2008, Murray et al., 2010). Finding ways to motivate and engage students in reading is an essential part of adolescent literacy instruction.

Motivation: Proficient Readers

Proficient readers who have a purpose for reading (and sufficient reading comprehension strategies to tackle the text they are reading) have more motivation and are engaged while reading, making reading enjoyable (Murray et al., 2010). For example, adolescent proficient readers who become engaged in reading a novel of their own choosing, or engaged in reading a set of complex instructions for how to set up a new computer, are more motivated and engaged because they are interested in what they are reading and learning from these texts. Proficient readers interact with text in a strategic way, use a variety of strategies to make meaning while reading, and read more. That reading, in turn, continues to increase their reading comprehension ability, and so these students are interested in and curious about topics and content in a wide variety of texts.

Lack of Motivation: Struggling Readers

Adolescent struggling readers, in contrast, often lack the motivation to read in school because they face increasingly difficult reading material and classroom environments that tend to deemphasize the importance of fostering motivation to read (Murray et al., 2010, citing Guthrie & Davis, 2003). They do not read as much as students with stronger motivation (Torgesen et al., 2007), and their lack of reading affects their ability to maintain fluency, expand vocabulary, and develop and strengthen effective reading strategies needed to learn from text. This in turn limits their exposure to important content information, world knowledge, and the ability to learn in all content areas (Murray et al., 2010). Struggling readers with low interest in reading prefer not to read and may engage in reading as a passive process without giving effortful attention to activating prior knowledge, using reading strategies, or employing other strategic thought processes. This results in low comprehension of text and may result in a lack of interest in exploring topics or content through reading.

For adolescent struggling readers, motivation and engagement are also impacted by text difficulty as well as both student and teacher expectations.

Text Difficulty Teachers should pay attention to the level of difficulty of the texts they assign (Moje, 2006; Torgesen et al., 2007). In many content-area classrooms, students are expected to read difficult text that can be overwhelming, particularly for struggling readers. This can have a significant negative effect on their motivation and willingness to stay engaged in reading such texts. One solution is to have texts that address similar content or themes at different levels of difficulty, or to provide opportunities for students to listen to text read aloud.

Student and Teacher Expectations The research guide *Improving Adolescent Literacy: Effective Classroom and Intervention Practices* (Kamil et al., 2008) points out the following roadblock to increasing motivation and offers suggested solutions:

> Adolescent students who struggle in reading do not expect to do well in class. As these students progress through school, most teachers do not expect them to do well either and often remark that they should have learned the material in earlier grades. Many adolescents do not express confidence in their own ability—they do not trust or value their own thinking. The strengths of students can be identified through interest surveys, interviews, and discussions, and through learning about and understanding students' reading histories. These activities will help teachers get to know their students.
>
> For many students, having a personal connection with at least one teacher can make a difference in their response to school. Knowing students' interests makes it easier for teachers to choose materials that will hook students and motivate them to engage in their own learning. Teachers should provide multiple learning opportunities in which students can experience success and can begin to build confidence in their ability to read, write, and think at high levels. (p. 30)

Practices That Support Motivation

1. Provide Content Goals for Reading

Establish meaningful and engaging content learning goals around the essential ideas of a discipline as well as the specific learning processes students use to access those ideas. A content goal is a question or purpose for reading. Content goals emphasize the importance of and increase interest in learning from what we read. Teachers can help students find a purpose for reading and foster their curiosity during reading. For example, a student who is reading to find out how panda bears are becoming extinct is more likely to read text carefully and to employ strategies that will help understand the text and answer the question. When teachers set goals to reach a certain standard or acquire particular information, students are more likely to sustain their efforts until they reach those goals. Learning goals can also be set by students, which may make them more apt to be fully engaged in reading to achieve them.

Recommended instructional practices:

- Facilitate the use of relevant background knowledge to increase interest in gaining content mastery.
- Arrange hands-on experiences or other stimulating tasks that lead students to want to find out more by reading.
- Make content goals interesting and relevant by having students read a variety of materials to pursue a theme over a period of time, "publish" a brochure related to a historical event or geographical location, or learn about a topic in order to teach it to someone else.
- Model the behaviors of a curious reader who is rewarded with new knowledge about an interesting topic.
- Involve students in creating content goals and tracking their progress in meeting those goals.
- Give students feedback on their progress in meeting content goals.

2. Provide a Range of Choices in Reading Activities

Provide a positive learning environment that promotes students' autonomy in learning. Allow students some choice of complementary books and types of reading and writing activities. When students choose what they read, what activities they engage in related to reading, and with whom they work, their motivation increases, as does the time they spend reading. They will assume greater ownership and responsibility for their engagement in learning. Students who can select their own reading material use more effective reading strategies and perform better on tests of comprehension.

Recommended instructional practices:

- Provide opportunities for students to choose which text they read by offering a list of appropriate readings.
- Give students control over some aspects of the task, such as where to work in the classroom, what type of product to produce (e.g., essay or poster), and which subjects to pursue.
- Allow students to select partners, join groups, or work alone.

3. Provide Students Interesting Texts for Reading Instruction

Students enjoy reading texts that they find interesting and choose to continue reading these texts during free time. Further, people remember interesting information more than information they find uninteresting. High-interest text increases motivation to read. It also increases comprehension and achievement. Texts can be chosen by the teacher or students. Teachers should try to make what students read and write about more relevant to their interests, everyday life, or important current events. This includes looking for opportunities to bridge literacy activities outside and inside the classroom.

Guidelines for selecting appropriate and interesting material:

- Choose texts on topics about which students possess background knowledge. Knowing something about a text's content makes it more interesting. The recommendation is not to avoid introducing new material, but rather to be mindful of the importance of motivation and the effect that unfamiliar content can have on students' engagement. This underscores the importance of giving students ample background knowledge before asking them to read texts that present new information.
- Texts that are visually pleasing and appear readable are more interesting and motivating. Pay attention to illustrations, layouts, graphics, and text sizes that are appealing and support text comprehension.
- Keep in mind that a text's relevance and interest is often an individual matter. Whereas some texts are interesting to just about everyone, other texts are interesting only when they support a reader's content goals.
- To generate interest, provide stimulating tasks related to reading topics prior to reading.

4. Increase Collaborative Reading

Increase opportunities for students to collaborate during reading. Adolescents are motivated by working together. When students can collaborate socially on reading and writing tasks, they find the work more motivating and often continue working even after completing the assigned task. Collaboration also increases the number of opportunities struggling readers have to respond, and when struggling readers are grouped with more capable peers, they are more likely to be successful in the learning task.

Figure 2.7. Practices that support motivation. (*Sources:* Guthrie & Humenick, 2004; Kamil et al., 2008; Murray et al., 2010.)

Recommended instructional practices:

- Allow students to collaborate by reading together, sharing information, and explaining and presenting their knowledge to others during reading and reading-related tasks.
- Teach collaborative group work skills such as appropriate group work behavior, how to provide feedback to group members, and maintaining individual accountability so that students benefit from working together.
- Use collaboration to foster a sense of belonging to the classroom community.

Figure 2.7. *(continued)*

Teaching Practices That Support Motivation

There is not a large body of research about effective instructional practices to motivate adolescent students to read, especially students who have difficulty. However, there is some consensus about four major instructional practices found to have significant effect sizes. These practices were summarized in 2004 by Guthrie and Humenick based on a meta-analysis of research, and updated in 2008 in the research guide quoted previously (Kamil et al.):

1. Provide content goals for reading.
2. Provide a range of choices in reading activities.
3. Provide students interesting texts for reading instruction.
4. Increase collaborative reading.

The four instructional suggestions are explained in detail in Figure 2.7.

SECONDARY LITERACY CHALLENGES

Integrating literacy instruction into content classroom teaching is challenging for a number of reasons, explained in the following section.

Limited Student Literacy Skills

The most obvious challenge is that many students in content classrooms have limited reading and writing skills. They lack experience reading lengthy expository text, do not effectively use comprehension strategies, and do not have sufficient content-specific vocabulary and background knowledge about the topics in text.

Lack of Teacher Training and Professional Development

Another key challenge is the lack of training of middle and high school educators to teach literacy skills. Most secondary teachers do not take sufficient pre-service coursework to be prepared to teach reading and writing instruction, especially content teachers (Bruisie, 2020; Johnston, 2020; Lesley, 2014). Once they are teaching, the opportunities for accessing high-quality, long-term professional development that includes implementation coaching are limited. Professional development for how to integrate literacy into content instruction must compete with numerous other topics and priorities for limited professional learning time.

The report *Time to Act: An Agenda for Advancing Adolescent Literacy for College and Career Success* (Carnegie Council on Advancing Adolescent Literacy, 2010) identifies teacher preparation and professional development as one of the major keys to successful adolescent literacy reform, noting the following:

> Determining what secondary school teachers need to know, ensuring they learn it, and supporting them in implementing that knowledge in classrooms is basic to achieving our goal of literacy for all. . . . Good teachers of adolescent students not only understand their own content-areas deeply, they also understand the specific literacy challenges created by the texts they assign. Such teachers are prepared to address the content learning needs of struggling readers as well as on-grade level readers in their classes. (p. 18)

Lack of Explicit Responsibility for Literacy Instruction

In most elementary schools, it is accepted that teachers are generalists, knowledgeable about literacy instruction as well as subjects. This is especially the case in the primary grades, where a major focus is on making sure young students develop basic literacy skills. However, it is not unusual in middle and high schools for the responsibility for teaching literacy skills to belong to no one in particular. Content teachers in these grades have traditionally been defined as specialists in their subject areas, with content being the focus rather than skills. This often includes English teachers who have students use reading and writing to study literature but do not necessarily teach these skills. Despite the calls over the last few decades for students to read and write more and content teachers to address literacy in content classrooms, evidence suggests that relatively little literacy instruction goes on in most content-area courses, and many middle and high school students do not engage in sufficient reading and writing (Graham, 2019; Heller & Greenleaf, 2007).

Lack of Resources

Another challenge is the lack of resources available to teachers to support content and disciplinary literacy instruction. Content teachers often must identify for themselves the specific reading, writing, or thinking process that must be applied to access the content and text they are using in their classes. They also must develop their own instructional materials, including scaffolds such as note taking guides and writing templates, as well as instructional materials.

Lack of Instructional Time

Incorporating literacy instruction into content classrooms can be time-consuming. If teachers assign complex reading and writing projects, they must spend time teaching students the skills needed to complete these tasks, and time reviewing, grading, and providing feedback about the completed assignments. In addition, most content teachers are under pressure to cover a significant amount of content information. It is not uncommon for them to express concern about how they will find enough time to meet the expectations placed on them to meet content requirements by the end of the school year.

Lack of Time to Collaborate

Insufficient time is available in many schools for content teachers to meet and work collaboratively with their peers to identify the reading and writing skills that are unique to their subject area, to prioritize which disciplinary literacy skills should be taught, and to determine the most effective way to provide that instruction. It is important for teachers to discuss how to provide the same approach to teaching literacy in science, versus history, versus mathematics, and so forth. Similarly, there is limited time for literacy coaches and specialists to meet with content teachers to share suggestions for integrating content literacy instruction into their classrooms.

SUMMARY

This chapter explores how *adolescent literacy* is defined by experts and explains how reading and writing demands change as students move into Grades 5–12. The distinction between content literacy and disciplinary literacy is explained, with examples of what this looks like in different subject areas. The chapter addresses the role of content teachers in developing middle and high school students' literacy with suggestions for integrating reading and writing instruction in the content-area classroom. The topic of adolescents' motivation and engagement in literacy is explored. The chapter concludes by identifying secondary literacy challenges.

REFLECTION QUESTIONS

1. What does the following sentence from the chapter mean to you? "In many ways, literacy is the gatekeeper to learning in any subject."
2. Explain how the focus of core literacy instruction in Grades 5–12 is different from kindergarten to Grade 4.
3. Describe content literacy and disciplinary literacy, and explain the difference.
4. Why might some adolescent struggling readers and writers have difficulty completing disciplinary reading and writing tasks?
5. What role can content teachers play in providing instruction for reading, writing, and discussion skills?
6. Select an instruction suggestion for teaching literacy in Grades 5–12 that resonates most with you. Briefly describe the suggestion and explain why you chose it.

Levels of Adolescent Literacy Instruction

<table>
<tr><td>Disciplinary literacy</td><td>Advanced reading and writing to learn

specialized strategies unique to subject areas</td><td rowspan="2">Tier 1 Instruction

provides accommodations, modifications, and scaffolds that ensure struggling readers and writers can access the same content knowledge as their peers</td></tr>
<tr><td>Content literacy</td><td>Reading and writing to learn

vocabulary, comprehension, writing strategies used across all subjects</td></tr>
<tr><td>Basic literacy</td><td>Learning to read and write

intervention for basic skills, including phonics, fluency, vocabulary, comprehension, basic writing skills</td><td>Tiers 2 and 3 Instruction

remediate to develop basic skills</td></tr>
</table>

From Sedita, J. (2004b). *Middle and high school reading achievement: A school-wide approach.* Keys to Literacy; reprinted by permission.

II

Literacy Instruction

3

Vocabulary Instruction

Vocabulary knowledge encompasses all the words we must know to access our background knowledge, express our ideas and communicate them to others, and learn new concepts. Students' word knowledge is linked strongly to academic success because students who have large vocabularies can understand new concepts more quickly than students with limited vocabularies. Marilyn Jager Adams sums up the need to develop vocabulary:

> Words are not just words. They are the nexus—the interface—between communication and thought. When we read, it is through words that we build, refine, and modify our knowledge. What makes vocabulary valuable and important is not the words themselves so much as the understandings they afford. (2009, p. 180)

This chapter explores the role vocabulary plays in overall academic success and in reading comprehension in particular, and the importance of learning academic vocabulary. The chapter provides an overview of what good, research-informed vocabulary instruction looks like in the classroom. It provides detailed guidance for specific recommended practices, including previewing vocabulary before reading, teaching targeted words in depth, teaching how to use the context and knowledge of word parts to determine the meaning of an unfamiliar word, and various strategies and templates teachers can use to help students build their vocabularies.

VOCABULARY AND ACADEMIC SUCCESS

The size of students' vocabulary is one of the strongest predictors of reading development (Moody et al., 2018). As students move from elementary to upper grades, the text they read contains more academic vocabulary they do not recognize, especially in the content areas. Vocabulary carries a large share of the meaning in text through specialized vocabulary, jargon, and discipline-related concepts. Learning these specialized vocabularies contributes to reading success among students.

Vocabulary instruction is necessary because of the vast number of words students must acquire each year to read and understand grade-level text and subject-area concepts. If students do not adequately and steadily build their vocabulary knowledge, reading comprehension and learning in general are affected. The good news is that growth in students' vocabulary is attainable when teachers in all subjects teach vocabulary. Research has shown that integrating explicit, multifaceted vocabulary instruction into the existing curriculum of content areas such as science and social studies enhances students' ability to acquire textbook vocabulary (Kamil et al., 2008; Moody et al., 2018).

Furthermore, for English learners (ELs), vocabulary instruction is essential. Because many ELs acquire English vocabulary later, they often enter school with fewer words than their English-speaking peers. Research finds that ELs are capable of eventually matching or even transcending native speaker levels of vocabulary knowledge, especially if they are exposed to vocabulary through a great deal of reading. There is also evidence that the same instructional practices that promote vocabulary learning in students with English as their primary language also promote vocabulary for ELs (Goldenberg & Cárdenas-Hagan, 2023; Snow & Kim, 2007).

Finally, developing students' vocabularies also supports writing ability. Many students have difficulty with writing because they lack sufficient knowledge of words needed to compose what they want to communicate in their writing. An extensive vocabulary is essential for writing longer, elaborated sentences. Word choice based on an awareness of the audience and purpose for a writing task is also important, but word choice is hampered for students with limited vocabularies. Vocabulary instruction supports writing as much as reading (Sedita, 2025).

THE VOCABULARY-COMPREHENSION CONNECTION

One of the oldest findings in educational research is the strong relationship between vocabulary knowledge and reading comprehension. Vocabulary knowledge is a significant predictor of reading comprehension. Vocabulary experts agree that students need to have some knowledge of between 90% and 95% of the words in text for adequate reading comprehension (Nagy & Scott, 2000; Samuels, 2002; Stahl, 1999). Knowing at least 95% of the words enables readers to get the main idea and guess correctly what any unfamiliar words mean. That may seem like a high percentage until one recognizes that there is a small set of very common words that account for most of the words in text, but a small percentage of uncommon words is what carries most of the meaning. Unfortunately, it is often this handful of unique words that are unfamiliar to students.

Simulation Activity: Vocabulary Gaps

The activity in Figure 3.1, which uses passages where some words are missing, is designed to help experience how comprehension is affected when 20% of the words are not known to the reader. Read the passages and answer the questions that follow. The full passages and the source of the texts are provided on page 56.

Simulation Activity

Sample Text #1

Just then the ___ line came ___ under his foot, where he had kept a ___ of the line, and he dropped his ___ and felt the ___ of the small ___ ___ pull as he held the line ___ and ___ to ___it in. The ___ ___ as he pulled in and he could see the blue back of the fish in the ___ and the ___ of his sides before he ___ him over the side and into the boat. He ___ in the ___ in the sun, ___ and ___ shaped, his big, ___ eyes ___ as he thumped his life out against the ___ of the boat with the quick ___ ___ of his neat, fast-moving tail.

Sample Text #2

Non-seed Plants: The division of non-seed plants is shown in Figure 21.6. These plants produce ___ reproductive cells called ___. Non-seed plants include vascular and ___ ___. ___ include small plants commonly called ___. Their flattened bodies resemble the ___ of an animal's liver. ___ are ___ plants that grow only in moist environments. Water and ___ move throughout the ___ by ___ and ___. Studies comparing the ___ of different plant divisions suggest that ___ may be the ___ of all plants.

Questions

1. What do you think these passages are about?
2. What did it feel like to read these passages without knowing some of the words?
3. Did you apply any strategies to help you make meaning?

Figure 3.1. Simulation activity showing how vocabulary gaps affect comprehension. (From Sedita, J. [2025]. *The key vocabulary routine.* Keys to Literacy; reprinted by permission.)

Vocabulary Gaps: Real-World Effects

What happens when students in elementary grades do not acquire enough vocabulary? Many of these students struggle with vocabulary when they are older, often due to a lack of reading across the grades. Upon entering school, students who have more vocabulary knowledge become better readers than those who have limited vocabulary (National Institute for Literacy, 2001). Learners with larger vocabularies tend to read more often, which contributes to the expansion of their vocabulary and improvement in their reading skill. This in turn enables them to read increasingly complex text, resulting in even more vocabulary growth. On the other hand, students who have lower vocabulary knowledge have difficulty getting meaning from what they read, and because they find reading difficult and tedious, they read less. As a result, they learn fewer words because they are not reading broadly enough to encounter and learn new words, and they fall behind compared to their peers.

Unfortunately, the gap in vocabulary knowledge between proficient and below-grade-level readers may grow exponentially if no intervention is provided—there can be as much as a 5-year difference between students by Grade 7 (Chall & Jacobs, 1983; Hirsch, 1996; Moody et al., 2018).

Students' reading comprehension and overall academic success also depends partly on their knowledge of academic vocabulary, as described in the following section.

ACADEMIC VOCABULARY

Academic vocabulary is referred to as *academic English,* or the *language of schooling.* A lack of academic vocabulary knowledge has consistently been identified as an obstacle to student success (Nagy & Townsend, 2012). Academic vocabulary facilitates communication and thinking about content-area information, and it is needed to convey abstract and technical ideas that do not come up in social or casual conversation. Estimates vary on how many words students need to learn every year. The suggested number ranges from 2,000 to 4,000 words per year after Grade 3 (Anderson & Nagy, 1992; Beck & McKeown, 1991; Blachowicz et al., 2013). The number of words high school graduates need to know is estimated to be between 50,000 and 100,000 (Graves, 2016; Hirsch, 2006; Snow & Kim, 2007).

Academic vocabulary includes words derived from Latin and Greek that tend to be longer due to prefixes and suffixes (Nagy & Townsend, 2012, p. 93). One reason that some ELs begin to have more difficulty with literacy beyond Grade 4 is that they have limited academic vocabulary knowledge even though they may have adequate vocabulary for everyday conversations.

Academic vocabulary includes general and subject-specific words, described in Figure 3.2 (Baumann et al., 2012; Nagy & Townsend, 2012; NGA/CCSSO, 2010).

Students acquire academic vocabulary primarily through reading, and so increasing reading time improves their academic vocabulary knowledge.

Academic Words

General academic words: These words include high-frequency words that appear regularly in written text across multiple subjects but are not frequently used in conversational language. They typically have different meanings depending on the content area or discipline in which they are used. A word's meaning may shift slightly in different contexts, although occasionally the shift is dramatic (e.g., ***factor*** used in mathematics versus ***factor*** used in history). General academic words are best taught in authentic contexts in multiple content areas so students can learn the different uses of the words.

Examples: *accentuate, decontextualize, delineate, discriminate, exemplify, investigate, hypothesize, paraphrase, plagiarize, tangential, valid*

Discipline-specific academic words: These words, also called domain-specific words, are words that are unique and essential to learning individual academic disciplines. They typically have just one meaning and are best taught in a single-subject, authentic context so students can make connections between the word and the related disciplinary concept.

Examples: *abolitionist, cytoplasm, diode, federalism, gerund, hypotenuse, isotope, macroeconomics, personification, polynomial*

Figure 3.2. Academic words. (*Sources:* Baumann et al., 2012; Nagy & Townsend, 2012; NGA/CCSSO, 2010.)

Reading Is the Main Way to Learn New Academic Words

Students will learn some new words through direct, explicit instruction provided by the teacher. However, given the limited time in the school day and the large number of words that must be acquired each year, teachers cannot possibly teach all the words students need to learn. Furthermore, students are limited in how much they can learn new academic words through classroom conversation because academic vocabulary is typically not used in everyday conversations. Therefore, the main way that students are exposed to new vocabulary is by reading or listening to academic text.

Teachers should provide all students across all grades with frequent access to high-quality, complex text that includes challenging vocabulary. Reading these kinds of texts enables students to grow their vocabularies and acquire knowledge that supports reading comprehension.

Sometimes, content teachers are hesitant to assign challenging reading tasks to students (or they use below–grade-level text) because some or many of their students do not have sufficient reading skills to independently read complex text. This hesitancy is understandable, but given how essential exposure to high-quality text is for developing vocabulary and reading comprehension ability, teachers must find ways to expose students who are not proficient readers to this kind of text by providing *scaffolds.* This includes enabling students to listen to text that is read by a peer or an adult or provided through the use of text-to-speech software. Studies show that students are able to learn word meanings from texts read aloud at the same rate at which students typically learn from written context (Stahl et al., 1991).

Increasing Reading Time Is Essential

The amount students read is strongly related to their vocabulary knowledge (National Reading Panel, 2000). As noted previously, the main way adolescents and adults learn new academic words is through exposure to written language during reading. Therefore, an important instructional goal in all subjects is to increase the amount of time students spend reading high-quality, complex text during and after school, as well as reading a broad variety of genres about varied topics, often described as *wide reading.* Research has determined that there is a significant difference in word exposure between students who read extensively each day and those who do not. For example, students who read for approximately an hour each day outside of school are exposed to about 4,300,000 words per year, while students who read only about 3 minutes per day are exposed to just 200,000 words (Anderson & Nagy, 1992).

Although reading is the primary means through which students acquire new vocabulary words, teachers in Grades 5–12 should also provide instruction in vocabulary. The sections that follow provide an overview of what good vocabulary instruction looks like in the classroom, then discuss specific instructional methods teachers can use.

WHAT GOOD VOCABULARY INSTRUCTION LOOKS LIKE

Vocabulary instruction research has found that there is no single best method for teaching vocabulary, that vocabulary should be taught both *directly* and *indirectly,* and that there is no best time or subject for vocabulary instruction (Baumann et al., 2003; Graves, 2016; National Reading Panel, 2000). In addition, good vocabulary instruction should develop both depth and breadth of vocabulary and provide students with multiple exposures to a new word.

Direct and Indirect Instruction

Direct instruction means focusing on specific words, such as previewing unfamiliar words prior to reading a selection, or selecting a set of subject-specific words to teach in depth. Direct instruction also includes teaching word-learning strategies, including explicitly teaching students to use the context or knowledge of word parts (roots, suffixes, prefixes) to determine the meaning of an unfamiliar word. *Indirect instruction* includes exposing students to lots of new words and having them read a lot. It also includes helping students develop an appreciation for words and experience enjoyment and satisfaction in their use.

Instruction Focused on Breadth and Depth

To sufficiently expand student vocabulary, instruction must also focus on *breadth* and *depth*. The goal of broad instruction is exposure to many words, whereas the goal of deep instruction is for students to thoroughly learn some words. When students increase their breadth of word knowledge, they increase the number of words for which they have some basic knowledge. When they increase vocabulary depth, they increase the number of words for which they have a deep understanding and which they can readily use in their spoken and written communication. In their review of the vocabulary instruction research, Pressley and colleagues (2007) found that students comprehend more when they are taught vocabulary taken from text they are reading. Focusing on words in content-area text also enables teachers to provide multiple encounters with the words and opportunities to use the words in discussions about the content.

Multiple Exposures

Students gradually learn a new word through multiple exposures to the word in context. The more often a student encounters a word, and the closer together the encounters occur, the greater the chance the word will be learned and remembered. Frequent exposures should be as meaningful as possible, including links to previous information about the word and student discussion about the word as it may relate to different situations. When lesson planning, teachers should try to find ways to repeatedly use new words in homework and classroom assignments, to point out and model the use of the words, and to do so over multiple days of instruction.

Summary of Vocabulary Instruction Research

Decades of research on effective vocabulary instruction has yielded several consistent findings. A summary of this research is provided in Figure 3.3. Teaching suggestions are grouped into general practices and more specific practices associated with previewing, teaching words directly, and teaching words indirectly.

The remaining sections of this chapter provide detailed guidance for how to implement several effective strategies for vocabulary instruction: previewing vocabulary, selecting and teaching targeted words in depth, using word-learning templates, helping students make connections among words, teaching word-learning strategies such as use of context clues and word parts, and fostering students' word consciousness.

PREVIEWING VOCABULARY PRIOR TO READING

Studies have shown that previewing and pre-teaching vocabulary improves comprehension (Billmeyer & Barton, 1998; Graves, 2016; Laflamme, 1997). Recall that if students are not familiar with at least 90% to 95% of the words in a text, their comprehension will be affected (Nagy & Scott, 2000; Samuels, 2002; Stahl, 1999). If students do not know some of the words in text, providing some familiarity with these words during previewing enables them to comprehend while reading, even if they are not deeply learning all the previously unknown words.

Levels of Word Knowledge

Over time, our knowledge of a word evolves and deepens. We gradually acquire words through repeated exposure in meaningful contexts. Each time a word is encountered in a new situation, our familiarity with it grows. The depth of knowledge for a word progresses through four stages (Beck et al., 2002; Graves, 2016): no prior knowledge, limited exposure, recognition of the word without the ability to use it, and a solid understanding with the ability to use the word appropriately. If a student has no prior knowledge of a word, previewing can slightly enhance their understanding.

Effective Vocabulary Instruction

General Instruction Practices

- Use a combination of direct and indirect instruction to help students develop their vocabularies.
- Teach vocabulary every day using content and text in the subject(s) you teach, and dedicate a portion of the regular classroom lesson to explicit vocabulary instruction.
- Immerse students in a rich array of collaborative language experiences in school so they learn words through listening, speaking, reading, and writing. This should include meaningful conversations around text and worthwhile content experiences.
- Increase the amount of reading students do of worthwhile texts that are filled with mature vocabulary, and engage students in authentic discussion about words in the text they read. Reading (or being read to) is the most important factor in increased word knowledge.
- Attend responsively to students' vocabulary needs, including monitoring when they are struggling to identify a word and finding ways to provide definitions of unfamiliar words.
- While most assistance provided for English learners and students who enter school with small vocabularies will not be different in kind from that provided English-only students, English learners will need to be taught more words, will need more intensive instruction, and will need to be given particular help in mastering word-learning strategies.
- Employ a consistent routine for teaching vocabulary that includes multiple components. Collaborate with teachers of the same grade or subject area to use the same routine.
- Teach relationships between words and connect words to background knowledge.

Previewing

- Help students assess their levels of familiarity with terms and help them attend to those that are most important, so they can devote their energy to learning those words that have been identified as central to the content. This can include having students rate their knowledge of the terms.
- Preview and provide some information about unfamiliar words at the initial stages of a unit and prior to reading, and provide definitions to students of potentially unfamiliar words.

Teaching Words Directly

- Select words that have the highest utility within a lesson or unit, and those that have generalizability across other units and subjects.
- Teach everything about a word including how it is spelled, definitions, attributes, examples, related words, visual representations, and use of the word in context.
- Provide multiple exposures to a targeted word in multiple oral and written contexts to increase the likelihood that students will understand and remember the word and use it more frequently.
- Help students deepen their understanding of the varied uses of a word, especially for words with multiple meanings.
- Use activities to help students develop strategies for remembering words and transferring new words to spoken and written vocabulary.

Teaching Words Indirectly

- Teach that the meaning of a word can sometimes be inferred from context clues.
- Teach the meaning of common word parts (roots, prefixes, suffixes) and provide practice in applying this knowledge to understand unfamiliar words.
- Make students word-conscious, and further their metalinguistic awareness of words and interest in words so they become eager word learners.

Figure 3.3. Effective vocabulary instruction. (*Sources:* Blachowicz et al., 2013; Butler et al., 2010; Graves, 2016; Kamil et al., 2008; National Reading Panel, 2000; Pressley et al., 2007; Young et al., 2022.)

Previewing and Background Knowledge

Previewing vocabulary also has benefits related to background knowledge. Research has determined that one's knowledge, including academic content knowledge and vocabulary, and the cultural knowledge developed through day-to-day activities, affects one's reading comprehension. A student with more expertise in a subject covered in a text will comprehend better than a student who has minimal or no knowledge (Hwang & Duke, 2020; Willingham, 2017).

Vocabulary previewing activities provide some basic information about unfamiliar vocabulary and provide an opportunity for students to make connections to the prior knowledge they have about the topic in the text, or to build knowledge if they do not have any. The teacher can provide basic, overall background knowledge about the topic by showing a brief video clip or a series of visuals related to the topic, or by reading a brief text passage.

The Goal: Temporary, Basic Familiarity

The goal of previewing is to offer temporary, basic familiarity with the meaning of the words in text to be read. This is not the same as deeply teaching specific words. Graves (2006) notes that during previewing, the teacher provides just enough information about a word "so students won't stumble over it when they see it in an upcoming passage." Previewing is more about attaching some basic meaning to new words than enabling deep learning of words. Goals for previewing include clearing up misconceptions about a word's meaning, clarifying the meaning of known words with multiple meanings, and helping students connect words to the topic of the text. Given these goals, teachers should not spend a lot of time teaching all the words that are chosen for previewing. Instead, they should select only a few words to teach deeply, something that is addressed later in this chapter.

Teachers should keep the following in mind as they identify words to preview and develop plans for how they will preview the words.

How to Select Words

Follow these guidelines:

- Choose words or phrases essential to understanding the text, including specialized academic words unique to the topic.
- Focus on words that are critical to understanding the major concepts in the text or related unit of study.
- Identify words unfamiliar to most of the students.
- Include words that have multiple meanings, focusing on the meaning relevant to the text.
- Include problematic phrases and figurative language.
- Exclude words that are clearly defined in context or can be understood through contextual clues.
- Base word selections on students' needs rather than solely relying on textbook word lists.

How to Preview Words

Try these activities:

- **Use visuals.** Provide visuals or help students create visuals such as illustrations, symbols, or pictures. This is especially helpful for visual learners and ELs.
- **Provide real-life examples.** Show students how a word is used in different contexts.
- **Use user-friendly definitions.** Avoid complex dictionary definitions that contain other words that are unfamiliar to students. Opt instead for simple, everyday language related to the use of the word in the associated text.
- **Provide synonyms and antonyms.** Introduce words with similar or opposite meanings to reinforce understanding. A thesaurus is helpful.
- **Use everyday language.** Explain words using everyday, connected language instead of dictionary definitions.

- **Offer multiple contexts.** Present words in various scenarios to reinforce meaning, including examples, situations, and questions that are interesting.
- **Use discussion.** Engage students in conversations about unfamiliar words. Asking them to suggest possible meanings enhances understanding.
- **Incorporate collaborative activities.** Have students work in small groups to explore word meanings and check each other's understanding.

Word Knowledge Rating Activities

Previewing activities that ask students to rate their knowledge of words are helpful, such as those described in the following section. These activities are quick and help students make connections to unfamiliar words, reinforce to them that words are learned incrementally, and remind them that they do not need deep knowledge of every word to comprehend while reading.

Thumbs Up, Thumbs Down This is a simple, quick activity. Students hold their thumb up if they know the word, down if they do not, and sideways if they are familiar with a word but cannot explain what it means.

Four Fingers Students hold up the number of fingers that best represent their knowledge of a word using this scale:

1. I have no prior knowledge of this word.
2. I have limited exposure to this word.
3. I recognize this word but cannot use it.
4. I have a solid understanding of this word and can use it.

Word Knowledge Checklists Students use a checklist to identify their levels of word knowledge (Beck et al., 2002). The teacher lists the words to be previewed in the first column. Students rate their knowledge of the words on four levels. View the example in Figure 3.4 that includes a column for students to add information about the words. (A blank copy of the Word Knowledge Checklist is included with the downloadable resources for this chapter.)

The first time students use a checklist, they sometimes rate their knowledge of the words as high because they think the task is something for which they will receive a grade. Teachers should explain that it is common to have minimal or no knowledge about some words encountered in text and encourage students to be honest about their levels of knowledge.

Teachers can use word knowledge checklists in several ways. The simplest is to have students complete the checklist independently in class or for homework. Another option is to have students work in pairs or small groups to discuss their knowledge of the words as they complete the checklist. Having to explain to a peer what is known about a word is helpful.

The checklist can also be used as a whole-class activity. The steps for this activity are listed here.

1. The teacher models correct pronunciation of the words.
2. Students independently rate their knowledge; the teacher reminds them to be honest about the level of knowledge.
3. In small groups, share and discuss word knowledge and identify those words that need clarification.
4. The teacher provides information for words needing clarification.

Previewing vocabulary helps students acquire temporary, basic familiarity with new words. However, it is often necessary for students to learn some new words in greater depth. The sections that follow provide guidelines for how teachers can first select, then teach, these words.

Word Knowledge Checklist

Word	Solid understanding, can use it	Recognition, cannot use it	Limited exposure	No prior knowledge	Notes: definition, synonym, example

Source: Beck et al. (2002).

 (page 1 of 1)

Figure 3.4. Word knowledge checklist. *Available on the Brookes Download Hub.* (*Source*: Beck et al., 2002.)

TEACHING WORDS IN DEPTH

Providing explicit, in-depth instruction for some words is essential for expanding vocabulary across all grade levels, but especially for students who have lower than grade-level vocabulary and reading difficulty. These students are less likely to read extensively, missing out on the opportunity to learn words through multiple exposures in text. Michael Graves explains the benefits of teaching some words in depth:

> Teaching individual words pays a number of important dividends. First, and most obviously, teaching a child a word leaves him with one less word to learn independently. Second, teaching individual words gives students a store of words that they can use to explore and understand their environment. Third, teaching individual words can increase students' comprehension of selections containing those words. Fourth, and very importantly, teaching individual words demonstrates our interest in words, and teaching them in engaging and interesting ways fosters students' interest in words. (2006, p. 59)

How to Select Words

Teachers should consider the following guidelines when targeting words for in-depth instruction (Sedita, 2025):

- Select words that are important to making meaning from the text and learning key concepts in the subject area. Students should be likely to encounter these words again as they read and learn more about the content topic.

- Unfamiliar words that are essential to comprehending the text but not essential to the instructional goal can be previewed but do not need to be selected for in-depth instruction.
- Select words that are uncommon in everyday spoken language but useful and practical to know in many situations because they will be frequently encountered in other reading material and may help in other content areas.
- Select words that provide good opportunities to practice word-learning strategies, such as using the context and analyzing word parts.
- Select a few words that are unique and will increase student curiosity and interest in learning new words.

Teachers should keep the particular needs of their students in mind and their instructional goals as they target and teach words in-depth. It can also be helpful to use a tiered model to categorize words as described in the following section.

A Three-Tier Model

There are too many words for students to learn for all of them to be explicitly taught in school. However, Beck and colleagues (2002) point out that not all words require direct instruction, as many will be learned through repeated exposures in context, including through extensive reading. They proposed a three-tiered model to help teachers select words for in-depth instruction.

- **Tier 1:** These are basic words that typically do not need explicit instruction, as most students already know them through everyday conversation. Examples for Grades 5–12 include *similar, sequence,* and *anticipate.*
- **Tier 2:** These are general academic words that appear frequently across multiple subject areas. Examples for Grades 5–12 include *saunter, verify, escalate,* and *redundant.*
- **Tier 3:** These are subject-specific academic words. Examples for Grades 5–12 include *federalism, aorta, palette,* and *personification.*

The authors of this model note that classifying words into these tiers is not always precise. The boundaries between the tiers may vary depending on individual students' vocabularies. For elementary grades, they recommend focusing on Tier 2 words for explicit instruction, as these words are versatile across various subjects. However, for middle and high school students, in addition to selecting Tier 2 words with broad applicability across subject, content-area teachers should consider teaching a few Tier 3 words to teach in-depth that are essential for understanding key concepts in their respective disciplines. The remaining Tier 3 words can be briefly previewed to give students the necessary context to better comprehend the texts they are reading.

How to Teach the Targeted Words

Knowledge of a word means knowing much more than its definition(s). Words can have multiple meanings depending on the context, function as different parts of speech, and share a root word with other words that have different suffixes and prefixes. Use the following evidence-based practices when teaching a targeted word in depth:

- Teach everything about a word, including how it is pronounced and spelled, definitions and multiple meanings, attributes, examples of use in context, related words, and visual representations of the word.
- Provide multiple exposures to the word in spoken and written contexts.
- Use teacher- and student-generated user-friendly definitions.

- Help students deepen their understanding of the varied uses of the word, especially for words with multiple meanings.
- Use activities to help students develop strategies for remembering and transferring new words to their own spoken and written vocabulary.

The sections that follow explore a few aspects of this type of in-depth instruction: providing multiple exposures, teaching multiple meanings, using synonyms and antonyms, providing visual references, and using the word in a sentence.

Provide Multiple Exposures in Meaningful Contexts Researchers have determined that students need multiple exposures to a word to learn it well (Graves et al., 2014; Swanson et al., 2017), estimating it can take as many as 17 exposures for a student to learn a new word (Kamil et al., 2008). Repeated exposure can be in the same lesson or passage, but the exposures will be most effective if they appear over an extended period of time. Another significant research finding is that these frequent exposures should be in meaningful contexts, including the use of discussion (Kamil et al., 2008; Swanson et al., 2017).

The goal for providing exposure to words in context is to help students deepen their understanding of the varied uses of a word. This includes activities that provide opportunities for active student engagement, including using, listening for, and writing new words. Research-based recommendations include introducing words using everyday explanations rather than dictionary definitions, using activities that provide opportunities for students to interact with word meanings through discussion and writing, and providing engaging examples, situations and questions about words (McKeown & Beck, 2004; Swanson et al., 2017). Figure 3.5 provides examples of activities aligned to these recommendations.

Teach Multiple Meanings Many English words are *polysemous*—that is, they have more than one meaning. For example, the word *development* is used in different ways depending on the subject and context, as shown in Figure 3.6. If students encounter a word for which they know only one meaning, their comprehension will be affected if the word has a different meaning within the context of the text. It is therefore important to teach multiple meanings for words targeted for in-depth instruction, and highlight the meaning aligned to the context of the content lesson or related text.

Use Synonyms and Antonyms Sometimes it is easier for students to learn a word by focusing on words that have similar meaning (synonyms) or opposite meaning (antonyms) such as the examples in Figure 3.7.

Provide Visual References Providing visuals that represent words is a good way to deepen the understanding of new words. Not all words can easily be represented using a visual,

Examples of Activities

- **Connect to an Experience:** Provide an opportunity for students to relate a word to their personal experience.
  - Example: Think of a place you have been that was ***boisterous***. What were the people doing that made the place boisterous?
  - Example: Describe something for which you are a ***novice***.
- **Thumbs Up or Down:** Use words in sentences that may or may not make sense. Students give a thumbs up or down to indicate if the sentence makes sense.
  - Example: Are snow skiers ***prevalent*** in tropical rainforests?
  - Example: Are elephants that move from place to place in the Serengeti Park ***nomadic***?
- **Pose a Question:** Pose a question that requires students to answer using knowledge of a word's meaning.
  - How do you think ***urbanization*** will affect cities in the United States?
  - What is an example of a ***schism***?

Figure 3.5. Examples of activities for providing multiple word exposures in meaningful contexts. (*Sources:* McKeown & Beck, 2004; Swanson et al., 2017.)

Development

1. Act of improving by expanding or enlarging or refining
   "They congratulated them on their development of a plan to meet the emergency."
   "They funded research and development."
2. A process in which something passes by degrees to a different stage (especially a more advanced or mature stage)
   "The development of this idea took many years."
   "the slow development of the author's skill as a writer"
3. (biology) The process of an individual organism growing organically; a purely biological unfolding of events involved in an organism changing gradually from a simple to a more complex level
   "The doctor explained bone development in children."
4. A recent event that has some relevance for the present situation
   "recent developments in the war"
   "What an exciting development!"
5. The act of making some area of land or water more profitable or productive or useful
   "the development of Alaskan resources"
6. A district that has been developed to serve some purpose
   "Such land is practical for small park developments."
7. A state in which things are improving; the result of developing (as in the early part of a game of chess)
   "After the voters saw the latest positive development in the economy, they changed their minds and became supporters of the bill."
   "In chess, you should take care of your development before moving your queen."
8. Processing a photosensitive material in order to make an image visible
   "The development and printing of the pictures took only two hours."
9. (music) The section of a composition or movement (especially in sonata form) where the major musical themes are developed and elaborated

Figure 3.6. Definitions for *development.* (Adapted from WordNet 3.0 Copyright 2006 by Princeton University. All rights reserved.)

but many can. Graphics, pictures, or drawings can be provided by the teacher or generated by students. For example:

- *fatigue:* a picture of someone who is very tired
- *rupture:* a picture of a ruptured pipe with water leaking
- *ensnared:* a picture of a sea turtle caught in a net

Use the Word in a Sentence One way in which teachers can actively engage students with words is to have them generate sentences that incorporate new words they are learning. Students can work independently or work collaboratively with peers to generate sentences. In addition to having students write one sentence for one word, teachers can assign tasks that require deeper critical thinking, such as the following:

- Students use two targeted words in the same sentence or paragraph. For example:
  - o The *suffragists* worked for decades to win the *franchise* in the United States.

Word	Synonym	Antonym
cautiously	carefully	carelessly
destitute	poor	*wealthy*
abundant	ample, bountiful	scarce
intentional	on purpose	accidental

Figure 3.7. Synonym and antonym examples. (From Sedita, J. [2025]. *The key vocabulary routine.* Keys to Literacy; reprinted by permission.)

- In order to *migrate* from England to the New World, early colonists needed *nautical* knowledge to sail across the Atlantic Ocean.

- The teacher uses two or more target words to form a question. Students then answer the question and share their explanations with partners or in small groups (O'Brien, n.d.). For example:
  - Can *incidents* cause *compassion?*
  - Do *territories* that are *possessions* have *autonomy?*

In-depth instruction may involve the use of word-learning templates, as described in the following section.

USING WORD-LEARNING TEMPLATES

Teachers can have students complete word templates that include different types of information about a word—for example, a Frayer Template (Frayer et al., 1969) or the modified Four-Square version, or the Two-Column Template (Sedita, 2015, 2025). Word-learning templates offer opportunities for students to engage deeply with words by integrating multiple types of information about a word. Depending on the template, this can include a visual, characteristics or attributes related to the word, use of the word in a sentence, related words or categories of words, part of speech, synonyms and antonyms, or examples and non-examples. The templates can be used in several ways:

- To introduce a new word
- As part of a class discussion about a word where the teacher and students fill in a template as they learn more about the word
- As a peer collaboration activity where students determine together the best information to add to the template
- As a tool for students to review vocabulary they have learned

Students can save copies of their templates in a personal vocabulary notebook where they can readily access the words to use them in their writing or review for a content vocabulary assessment.

Frayer and Four-Square Templates

The Frayer Method uses a well-researched template that encourages students to analyze a word's meaning and essential attributes and provide examples and non-examples of the word (Frayer et al., 1969). The word is placed at the top of the template or in the center of four squares. An example is shown in Figure 3.8 for the word *nautical.*

The *example/non-example* part of the Frayer Template is sometimes difficult to complete for some words. Teachers can use a modified Four-Square version instead. With this option, teachers and students use the squares for other kinds of information such as multiple meanings, antonyms or synonyms, related words, or a visual that represents the word. (Blank, reproducible copies of both the Frayer and the Four-Square templates are included with the downloadable resources for this chapter on the Download Hub.)

The Two-Column Template

With the Two-Column Template (Sedita, 2015, 2025), the teacher or student places a word in the left column and lists information about the word in the right column (i.e., definition, part of speech, synonym or antonym, example and non-example, multiple meanings, use in a sentence). A visual representation of the word can be included in the left column under the word. Not all the items in the right column are applicable to every word. An example is shown in Figure 3.9 for the word *nautical.* (A blank copy of the Two-Column Template is included with the downloadable resources for this chapter.)

Concept Word: *nautical*

Define the word, include picture if possible – *related to shipping or navigation*	List key characteristics and attributes – *associated with the ocean* – *describes ships, sailors* – *things that help travel over water*
Example – *rigging* and *sails* – *seaman* – *rudder*	Non-example – *mountains* – *train* – *paved roads*

Figure 3.8. Frayer Template example. *Blank version available on the Brookes Download Hub.* (Adapted from Frayer, D.A., Frederick, W.D., & Klausmeier, H.J. [1969]. A schema for testing the level of concept mastery [Technical Report No. 16]. University of Wisconsin, Wisconsin Center for Education Research. As shown in Sedita, J. [2025]. *The key vocabulary routine.* Keys to Literacy; reprinted by permission.)

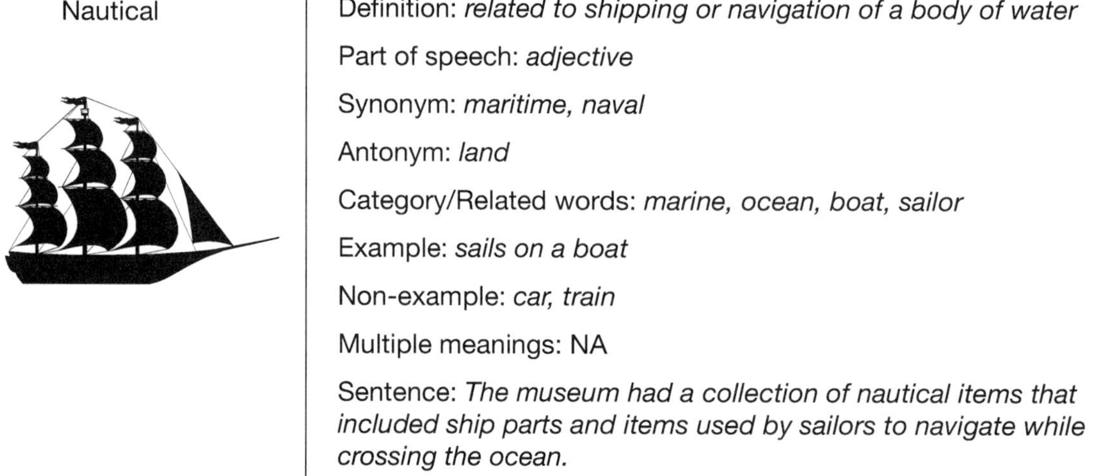

Figure 3.9. Two-Column Template example. (*Key:* NA, not applicable.) *Blank version available on the Brookes Download Hub.* (Reprinted by permission from Sedita, J. [2015]. *The key comprehension routine.* Keys to Literacy; and Sedita, J. [2025]. *The key vocabulary routine.* Keys to Literacy.)

MAKING CONNECTIONS AMONG WORDS

Connecting existing background knowledge to text supports reading comprehension, and word meanings are part of larger knowledge structures, described as *schema*. A *schema* is a mental map that represents and organizes one's understanding of a particular topic and the vocabulary used to represent that knowledge. Word learning is most efficient when a connection to existing schema can be made. Activities that have students associate new words with other related words help them learn these words by making connections to their schemas (Graves, 2006). Many words have multiple meanings and different connotations depending on the subject area. They can also be different parts of speech. When a new word is taught in relation to other words, information becomes available that is unique to how that word is being used in context.

Categorizing, semantic mapping, and *semantic feature analysis* can be used to teach words in relation to other words. These activities help students make connections between new and known words and to background knowledge and existing schemas. The discussion that takes place about words during these activities provides opportunities for rich discussion about words and pushes students to go beyond simply learning definitions to active thinking about how the related words are the same and different.

Categorizing

To generate a categorizing activity, the teacher creates a list of words related to a text or a unit of study. (The activity should only be used if most of the words can be grouped into categories, and it is best used after students have some knowledge of the word meanings.) Students sort the words into teacher-provided categories, or to increase the challenge, students can be asked to generate the categories. A categorizing activity is more effective if students can work collaboratively with peers to generate categories and sort the words. Figure 3.10 shows examples in which the words have already been sorted into categories.

Examples of Categorizing

Social Studies Example

Topic: Egypt

Categories:

- Words related to the Nile River: *cataracts, delta, inundation, tributary, papyrus*
- Words related to the afterlife: *canopic jars, mastaba, natron, Anubis, sarcophagus, shroud, Luxor*
- People: *Hatshepsut, Menes, pharaoh, scribes, Imhotep, artisans*

Mathematics Example

Topic: Geometry

Categories:

- Lines and angles: *ray, vertex, parallel, perpendicular, bisect, midpoint, line segment, adjacent, endpoint*
- Quadrilaterals: *parallelogram, rectangle, rhombus, trapezoid, square*
- Other polygons: *triangle, pentagon, hexagon, octagon, decagon*
- Triangle: *acute, obtuse, isosceles, equilateral, scalene, right*
- Circle: *chord, radius, diameter, center, semicircle, central angle*

Science Example

Topic: Cell Biology

Categories:

- Types of cells: *stem, bone, muscle, nerve, neutrophils, basophils, red and white blood, fat*
- Parts of cells: *cytoplasm, plasma membrane, mitochondrion, nucleus, platelets, organelles, ribosomes*
- Immune system cells: *antibodies, white blood cells, lymphocyte, cytokines, B cells, T cells, macrophages*
- Blood cell diseases: *HIV, sickle cell anemia, hemophilia, anemia, leukemia, myeloma*

Figure 3.10. Examples of categorizing. (From Sedita, J. [2025]. *The key vocabulary routine.* Keys to Literacy; reprinted by permission.)

Semantic Mapping

Semantic mapping (Heimlich & Pittelman, 1986) is a well-researched activity that helps students draw on background knowledge of a topic and make connections among ideas and words related to that topic. It is also highly interactive. A semantic map is usually constructed prior to learning the new words associated with a text or unit of study.

There are two parts to a semantic mapping activity. The first is a brainstorming activity. The teacher chooses a key concept word that is central to the topic covered in the text or unit of study and writes this word on the board or a piece of chart paper. Students are asked to brainstorm any words they know associated with the key word. This brainstorming is best done as a whole class or in small cooperative groups. Then the teacher or a student scribe writes the words on the semantic map. Using the social studies example from Figure 3.10, the teacher might use *Egypt* as the key word. Students might generate some common terms such as *pharaoh, Nile River, Sphinx, desert, pyramids,* and so forth.

The second part is a categorizing activity. Once students have generated a significant number of words, they are asked to make connections among the words, group them, and assign categories for these groupings. The categorizing step is more effective if students collaborate with peers to generate the categories. Teachers can scaffold a semantic mapping activity by providing some words to get students started, posing questions to elicit more words, and providing categories to sort the words. Once students have learned new words from the text or completed the unit of study, the teacher can return to the semantic map and ask students to add more words.

Figure 3.11 is an example of a semantic mapping activity from a high school chemistry class.

Semantic Mapping Example

Key word: *chemical reactions*

Words generated by the students: *macro, properties, bubbles, formula, particles, changes, molecules, liquids, gas, solids, density, atoms, dissolve, evaporate, test, ingredients, comparing, flammability, before/after, test*

Categories: *properties, experiments, particle levels, words related to change*

Figure 3.11. Semantic mapping example.

Semantic Feature Analysis

Semantic feature analysis (Baldwin et al., 1981) is another well-researched activity that helps students recognize similarities and differences among related words. A relational matrix, or grid, is used to show how related words are alike and different. Some knowledge of the words is necessary, so it is best to do this activity after the words have been previewed or after students have learned something about the words.

To generate a semantic feature analysis matrix, the teacher selects a list of related vocabulary words and places them along the left column of the grid. Across the top, opposing axis of the grid, the teacher supplies features that highlight how these words might be similar and different. To complete the grid, students consider each word and determine if each feature applies to the word. A plus sign (+) is placed in the corresponding block on the grid if the feature is associated with the word, and a minus sign (–) is placed if it is not. If students are unsure, a question mark (?) can be placed in the block. Depending on the context in which a word is used, students may determine that both a plus and minus sign can be assigned. This activity is best done by having students work collaboratively to provide an opportunity to discuss words.

Figure 3.12 shows a basic example using animals. It is an example of how a semantic feature analysis causes one to make connections to prior knowledge and schema, as well as how decisions about features are affected by context.

TEACHING WORD-LEARNING STRATEGIES FOR READING

Use of the context and knowledge of meaningful word parts (roots, prefixes, suffixes) to determine the meaning of an unfamiliar word are two research-based word-learning strategies that support vocabulary development (Blachowicz et al., 2013; Graves, 2016). Proficient readers integrate both strategies as they read. When used in tandem, context (outside the word) and word parts (inside the word) can be helpful as students encounter unfamiliar words when reading.

	herbivore	carnivore	fur	scales	feathers	live underwater	live on land
raccoon	+	+	+	–	–	–	+
whale	–	+	–	–	–	+	–
frog	–	+	–	–	–	+	+
seagull	+	+	–	–	+	–	+
ant	+	+	–	–	–	–	+
rabbit	+	-	+	–	–	–	+
fish	+	+	–	+	–	+	–
ostrich	+	+	–	–	+	–	+
snake	–	+	–	+	–	+	+

Figure 3.12. Semantic Feature Analysis example.

Teach Use of Context

Readers use context by locating words or phrases in the text that give clues to the meaning of an unknown word. Sometimes graphics or visuals in the text can also provide clues to meaning. Expository, nonfiction text tends to offer more context clues than narrative text. Multiple studies have shown that when students are taught to use context clues, they become better at figuring out the definitions of words compared to students who are not directly taught this skill (Blachowicz et al., 2013; Graves, 2016; Kuhn & Stahl, 1998).

Context clues may appear within the same sentence as the target word, as in this example:

> The nation was undergoing *urbanization,* the movement of people into cities.

Or, the surrounding sentences may provide context clues, as in this example:

> In 1922, Howard Carter and his crew were the first team to find King Tut's tomb. They came across many *obstacles* while searching. One was that the daily temperature reached as high as 120 degrees. Another was that the tomb is in the desert where there is nothing to protect people from the hot sun. To make things worse, there was a lot of sand and rock around the tomb that were difficult to remove because the summer sun made them very hot to touch. (Vaughn et al., 2022)

To teach students how to use context clues during reading, teachers should share examples from classroom texts and explicitly teach the different types of context clues. It is also important to teach students the limitations of this strategy.

Share Examples in Classroom Text The best way to teach students how to use the context is to provide many examples from content reading. Before students read a text, the teacher can identify a few examples where the text provides clues to the meaning of words, preferably words unfamiliar to students that are targeted for in-depth instruction. Before reading, the teacher asks students to read the sentence containing the word and any surrounding text or visuals that provide clues to making meaning. A quick discussion follows about what is in the text that provides information about the word.

Graves (2006, p. 99) suggests teaching students the following four-step strategy for inferring words from context:

1. Read carefully and ask yourself, "Does this make sense?"
2. Notice when you don't know the meaning of a word and slow down. Read that sentence at least once more, looking for clues.
3. If necessary, go back and reread the preceding sentence, looking for clues that help you figure out what the word might mean.
4. When you figure out what the word might mean, substitute your guess for the difficult word and see if it makes sense. If it does, keep on reading. If it doesn't, try again.

Teach Different Types of Context Clues There are six different types of context clues, identified in Figure 3.13 with examples: definition, description, synonym, comparison, contrast, and example.

Types of Context Clues

Type of clue	Explanation	Example
Definition	The word is defined directly in the sentence.	***Diffusion*** is the net movement of the particles of a substance from where they are more concentrated to where they are less concentrated.
Description	The word is described by information in the context.	***Pollination*** occurs when a pollen grain from a male plant lands on the stigma of a female plant.
Synonym	A word that is similar is provided.	It was a ***triptych***, or three-paneled, painting.
Comparison	The word is compared with something similar.	***Cumulus*** clouds look like a pile of cotton balls.
Contrast	The word is contrasted with another word, usually an antonym.	Unlike a compound, an ***element*** cannot be broken down into simpler materials.
Example	Examples related to the word are provided.	Phil's statement about everything and everybody having a good side showed that he was an ***optimist***.

Figure 3.13. Types of context clues. (From Sedita, J. [2025]. *The key vocabulary routine.* Keys to Literacy; reprinted by permission.)

Discuss Limitations of This Strategy It is important to point out that contexts vary in how much information they provide a reader and are not always helpful. The first example that follows provides only partial clues. In the second example, the context is misleading.

> In order to gain active immunity to a disease, one of two things must occur—either you come down with the disease, or you receive a *vaccination*.

In this example, the student may guess that a vaccination has something to do with preventing disease, but there is not enough information to discern just what a vaccination is.

> "Sandra had won the dance contest, and the audience's cheers brought her to the stage for an encore. 'Every step she takes is so perfect and graceful,' Ginny said *grudgingly* as she watched Sandra dance." (Beck et al., 2002)

In this example, the student might wrongfully assume that Ginny admired Sandra's dancing.

Teach Use of Word Parts

When students encounter an unknown word, they can sometimes use their knowledge of the individual units of meaning (roots, prefixes, suffixes) to help determine the meaning of the word. This is called *structural analysis* or *morphemic analysis*. Research finds that using this strategy to determine the meaning of words improves vocabulary and reading comprehension (Goodwin & Ahn, 2013). For example, in the sentence that follows, knowing that *bi* means *two* and *sect* means *cut*, together with the context clue *two equal slices*, helps determine that the word *bisect* means *cut in two*.

With the skill of a surgeon, the chef will *bisect* the pie into two equal slices.

This vocabulary strategy is especially helpful in upper grades because a large percentage of unfamiliar, content-area words encountered in Grade 5 and above are multisyllabic words derived from Latin and Greek that may be difficult to read (Carlisle, 2007; Kearns, 2015). Nagy and Anderson (1984) estimated that 60% of the unfamiliar words middle school students encounter in books are derived words whose meaning could be figured out by analysis of word structure and their use in the passage.

For example, the root *bio* (meaning *life, living organisms*) reappears again and again in science text (e.g., *biology, biologist, biosphere, biodegradable, biochemical, biohazard*). In the word *monotheism*, if students recognize the prefix *mono-* (meaning *one, alone, single*) and the base word *theism* (meaning *belief in the existence of a god or gods*), they can infer that *monotheism* means the belief in one god. Other examples of common word parts include the following:

- tri = three (triangle)
- trans = across, through (transport)
- contra = opposite (contradiction)
- logy/ology = study of (psychology)
- spect = look, observe (inspect)
- graph = write, record (photograph)

Teach Students to Deconstruct Words To use knowledge of word parts to determine the meaning of an unknown multisyllabic words, students need to *deconstruct* a word into its meaningful parts. Teachers can instruct students to find prefixes, suffixes, and roots in the word and then ask themselves if they know the meaning of any of the word parts. Figure 3.14 includes three examples of words that have been deconstructed into meaningful parts. Chapter 8, "Advanced Word Study and Fluency," includes additional suggestions for teaching word parts.

transportable	introspective	hypothermia
trans: *to the other side of, across, through* port: *to carry* able: *capable of being* Definition: *capable of being carried across or through to somewhere else*	intro: *in, within, to the inside* spect: *to look* ive: *quality or nature of* Definition: *looking inside oneself*	hypo: *under, below* therm: *measurement of heat* ia: *state of, condition of* Definition: *a state in which the unit of heat is below expected*

Figure 3.14. Examples of meaningful word parts. (From Sedita, J. [2025]. *The key vocabulary routine.* Keys to Literacy; reprinted by permission.)

Discuss Limitations of This Strategy Keep in mind that there are some limitations to structural analysis. Recognition of a meaningful word part typically provides the gist of an unfamiliar word, not an exact definition. When a reader combines this with use of the context, it may be sufficient to understand enough about the word's meaning to support reading comprehension. However, teachers must also make students aware that structural analysis does not always work. This is because some prefixes are not consistent in meaning (e.g., *in-* means both *not* and *in*) and because the meanings of many Greek and Latin roots have changed substantially over hundreds of years, and they no longer lend themselves to literal translation.

FOSTERING WORD CONSCIOUSNESS

When students develop word consciousness, they develop an interest in learning and using new words and becoming more skillful and precise in word usage. Promoting word consciousness is an essential way to motivate students to read and build their vocabularies (Graves, 2006, 2016). Teachers can help students become interested in words on both a cognitive and an emotional level by sharing their enjoyment of learning new words. A word-conscious classroom is full of unusual, interesting, new words. Figure 3.15 includes suggestions for creating what Beck and colleagues (2002, 2004) describe as a "word-rich classroom" that fosters word consciousness.

Teach Etymology

Etymology is the study of the origin and historic development of a word. Discovering the earliest known use of a word, its changes in form and meaning, and its transmission from one language to another can be used to build students' curiosity about words. Teachers can use online resources with students to discover the history of a word. Figure 3.16 includes some examples of words with interesting histories.

Engage in Word Play

Research finds that incorporating different types of word play in the classroom goes a long way to promote an interest in words (Blachowicz & Fisher, 2004; Lehr et al., 2004). Word play includes word jokes and riddles, puns, idioms, word-category games, and word manipulations such as anagrams (rearranging letters in a word). These activities develop domains of word meaning and relatedness as they engage students in practice and rehearsal of words (Graves, 2016).

Suggestions for Fostering Word Consciousness

- Share with students your favorite words, how you recently learned a new word, or how you had a misunderstanding about a new word.
- Instruct students to keep a record of words they have learned, perhaps in the form of a personal word journal.
- Be a model for how new or unique words are used by replacing simple terms with more sophisticated and precise terms when talking to students.
- Encourage students to make connections with new words outside the classroom by finding examples in books, other paper or digital texts, and video or television. Finding words outside of class can be required or for extra credit.
- Create a suggestion box for students to place possible words for expanding the classroom word pool.
- Provide resources in the classroom for learning about new words, including a user-friendly online dictionary and thesaurus.
- Find opportunities to make connections between words that share the same roots or prefixes.

Figure 3.15. Fostering word consciousness.

General academic words:

phony: not real or genuine, fake

Comes from the English word *fawney*, which before 1900 referred to a gilt brass ring used by swindlers. The swindlers would say the rings were made of real gold, but they were fakes.

hazard: an unavoidable danger or risk

Comes from the 12th-century Old French word *hasard*, or *hasart*, which meant a game of *chance played with dice*. The word evolved to mean *chances in gambling* and eventually *chance of loss*, *harm*, *risk* in English in the 1500s.

Figure 3.16. Etymology examples.

SUMMARY

This chapter emphasizes that vocabulary knowledge is foundational to academic success, particularly in reading and writing. Students with extensive vocabularies comprehend texts more easily, learn new concepts more rapidly, and communicate more effectively. As students progress through school, they encounter increasingly complex academic vocabulary, which is essential for learning across content areas. Effective vocabulary instruction should include both direct teaching of selected words and indirect exposure through reading. Instructional suggestions include previewing words before reading, selecting, and teaching targeted words in-depth, using activities to make connections among words, teaching word-learning strategies (like context clues and word parts), and fostering word consciousness.

REFLECTION QUESTIONS

1. Explain the connection between vocabulary knowledge and reading comprehension.
2. How is academic vocabulary different from the vocabulary used in everyday conversations? Give some examples of academic vocabulary from the content and texts you use with students.
3. Explain what is meant by direct and indirect instruction, and the difference between vocabulary instruction focused on breadth versus depth of word knowledge.
4. What are the benefits of previewing unfamiliar words before reading? How might you incorporate one of the suggestions for previewing into your instruction?
5. What are two suggestions for selecting words to teach in depth that are most helpful to you? What are three suggestions for teaching words in depth that you would like to use in your instruction?
6. Describe the kinds of information about a word that are provided in a Frayer/Four-Square Template and Two-Column Template.
7. Categorizing, semantic mapping, and semantic feature analysis are activities that can help students make connections between words. Which of these would be most helpful for supporting your teaching goals?
8. What is the advantage of integrating both use of context and knowledge of meaningful word parts to determine the meaning of an unfamiliar word when reading? Find at least one clear example for each of these strategies in the text you use with students.
9. What can you do to foster word consciousness for the students you work with?

////////////

Simulation Activity: Full Passages

The first passage is from the novel *The Old Man and the Sea* by Ernest Hemingway (1952). The second passage is an example of a high school science text. The words that were missing from both passages are underlined.

Sample Text #1

Just then the <u>stern</u> line came <u>taut</u> under his foot, where he had kept a <u>loop</u> of the line, and he dropped his <u>oars</u> and felt the <u>weight</u> of the small <u>tuna's</u> <u>shivering</u> pull as he held the line firm and commenced to <u>haul</u> it in. The <u>shivering</u> <u>increased</u> as he pulled in and he could see the blue back of the fish in the <u>water</u> and the <u>gold</u> of his sides before he <u>swung</u> him over the side and into the boat. He <u>lay</u> in the <u>stern</u> in the sun, <u>compact</u> and <u>bullet</u> shaped, his big, <u>unintelligent</u> eyes <u>staring</u> as he thumped his life out against the <u>planking</u> of the boat with the quick <u>shivering</u> <u>strokes</u> of his neat, fast-moving tail.

Sample Text #2

Non-seed Plants: The division of non-seed plants is shown in Figure 21.6. These plants produce <u>hard-walled</u> reproductive cells called <u>spores.</u> Non-seed plants include vascular and <u>nonvascular</u> <u>organisms</u>. <u>Hepaticophyta</u> include small plants commonly called <u>liverworts</u>. Their flattened bodies resemble the <u>lobes</u> of an animal's liver. <u>Liverworts</u> are <u>nonvascular</u> plants that grow only in moist environments. Water and <u>nutrients</u> move throughout the <u>liverwort</u> by <u>osmosis</u> and <u>diffusion</u>. Studies comparing the <u>biochemistry</u> of different plant divisions suggest that <u>liverworts</u> may be the <u>ancestors</u> of all plants

Four-Square Template

Word: ____

Frayer Template

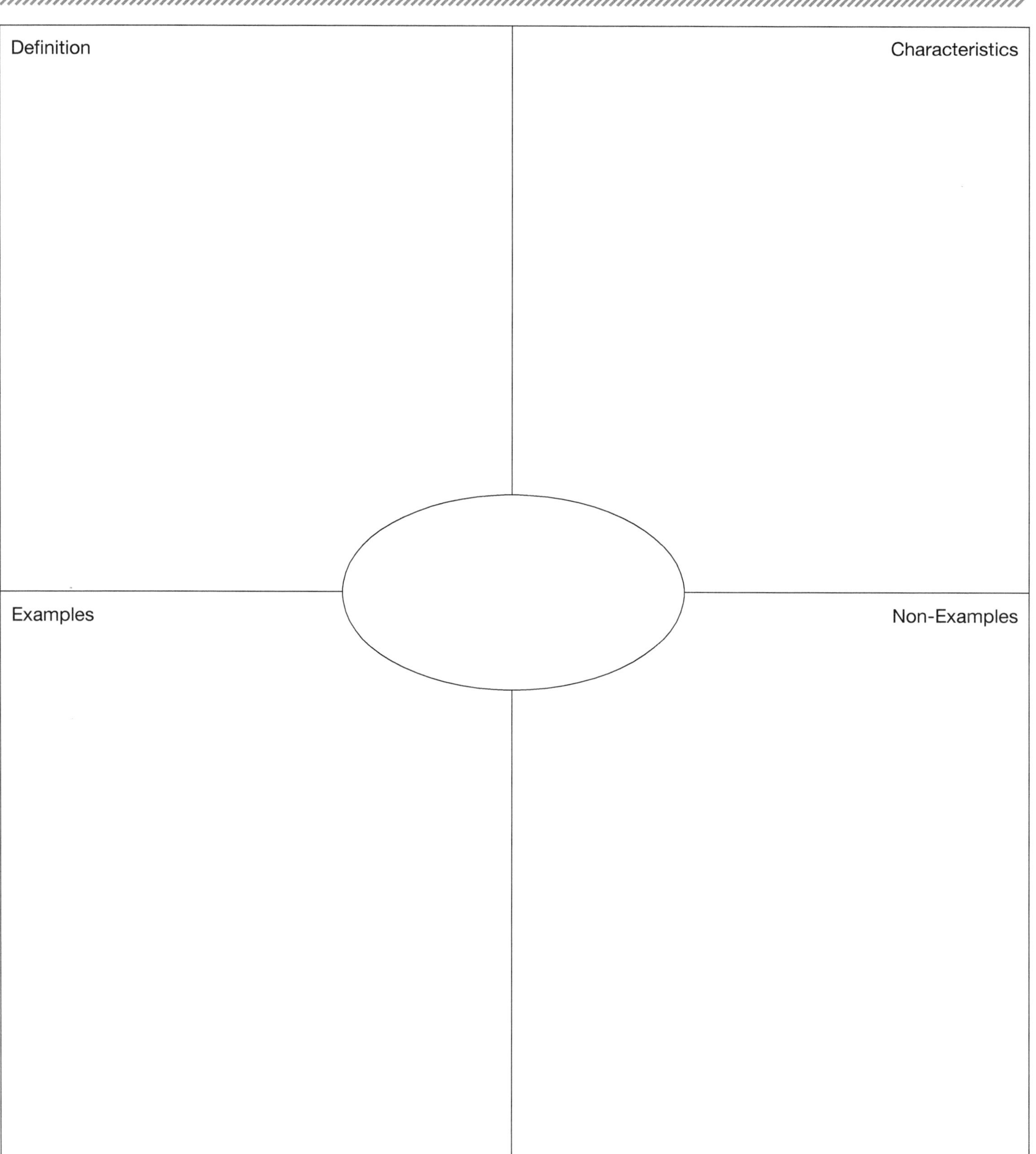

Adapted from Frayer, D.A., Frederick, W.D., & Klausmeier, H.J. (1969). A schema for testing the level of concept mastery (Technical Report No. 16). University of Wisconsin, Wisconsin Center for Education Research. As shown in Sedita, J. (2025). *The key vocabulary routine*. Keys to Literacy.

Two-Column Notes Template

word	Definition: Part of speech: Synonym: Antonym: Category/Related words: Example: Non-example: Multiple meanings: Sentence: Illustration:

Reprinted by permission from Sedita, J. (2015). *The key comprehension routine.* Keys to Literacy; and Sedita, J. (2025). *The key vocabulary routine.* Keys to Literacy.

Word Knowledge Checklist

Word	Solid understanding, can use it	Recognition, cannot use it	Limited exposure	No prior knowledge	Notes: definition, synonym, example

Source: Beck et al. (2002).

4

Comprehension Instruction

The National Reading Panel's (2000) review of research related to reading comprehension found that reading comprehension is a complex, active process that requires intentional and thoughtful interaction between the reader and the text, and vocabulary knowledge plays a significant role in understanding what is read.

Since 2000, reading researchers and experts have confirmed these findings and identified additional factors with implications for comprehension instruction. Catts (2021–2022) points out that reading comprehension is more than a single construct that can be measured with one general reading test; it is a complex activity that depends on a wide range of knowledge and skills. Duke and colleagues (2021) summarize comprehension research findings as follows:

- Teaching foundational word-reading and bridging skills supports reading comprehension development (phonological awareness, phonics and word recognition, morphological awareness, fluency).
- Teaching text structures and features fosters reading comprehension development.
- Vocabulary and knowledge building support reading comprehension development.
- Comprehension strategy instruction improves reading comprehension.
- Supporting engagement with text fosters comprehension development (reading widely and in volume, discussing and analyzing texts, or writing about texts).

This chapter begins by exploring the factors that contribute to reading comprehension and the importance of making sure all students have access to high-quality, grade-level text. Instructional suggestions are then provided for developing students' reading comprehension abilities. The chapter ends with suggestions for planning and conducting a close reading lesson.

FACTORS THAT CONTRIBUTE TO READING COMPREHENSION

Comprehension is affected if words are incorrectly recognized, if the text includes words that the reader does not know, if the linguistic structure of the sentences is overly complex, or if the topic of the reading material is so unfamiliar that the reader cannot make inferences that are necessary to understanding the text (Snow et al., 1999). Fluency, metacognition, knowledge, text structure, and language structures each play a role in enabling reading comprehension.

Fluency

The ability to read fluently, including with accuracy and prosody at a sufficient pace, is essential for reading comprehension. Students who have not developed fluent decoding skills by the end of Grade 3 must devote so much cognitive attention to these foundational skills that they are not able to focus on the critical thinking needed to comprehend while reading.

Metacognition

When students are metacognitive, they are aware of themselves as readers, they realize when they are not comprehending, and they know how to use comprehension strategies to support their understanding. The ability to make inferences to *read between the lines* is also essential.

Background Knowledge

Comprehension is affected when students do not know the meaning of most of the words in the text they are reading. It is also affected when they do not have sufficient background knowledge about the topics in the text gained from life experiences or subject-area learning.

Text Structure

When they first learn how to read, students must develop knowledge of how print works. As they move past the primary grades, they must also learn how text structure at the paragraph level and longer text levels supports understanding while reading.

Language Structures

Syntactic awareness (awareness of the rules of grammar) and semantic knowledge (the relationships of word meaning at the phrase, sentence, or text levels) are important contributing factors for comprehending while reading.

Understanding how these factors contribute to comprehension contributes to our understanding of the key components of good comprehension instruction.

ACCESS TO HIGH-QUALITY, GRADE-LEVEL TEXT

Students across all grades and subjects should be provided access to high-quality, grade-level texts that offer opportunities to develop academic language (vocabulary and syntactic awareness) and acquire knowledge about the world, both of which contribute to development of reading comprehension. As students move through the grades, they should regularly read increasingly complex, grade-level text on their own, with scaffolds provided for students who need assistance.

To provide students with access to appropriate texts, teachers in Grades 5–12 will need to measure text difficulty, select texts, and plan supports for challenging texts.

Measuring Text Difficulty

Text complexity is determined by a range of quantitative and qualitative features and depends on the reader and task for which it is selected. Teachers must consider three aspects to measuring complex text in tandem when they identify text to use with students: quantitative dimensions, qualitative dimensions, and reader and task considerations (NGA/CCSSO, 2010).

Quantitative Dimensions of Text Complexity *Quantitative dimensions* refers to those aspects of text complexity, such as word length or frequency, sentence length, and text cohesion, that are difficult for a human reader to evaluate efficiently, especially in long texts. These text aspects are typically measured by a computer, using measurements such as *Lexile* levels or readability formulas such as Flesch-Kincaid and Dale Chall.

Qualitative Dimensions of Text Complexity *Qualitative dimensions* refers to those aspects of text complexity best measured by a human reader, such as levels of meaning or purpose; format and text structure; language and conventionality and clarity (vocabulary, sentence structure); and knowledge demands. Questions for teachers to consider include:

- How much of the text language is conversational and how much is academic?
- How much is literal and how much is figurative?
- Does the text contain singular or multiple themes or themes that are complex?
- Does the text require everyday or familiar knowledge, or knowledge outside the familiar?

Reader and Task Considerations While quantitative and qualitative elements focus on the inherent complexity of text, teachers must also consider variables specific to particular readers (such as motivation, knowledge, and experiences) and to particular tasks (such as purpose and the complexity of the task assigned and the questions posed) when determining whether a text is appropriate for a given student. Such assessments are best made by teachers employing their professional judgement, experience, and knowledge of their students and the subject (NGA/CCSSO, 2010).

Questions to consider include:

- Will the student be interested and motivated to read the text?
- What level of previous knowledge does the student have about the topic of the text?
- What background knowledge might need to be provided about the topic of the text?
- What level of reading skills is required, and are scaffolds needed to support independent reading of the text?

Selecting Text

Teachers should consider two types of qualitative measures when selecting text to use with students. The first is the complexity of the language: the difficulty level of the vocabulary, complex sentences, and challenging cohesion and cross-reference between sentences. The second is the complexity of meaning: the level of background knowledge required, degree of inference required, and complexity of the ideas. Teachers should consider all of the following qualitative measures when selecting text: figurative language, language conventions and clarity, text density and complexity, purpose for reading the text, text features including graphics, vocabulary, and variations of standard English.

Supports for Challenging Text

Teachers can help students who have reading difficulty access and understand the concepts in text by thinking aloud and explaining what the text is saying, summarizing text information, posing guiding questions, and providing opportunities for collaborative, peer discussion about the text.

By providing explicit instruction of vocabulary and comprehension strategies and giving students opportunities to practice using these strategies with teacher guidance, content-area teachers can give students the tools they need to navigate texts independently. Detailed suggestions for comprehension strategies are provided in this chapter (analyzing text and close reading, graphic organizers, note taking, summarizing, using questions). Other strategies that support comprehension are found in Chapter 3, "Vocabulary Instruction," Chapter 5, "Teaching Text Structure," and Chapter 7, "Supporting Learning Through Discussion."

WHAT GOOD COMPREHENSION INSTRUCTION LOOKS LIKE

Instruction to help students' reading comprehension can be organized into several categories: writing about text, vocabulary, text structure, background knowledge, inferencing, metacognition, and comprehension strategies.

Use Writing to Support Comprehension

Recall from Chapter 1 that writing about text supports comprehension (Graham & Perin, 2007; Graham et al., 2015, 2020). Graham and Hebert (2010, p. 13) note that writing enhances reading comprehension because it affords greater opportunities to think about ideas in a text, requires students to organize and integrate those ideas into a coherent whole, fosters explicitness, facilitates reflection, encourages personal involvement with texts, and involves students transforming ideas into their own words.

Based on their research meta-analysis, they recommend the following activities, which are addressed in greater depth later in this chapter and in Chapter 6, "Writing Instruction":

- Have students respond to text by writing personal reactions, analyzing, and interpreting the text.
- Have students write summaries of a text.
- Have students write notes about a text.
- Have students answer questions about a text in writing, or create and answer questions about a text in writing.

Develop Vocabulary

Vocabulary development plays an important role in improving students' comprehension of text. As noted in Chapter 3, vocabulary knowledge is a significant predictor of reading comprehension. Students need to be familiar with 90%–95% of the words in a text to fully understand what they are reading (Nagy & Scott, 2000; Samuels, 2002), and teaching students the meanings of words in text supports their comprehension of that text (Duke et al., 2021). Vocabulary instruction should be integrated throughout the school day in all subjects and should combine direct and indirect instruction. It should also focus on breadth and depth of word learning, as discussed in Chapter 3.

Teach Text Structure

Awareness of a text's structure provides clues to making meaning and the features of written text have a significant impact on reading comprehension. Complex or disorganized text structure at the sentence, paragraph, passage, or book level can negatively affect comprehension. Awareness of text structure also supports writing, enabling students to better organize the content of their writing pieces. Research finds that students benefit from instruction in common structures and elements of narrative and informational text (Duke et al., 2021). Instruction about text structure can focus on several levels (Sedita, 2020d):

- Overall structure for the three main types of text (opinion/argument, informational, narrative), including introductions, conclusions, and body development
- Paragraph structure
- Patterns of organization (description/explanation, sequence, cause and effect, compare and contrast, problem and solution)

Chapter 5, "Teaching Text Structure," provides additional details and instruction suggestions.

Develop Background Knowledge

Research has determined that students' knowledge, including academic content knowledge and the cultural knowledge developed through day-to-day activities, affects their reading comprehension. A student with more expertise in a subject covered in a text will comprehend better than a student who has minimal or no knowledge of the subject (Cervetti & Hiebert, 2019; Hwang & Duke, 2020; Willingham, 2017).

Knowledge about the content in text provides a scaffold for learning, enabling students to deepen their existing knowledge, better retain new ideas and knowledge from the text, and increase vocabulary knowledge. Recall from Chapter 3 that background knowledge is organized in a *schema,* a mental map that represents and organizes one's understanding of a particular topic, including concepts and the words used to represent those concepts. If students have a well-developed schema about a subject in text they are reading, it will be easier to recognize the vocabulary and understand similar applicable knowledge. Teachers can support students by providing opportunities to make connections to knowledge they already have about the subject of a text, or by providing some basic knowledge prior to reading.

There are several ways teachers can activate or provide background knowledge.

Provide Some Background Knowledge Even students who have developed significant background knowledge about a lot of topics will encounter text about which they have little or no knowledge. Teachers can provide basic information such as showing a brief video or a series of visuals related to the topic, or reading a brief text passage.

Preview Unfamiliar Vocabulary Prior to reading, the teacher should identify words in the text that might be unfamiliar to students. Remember, the goal of previewing is to provide just enough knowledge about the words so students do not *stumble* over them while they read (Graves, 2006), rather than deeply teaching the words. There are many ways teachers can provide basic information for words in a preview list: provide a visual representation of the word, use the word in a sentence, provide a user-friendly definition, provide synonyms or antonyms, use everyday examples of how the word is used, or conduct a discussion on what students already know about the words.

Share the Big Ideas A basic outline or graphic organizer that presents the topics, subtopics, and main ideas from the text helps students see the big picture of what they are about to read. Prior to reading, the teacher can ask students if they are familiar with any of the topics or main ideas.

Pose Prereading Questions The teacher can pose questions related to the content of the text and ask students to think about finding the answers to these questions as they read. This type of prereading activity helps students activate any prior knowledge they have about the text and gives them a focus and purpose for their reading.

Use a Prediction Task Prediction is a strategy that leads readers to anticipate what the author will reveal. After the teacher provides some information about the text using any of the activities listed previously, the teacher asks students to make some predictions about what they think they may learn based on that information. Predicting is a tool readers can apply in certain reading situations, but it can only work if there is some relevant knowledge available. This might be provided by the teacher (Shanahan, 2023).

Teach Inference-Making

When middle and high school students read grade-level texts, they often need to make inferences about things that are not directly stated in the text. Inferences are made by reaching conclusions based on clues and reasoning. For example, we apply our knowledge and experience to infer that something has happened even if we do not actually see or hear the event. Based on what we know, it makes sense to think that what we have inferred has happened. Similarly, a reader makes inferences by establishing appropriate, meaningful connections between separate pieces of information literally stated in the text and the reader's background knowledge. It is sometimes called *reading between the lines.*

Inference is essential to understanding text passages because authors do not always explicitly state information or explain concepts. Comprehending while reading is explained as the construction of a *mental model* that requires readers to integrate information from the text with their own experiences and background knowledge to make full sense of what they read. This is also described as a *situation model* (Bower & Morrow, 1990; Kintsch, 1998; Zwaan, 2016).

Knowledge-based inferences enable readers to establish causality, draw conclusions, and infer important relationships. These inferences require students to search their memories and connect knowledge from outside the text with information in the text (The Meadows Center, 2018).

Weak comprehenders generate fewer inferences than their more skilled peers and are less likely to engage in integrative processing (Oakhill & Cain, 2016).

Basic Examples

Review the two examples that follow and consider how the reader must integrate the information in the text with prior knowledge to be able to comprehend (Oakhill & Cain, 2016). Use the questions to guide your thinking.

Example 1 Johnny carried a jug of water. He tripped on a step. Mom gave him a mop.

- Why did Johnny's mother give him a mop?
- What background knowledge is needed?

Example 2 Bobby was busy with his bucket and spade. The sandcastle was nearly complete. Then a huge wave crashed onto the shore. On seeing that his day's work had been ruined, Bobby started to cry.

- Why did Bobby start to cry?
- What inference must be made about the sandcastle that is not explicitly stated?
- What background knowledge is needed?

Advanced Examples

Review the sample science and literature passages found in Chapter 2, Figure 2.4. Consider the following inferences that can be made.

Inferences from the science text:

- Placing dihydroartemisinic acid (DHAA) under ultraviolet (UV) light is the most effective way to produce artemisinin to be used against malaria.
- DHAA should not be kept under UV light for longer than 8 days.

Inferences from the literature passage:

- The man and his family were very poor.
- Al was more sympathetic and charitable than Mae.
- The family could not afford shoes or clothing for the children.
- The children often went hungry.

Teaching Suggestions

The Meadows Center for Preventing Risk (2018) suggests using the metaphor of an iceberg to explain inference-making to students:

> When we look at an iceberg from a boat, we only see just a small part of it that floats above the water. Most of the iceberg is below the water's surface. Reading is similar to looking at an iceberg. The words on the page are just the tip of the meaning. To understand the full meaning of the text, you have to look beneath the surface of the words. This involves thinking hard and digging into your knowledge about people and the world, and making educated guesses about what is going on in the text. These educated guesses are based on information in the text and information from your background knowledge.

Before students read, teachers should preview the text to identify where inference is required and make sure students have the related background knowledge needed to make the inference. If they do not, the teacher should provide some background knowledge and raise their awareness of where inferences must be made. Using an example in the text, the teacher should model and explicitly teach how to look for clues to work out critical pieces of information that are not stated. See the example in Figure 4.1.

Many studies of inference instruction have found providing students with opportunities to answer inference questions to be effective (Nice et al., 2024). This includes using explicit instruction with the teacher modeling and providing feedback for how to use questions (Hall, 2016). Following the Gradual Release of Responsibility model (Pearson & Gallagher, 1983), the teacher starts by modeling their own thinking about how to answer an inference question. Students are then given an opportunity to answer

Inference Example

A small group of adults were standing and sitting in the small shelter on the corner of the city street. Several of them rubbed their hands together and stamped their feet on the frozen sidewalk. One person glanced at the schedule on the wall of the shelter. It was seven o'clock in the morning and the people had briefcases and lunch bags.

Possible inferences: it was winter, they were waiting for a bus, some of them were taking a bus to work

What were the clues?

- **Winter:** in the small shelter, rubbed hands together, frozen sidewalk
- **Waiting for a bus:** shelter on corner of the city street, person glanced at the schedule
- **Bus to work:** seven o-clock in the morning, had briefcases and lunch bags

Figure 4.1. Inference example.

inference questions with scaffolding as needed. Eventually, students reach independence when they are able to answer questions on their own.

Basic questions such as *who, where, why,* and *when* are useful (Barth & Thomas, 2022), as well the following types of questions (Nice et al., 2024):

- Questions focused on word meaning (e.g., "What does this word/phrase mean in this passage?")
- Questions focused on integrating pieces of information to gain meaning (e.g., "How is this flood similar to other flooding disasters?")
- Questions related to more elaborate inferences that require making a background knowledge-based inference (e.g., "Based on what you know about ______, why do you think ______?")

Teaching students to generate their own questions about text has also been identified as effective in inference instruction studies. Student-generated questions can support inference-making, help students get better at answering questions in general, and improve their metacognition—that is, their awareness of whether they understand what they read (Nice et al., 2024). Suggestions for teaching students how to generate questions to support comprehension are provided later in this chapter.

Develop Metacognition

Metacognition is the process of considering and regulating one's own learning. When students are metacognitive while reading, they are thinking critically about their own understanding as they read. It is often described as *thinking about thinking.*

- Proficient comprehenders constantly monitor whether or not they are understanding as they read and catch themselves when they make an error. They then apply a strategy to get their understanding on track.
- Students who struggle with comprehension often are not aware that they are not comprehending. If they do realize they are not understanding, they do not have strategies to do something about it.

Students benefit from explicit instruction for how to be aware when they are having difficulty making sense of what they are reading. The cause of that difficulty may be that they have incorrectly decoded a word(s), there are unfamiliar words, or they cannot understand information or concepts in the text.

Vaughn and colleagues (2022) suggest teachers help students determine when they do not understand the text, teach them to ask themselves questions as they read to check their understanding, and provide opportunities for them to reflect on what they have learned from the text. They can model using think-aloud what a strategic reader might do to recognize and address the problem. View the examples of questions in Table 4.1 to share with students to help them monitor their comprehension while reading.

The previous sections explain how students' comprehension is strengthened through instruction in vocabulary, text structure, inference-making, and metacognition, as well as through the development of background knowledge and opportunities to write about text. The sections that follow provide detailed guidance about teaching comprehension strategies.

Table 4.1. Questions to support comprehension monitoring

Before	• What do I already know about this topic?
During Stop after every 1–3 paragraphs and ask:	• Do I understand this? • What is the main idea and the most important information? • What is confusing? • Should I ask for help?
After	• What did I do to make sense of the text? • Can I explain what I learned?

Source: Vaughn et al. (2022).

TEACHING COMPREHENSION STRATEGIES

Comprehension strategies are plans or procedures that readers use and apply when they read. They are intentional mental actions during reading that improve comprehension—deliberate efforts to better understand or remember (Shanahan et al., 2010). There are decades of research on the positive effects of comprehension strategy instruction. Some of the most commonly used strategies include, but are not limited to, identifying and stating main ideas, making inferences, developing awareness of text structure, retelling, summarizing, self-monitoring strategies such as self-questioning, using graphic organizers, and question generation and answering (Duke et al., 2021; Kamil et al., 2008; National Reading Panel, 2000; Oakhill et al., 2015; Torgesen et al., 2007; Vaughn et al., 2022). Middle and high school teachers should provide strategy instruction across the content areas, teach the strategies explicitly, and create classroom routines around the use of these strategies.

Provide Strategy Instruction in the Content Areas

Instruction to support comprehension should not be limited to English language arts classes. Comprehension strategies are best taught and practiced in natural learning settings and content areas using content-area text by a classroom teacher who demonstrates, models, and guides students in their acquisition and use. Comprehension instruction embedded in content teaching need not detract from content learning or knowledge building (Duke et al., 2021; National Reading Panel, 2000).

Comprehension strategies are often organized into before, during, and after reading activities. Some strategies, such as predicting, are best used before reading, while others support comprehension during and after reading. For example, focusing on main ideas is a during-reading strategy, but it is also used for summarizing as an after-reading strategy. Graphic organizers can be used before students read to activate prior knowledge, during reading to help them make connections among topics, and after to review key concepts. A number of strategies integrate writing, such as taking notes, writing summaries, and generating and answering questions in writing.

Provide Explicit Instruction

The goal of comprehension strategy instruction is to make strategies understandable to students so they can apply them when reading. Explicit strategy instruction includes explaining a strategy and the sub-skills involved, modeling how to apply the strategy, and providing many examples of the strategy applied to text. Explicit instruction also includes the following:

- Students engage in guided practice as they apply the strategy to a variety of text types.
- Students eventually use the strategy independently, in combination with other comprehension strategies, to support understanding of a wide variety of texts from different subjects.

Keep in mind that strategies are not activities using worksheets that provide isolated practice with skills such as sequencing or drawing conclusions. These kinds of activities lack explicit instruction and how to think using real text. An effective instructional practice identified by the National Reading Panel (2000) is the use of cooperative learning in which students work together to learn and apply strategies in the context of reading.

Teach Comprehension Strategy Routines

Instruction that focuses on just one strategy and instruction that involves teaching the use of multiple strategies in concert have both been found to be effective (Duke et al., 2021; Shanahan et al., 2010). The National Reading Panel findings (2000) came out in favor of teaching a comprehension strategy routine that bundles several strategies. Multiple strategy instruction should teach students to be flexible as to which strategies are used and when. *Reciprocal Teaching* (Palinscar & Brown, 1984), *Collaborative Strategic Reading* (Klingner et al., 2001), and *The Key Comprehension Routine* (Sedita, 2015) are examples of multiple strategy routines that combine several evidence-based instructional practices. Figure 4.2 provides details about each routine.

Five comprehension strategies teachers can teach their Grades 5–12 students are 1) using graphic organizers, such as a Top-Down Topic Web, to create a visual hierarchy of topics, 2) identifying main ideas, 3) note taking, 4) summarizing, and 5) answering and generating questions.

STRATEGY 1: USE A TOP-DOWN TOPIC WEB

Graphic organizers employ illustrations or diagrams to represent relationships between information or concepts. They are sometimes called graphs, charts, maps, webs, or grids. Research has long supported the use of graphic organizers as a tool to support reading comprehension and achievement in the content areas (Klingner & Vaughn, 2004; Manolie & Papadopoulou, 2012; National Reading Panel, 2000). Graphic organizers assist students in learning because they give them a way to organize and prioritize the relationships among underlying ideas in text and content presented in subject-area classrooms.

A plethora of graphic organizers can be used to represent information and text structures. Teachers should use any graphic organizer that is helpful to students. However, many graphic organizers are designed for a specific purpose, and some students become overwhelmed when they are asked to use many different graphic organizers. Figure 4.3 is an example of a generally useful graphic organizer called a Top-Down Topic Web (Sedita, 2015). The number and types of shapes in this type of graphic organizer change, depending on the content it is representing.

Format

As shown in Figure 4.3, levels of topics and subtopics are arranged in a top-down, hierarchical format. Notice that the shapes and placement of items are purposeful. The broadest topic is placed at the top of the web, subtopics beneath that, and more subordinate subtopics beneath those subtopics. Different shapes are used to denote the level of subtopics. For example, the broadest topic at the top might be in a rectangle, subtopics in circles or ovals, and the subordinate subtopics in a different shape such as another rectangle or a triangle. Although the choice of shapes does not matter, the same shape should be used consistently across each level. Arrows can be added to accentuate the connections among topics.

Classroom Examples and Uses

The Top-Down Topic Web format is flexible and can be used to represent just about anything that is *read, said,* or *done* in any subject area. Figure 4.4 includes classroom examples from a variety of subjects.

Topic webs can be used to support comprehension before, during, and after reading. They frame student learning by showing them the big picture of what they are learning. When students generate their own topic webs, they become more aware of the connections among topics. They are especially helpful as a scaffold for students who have difficulty with reading comprehension and for English learners because they provide a way for teachers to share the essential topics being taught while reducing the language load. The following are suggestions for using topic webs before, during, and after learning, including questions to help students use a topic web to support comprehension.

Comprehension Strategy Routines

Reciprocal Teaching (Palinscar & Brown, 1984)

Reciprocal Teaching is a comprehension strategy routine in which students become the teacher in small-group reading lessons. Teachers model and then help students learn to guide group discussions using four strategies. Once students have learned the strategies, they take turns assuming the role of teacher in leading a dialogue about what has been read.

1. **Prediction**

   Students predict what they think the reading may be about.

2. **Question as you go**

   Students generate questions as they listen and read. Questions can be right-there (answer in the text), between-the-lines (inference needed), and critical thought (require their opinion).

3. **Clarify**

   Students ask themselves what words and phrases are unclear.

4. **Summarize**

   Students summarize verbally with peers and then record the summary.

Collaborative Strategic Learning (Klingner et al., 2001)

Students work in small collaborative groups and apply four comprehension strategies. This routine is mostly used with informational text but can also be used with narrative text.

1. **Preview the text**
   - Students read the title, subtitles, and keywords.
   - Students ask, "What do I already know?"
   - Students predict, "What will I learn?"
2. **Click and clunk**
   - Students look for "clunks"—words or ideas they do not understand.
   - Students use "fix-up" strategies, such as reading the sentence with the clunk, reading the sentences before and after the clunk, and looking for meaningful word parts.
3. **Get the gist**
   - Students find and write the main ideas (the most important who or what and information about the who or what).
4. **Wrap up**
   - Students generate and answer questions.
   - Students identify the most important information by asking, "What did we learn?"

The Key Comprehension Routine (Sedita, 2015)

Students are taught a set of comprehension strategies that can be used individually or in combination to support comprehension of informational or narrative texts.

1. **Categorizing and main idea**

   Students learn how to identify the "big ideas" of text along a continuum that includes:
   - Categorizing, paragraph main idea, central main idea of multi-paragraph for informational text
   - Main events and theme for narrative text
2. **Top-Down Topic Web**
   - A graphic organizer that identifies the topics and subtopics found in text
   - Used before reading to help students activate prior knowledge and make predictions
3. **Two-Column Notes**
   - A graphic organizer used during reading to support metacognition and self-monitoring as students identify and write the main ideas and supporting details while reading
4. **Summarizing** (Retell for primary grades)
   - Using the main ideas to generate an oral or written summary of any type of text
5. **Generating questions**
   - Generating questions related to the text along a continuum of thinking based on Bloom's Taxonomy (remember, understand, apply, analyze, synthesize, create)

NOTE: These strategies are not limited to use with just text. They can be used to support comprehension of anything that is read, said, or done in the classroom.

Figure 4.2. Comprehension strategy routines. (*Sources:* Klingner et al., 2001; Palinscar & Brown, 1984; Sedita, 2015.)

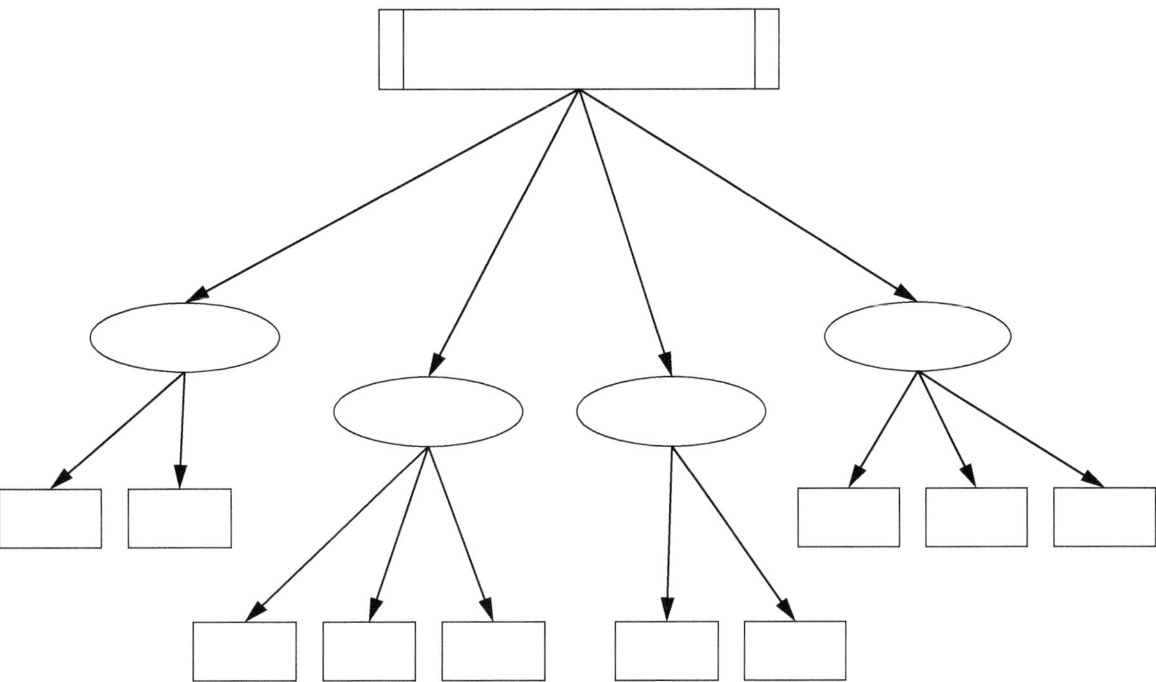

Figure 4.3. Top-Down Topic Web: Blank example. (From Sedita, J. [2015]. *The key comprehension routine.* Keys to Literacy; reprinted by permission.)

Before Learning Teachers can use topic webs before learning for these purposes:

1. **Provide students with a topic road map:** A Top-Down Topic Web introduces students to how the topics in the text are organized and enables them to create a mental overview (schema) of the information before they start reading.
2. **Activate students' background knowledge and vocabulary:** When students have an opportunity to discuss a topic web before they read, it makes it easier to activate their existing background knowledge and provides an opportunity to use known vocabulary and preview new vocabulary related to the topics.
3. **Support students in making predictions:** One strategy that supports comprehension is generating informed predictions about the content of a text prior to reading and then monitoring those predictions when reading to see if they are accurate (Elleman, 2017; Reed, 2019, citing Elbro & Buch-Iversen, 2013). Making predictions helps students think ahead, set a purpose for reading, and make connections between their existing knowledge and new information from the text. Students can make some predictions about a text's content by looking at the title, headings, and graphics. However, a topic web enables students to make stronger, more accurate predictions because they can also preview the main topics and subtopics. Teachers can pose the following questions before students read:
    - What do you know about any of the topics on this topic web?
    - Can you create a question you would like answered about something on this topic web?
    - Can you make a prediction about something you will learn from the text?

During Learning During reading, the construction of mental representations enhances comprehension. These mental pictures involve not only descriptive images, but also representations of relationships between ideas. Such mental images help students to understand the processes or events in the text as well as remember more abstract concepts (Gambrell & Bales, 1986).

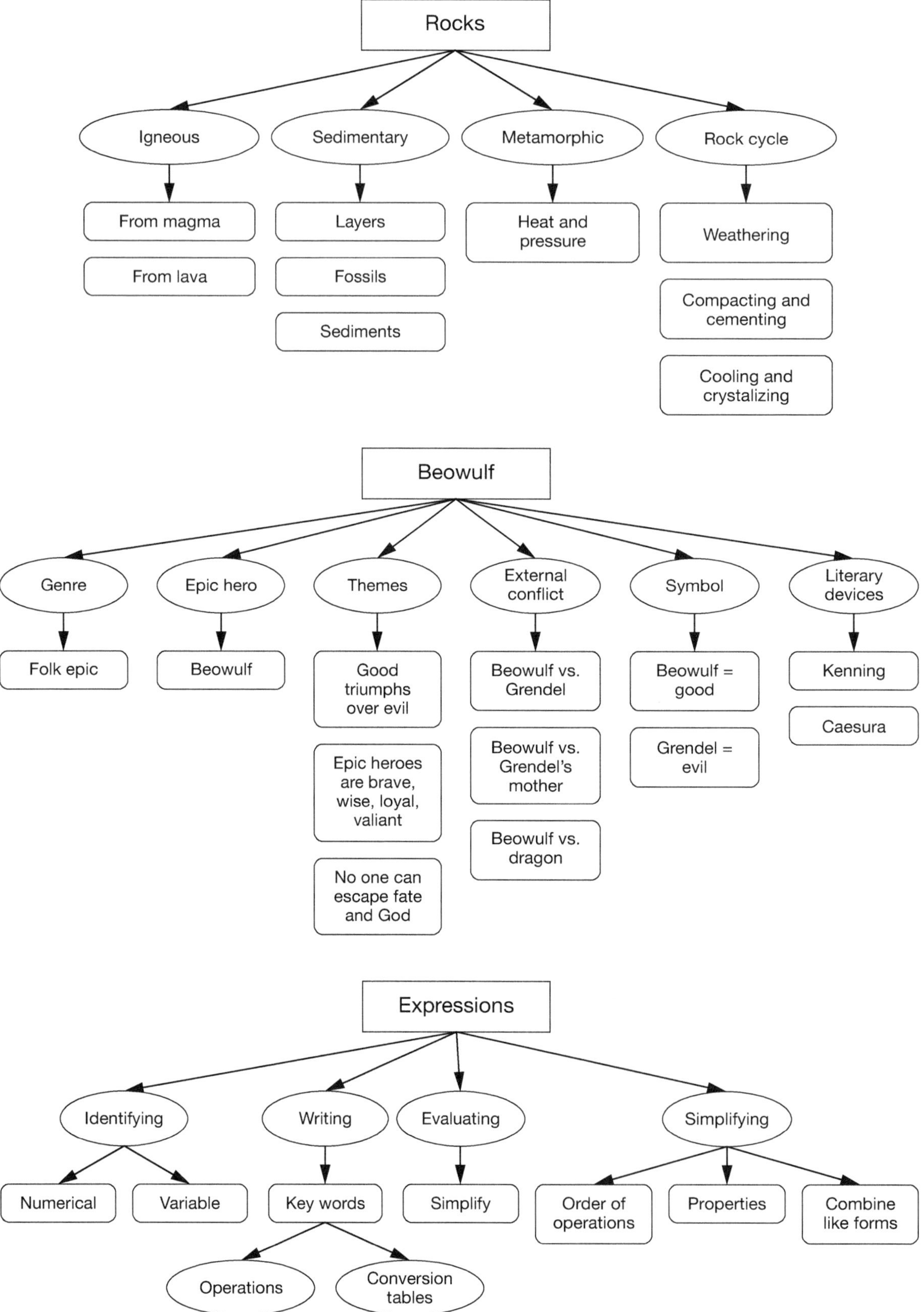

Figure 4.4a. Classroom examples of Top-Down Topic Webs.

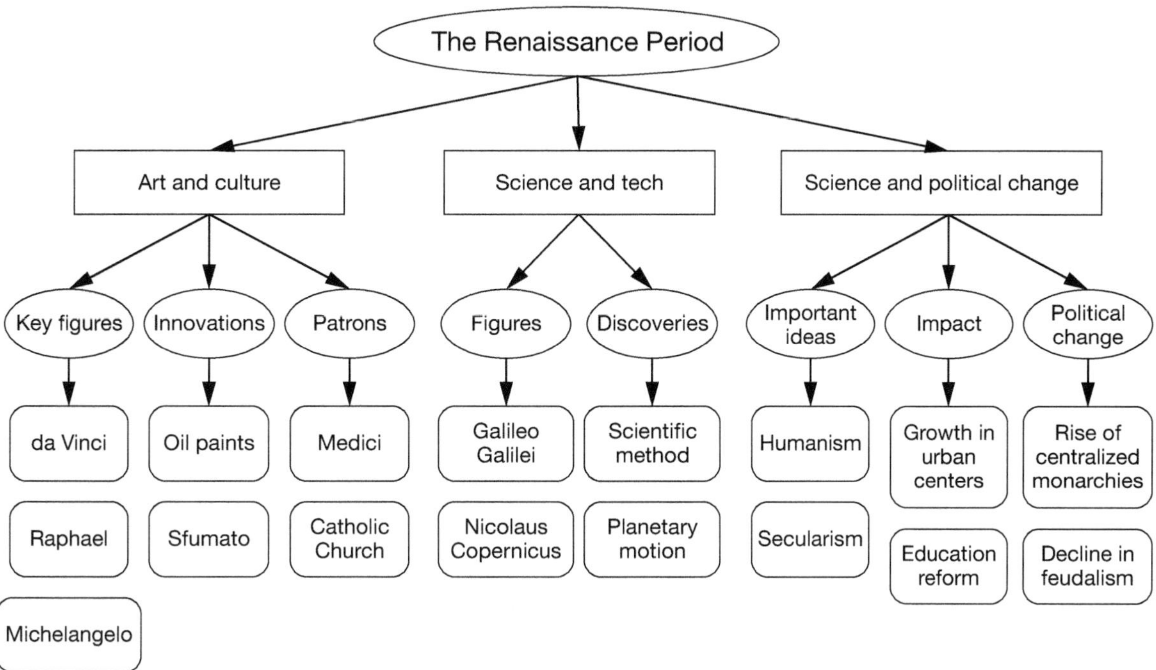

Figure 4.4b. *(continued)*

The format of a Top-Down Topic Web lends itself to representing mental images of the relationships among ideas. A topic web essentially chunks information into manageable units to be learned in sections and then joined together again in a big picture. It is important to review the topic web several times during reading or at various stages during a unit of study to help students understand how the pieces of the topic web are related. Teachers can pose the following questions during reading:

- Find your place on the topic web. What topics will be covered in this part of the text?
- How does what you will read now connect with other parts of the topic web?

After Learning The topic web is a helpful after-reading strategy, serving as a general study guide. Students can review the topics and subtopics to help study for a test. The items on a topic web can also be used to support generation of questions at various levels of thinking or to generate a summary. Teachers can pose the following questions after students read:

- How can you use the topic web to generate a summary of what you read?
- Can you create questions about the text using the topics in the topic web?

A Closer Look at Format

Seemingly minor formatting choices—shapes, color, stacking elements—can make a big difference in how clearly a topic web visually represents the relationships among ideas.

Changing Shapes View the comparison of the first two Top-Down Topic Webs in Figure 4.5. They have the same number of topics and subtopics, but all the shapes in the first example are the same while the shapes change in the second example to better reflect that the third level of subtopics (the rectangles) are subordinate to the second level (the ovals).

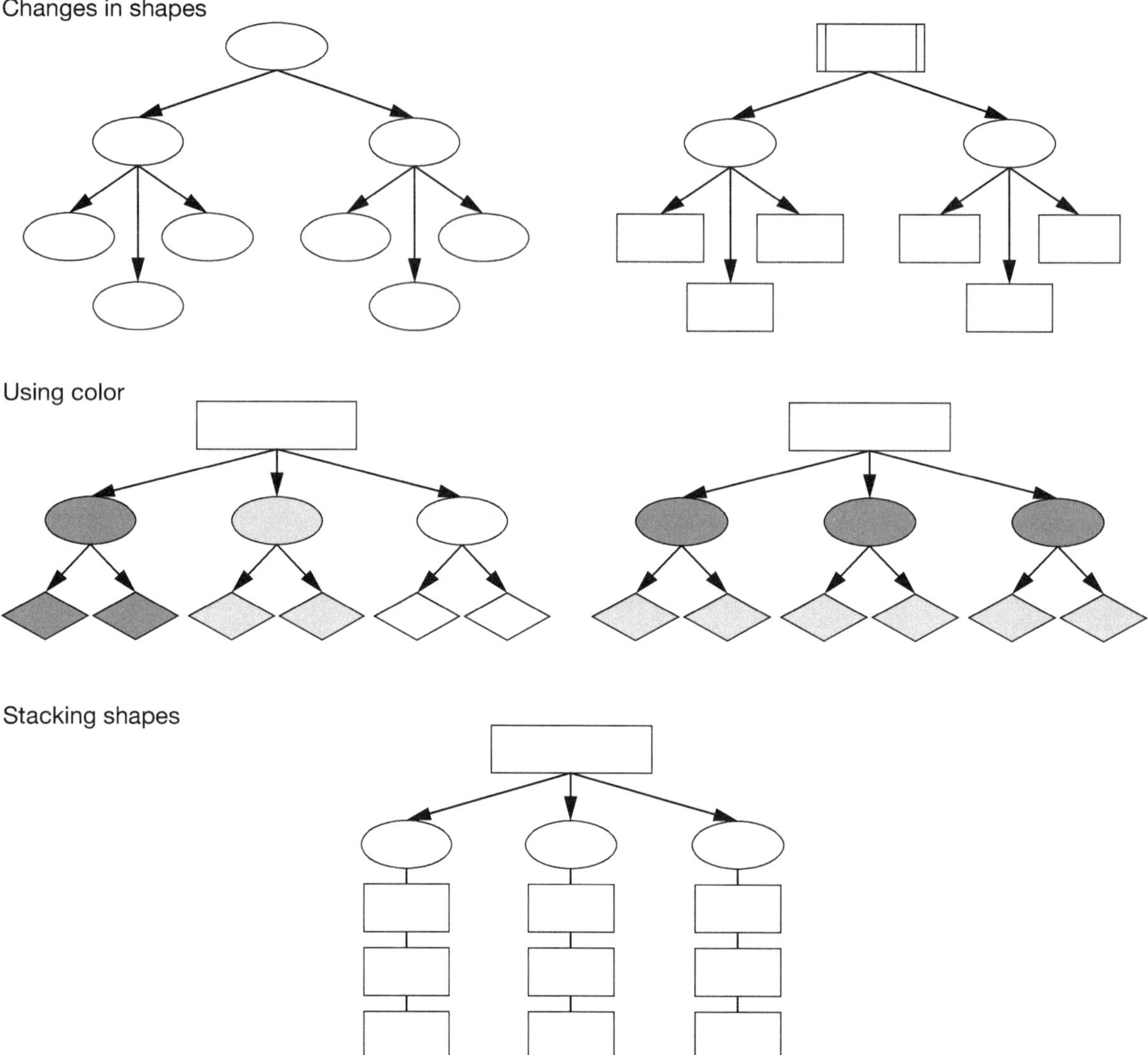

Figure 4.5. Top-Down Topic Web format. (From Sedita, J. [2015]. *The key comprehension routine.* Keys to Literacy; reprinted by permission.)

Using Color View the next two examples in Figure 4.5 to see how color (represented here by shades of gray) can be used to further emphasize the relationships among ideas in a topic web. Color can be used vertically (the same color for one topic and all of its subtopics) or horizontally (the same color for all the subtopics on one level, and a different color for the subordinate subtopics at a lower level).

Stacking One way to save space when there are a lot of topics is to stack shapes representing the same topic level under a broader topic of a different shape, as shown in the last example in Figure 4.5.

Gradual Release of Responsibility

At first, teachers will generate Top-Down Topic Webs, but ultimately the goal is to have students independently generate their own topic webs. Using think-aloud, the teacher should model how to generate a topic web and use it before, during, and after students read, and then gradually shift the responsibility for generating topic webs to students. Until students can independently generate topic webs, teachers can use two scaffolds. The first is to provide a partially completed topic web, with some topics included in the shapes, and then have students fill in the topics for blank shapes. The second is to provide a list of all the topics and subtopics that students must organize into a topic web.

STRATEGY 2: IDENTIFY MAIN IDEAS

Research finds that identifying and stating main ideas is a beneficial reading comprehension strategy (Boardman et al., 2015; Filderman et al., 2021; Peng et al., 2023; Scientific Advisory Committee, 2023; Vaughn et al., 2022). Being able to pause and identify the main idea, or gist, of a paragraph or longer piece of text is essential for self-monitoring while reading, being able to take notes and generate summaries, and generating higher-level questions about text. It is also an important part of recognizing text structure—that is, grasping how sections of information text are organized into main topics and subtopics, and how narrative text progresses as a series of main events. Main idea skills enable students to group or "chunk" information into manageable units by topics. The ability to state a main idea and support it with relevant details is also an essential writing skill (Sedita, 2020d).

Main idea skills range from a basic categorizing level to more challenging tasks such as identifying the central idea or theme of a complex text passage. Main idea instruction can begin in the elementary grades, but content teachers play an important role in helping students in upper grades apply main idea skills to increasingly more complex texts and varied genres. Vaughn and colleagues (2022, p. 47) explain the value of teaching main idea skills:

> Generating the gist of a short portion of text is an essential component of building students' comprehension. Some refer to it as the main idea. Gist statements can help students understand what they read and remember the most important information. Generating the gist provides an opportunity for students to separate important information from irrelevant information and to integrate important ideas and connections in the text to determine what the author meant.

They also point out that having several easy steps to follow in a routine will help students identify main ideas. View their suggested routine for generating a gist statement:

1. Identify and mark the most important person (referred to as the who), place, or thing (referred to as the what) in a section of text.
2. Mark and then list the important information about the most important person, place, or thing.
3. Synthesize or piece together the important information to formulate a gist statement.
4. Write the gist statement in your own words.
5. Check that the gist statement includes all the important information in a short, complete sentence that makes sense. (2022, p. 48)

STRATEGY 3: TAKE NOTES

As noted previously in this chapter, taking notes about text enhances comprehension as students process, organize, and restate the information in their own words (Graham & Hebert, 2020). It also encourages metacognition as they actively search for main ideas and key supporting details.

Two-Column Notes (Sedita, 1989, 2003, 2015) is a note-taking format that is an adaptation of the Cornell Note System originally developed in the 1950s at Cornell University for use with college students (Pauk, 1997). Figure 4.6 provides details about the two-column format. (A full-size, reproducible version of the notes template is included with the downloads for this chapter.)

Classroom Examples

Two-Column Notes are flexible and can be used to represent anything that is *read, said,* or *done* in any subject area. Figure 4.7 includes classroom examples from a variety of subjects.

Paragraph-Level Notes

Students benefit from explicit instruction that teaches them how to take notes focused on main ideas and supporting details as they move from paragraph to paragraph when reading. Sometimes the main

Two-Column Notes

Topic: ______________________________

Big Ideas	Supporting Details

From Sedita, J. (2020d). *Keys to content writing* (4th ed.). Keys to Literacy; reprinted by permission.

In *The Essentials of Adolescent Literacy: Integrating Evidence-Based Reading and Writing Instruction in Grades 5–12*, by Joan Sedita (2026, Keys to Literacy, LLC). Published by Brookes Publishing Co. (page 1 of 1)

Figure 4.6. Two-Column Notes. (From Sedita, J. [2020d]. *Keys to content writing* [4th ed.]. Keys to Literacy; reprinted by permission.)

idea of a paragraph is easy to identify because it is stated within the paragraph as a topic sentence at the start of the paragraph. Other times it can be more challenging to determine the main idea, especially if it is not stated and must be inferred by analyzing details in the paragraph.

Teachers should model how to add main ideas and relevant details to notes from paragraphs in classroom text, especially for students who have difficulty with reading and writing. Figure 4.8 includes examples of Two-Column Notes for the history, science, and math samples of text from Figure 2.4 in Chapter 2.

Teaching Note Taking Skills

Beyond the two-column format, the more challenging part of note taking instruction is teaching students the underlying skills needed to take notes effectively, including the following:

- Identifying and stating the main ideas
- Distinguishing between relevant and irrelevant details
- Paraphrasing
- Writing concisely and using abbreviations
- Using visual cues such as arrows, stars, brackets, and underlines to organize notes
- Listening skills for taking notes from a lecture, audio, or video source
- Integrating information into notes from multiple sources

Students benefit when teachers model how to take notes about the texts and content they teach. Teachers can give students partially completed Two-Column Notes as a scaffold for which students add their own wording in the left or right columns. The amount of information provided by the teacher will vary depending on the difficulty of text content and the students' note taking abilities.

STRATEGY 4: SUMMARIZE

A summary is a shorter, condensed restatement in the student's own words of the main ideas or events from a text or non-text source. Summaries can include a few details that are essential to explain the main ideas. A summary gives an accurate, objective representation of the source and does not include the student's opinion or interpretation (Sedita, 2003, 2015). Research has consistently identified summarizing as a highly effective strategy for supporting comprehension, as well as for improving writing skills (Graham & Hebert, 2010; Kamil et al., 2008; National Reading Panel, 2000; Stevens et al., 2019).

Summarizing supports critical thinking because it requires higher-order processing skills to support both a selection process (deciding what is important) and a reduction process (condensing information) (Anderson & Hidi, 1988–1989; Maria, 1990). To summarize, students must do the following:

- Identify and combine main ideas and essential information.
- Delete, generalize, or minimalize details.

Topic: What Blood Cells Do	
Red cells	• have hemoglobin—picks up oxygen when you breathe • carry oxygen around body • 1 drop = 5 mil. cells • made in bone marrow
White cells	• made in bone marrow • larger than red cells • fewer of them (1 for every 700 red) • defend body against infection from germs, viruses, bacteria • travel to infected areas • can even destroy cancer
Platelets	• like tiny disks • make chemicals to help blood clot • clotting makes blood thicken to stop bleeding • platelets stick together to clot • white cells then fight bacteria that enters wound
Plasma	• liquid part of blood, has no cells • 90% water, 50% to 60% of blood • carries nutrients and waste products

Topic: Graphing a Line	
Find ordered pairs	• choose *x*, find corresponding *y* in equation • form 3 ordered pairs • make a table
Plot ordered pairs	• draw *x* and *y* axis • label *x* and *y* axis • plot points & label ordered pairs
Draw line	• use ruler to draw line through points • label line with equation
Identify *x* and *y* intercepts	• find where graph intersects *x* axis, label as ordered pair (*x*, 0) • find where graph intersects *y* axis, label as ordered pair (0, *y*)

Topic: Civil War	

Events leading to the Civil War	• N & S argue about states' rights
	• expansion of territory, border states, & slavery
	• disputes over federal taxation
	• election of Abraham Lincoln
	  ◦ from IL, famous speech
	  ◦ memorial in DC

Important Civil War battles	• Antietam—very bloody • Gettysburg—turning point of war • Shiloh
Important figures of the Civil War	• Abraham Lincoln: president, wrote Emancipation Proc • Ulysses Grant: general for the Union, president during reconstruction • Robert E. Lee: general for the Confederacy • Meade: Leader for the Union at Gettysburg • J. Wilkes Booth: arrested for assassination of Lincoln
American minorities	• South dependent on slaves for economy • freed slaves migrate to northern cities • Hispanics were involved in both sides • Were Native Americans involved?

Figure 4.7. Classroom examples of Two-Column Notes. (From Sedita, J. [2015]. *The key comprehension routine.* Keys to Literacy; reprinted by permission.)

Topic: Plot Summary, Steinbeck's *Of Mice and Men*	
Event 1: George & Lennie's dream	• dream of owning a farm & Lennie tending rabbits • dream symbolizes hope & freedom • success depends on saving $ at the ranch
Event 2: Arrival at ranch	• meet Candy, who shares ranch insights • Curley: hostile toward Lennie due to his size • Curley's wife seeks attention, creates tension
Event 3: Conflict with Curley	• Curley jealous, picks fights • Lennie crushes Curley's hand in fight • escalates tension & foreshadows trouble
Event 4: Friendship with Candy & Crooks	• Candy offers his savings to join their dream • Crooks briefly believes in the dream • their shared hope shows their vulnerability

Figure 4.7. *(continued)*

Chinese scholar-officials	
Represented backbone of Chinese state & bureaucracy	• no hereditary aristocracy • merchant class not political • SO's got power form education and government office • checked power of emperor • had to pass difficult exams • quotas ensured no regional dominance • low passing rates ensured only best became SOs

Solving 1-step linear equations	
Find the missing part of the equation	• important algebra skill • problem where answer known, but missing a part • Ex.: $4x + 16 = -4$ • x is unknown • solution is –5 • solution works: $4(-5) + 16 = -4$ Multiply 4(–5) $-20 + 16 = -4$ Add –20 + 16 $-4 = -4$ True!

Experiment: antimalarial medicine	

How to make antimalarial medicine faster	• artemisinin—natural plant medicine made from DHAA
	• Study: affects of heat, light, or amount/composition of DHAA
	• Experiment: DHAA sample conditions:
	  ◦ infared light, hot oil bath, UV light for 2.5 hrs
	  ◦ UV lamp for 8 days
	• Results:
	  ◦ 2.5 hr UV sample—larger amounts
	  ◦ 8 days UV—decrease became SOs

Figure 4.8. Examples of paragraph-level notes. (*Key:* DHAA, dihydroartemisinic acid; SOs, scholar-officials; UV, ultraviolet.)

- Substitute their own words to state the essential information.

Summarizing is an important strategy for several reasons:

- Summarizing ensures that students understand the information source in its entirety.
- Writing key ideas in their own words enables students to process material more deeply and makes it more memorable, resulting in better learning (Graham & Harris, 2007; Graham & Hebert, 2010; Maria, 1990).
- Summary generation can serve as an instrument for self-review and be used to refresh memory after time has passed, such as when studying for a test.
- Student summaries can be useful formative assessment tools for teachers to assess how well students understand what they are reading and learning. Reviewing summaries can alert teachers to gaps in students' understanding, which can then be addressed in instruction.

Classroom Examples: Tasks and Text Types

A summary can be generated from anything that is *read, said,* or *done,* and from text sources of all types and lengths. Figure 4.9 lists examples of classroom summarizing tasks.

When students recognize the structure of text they are summarizing, they can more readily identify the key information. Text features such as titles and headings also provide clues. View the questions in Figure 4.10 that students can consider when writing a summary for the three basic types of text.

Teaching Suggestions

Start by having students write summaries of easy text where the ideas are familiar. This allows students to practice summarizing without having to simultaneously comprehend unfamiliar content from a text source. Begin with a short, multiparagraph text passages with main ideas that are easy to identify. For some students, it is easier to start summarizing narrative text because main events are easier to identify sometimes than main ideas in expository text.

Find opportunities for students to work with partners or in small groups to identify key ideas from sources and write summaries. Research about best practices for comprehension instruction finds that

Examples of Classroom Summarizing Tasks

Science: major types of erosion; the stages of human development; how the periodic table is organized; the process of photosynthesis; the seven types of stars; three ways that color is used by animals of the coral reef; the stages of the water cycle; ways bacteria can be helpful to humans

Social Studies/History: the three major social reforms of the late Roman empire; major reasons why people immigrate; ways that mills provided opportunity for workers in the 1800s; the three branches of the government, including their main purposes; how early humans were able to survive the harsh conditions of the Ice Age; the three major changes brought to Japan by the occupation of American troops; four acts of British Parliament that angered the colonists

English Language Arts: the main character's traits at the start of the novel; the seven major stages of an epic; how the two settings in the chapter are different and similar; the persuasive writing techniques used in the sample; the major events in Chapter 10 of the novel

Mathematics: the rules for exponents; four ways of displaying data used in class this week; similarities and differences of mean, median, mode; types of angles; the steps to making a line graph; the steps to simplify a rational expression; major types of quadrilaterals; the rules of probability; ways to classify fractions

Figure 4.9. Examples of classroom summarizing tasks. (From Sedita, J. [2015]. *The key comprehension routine.* Keys to Literacy; adapted by permission.)

Questions to Support Summarizing

Summarizing Informational Text

- How are the paragraphs organized?
- Are you summarizing a section of the text or the entire text?
- What are the main ideas of each paragraph?
- Identify 1 to 2 key details that might be used to explain each main idea.
- What are the central ideas of each section?

Summarizing Argumentative Text

- What claim (position) does the author make?
- What are the main reasons provided to support that claim?
- Identify 1 to 2 key pieces of evidence that might be used to explain each reason.
- Is there a counterclaim?
- If so, identify 1 to 2 key points presented to rebut the counterclaim.

Summarizing Narrative Text

Overall Summary

- Who are the main characters?
- What is the main setting(s)?
- What was the main problem and solution?
- Was there a theme(s) or moral to the story?

Plot Summary

- Are you summarizing a section, a chapter, or the whole story?
- What are the main events in each section or chapter?
- Identify 1 to 2 key details that might be used to describe each event.

Literary Element Summary

- What is the literary focus of the summary (characters, setting, problem/solution, or theme)?
- Identify key points about this literary focus.
- Identify 1 to 2 details to support each key point.

Figure 4.10. Questions to support summarizing. (From Sedita, J. [2015]. *The key comprehension routine.* Keys to Literacy; reprinted by permission.)

students who learn and practice comprehension strategies, such as summarizing, in collaboration with other students learn them faster, and collaborative writing has a strong impact on writing quality and motivation to write (Graham & Perin, 2007; National Reading Panel, 2000).

How to Write a Summary: Steps Students benefit from a simple set of instructions for generating a summary from text. Teachers should provide the following set of steps for writing a summary (from Sedita, 2003, 2015).

1. Read the material and identify the main ideas.
2. Distinguish the main ideas from the details.
3. Write the main ideas in phrase form.
4. Begin the summary with an introductory statement that includes the topic of the summary.
5. Turn the main ideas into sentences, including a few details when it is necessary to convey the main idea.
6. Combine the sentences into one or more paragraphs.
7. Use transitions to connect sentences and paragraphs.

A full-size, reproducible version of these steps is included with the downloads for this chapter. Present these additional guidelines when sharing the steps with students:

- The first sentence of the summary should be a general statement that introduces the overall topic of the summary.
- Although the summary should be developed primarily from main ideas, some details need to be included to adequately convey a main idea.
- Each main idea may not correspond precisely to one sentence. Two related ideas can be combined into one sentence, and more than one sentence may be required to explain a single main idea.
- The length of a summary depends on the length of the material being summarized; it can range from one sentence to multiple paragraphs.

Transition Words and Phrases Students should include transition words and phrases in their summaries to link the main ideas within a summary. Examples include *another, in addition, furthermore, initially, lastly, similarly, for instance, to sum up.* Transition words and phrases are addressed in more detail in Chapter 5, "Teaching Text Structure."

Scaffold: Summary Template Figure 4.11 shows a summary template that teachers can use to support students who have difficulty writing summaries. (A full-size, reproducible version is included with the downloads for this chapter.) Note how each section of the template corresponds to one of the steps for writing a summary and that a small set of transitions is included at the bottom. When teachers provide the template, they have a choice of asking students to write out the full summary on another page after completing the template, or accepting the template as a finished summary. Not all students will need a summary template.

Summary Template

1. List the main ideas in phrase form.
   - ____
   - ____
   - ____
   - ____
   - ____
2. Write an introductory sentence that states the topic of the summary.
3. Turn the main ideas into sentences using your own words. You can combine some of the main ideas into one sentence.
4. Add transition words from the list below or from the transition poster.
   first, next, finally, before, after, during, later, also, another, in addition, in conclusion, to sum up, similarly, however, on the contrary, most important, for example, as a result, therefore
5. Proofread and edit your summary.

From Sedita, J. (2023). *The writing rope: A framework for explicit writing instruction in all subjects.* Paul H. Brookes Publishing Co.; reprinted by permission.

Figure 4.11. Summary template. (From Sedita, J. [2023]. *The writing rope: A framework for explicit writing instruction in all subjects.* Paul H. Brookes Publishing Co.; reprinted by permission.)

STRATEGY 5: ANSWER AND GENERATE QUESTIONS

Research finds that having students answer questions about their reading and teaching them how to generate their own questions improves comprehension (Kamil et al., 2008; National Reading Panel, 2000; Vaughn et al., 2022). Proficient readers engage in critical thinking by asking themselves questions to make sense of what they read. Students who have questions on their mind are thinking critically, and the quality and level of the questions determines the quality and level of their thinking.

Teacher-Generated Questions

Teachers can pose questions before reading about the topics in the text to help students make predictions and make connections to their background knowledge. They can use questions to help students read with a purpose, alert them to information in the text, and prepare them to be actively engaged during reading. Teachers can pose questions after reading to help students think critically about what they read and save concepts and information in long-term memory.

It is helpful to teach students about different kinds of questions. When teachers ask questions about text, some students are able to answer *literal* questions (those that have responses that are directly stated in the text), but not *inferential* questions (those that have responses that are indirectly stated or require other information) or *evaluative* questions (those that require formulating a response based on opinion). The *question-answer-relationship* (QAR) model identifies four types of questions, described in Table 4.2 (Raphael & Au, 2011). Students benefit from instruction on how to identify and answer each type of QAR question using modeling through think-aloud and guided practice. They also benefit from working collaboratively with peers to practice answering the different types of questions based on text they are reading.

Table 4.2. Question-answer-relationship (QAR) model

Right There questions	Think & Search questions	Author & Me questions	On My Own questions
These are literacy questions whose answers can be found in the text and usually easy to find. Students can find the answer in one place.	The answer is in the text, but students need to pull different pieces of information that come from different places in the text.	Involves inferencing because the answer is not explicitly stated in the text. Students need to think about what they already know, what the author tells them in the text, and how it fits together. The answer is not directly in the text, but students must have read it to answer the question.	The answer is not text-based. Students must use their own experiences and background knowledge to answer the question.

Source: Raphael and Au (2011).

Student-Generated Questions

Having students generate questions increases their comprehension as the responsibility for learning shifts from the teacher to the student. Students can generate questions before, during, and after reading:

- *Before:* Similar to teacher questions, when students pose questions before they read, it helps them make predictions about the text and connect to prior knowledge.
- *During:* By posing questions to themselves during reading, students can self-monitor their understanding and check predictions. Posing questions helps them actively engage with text and connect what they already know with new information in the text.
- *After:* After-reading questions help students process information from the text and study in preparation for quizzes and tests.

Basic and Advanced Levels of Questions

The most basic level of question generation uses *who, what, where, when, why,* and *how* questions. Generating questions does not come naturally to many students. Encouraging students to ask simple "W" questions is a good starting point as they leave the elementary grades, but as they move into high school, they must learn to generate the kinds of questions that require them to go beyond readily available facts in texts to support deeper critical thinking. For more advanced question generation, students and teachers can use a continuum of thinking, such as *Bloom's Taxonomy* (Bloom, 1956). Table 4.3 summarizes the levels of thinking in Bloom's Taxonomy.

Classroom Examples

View the examples in Figure 4.12 of questions using the QAR and Bloom's Taxonomy frameworks applied to the samples of text from Figure 2.4 in Chapter 2.

Table 4.3. Bloom's Taxonomy

Remembering	Recalling information (facts)	Recognizing, listing, identifying, retrieving, naming, finding
Understanding	Explaining ideas or concepts (in your own words)	Summarizing, paraphrasing, describing, explaining
Applying	Using information in another familiar situation (use, do it)	Implementing, carrying out, executing
Analyzing	Breaking information into parts to explore understandings and relationships	Comparing, contrasting, organizing, deconstructing, distinguishing, arranging
Evaluating	Examining information and making judgments (fair/unfair, right/wrong, ranking)	Debating, hypothesizing, critiquing, appraising, judging
Creating	Generating new ideas, products, or ways of viewing things (what if?)	Designing, constructing, planning, producing, inventing

Source: Bloom (1956).

Examples of Questions Using the Question-Answer Relationship (QAR) Model and Bloom's Taxonomy

History

QAR:

- **Right There:** What texts were the civil service examinations based on?
- **On My Own:** Why would the children of wealthy families have an advantage to become a scholar-official?

Bloom's Taxonomy:

- **Understanding:** Explain the effects of quotas of scholar-officials from each province.
- **Analyzing:** How is the Ming Dynasty system of scholar-officials as public servants similar to and different from public servants in the U.S. federal government?

Mathematics

QAR:

- **Think & Search:** Which example has a solution with a correct answer, and which example has an incorrect answer?
- **Author & Me:** How would the correct answer change if the number 16 in the Example 1 equation changed to 8?

Bloom's Taxonomy:

- **Applying:** Based on the examples, solve this linear equation: $5x + 15 = -5$
- **Creating:** Create your own one-step equation.

Science

QAR:

- **Right There:** Where does artemisinin come from?
- **Think & Search:** Describe the results of placing samples of DHAA under UV light for 2.5 hours and for 8 days.

Bloom's Taxonomy:

- **Remembering:** How long did the samples of DHAA remain in infrared light, a bath of hot oil, and under a UV light?
- **Evaluating:** Do you think the time of 2.5 hours was too little, too much, or just right for this experiment? Explain why.

Literature

QAR:

- **Author & Me:** What lines in the passage indicate that the man and his boys were poor?
- **On My Own:** What do you think Al was feeling when he growled, "God Almighty, Mae, give 'em bread." Why do you think this?

Bloom's Taxonomy:

- **Understanding:** Explain why Mae was hesitant to sell the man a loaf of bread for just a dime.
- **Evaluating:** Do you think Mae should have sold the bread to the man for a dime? Justify your answer.

Figure 4.12. Examples of questions using the question-answer relationship (QAR) model and Bloom's Taxonomy. (*Key:* DHAA, dihydroartemisinic acid; UV, ultraviolet.) (*Source:* Bloom, 1956; Raphael & Au, 2011.)

Question Terms

Remembering	Understanding	Applying	Analyzing	Evaluating	Creating
cite	describe	adapt	analyze	appraise	assemble
define	discuss	apply	arrange	assess	compile
find	explain	compute	categorize	choose	compose
give an example	interpret	demonstrate	compare	conclude	concoct
identify	paraphrase	dramatize	contrast	criticize	construct
label	report	draw	deconstruct	critique	create
list	restate in own words	illustrate	detect	debate	design
locate	retell	implement	dissect	deduce	develop
match	summarize	interview	distinguish	defend	devise
name	translate	make	examine	hypothesize	formulate
quote		operate	group	judge	generate
recall		practice	inspect	justify	imagine
recite		role play	integrate	prioritize	invent
recognize		sequence	organize	rank	make
retrieve		solve	probe	rate	originate
show		use	research	reject	prepare
			separate	validate	produce
			sift		set up
					what if?

Source: Bloom (1956), and reprinted by permission from Sedita, J. (2015). *The key comprehension routine.* Keys to Literacy.

Figure 4.13. Question terms. (*Source:* Bloom [1956], and reprinted by permission from Sedita, J. [2015]. *The key comprehension routine.* Keys to Literacy.)

Question Terms and Prompts

Some students are not able to generate or effectively answer questions, including those on standardized tests, because they are not familiar with question terms. An important part of instruction for question generation is making sure students know the meanings of question terms. Note that questions do not always have to end with a question mark, as shown in the examples that follow. The key question prompt is shown in bold in each example.

- **Compare and contrast** the transfer of energy as it relates to consumers and decomposers.
- **Describe** the pattern of one of your graphs.
- **Explain** what might be an alternative ending to the story.
- **Recite** the first four lines of the poem.

Figure 4.13 lists question terms organized by levels of Bloom's Taxonomy. (A full-size, reproducible version of these terms is included with the downloads for this chapter.)

INSTRUCTION BEFORE, DURING, AND AFTER READING

Figure 4.14 lists a number of suggestions that draw on the content from this chapter. (A full-size, reproducible version of these suggestions is included with the downloads for this chapter.)

ANALYZE TEXT AND TEACH CLOSE READING

Students benefit when their content teachers explicitly demonstrate how to tackle a challenging piece of text. One of the instructional suggestions in Chapter 2 for helping students read content-area text is to analyze text with students and teach close reading skills.

Close reading is something readers do to figure out a challenging text. It includes an intensive analysis of the text to determine what it says, how it says it, and what it means. It is sometimes referred to as *deep reading, critical reading, unpacking or dissecting the text,* and *reading like a detective.* During a close reading lesson, teachers demonstrate how to go about reading a text, and students practice close reading strategies using multiple readings, peer discussion, and text-embedded questions (Sedita, 2020b).

Content-area teachers are in the best position to teach and demonstrate close reading because, as disciplinary experts, they have a unique scientific, historical, mathematical, or literary lens and recognize the challenges related to text in their subject area. The characteristics of a close reading lesson include the following:

- It uses a short passage, typically one to several paragraphs.
- It is student centered and includes highly collaborative discussion.

- It combines independent, partner or small-group, and whole-group activities.
- It uses reading, thinking, and talking during multiple reads.
- It includes text-dependent questions.
- It includes the teacher modeling and thinking aloud (sharing verbally) the mental processes they use to read closely.
- It can culminate in a text-based writing task.

Planning a Close Reading Lesson

Teachers begin developing a close reading lesson by selecting a challenging text passage and determining what about the text is unique to their discipline and what might be particularly difficult for students. The focus areas and objectives for the multiple close readings can include any of the following:

1. Challenging vocabulary
2. Difficult phrasing and sentences
3. The author's point of view
4. The central or main ideas
5. Any additional challenging areas of the text

Supporting Comprehension

Before Reading

- Preview unfamiliar vocabulary and provide support for comprehending complex sentences.
- Activate and build background knowledge.
- Preview the structure of the text as well as the topics or concepts with the aid of a graphic organizer.
- Set a purpose for reading.
- Pose prereading questions.
- Ask students to predict what they are going to read based on text features such as title, headings, and key words.
- Use discussion to support these suggestions.

During Reading

- Ask students to use teacher-generated questions to support comprehension.
- Encourage students to be metacognitive by generating their own questions, identifying words and concepts they do not understand, and seeking clarification for confusing aspects about what they read.
- Ask students to identify main ideas and relevant details when reading.
- Ask students to take notes focused on essential information.
- Remind students to use inference-making strategies when appropriate.
- Remind students to utilize text structure to support comprehension.
- Encourage students to use word learning strategies (use of context and knowledge of meaningful word parts) to determine the meaning of unfamiliar words.
- Use discussion to support these suggestions.

After Reading

- Ask students to review and revise notes.
- Ask students to summarize text.
- Encourage students to use acquired vocabulary in discussions and writing.
- Encourage and provide time for students to ask and answer questions, orally or in writing.
- Use discussion to support these suggestions.

Figure 4.14. Supporting comprehension.

Include Text-Dependent Questions Close reading lessons are driven by text-dependent questions planned by the teacher ahead of time. These are evidence-based questions that students can answer only by referring explicitly back to the text being read. They should not be based on information extraneous to the text or based on students' personal beliefs. Consider the two questions about Lincoln's Gettysburg Address. The first is a text-dependent question, the second is not.

1. In the address, what does Lincoln say the living who were there that day should do?
2. Lincoln says that the nation is dedicated to the proposition that "all men are created equal." Why do you think equality is an important value to promote?

Text-dependent questions can be related to any of the five focus areas listed previously. The teacher develops these questions to be asked at critical junctures in the text—points at which students must decipher the meanings of words, sentences, and inter-sentence connections, as well as consider text structure or make inferences in order to understand the text. Depending on the text being used for a close reading lesson, there are many types of questions teachers might generate. Figure 4.15 lists generic questions that can be customized for use with text in any subject. (A full-size, reproducible version is included with the downloads for this chapter.)

Assign a Culminating Writing Task The benefits of writing about text were noted previously in this chapter. As a follow-up to a close reading lesson, teachers can assign a writing task to complete

Examples of Text-Dependent Questions

Vocabulary

- What words grab your attention?
- What are the most important/challenging words in this text?
- What does the word __________ mean in the context it appears in the text? Can it be used in another way?
- What clues to meaning are available for the word __________ within the sentence or within the text?
- Are there any meaningful word parts you recognize that can help you determine what the word __________ means?
- Why do you think the author chose to use this word?
- What does the word __________ mean?

Difficult Phrases or Sentences

- Does the author do anything unusual with the language in this sentence?
- What role does this phrase/sentence play in the text?
- What makes this phrase/sentence challenging to understand?
- How many major ideas are included in this sentence?
- Can you break this sentence into more manageable, shorter sentences?
- What does the figurative language in this phrase/sentence mean?
- Does the author use any transition words or phrases that help transition from sentence to sentence or paragraph to paragraph?
- What do you notice about the author's use of punctuation?

Central Ideas and Key Details

- What is the most important part of paragraph/section __________?
- What is the central idea/theme of the text? Is it stated or implied?
- Explain the central idea/theme in your own words.
- Are there any main ideas that contribute to the central idea?
- Identify the claim about __________ that is most supported by the evidence within the text.
- What details stand out most to you?
- What are the most relevant details needed to understand the text?
- What key details support the central/main idea __________?
- Cite evidence from the text that tells you __________.

Author's Point of View or Purpose

- Who is the author/narrator?
- What is the author's overall message/point of view/purpose?
- What does the author want the reader to understand about __________?
- How does the author's choice of words support the author's message or point of view?

From Sedita, J. (2020b). *Creating a close reading lesson.* Keys to Literacy; adapted by permission.

 (page 1 of 2)

Figure 4.15. Examples of text-dependent questions. (From Sedita, J. [2020b]. *Creating a close reading lesson.* Keys to Literacy; adapted by permission.)

in class or for homework. Examples of writing tasks include a personal reaction to the text, a summary, or a response to a question related to the text.

Conducting a Close Reading Lesson: Multiple Reads

A close reading lesson includes a repeating cycle where students *read a little, think a little, talk a little,* and *write a little* as they focus on the different aspects of the text using text-dependent questions as a guide. Students apply discussion strategies during the opportunities in this cycle to talk with peers. During a close reading lesson, students read the text several times.

First Read For the first read, students read the full text independently. Their goal is to become familiar with the text and determine what they are able to understand before interacting with the teacher and peers. The teacher starts the lesson by stating the purpose(s) for the first reading and posing one or two initial questions to help focus the first read. As students read, they annotate the text by highlighting what they think are important parts, identifying parts that are difficult, and posing questions.

This independent reading is followed by a partner or small-group discussion where students discuss what they have learned and noticed about the text. Some of the text-dependent questions are used to facilitate this discussion.

Second Read For the second read, the students listen to the teacher read the text aloud, modeling fluent reading and pausing at critical junctures to pose questions and verbally share the mental processes they are using as they closely read the text. This includes sharing their wonderings and questions related to the text. Students take notes and expand their text annotations as they listen.

Third Read For the third read, the teacher asks students to read a section of the text that has been identified as a focus area (i.e., vocabulary, challenging phrases or sentences, central idea and key details, author's point of view or purpose, and any additional challenging aspects of the text). The teacher asks students to answer text-dependent questions related to that focus area. Students read the passage with a partner or in a small group and then participate in collaborative discussion about what they gleaned from the text and responses to the questions. This is followed by a whole class discussion facilitated by the teacher where partners or small groups share their responses.

The cycle for the third read is continued for each section of the text.

A close reading lesson can be completed over one or more lessons, depending on the length of the text and number of focus areas covered. The goal of analyzing text with students and conducting close reading lessons is for students to read complex texts independently. Some students will achieve this goal sooner than others.

SUMMARY

This chapter begins by discussing factors that contribute to reading comprehension and emphasizes the importance of ensuring that all students have access to high-quality, grade-level texts. It offers instructional suggestions for enhancing students' comprehension, including developing background knowledge before reading, making inferences, and fostering metacognitive awareness. Additional suggestions are provided for comprehension strategies, including Top-Down Topic Webs, Two-Column Notes, summarizing, and answering and generating questions. The chapter concludes with suggestions for teaching close reading skills.

REFLECTION QUESTIONS

1. Briefly describe each of the factors that contribute to reading comprehension.
2. Why is it important for all students, including those with below–grade-level reading skills, to access high-quality, grade-level text?
3. Why is it helpful for students to activate background knowledge prior to reading? What are some of the suggestions from the chapter for activating or providing background knowledge?
4. Why is inference essential to understanding text, and how do readers make inferences?
5. What comprehension strategies do you already use to help students comprehend text? What is the advantage of having teachers from different content areas in the same school teach a consistent set of strategies?
6. What is the difference between a Top-Down Topic Web and Two-Column Notes? Do you think your students would benefit from learning how to use one or both of these comprehension strategies?

7. What is a summary? How does summarizing support comprehension of text and content learning?
8. Explain the similarities and differences for these two question frameworks: question-answer-relationship (QAR), Bloom's Taxonomy.
9. Explain close reading and summarize the suggestions provided in the chapter for planning and conducting a close reading lesson.

Examples of Text-Dependent Questions

Vocabulary

- What words grab your attention?
- What are the most important/challenging words in this text?
- What does the word __________ mean in the context it appears in the text? Can it be used in another way?
- What clues to meaning are available for the word __________ within the sentence or within the text?
- Are there any meaningful word parts you recognize that can help you determine what the word __________ means?
- Why do you think the author chose to use this word?
- What does the word __________ mean?

Difficult Phrases or Sentences

- Does the author do anything unusual with the language in this sentence?
- What role does this phrase/sentence play in the text?
- What makes this phrase/sentence challenging to understand?
- How many major ideas are included in this sentence?
- Can you break this sentence into more manageable, shorter sentences?
- What does the figurative language in this phrase/sentence mean?
- Does the author use any transition words or phrases that help transition from sentence to sentence or paragraph to paragraph?
- What do you notice about the author's use of punctuation?

Central Ideas and Key Details

- What is the most important part of paragraph/section __________?
- What is the central idea/theme of the text? Is it stated or implied?
- Explain the central idea/theme in your own words.
- Are there any main ideas that contribute to the central idea?
- Identify the claim about __________ that is most supported by the evidence within the text.
- What details stand out most to you?
- What are the most relevant details needed to understand the text?
- What key details support the central/main idea __________?
- Cite evidence from the text that tells you __________.

Author's Point of View or Purpose

- Who is the author/narrator?
- What is the author's overall message/point of view/purpose?
- What does the author want the reader to understand about __________?
- How does the author's choice of words support the author's message or point of view?

From Sedita, J. (2020b). *Creating a close reading lesson*. Keys to Literacy; adapted by permission.

How to Write a Summary

1. Read the material and identify the main ideas.
2. Distinguish the main ideas from the details.
3. Write the main ideas in phrase form.
4. Begin the summary with an introductory statement that includes the topic of the summary.
5. Turn the main ideas into sentences, including a few details when it is necessary to convey the main idea.
6. Combine the sentences into one or more paragraphs.
7. Use transitions to connect sentences and paragraphs.

From Sedita, J. (2015). *The key comprehension routine.* Keys to Literacy; used by permission.

Question Terms

Remembering	Understanding	Applying	Analyzing	Evaluating	Creating
cite	describe	adapt	analyze	appraise	assemble
define	discuss	apply	arrange	assess	compile
find	explain	compute	categorize	choose	compose
give an example	interpret	demonstrate	compare	conclude	concoct
identify	paraphrase	dramatize	contrast	criticize	construct
label	report	draw	deconstruct	critique	create
list	restate in own words	illustrate	detect	debate	design
locate	retell	implement	dissect	deduce	develop
match	summarize	interview	distinguish	defend	devise
name	translate	make	examine	hypothesize	formulate
quote		operate	group	judge	generate
recall		practice	inspect	justify	imagine
recite		role play	integrate	prioritize	invent
recognize		sequence	organize	rank	make
retrieve		solve	probe	rate	originate
show		use	research	reject	prepare
			separate	validate	produce
			sift		set up
					what if?

Source: Bloom (1956), and reprinted by permission from Sedita, J. (2015). *The key comprehension routine.* Keys to Literacy.

Summary Template

1. List the main ideas in phrase form.

- ______________________________
- ______________________________
- ______________________________
- ______________________________
- ______________________________

2. Write an introductory sentence that states the topic of the summary.

____

____

____

3. Turn the main ideas into sentences using your own words. You can combine some of the main ideas into one sentence.

____

____

____

____

____

____

____

____

____

4. Add transition words from the list below or from the transition poster.
first, next, finally, before, after, during, later, also, another, in addition, in conclusion, to sum up, similarly, however, on the contrary, most important, for example, as a result, therefore

5. Proofread and edit your summary.

Supporting Comprehension

Before Reading

- Preview unfamiliar vocabulary and provide support for comprehending complex sentences.
- Activate and build background knowledge.
- Preview the structure of the text as well as the topics or concepts with the aid of a graphic organizer.
- Set a purpose for reading.
- Pose prereading questions.
- Ask students to predict what they are going to read based on text features such as title, headings, and key words.
- Use discussion to support these suggestions.

During Reading

- Ask students to use teacher-generated questions to support comprehension.
- Encourage students to be metacognitive by generating their own questions, identifying words and concepts they do not understand, and seeking clarification for confusing aspects about what they read.
- Ask students to identify main ideas and relevant details when reading.
- Ask students to take notes focused on essential information.
- Remind students to use inference-making strategies when appropriate.
- Remind students to utilize text structure to support comprehension.
- Encourage students to use word learning strategies (use of context and knowledge of meaningful word parts) to determine the meaning of unfamiliar words.
- Use discussion to support these suggestions.

After Reading

- Ask students to review and revise notes.
- Ask students to summarize text.
- Encourage students to use acquired vocabulary in discussions and writing.
- Encourage and provide time for students to ask and answer questions, orally or in writing.
- Use discussion to support these suggestions.

Two-Column Notes

Topic: ____

Big Ideas	Supporting Details

From Sedita, J. (2020d). *Keys to content writing* (4th ed.). Keys to Literacy; reprinted by permission.

5

Teaching Text Structure

Text structure refers to how information and ideas are organized in text. When authors write text, they develop and follow plans for how the text will be built, similar to what an architect does. Language and text structure is processed to gain (comprehend) or convey (write) intended meanings. As students advance into middle and high school grades, text structure becomes increasingly more complex and unique to each discipline, which is why content teachers are in the best position to teach students how text is structured in their subject area.

This chapter presents an overview of how teaching text structure supports reading and writing, and what elements of text students and teachers can use to understand text structure. The chapter then describes how to teach students about text structure at successively narrower levels—broad genres or types of text, typical patterns of text organization, paragraph structure, and sentence structure.

TEXT STRUCTURE: READING AND WRITING

Teaching text structure supports both reading and writing. The structure and features of written text have a significant impact on comprehension. Awareness of a text's structure provides clues to making meaning, and disorganized text can negatively affect comprehension. Readers who are familiar with text structures recognize how information is unfolding (Akhondi, 2011; Snow, 2002). Research has long found that students benefit from instruction in common structural elements of narrative and informational text to support comprehension (Duke et al., 2021). If students do not consider text structure when writing, their writing pieces will be disorganized and of a lower quality. The use of mentor text (sometimes described as *written exemplars*) to highlight structure and key features of texts has been found to develop effective writing skills for students in Grades 6–12 (Graham et al., 2016).

Showing students the connection between reading and writing helps them develop and transfer text structure awareness for reading to writing and vice versa (Graham et al., 2016). Consider these examples of transferring awareness of compare-and-contrast text structure:

- Reading to writing: If students learn to recognize a compare-and-contrast pattern of organization while reading, they can use this as a model to write a comparison of two primary source documents in a history class.
- Writing to reading: If students learn how to include compare-and-contrast transition words and phrases when writing (e.g., *likewise, similarly, in like manner, in contrast, however, on the other hand*), they will be more aware of them when reading.

Understanding text structure, as a reader or as a writer, includes awareness of multiple levels of text structure and awareness of text features.

Multiple Levels of Text Structure

Instruction for text structure addresses several areas: sentence structure, paragraph structure, patterns of organization, transition words and phrases, text features (e.g., title, headings), and structure for the three major text genres (narrative, informational, argument). This chapter shares instructional suggestions for each of these areas to support students' reading comprehension and writing.

Across these multiple levels, language and text structure is processed to gain (comprehend) or convey (write) intended meanings. Table 5.1 identifies different ways in which people process language and text structure during reading comprehension and writing, two complementary aspects of language use (Moats & Sedita, 2004; Sedita, 2004b).

Text Features

Text features include titles, headings and subheadings, graphics (charts, pictures, maps), captions, and bold or italic print. Text features support reading comprehension by helping students identify the topic and overall organization of ideas. Headings represent topical sections of text, making it easier for students to work their way through longer text passages. Graphics and captions highlight important details and present an alternative representation of information.

The use of text features when writing helps students make clear the topic of their writing and helps them organize the content of the writing. Students can use headings and incorporate graphics and captions to help readers of their writing understand what they have to say.

THREE TYPES OF TEXT (GENRES)

Genre is a stylistic category of writing characterized by similar style and form. Most state English language arts standards identify three major text genres (also described as *types of text*) that students must learn to write: *informational, argument,* and *narrative.* Informational and argument text are sometimes categorized together as expository text. Awareness of the differences in structure among these three types of text also supports reading comprehension. The chart in Figure 5.1 describes each type of text, including details about each one's purpose and structure; a full-size, reproducible version is included with the downloads for this chapter.

Text that is read or written by students can incorporate a combination of these types; as noted in the Common Core State Standards (NGA/CCSSO, 2010, p. 24), "skilled writers many times use a blend of these three types of text to accomplish their purposes." For example, a newspaper editorial might begin with informational writing to present facts about a topic and then switch to narrative writing to recall a series of events related to the topic. The piece might shift again at the end to argument writing as the editor states a claim (position) about the topic and provides reasons with evidence to support that claim.

Teaching the Three Types of Text for Reading

Teachers of all subjects can find opportunities to note the differences among the types of text students read. This is sometimes called *reading like a writer.* Teachers and students should analyze how the author of a text used text structure, vocabulary, and various writing techniques to produce the text. Teachers can point out the type of text used by the author before reading, or they can ask students after they read to identify the type. Teachers can use the following questions to support text analysis; a reproducible copy is also provided with the chapter downloads.

- Is the text informational, narrative, or argument?
- Is there anything unique about the format of the text?

Table 5.1. Language and text structure roles in reading and writing

Language structure	Role in comprehension	Role in writing
Sentence structure (syntax and the rules of grammar)	The reader uses knowledge of syntax to chunk parts of sentences into meaningful units, to confirm the recognition of words, and to infer the meaning of unfamiliar words.	The writer uses knowledge of syntax to vary the sentence structure, to create compound and complex sentences, and to make the writing richer through the use of advanced parts of speech.
Rules of capitalization and punctuation	Assist the reader to identify proper nouns and the beginning and ending of sentences. Provide information about phrasing and emphasis.	Enable the writer to offer the reader clues about sentence structure, phrasing, and emphasis.
Paragraph structure (organizing text content into units based on main ideas)	The reader uses paragraph structure to identify main ideas (stated or implied) and supporting details. Attending to main ideas while reading supports metacognition and critical thinking.	The writer uses paragraph structure to organize the writing into main idea units and indents at the start of a new paragraph to convey the change in main idea.
Patterns of organization (describe/explain, sequence, cause and effect, compare and contrast, problem and solution)	Recognizing these patterns aids reading comprehension.	Knowledge of these patterns helps students select the best structure for presenting what they want to say in their writing.
Transition words and phrases (used to connect parts of text and to signal patterns of organization)	Serve as signals to the reader to anticipate the text structure and the relationships between ideas in sentences and paragraphs.	Enable the writer to present ideas in a more organized format, to link ideas in the text, and to signal to the reader patterns of organization.
Narrative story structure	The reader uses story structure to identify the characters, setting, sequence of events, and plot/theme.	The writer uses story structure to convey information about the characters, setting, sequence of events and plot/themes of the story. The writer also uses story structure to let the reader know the type of narrative text (e.g., folktale, biography, short story).
Informational structure	The reader accesses information by attending to the hierarchical structure used to organize information into topics, sub-topics, and main ideas.	The writer presents information using a hierarchical structure that organizes information into topics, sub-topics, and main ideas.
Opinion & argument structure	The reader determines the opinion or argument expressed in the text by attending to the claim, reasons, evidence, counterclaim, and rebuttal.	The writer gives an opinion or makes an argument to convince or persuade the reader by using the structural elements of claim, reasons, evidence, counterclaim, and rebuttal.
Expository text markers (headings, subheadings, other visual clues)	Provide clues and a framework for chunking reading into manageable units; help the reader identify the hierarchy of main ideas and subordinate ideas.	The writer can use headings and subheadings to organize ideas during writing and provide the reader with a guide for identifying the hierarchy of ideas.

Adapted by permission from Sedita, J. (2004). *The comprehension-writing connection.* Sedita Learning Strategies; and Moats, L. C., & Sedita, J. (2004). *Writing: A road to reading comprehension.* LETRS Module 11. Sopris West.

- Did the author include an introduction and conclusion, and how do these structures support comprehension?
- How did the author organize the body of the piece?
- For informational text, how did the author organize the topics and subtopics?
- For narrative text, how did the author sequence the events?
- For argument text, how did the author organize the reasons, evidence, counterclaim, and rebuttal?
- Did the author use text features (e.g., title, headings, subheadings) to support the structure of the text?

Three Types of Text

Type of text	What it does	Text structure	Examples
Argument	Makes an argument to convince the reader that a point of view is valid or to persuade the reader to take a specific action	Organized around these components: claim, reason, evidence, counterclaim, rebuttal	Persuasive letters, editorials, argument essays, reviews of books or movies, claims about the worth or meaning of a literary work
Informational	Examines previously learned information or provides new information	Organized into sections and sub-sections that include paragraph main ideas; tends to be organized hierarchically	Textbook, article, letter, speech, manual, directions, subject area report, summary of information, workplace memo, job application, resume
Narrative	Tells a story (real or imagined) of an experience, event, or sequence of events	Organized around literary elements such as setting, characters, events, problem/solution; also organized by order of events	Diary entry, biography, autobiography, personal narrative, memoir, folktales, fairytales, fables, myths, creative fiction stories, science fiction, poems, plays, eyewitness accounts, plot summary, short story

From Sedita, J. (2020d). *Keys to content writing.* Keys to Literacy; reprinted by permission.

Figure 5.1. Three types of text. (From Sedita, J. [2020d]. *Keys to content writing.* Keys to Literacy; reprinted by permission.)

- Did the author use a specific pattern of organization within the text (i.e., description/explanation, sequence, compare and contrast, cause and effect, problem and solution)?
- Did the author use transition words or phrases to connect sentences or parts of the text or to signal a pattern of organization? If yes, how do they support comprehension?
- Do most of the paragraphs have stated main ideas, or are the main ideas implied?
- How complex are the sentences in the text?

Teaching the Three Types of Text for Writing

As noted previously, most states have writing standards that require students to compose informational, argument, and narrative writing pieces. For students in the elementary grades, many standards suggest student writing be distributed equally across the three types, with more informational and argument writing incorporated into science, history, and other content areas to balance out the common emphasis on narrative writing in English language arts classes. Between middle and high school, however, it is expected that this balance will shift to 40% informational, 40% argument, and 20% narrative.

Introductions and Conclusions For any type of writing, most state writing standards also require students to include introductions and conclusions in their compositions. The main purpose for an introduction in informational writing is to introduce the topic. For argument writing, the purpose is to introduce the topic and state the claim (position). For narrative text, the purpose is to orient the reader by establishing a situation or context or introducing a narrator or character. The main purpose of a conclusion for all three types of text is to provide some closure.

In Chapter 6, "Writing Instruction," you will learn about a graphic organizer that students can use as a prewriting tool to plan the structure of their writing pieces that includes sections for an introduction and a conclusion.

A Closer Look at Argument Writing Argument writing can be challenging, even for proficient writers. As students progress into the upper grades, they are expected to write more sophisticated arguments. These assignments require students to develop strong reasons and evidence to support a claim, as well as thoughtfully address counterclaims with effective rebuttals.

An argument is a reasoned, logical way of demonstrating that the writer's position, belief, or conclusion is valid. This type of writing has several purposes:

- to change someone's point of view
- to bring about some action
- to convince someone to accept the writer's explanation or evaluation of a concept, issue, or problem

The structure of argument text is organized around five main components described in Figure 5.2. (A full-size, reproducible version of this list is included with the chapter downloads.)

PATTERNS OF ORGANIZATION AND TRANSITIONS

Patterns of organization are specific text structures embedded in expository or narrative text. The most common patterns are *description/explanation, sequence* (also called *chronology*), *cause and effect, compare and contrast,* and *problem and solution.* There may be multiple patterns within a text. *Transition words and phrases,* also called *linking words,* connect sentences, paragraphs, or sections in a text. They also are used to signal patterns of organization.

Awareness of patterns of organization and transitions when reading supports comprehension, and the quality of writing pieces is improved when students incorporate them. Review the chart in Figure 5.3 that describes the purpose of each common pattern along with related transitions. (A copy of this chart is included with the downloadable resources for this chapter.) A longer list of transitions that can be used for multiple purposes is available in Figure 5.4; a full-size, reproducible version of the list is included with the chapter downloads.

Argument Writing Components

- **Claim:** the position taken by the writer; what the writer is trying to prove or argue
  - *What do I think?*
- **Reason:** provided to support a claim; reasons are supported by evidence
  - *Why do I think it?*
- **Evidence:** used to support or prove a reason; statistics, facts, quotations, surveys, etc.
  - *How do I know (proof)?*
- **Counterclaim:** opposing position, counterargument
  - *What is the other side?*
- **Rebuttal:** refutes or disproves the counterclaim; addresses the criticism of the claim
  - *What is my response to the other side?*

From Sedita, J. (2020d). *Keys to content writing.* Keys to Literacy; reprinted by permission.

Figure 5.2. Argument writing components. (From Sedita, J. [2020d]. *Keys to content writing*. Keys to Literacy; reprinted by permission.)

Teaching Patterns and Transitions for Reading

Students who are able to recognize patterns of organization while reading are better able to find information to support comprehension (Williams, 2017). Students benefit when teachers point out these structures in the texts students are reading, including the transitions that signal them.

Teaching Patterns and Transitions for Writing

Depending on the purpose of a writing task, students must make decisions about which pattern(s) will best convey what they are trying to say in their writing. They benefit from a clear explanation about each pattern that includes examples provided by the teacher that they can emulate.

PARAGRAPH STRUCTURE

A *paragraph* is a section of a piece of text, indicated by a new line or indentation. A basic paragraph consists of several sentences focused on a main idea. The start of a new paragraph signals a shift from one main idea to another. A multi-paragraph piece of text typically centers around one topic, with each paragraph focused on a more specific main idea related to that topic. Students who are aware of paragraph structure when reading recognize that each new paragraph signals a new main idea, which supports their comprehension. For writing, grouping ideas and information into paragraphs helps students produce more organized, better structured writing pieces.

Common Patterns of Organization

Pattern	Purpose	Common transitions
Description, explanation	Describe a person, place, or thing; explain a topic or idea	*for instance, such as, another, in addition, for example, furthermore, also*
Sequence, chronology	Present items, events, or steps in order	*first, second, initially, before, next, following, after, then, finally, lastly*
Problem and solution	What went wrong and how it was or could be fixed	*the problem is, the question is, a solution is, therefore, if...then*
Cause and effect	What happened and why it happened	*because of, as a result, caused by, consequently, for that reason, that is why, therefore, thus*
Compare and contrast	How two or more things are alike and/or different	*by comparison, compared to, in like manner, likewise, similarly, but, however, in contrast, on the contrary, on the other hand, unlike*

From Sedita, J. (2015). *The key comprehension routine*. Keys to Literacy; reprinted by permission.

Figure 5.3. Common patterns of organization. (From Sedita, J. [2015]. *The key comprehension routine.* Keys to Literacy; reprinted by permission.)

Teaching Basic Paragraph Structure

Most students learn about paragraph structure in the elementary grades. However, some older students who struggle with reading and writing may not have a solid understanding of paragraph structure. The information that follows can be shared with secondary students who do not have well-developed paragraph awareness.

- *Topic sentences* state the main idea of a paragraph. They can be located in the beginning, middle, or end of a paragraph. Some paragraphs do not include a topic sentence; the main idea is implied. These kinds of paragraphs are more difficult to comprehend when reading. Students should be encouraged to include topic sentences when they write paragraphs.
- *Supporting sentences* contain details that support the main idea. The number of supporting sentences in a paragraph varies considerably.
- *Concluding sentences* provide some closure to a paragraph. They are often not encountered at the end of every paragraph when reading multi-paragraph texts, nor must students include a conclusion sentence for every paragraph when writing multi-paragraph pieces.

View the examples in Figure 5.5 of well-structured paragraphs at the middle and high school level. Where is the topic sentence? Which are the supporting sentences?

Color Coding

This activity uses three colors to highlight basic paragraph parts: green for topic sentences, yellow for supporting sentences, and red for concluding sentences. Teachers find examples of well-structured paragraphs from content-area text. After modeling how to color code these samples, teachers provide opportunities for students to color code paragraphs collaboratively with peers and then on their own. Eventually, students color code the paragraphs they write.

Finding a Paragraph's Main Idea: Activities

One of the reasons some students struggle with paragraphs is that they have not developed proficient main idea skills, as discussed in Chapter 4. The ability to identify and state main ideas is essential for taking notes and generating summaries. It is also needed to develop topic sentences when writing. The following activities are especially helpful for teachers who want to help students more readily attend to paragraph main ideas when reading or writing: identify the topic sentence, identify the sentence that does not belong, or create a topic sentence.

Identify the Topic Sentence For this activity, students are given several sentences out of order from one paragraph. They are asked to determine which sentence is the topic sentence that states the main idea and which sentences support the main ideas by providing details. The topic sentence has been italicized in the following example.

- Wealthy people in the city-state of Florence wanted to reproduce ancient Greek dramas.
- The first real opera was probably a recitative work titled *Dafne* written in 1594 or 1597.
- *Opera began in the late 16th century in Italy.*
- Italian composers like Claudio Monteverdi expanded opera with more complicated songs.
- As more people heard operas, they spread throughout Italy.

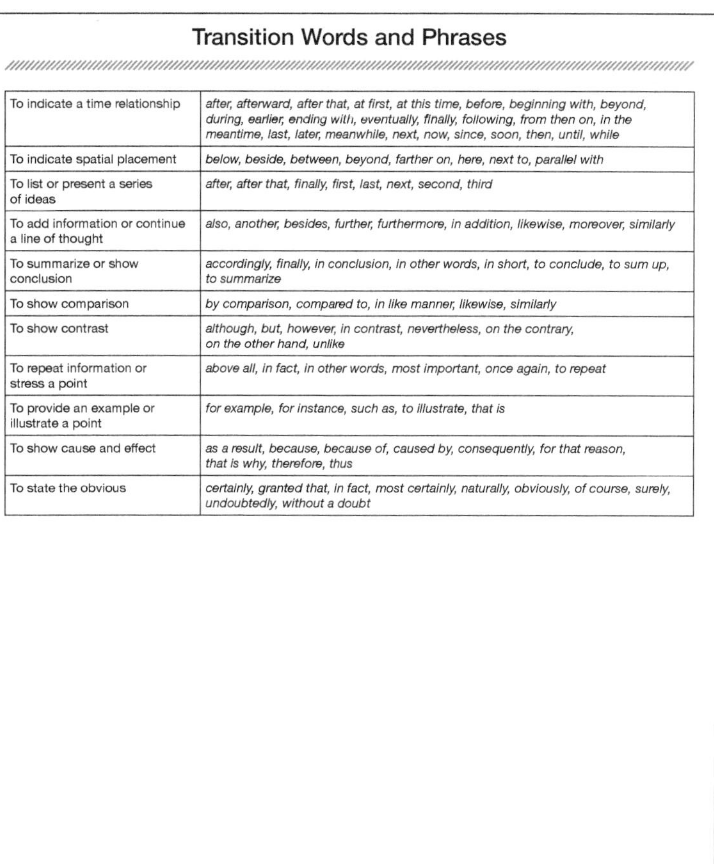

Transition Words and Phrases

To indicate a time relationship	*after, afterward, after that, at first, at this time, before, beginning with, beyond, during, earlier, ending with, eventually, finally, following, from then on, in the meantime, last, later, meanwhile, next, now, since, soon, then, until, while*
To indicate spatial placement	*below, beside, between, beyond, farther on, here, next to, parallel with*
To list or present a series of ideas	*after, after that, finally, first, last, next, second, third*
To add information or continue a line of thought	*also, another, besides, further, furthermore, in addition, likewise, moreover, similarly*
To summarize or show conclusion	*accordingly, finally, in conclusion, in other words, in short, to conclude, to sum up, to summarize*
To show comparison	*by comparison, compared to, in like manner, likewise, similarly*
To show contrast	*although, but, however, in contrast, nevertheless, on the contrary, on the other hand, unlike*
To repeat information or stress a point	*above all, in fact, in other words, most important, once again, to repeat*
To provide an example or illustrate a point	*for example, for instance, such as, to illustrate, that is*
To show cause and effect	*as a result, because, because of, caused by, consequently, for that reason, that is why, therefore, thus*
To state the obvious	*certainly, granted that, in fact, most certainly, naturally, obviously, of course, surely, undoubtedly, without a doubt*

From Sedita, J. (2020d). *Keys to content writing.* Keys to Literacy; reprinted by permission.

Figure 5.4. Transition words and phrases. (From Sedita, J. [2020d]. *Keys to content writing* [4th ed.]. Keys to Literacy; reprinted by permission.)

Identify the Sentence That Does Not Belong For this activity, students are given all the sentences from a paragraph, plus one extra sentence that does not belong in the paragraph because the detail is not as related to the main idea as the other sentences. They are asked to review each supporting sentence and choose the one that does not belong. The sentence that does not belong has been italicized in the following example.

Topic sentence: Long ago, cats evolved from wildcats that started hunting for prey around human settlements.

- DNA from more than 2,000 cats from around the world has been analyzed.
- The DNA of cats tells a story that follows ancient human travels.
- *The average age for an indoor cat is 15 years.*
- Wildcats were most likely first domesticated in the eastern Mediterranean region.
- Cats spread out to the rest of the world as traders and sailors brought them on their journeys.

Create a Topic Sentence For this activity, students are given several supporting sentences. They are asked to identify the main idea and then write a topic sentence that states the main idea. A topic sentence for the following example would be *Early Mesopotamian farmers grew different types of crops.*

Topic sentence:

____

____

If you were to go back in time to Mesopotamia, you would see fields of wheat and barley, the region's most important crops. You would also see gardens of beans, onions, lettuce, cucumbers, and spice plants. Ancient farmers also grew date palm, apple, and pomegranate trees.

Grade 6 Example
Three major seas played an important role in the life of ancient Greece. The Mediterranean Sea, the Ionian Sea, and the Aegean Sea connected most parts of Greece to each other and were central to trade, travel, and communication. These seas connected Greece to other cultures, allowing the exchange of goods, ideas, and technologies. The seas also provided resources like fish, which were important for the Greek diet. As a result, the seas helped shape Greek society, economy, and culture.

Grade 8 Example
Meteorologists play a crucial role in studying and predicting weather patterns. They observe various factors, including sky conditions, cloud formation, temperature, and wind speed, to understand weather trends. Using specialized instruments such as barometers, anemometers, and radar, they collect data that helps forecast weather events. By analyzing this information, meteorologists can predict conditions like storms, temperature changes, and precipitation. Their forecasts are essential for informing the public about potential weather hazards, allowing people to make preparations for changing conditions.

Grade 11 Example
During World War II, roughly 350,000 women served in the U.S. military, both within the country and overseas, while many more filled jobs in civilian industries. Among them were the Women's Airforce Service Pilots, recipients of the distinguished Congressional Gold Medal. With large numbers of men entering military service, industries faced severe labor shortages. From 1940 to 1945, the proportion of women in the American workforce rose from about 27% to almost 37%, and by the end of the war, close to one in four married women were employed outside the home. Alongside their contributions in factories and other civilian roles, approximately 350,000 women enlisted in the Armed Forces. Encouraged by First Lady Eleanor Roosevelt and various women's organizations, Congress established the Women's Auxiliary Army Corps, which was later reclassified as the Women's Army Corps (WAC) with full military standing. In the Navy, the Women Accepted for Volunteer Emergency Service (WAVES) held the same rank and privileges as naval reservists, providing critical shore-based support. Despite their essential service, women continued to earn significantly less than men, often receiving no more than half the wages paid to male workers.

Figure 5.5. Paragraph examples at the middle and high school levels. (*Sources:* Houghton Mifflin Harcourt, n.d.; National Geographic, n.d., History.com, n.d.)

SENTENCES AND SYNTACTIC AWARENESS

A *sentence* is a collection of words that come together to express a complete thought. Some sentences are short, and some are quite long, depending on how many ideas are included in the sentence. To comprehend a sentence, a reader must process, store in working memory, and integrate a variety of syntactic and word-meaning information (Paris & Hamilton, 2009). A writer must be able to manipulate and add words to write a high-quality, elaborated sentence. Many students who have difficulty with reading and writing in middle and high school benefit from instruction about sentences.

Syntax is the study and understanding of grammar—the system and arrangement of words, phrases, and clauses that make up a sentence. Syntax represents the structure of a sentence and conveys its meaning. *Syntactic awareness* means having the ability to monitor the relationships among the words in a sentence to understand while reading or composing. Students build syntactic awareness through exposure to oral language when they are young and especially through exposure to written language as they independently read challenging texts across the grades that include lengthy, complex sentences.

Sentences and Reading Comprehension

The ability to understand at the sentence level is in many ways the foundation for being able to comprehend text. One by one, sentences communicate ideas that add up to making meaning. The complexity of a text's syntax (grammar) is one predictor of a text's comprehensibility (Eslami, 2014; Frantz et al., 2015; Shanahan et al., 2012), and efficient processing of sentence structure is necessary for overall comprehension (Zipoli, 2016). Effective readers have knowledge of phrase structures, parts of sentences, and how they work (Scott, 2004).

Sentences that are complex, contain a large number of ideas, or have unusual word order will make it difficult for students to comprehend what they are reading, especially students who struggle with reading. As students move into middle school, they begin to encounter longer and more complex sentences, sometimes made more challenging because the sentences are written in a style that is unique to science, history, mathematics, or literature.

Consider the following examples. Why might they be challenging for students? What might a teacher do to provide some support?

- "Many miles downstream on the side to which the dogs had crossed, a small cabin stood near the bank of the river, surrounded by three or four acres of cleared land, its solid uncompromising appearance lightened only by the scarlet geraniums at the window sills and a bright blue door." (Burnford, 1961)
- "The grueling process of the exams, the writing of essays, the drafting of mock state papers and edicts, and commenting on Confucian texts, coupled with the meager passing rates, ensured that those who advanced would be adept public servants capable of administering the Chinese state." (Rankin & Weise, 2022, p. 30)
- "The boys edged behind him and they went immediately to the candy case and stared in—not with craving or with hope or even with desire, but just with a kind of wonder that such things could be." (Steinbeck, 1939, Ch. 15)

Sentences and Writing

Sentences, along with paragraphs, are the building blocks of writing in any subject. Composing each sentence, the writer combines ideas to make meaning. The writer then groups sentences related to the same main idea into paragraphs, and then groups paragraphs to build longer, cohesive text. As students move into upper grades, they need to develop more complex and elaborated sentences that represent the higher levels of critical thinking used to learn in different content areas. This is not an easy task, as Bruce Saddler explains: "Of the many difficulties writers encounter when engaged in the complex act of writing, crafting sentences that accurately convey the intended meaning is particularly challenging . . . manipulating sentences is both effortful and critical" (2005, p. 1).

Students with limited sentence writing skills in Grades 5–12 tend to write sentences that are shorter, are not complex, and represent lower overall quality of ideas. Their sentences contain less unusual vocabulary and frequent grammatical errors.

Sentence Activities

The goal for sentence instruction in Grades 5–12 is to develop students' syntactic awareness so they can more successfully comprehend challenging sentences when reading and write more high-quality, elaborated sentences. There are three activities that support these goals: *sentence combining, sentence deconstruction,* and *sentence elaboration.* Teachers should use content information and sample sentences from classroom text as the basis for developing these activities.

Sentence Combining for Reading and Writing Developed in the 1960s and studied for decades, sentence combining is an effective method for helping students across all grades and into college develop syntactic awareness to support comprehension and writing of sentences (Graham & Perin, 2007; Saddler, 2012; Strong, 1986). Sentence combining provides practice with manipulating and rearranging words in sentences, expanding sentences, and clarifying sentence meaning. Teachers of any subject area can assign sentence combining activities.

How It Is Done Students are given two or more sentences they must combine into one grammatically correct sentence. They can add or delete words and change the order of words from the original sentences, as long as all of the information and meaning is included in the new sentence. Figure 5.6 includes several examples.

Examples of Sentence Combining

Two sentences:

- Antarctica is the coldest of the seven continents.
- Antarctica receives very little precipitation.
- Combined: *Antarctica is the coldest of the seven continents and receives very little precipitation.*

Four sentences:

- Antarctica is the coldest of the seven continents.
- Antarctica's average annual temperature in the interior is below –50C.
- Antarctica receives very little precipitation.
- Antarctica is technically a desert!
- Combined: *Antarctica, the coldest of the seven continents, with an average annual temperature below –50C in the interior, receives so little precipitation that it is technically a desert!*

Figure 5.6. Examples of sentence combining. (*Source:* Sedita, 2023.)

Instructional Suggestions When introducing sentence combining to students, teachers can point out that these activities will help their reading comprehension and improve their writing. Teachers should start by asking students to combine just two basic sentences and then gradually increase the challenge to more than two sentences and by making the sentences to be combined longer. Teachers can use sample sentences from classroom text or those related to content as the basis for developing a sentence combining activity. One option is to select a longer complex sentence from text and then break it into smaller sentences for the students to combine. Teachers may also do the following:

- Label basic parts of speech (noun, verb, adjective, adverb), but do not make this the focus of the activity.
- Provide opportunities for students to collaborate with peers to combine sentences.
- Practice sentence combining at least two or three times per week.

Encouraging Discussion About Sentence Combinations Students benefit from discussion about how and why they are combining their sentences, as well as evaluation of the resulting sentences. The practice, supportive discussions, and comparisons of student-generated sentences help them understand the possible options in writing revision (Saddler, 2012). Use the following questions to support discussion:

- What process did you follow to combine the sentences?
- Which combination sounded best? Why?
- Which combination seems the clearest?

Sentence Deconstruction to Support Comprehension Proficient readers intuitively break longer sentences down into manageable parts and then combine the meaning of the individual parts for effective comprehension of the whole sentence. Sentence deconstruction is an instructional strategy that helps students build the ability to do this. It is the opposite of sentence combining. Instead of combining smaller sentences into one sentence, deconstruction breaks one sentence into smaller sentences.

For example, in the sentence that follows, there are three key parts:

1. colonial soldiers wore camouflaged clothing
2. British soldiers wore bright red uniforms
3. during the American Revolution

During the American Revolution, the colonial soldiers wore clothing that camouflaged them, unlike the British soldiers, who wore bright red uniforms.

How It Is Done First, the teacher selects a challenging sentence from the text students are reading that has multiple parts. Using think-aloud, the teacher then models how to identify the different parts and list them. The teacher turns each part into a phrase or a full sentence, making it easier for students to comprehend each part of the sentence.

Teachers should start with sentences that have only a few parts, and then gradually make the task more challenging by increasing the number of parts. As students develop proficiency, the teacher can have students work collaboratively with peers to deconstruct sentences, with a goal of completing the task independently. As an extension, after deconstructing a sentence, students can combine the parts back into a single sentence. The resulting sentence may be similar to the original sentence, or students might rearrange phrases and clauses to produce a different version.

Sentence Deconstruction Examples Figure 5.7 includes several examples. Each part of the sentence is listed on the left and turned into a simple sentence on the right.

Examples of Sentence Deconstruction

Example 1: The penguin is an ocean bird, living in and near the ocean, comfortably swimming in the sea for months at a time, but while on land, it walks along slowly with limited mobility.

penguin is an ocean bird	The penguin is an ocean bird.
lives in and near the ocean	Penguins live in and near the ocean.
swim in the sea	Penguins swim in the sea.
swim for months at a time	They can swim for months at a time.
walk slowly on land	Penguins walk slowly on land.
have limited mobility	They have limited mobility on land.

Example 2: The grueling process of the exams, the writing of essays, the drafting of mock state papers and edicts, and commenting on Confucian texts, coupled with the meager passing rates, ensured that those who advanced would be adept public servants capable of administering the Chinese state.

grueling exam process	The exam process was grueling.
written essays	There were written essays.
mock state papers and edicts	Mock state papers and edicts were drafted.
comments on Confucian texts	Comments on Confucian texts were made.
meager passing rates	There were meager passing rates
those who advanced became adept public servants	These things ensured that those who advanced became adept public servants.
capable to administer the Chinese state	Those who advanced would be capable of administering the Chinese state.

Figure 5.7. Examples of sentence deconstruction. (From Sedita, J. [2020d]. *Keys to content writing* [4th ed.]. Keys to Literacy; reprinted by permission.)

Sentence Elaboration for Writing Teachers can use sentence elaboration activities to help students learn to write longer, more sophisticated, and detailed sentences. Although these activities are focused more on writing sentences, the practice students receive while elaborating their sentences does improve syntactic awareness, which in turn supports reading comprehension.

The "W" Questions The simplest way to have students write longer sentences is to ask them to respond to *who, what, when, where, why, which,* and *how* questions. The teacher provides a simple subject and then poses questions to help students expand it into a longer sentence. Students can use any combination of these questions to expand a simple sentence. Figure 5.8 includes two examples.

Expanding Sentences With *W* Questions

Example 1: The Pilgrims

Did **what**?	The Pilgrims arrived.
Where did they arrive?	The Pilgrims arrived at Plymouth Rock.
How did they arrive?	The Pilgrims arrived by boat at Plymouth Rock.
When did they arrive?	The Pilgrims arrived by boat at Plymouth Rock in 1620.
Why did they arrive?	The Pilgrims arrived by boat at Plymouth Rock in 1620 to live in a new land.

Example 2: The U.S. Constitution

Does **what**?	The U.S. Constitution establishes a separation of powers.
How?	The U.S. Constitution establishes a separation of powers by creating three branches of government.
When?	The U.S. Constitution, ratified in 1788, establishes a separation of powers by creating three branches of government.
Who?	The U.S. Constitution, ratified in 1788, establishes a separation of powers by creating three branches of government represented by the president, Congress, and the Supreme Court.

Figure 5.8. Expanding sentences with *W* questions. (From Sedita, J. [2020d]. *Keys to content writing* [4th ed.]. Keys to Literacy; adapted by permission.)

Alternatively, the teacher can ask students to take sentences they have already written and pose *W* questions to themselves to expand their sentences.

Expanded Kernel Sentences for Writing

This more advanced activity, adapted from the work of Jennings and Haynes (2002), gives students the opportunity to identify parts of speech. The kernel sentence is small at first, but as students add different sentence elements, the sentence expands. The teacher can ask students to follow some or all of the steps in the kernel sentence process shown in Figure 5.9, which includes two examples. (A copy of this process and the examples is included with the downloadable resources for this chapter.) Once students begin writing longer sentences with multiple phrases and clauses, it is important for them to learn how to incorporate commas and other types of punctuation.

Kernel Sentence Expansion

Steps:

1. Start with a noun and a verb.
   - *The turtle dives.*
   - *Meteorologists study.*
2. Elaborate the subject (e.g., add articles, adjectives).
   - *The* ***green and brown leatherback*** *turtle dives.*
   - ***Local and national*** *meteorologists study.*
3. Elaborate the predicate (add adverbs).
   - *The green and brown leatherback turtle dives* ***gently and slowly.***
   - *Local and national meteorologists* ***constantly*** *study.*
4. Add a phrase.
   - *The green and brown leatherback turtle dives gently and slowly* ***into the dense seaweed.***
   - *Local and national meteorologists constantly study* ***weather and the atmosphere****.*
5. Compound the subject.
   - *The green and brown leatherback turtle* ***and a smaller baby turtle*** *dive gently and slowly into the dense seaweed.*
   - *Local and national meteorologists and* ***dedicated forecasters*** *constantly study weather and the atmosphere.*
6. Compound the predicate.
   - *The green and brown leatherback turtle and a smaller baby turtle* ***hold their breath*** *as they dive gently and slowly into the dense seaweed.*
   - *Local and national meteorologists and dedicated forecasters constantly study weather and the atmosphere* ***and make predictions.***
7. Add a dependent clause to make a complex sentence.
   - ***Because they are in search of food,*** *the green and brown leatherback turtle and a smaller baby turtle hold their breath as they dive gently and slowly into the dense seaweed.*
   - *Local and national meteorologists and dedicated forecasters constantly study weather and the atmosphere and make predictions* ***based on factors like temperature, humidity, and air pressure.***
8. Combine two sentences into a compound sentence.
   - *Because they are in search of food, the green and brown leatherback turtle and a smaller baby turtle hold their breath as they dive gently and slowly into the dense seaweed,* ***but they must return to the surface for air.***
   - *Local and national meteorologists and dedicated forecasters constantly study weather and the atmosphere and make predictions based on factors like temperature, and air pressure,* ***but they also rely on observation of the sky and clouds.***

Source: Jennings and Haynes (2002).

Figure 5.9. Kernel sentence expansion. (*Source:* Jennings & Haynes, 2002.)

SUMMARY

This chapter explains how multiple levels of text structure support both reading and writing, beginning with the structure of the three main text genres: informational, argument, and narrative. Suggestions are provided for teaching paragraph structure, patterns of organization, and transition words and phrases that can be used to signal these patterns and connect sections of text. The important role of syntactic awareness in both reading and writing is also addressed, along with activities designed to develop this awareness, such as sentence combining, sentence deconstruction, and sentence elaboration.

REFLECTION QUESTIONS

1. Summarize why teaching text structure supports both reading and writing.
2. What are the three types (genres) of text described in the chapter? What are the differences between their purposes and overall text structures?
3. What are the five patterns of organization? What is the purpose for each pattern?
4. Explain how awareness of transition words and phrases helps students comprehend while reading and produce more high-quality writing pieces.
5. How are identifying and stating main ideas related to paragraph structure?
6. Briefly explain the terms *syntax* and *syntactic awareness.* How do sentence-based activities such as sentence combining, sentence deconstruction, and sentence elaboration help students read and write sentences?

Argument Writing Components

- **Claim:** the position taken by the writer; what the writer is trying to prove or argue
  - *What do I think?*
- **Reason:** provided to support a claim; reasons are supported by evidence
  - *Why do I think it?*
- **Evidence:** used to support or prove a reason; statistics, facts, quotations, surveys, etc.
  - *How do I know (proof)?*
- **Counterclaim:** opposing position, counterargument
  - *What is the other side?*
- **Rebuttal:** refutes or disproves the counterclaim; addresses the criticism of the claim
  - *What is my response to the other side?*

From Sedita, J. (2020d). *Keys to content writing.* Keys to Literacy; reprinted by permission.

Common Patterns of Organization

Pattern	**Purpose**	**Common transitions**
Description, explanation	Describe a person, place, or thing; explain a topic or idea	*for instance, such as, another, in addition, for example, furthermore, also*
Sequence, chronology	Present items, events, or steps in order	*first, second, initially, before, next, following, after, then, finally, lastly*
Problem and solution	What went wrong and how it was or could be fixed	*the problem is, the question is, a solution is, therefore, if...then*
Cause and effect	What happened and why it happened	*because of, as a result, caused by, consequently, for that reason, that is why, therefore, thus*
Compare and contrast	How two or more things are alike and/or different	*by comparison, compared to, in like manner, likewise, similarly, but, however, in contrast, on the contrary, on the other hand, unlike*

From Sedita, J. (2015). *The key comprehension routine*. Keys to Literacy; reprinted by permission.

Kernel Sentence Expansion

Steps:

1. Start with a noun and a verb.
   - *The turtle dives.*
   - *Meteorologists study.*
2. Elaborate the subject (e.g., add articles, adjectives).
   - *The* ***green and brown leatherback*** *turtle dives.*
   - ***Local and national*** *meteorologists study.*
3. Elaborate the predicate (add adverbs).
   - *The green and brown leatherback turtle dives* ***gently and slowly.***
   - *Local and national meteorologists* ***constantly*** *study.*
4. Add a phrase.
   - *The green and brown leatherback turtle dives gently and slowly* ***into the dense seaweed.***
   - *Local and national meteorologists constantly study* ***weather and the atmosphere****.*
5. Compound the subject.
   - *The green and brown leatherback turtle* ***and a smaller baby turtle*** *dive gently and slowly into the dense seaweed.*
   - *Local and national meteorologists and* ***dedicated forecasters*** *constantly study weather and the atmosphere.*
6. Compound the predicate.
   - *The green and brown leatherback turtle and a smaller baby turtle* ***hold their breath*** *as they dive gently and slowly into the dense seaweed.*
   - *Local and national meteorologists and dedicated forecasters constantly study weather and the atmosphere* ***and make predictions.***
7. Add a dependent clause to make a complex sentence.
   - ***Because they are in search of food,*** *the green and brown leatherback turtle and a smaller baby turtle hold their breath as they dive gently and slowly into the dense seaweed.*
   - *Local and national meteorologists and dedicated forecasters constantly study weather and the atmosphere and make predictions* ***based on factors like temperature, humidity, and air pressure.***
8. Combine two sentences into a compound sentence.
   - *Because they are in search of food, the green and brown leatherback turtle and a smaller baby turtle hold their breath as they dive gently and slowly into the dense seaweed,* ***but they must return to the surface for air.***
   - *Local and national meteorologists and dedicated forecasters constantly study weather and the atmosphere and make predictions based on factors like temperature, and air pressure,* ***but they also rely on observation of the sky and clouds.***

Source: Jennings and Haynes (2002).

Questions to Analyze Text Structure

- Is the text informational, narrative, or argument?
- Is there anything unique about the format of the text?
- Did the author include an introduction and conclusion, and how do these structures support comprehension?
- How did the author organize the body of the piece?
- For informational text, how did the author organize the topics and subtopics?
- For narrative text, how did the author sequence the events?
- For argument text, how did the author organize the reasons, evidence, counterclaim, and rebuttal?
- Did the author use text features (title, headings, subheadings) to support the structure of the text?
- Did the author use a specific pattern of organization within the text (i.e., description/explanation, sequence, compare and contrast, cause and effect, problem and solution)?
- Did the author use transition words or phrases to connect sentences or parts of the text or to signal a pattern of organization? If yes, how do they support comprehension?
- Do most of the paragraphs have stated main ideas, or are the main ideas implied?
- How complex are the sentences in the text?

Three Types of Text

Type of text	What it does	Text structure	Examples
Argument	Makes an argument to convince the reader that a point of view is valid or to persuade the reader to take a specific action	Organized around these components: claim, reason, evidence, counterclaim, rebuttal	Persuasive letters, editorials, argument essays, reviews of books or movies, claims about the worth or meaning of a literary work
Informational	Examines previously learned information or provides new information	Organized into sections and sub-sections that include paragraph main ideas; tends to be organized hierarchically	Textbook, article, letter, speech, manual, directions, subject area report, summary of information, workplace memo, job application, resume
Narrative	Tells a story (real or imagined) of an experience, event, or sequence of events	Organized around literary elements such as setting, characters, events, problem/solution; also organized by order of events	Diary entry, biography, autobiography, personal narrative, memoir, folktales, fairytales, fables, myths, creative fiction stories, science fiction, poems, plays, eyewitness accounts, plot summary, short story

From Sedita, J. (2020d). *Keys to content writing.* Keys to Literacy; reprinted by permission.

Transition Words and Phrases

To indicate a time relationship	*after, afterward, after that, at first, at this time, before, beginning with, beyond, during, earlier, ending with, eventually, finally, following, from then on, in the meantime, last, later, meanwhile, next, now, since, soon, then, until, while*
To indicate spatial placement	*below, beside, between, beyond, farther on, here, next to, parallel with*
To list or present a series of ideas	*after, after that, finally, first, last, next, second, third*
To add information or continue a line of thought	*also, another, besides, further, furthermore, in addition, likewise, moreover, similarly*
To summarize or show conclusion	*accordingly, finally, in conclusion, in other words, in short, to conclude, to sum up, to summarize*
To show comparison	*by comparison, compared to, in like manner, likewise, similarly*
To show contrast	*although, but, however, in contrast, nevertheless, on the contrary, on the other hand, unlike*
To repeat information or stress a point	*above all, in fact, in other words, most important, once again, to repeat*
To provide an example or illustrate a point	*for example, for instance, such as, to illustrate, that is*
To show cause and effect	*as a result, because, because of, caused by, consequently, for that reason, that is why, therefore, thus*
To state the obvious	*certainly, granted that, in fact, most certainly, naturally, obviously, of course, surely, undoubtedly, without a doubt*

From Sedita, J. (2020d). *Keys to content writing.* Keys to Literacy; reprinted by permission.

6

Writing Instruction

Writing, like reading, is a relatively new cultural development. It does not come naturally the way speaking does, and it is a demanding and highly complex process. There is wide variation in writing ability among students. Students who have difficulty with reading typically have difficulty with writing, but it is not unusual for students who have grade-level or above reading skills to have difficulty with writing. All students benefit from writing instruction, even those for whom learning to write seems to come effortlessly. The ability to write is essential to learning, as Graham and Perin (2007) note in the *Writing Next* report:

> Writing is not just an option for young people—it is a necessity. Along with reading comprehension, writing skill is a predictor of academic success and the basic requirement for participation in civic life and the global economy. . . . All students need to become proficient and flexible writers. (p. 19)

This chapter begins by describing how students in Grades 5–12 move from learning to write, to writing to learn content. It then presents principles, practices, and frameworks that constitute a research-based understanding of what good writing instruction looks like in the classroom. The chapter goes on to explain how content-area teachers can use different types of assignments and mentor texts to teach writing within their academic discipline. Detailed recommendations are presented for teaching each stage of the writing process and planning assignments.

LEARNING TO WRITE, WRITING TO LEARN

Elementary students are *learning to write* as they acquire foundational writing skills, including transcription skills (spelling and handwriting/keyboarding), the ability to write sentences and paragraphs, and the differences in purpose, use, and structure of narrative, informational, and opinion text. They also start building strategies to support the stages of the writing process such as using pre-planning tools and revision strategies.

As students move into middle school, an assumption is made that these foundational skills have been learned and the focus for writing instruction shifts to learning more sophisticated writing skills and using *writing to learn*. This includes learning about what is unique about writing in specific subjects—that is, how to write like a mathematician, scientist, historian, or literary expert. This shift works for students who have grade-level writing ability. However, there are large numbers of adolescent learners who have difficulty with writing. In addition to instruction for advanced writing skills, struggling writers need supplemental instruction to fill in the gaps in foundational skills. This instruction will vary based on the individual needs of students. Intervention suggestions are shared in Chapter 9, "Adolescent Learners With Literacy Difficulties."

Teaching Principles for Writing

Gradual release of responsibility	This model of instruction is also referred to as an I do it, We do it, You do it approach to teaching. It includes explicit instruction using a direct approach to introduce and teach a new writing skill and gradually releasing support with a goal of independent use by students (Pearson & Gallagher, 1983).
Explicit instruction of writing strategies	Explicit instruction involves using structured and sequenced steps to teach a specific skill. It includes the teacher explaining a skill and modeling how it is applied using think-aloud and providing guided practice with feedback. Teaching students strategies for planning, revising, and editing their compositions has shown a dramatic effect on the quality of students' writing. Strategy instruction may involve teaching more generic processes, such as brainstorming or collaboration for peer revising, or it may involve strategies for accomplishing a specific type of writing task, such as writing an opinion or argument piece (Graham & Perin, 2007).
Differentiated instruction	Differentiated instruction calls for designing instruction to suit individual student needs rather than using a standardized approach to instruction that assumes all students learn to write the same way.
Scaffolding	Scaffolding is assistance offered by a teacher or a peer to support learning a writing skill that a student is initially unable to grasp independently, and then removal of the assistance once the skill is learned. This is not the same as doing the work for the student. Scaffolding is a hallmark of differentiated instruction. Examples of writing scaffolds include graphic organizers, writing templates, and lists of words such as transitions.
Opportunities for collaboration	Writing is a social activity and is best learned in a community. Collaborative writing has been found to have a significant effect on improving student writing and engagement in writing (Graham & Perin, 2007). It involves instructional arrangements whereby students work together to plan, draft, revise, and edit their writing pieces.
Mentor text as models for writing	Writing models, also referred to as mentor text, should be used to show students what high-quality writing looks like so they can emulate the style, language, and structure of the text.
Increasing the amount students write in all subjects	Adequate time for students to write is essential to the development of writing skills, and that time can occur during content instruction (Graham et al., 2012). Writing is one of the major strategies to extend critical thinking about a subject-area topic. Many state writing standards call for students to write routinely in all subject areas, including short- and long-term writing tasks.

Sources: Graham and Perin (2007), Graham et al. (2012), and Pearson and Gallagher (1983).

Figure 6.1. Teaching principles for writing. (*Sources:* Graham & Perin, 2007; Graham et al. 2012; Pearson & Gallagher, 1983.)

WHAT GOOD WRITING INSTRUCTION LOOKS LIKE

To deliver effective writing instruction, teachers should keep in mind certain general teaching principles as well as specific teaching practices, all based in research. Writing research also informs two instructional models discussed in this chapter, The Writing Rope (Sedita, 2019) and The Not-So-Simple View of Writing (Berninger & Winn, 2006).

Teaching Principles

There are several teaching principles informed by writing research that teachers should keep in mind as they teach and use writing in any subject (Sedita, 2020d). These include gradually releasing responsibility, explicitly teaching writing strategies, differentiating instruction, scaffolding learning, providing opportunities for collaboration, using mentor texts as writing models, and increasing writing across all subjects. Review these principles in Figure 6.1 and note that some of the items are included in the broader principles of literacy instruction introduced in Chapter 1. (A full-size, reproducible version of this list is included with the downloads for this chapter.)

Teaching Practices

Researchers and practitioners have been studying writing instruction for many decades to identify effective instructional practices. Figure 6.2 lists teaching practices that are consistently identified as effective across all grades, several of which are incorporated into the teaching principles described in Figure 6.1.

Effective Teaching Practices

- Teach students that there are different purposes for writing.
- Assign writing tasks for real audiences that are relevant to students' everyday lives.
- Teach the stages of the writing process.
- Explicitly teach writing skills, strategies, and techniques.
- Provide procedural scaffolds.
- Provide opportunities for students to collaborate with peers and the teacher.
- Use mentor models of text for students to emulate.
- Provide actionable feedback.
- Increase the amount of time students write and time spent on writing instruction.
- Create a supportive, engaging writing environment.

Figure 6.2. Effective teaching practices. (*Sources:* Boscolo & Gelati, 2007; Chapman, 2006; Coker, 2007; Donovan & Smolkin, 2006; Hidi & Boscolo, 2006; MacArthur, 2007; Pritchard & Honeycutt, 2007.)

The findings and recommendations from three guides based on meta-analyses of writing research are summarized here.

1. *Teaching Secondary Students to Write Effectively* (Graham et al., 2016): Explicitly teach appropriate writing strategies using a Model-Practice-Reflect instructional cycle. Integrate writing and reading to emphasize key writing features. Use assessments of student writing to inform instruction and feedback.
2. *Writing to Read—Evidence for How Writing Can Improve Reading* (Graham & Hebert, 2010): Have students write about the texts they read. Teach students the writing skills and processes that go into creating text. Increase how much students write.
3. *Writing Next—Effective Strategies to Improve the Writing of Adolescents in Middle and High Schools* (Graham & Perin, 2007): Incorporate 11 elements of writing instruction found to be effective for helping students in Grades 4–12 learn to write well and use writing as a tool for learning, including writing strategies, summarizing, collaborative writing, specific product goals, word processing, sentence combining, prewriting, inquiry activities, process writing approach, study of models, and writing for content learning.

In addition, a more recent 2023 meta-analysis examining effective writing instruction specifically for students in Grades 6–12 found the following effective for enhancing student writing, confirming earlier findings (Graham et al., 2023): strategy instruction, digital writing tools, transcription instruction, computer-assisted instruction, teaching critical/creative thinking skills for writing, emulating good models of writing, feedback, goal setting, prewriting activities, grammar instruction, sentence instruction, inquiry, observing writers/readers, peer assistance, summarization instruction, and text structure instruction.

The Writing Rope

The Writing Rope (Sedita, 2019, 2023) was introduced in Chapter 1. This framework for teaching writing across all grades is shown again in Figure 6.3 and included in the downloadable resources for this chapter. The Writing Rope organizes writing skills, strategies, and techniques students must learn to become proficient writers into five components, represented as strands in a rope. Details about each strand are provided in the following section.

Critical Thinking This strand draws significantly on critical thinking and executive function skills, as well as the ability to develop background knowledge about a writing topic. Students engage in critical thinking as they think about what they want to communicate through their writing. If they are composing an informational or argument piece, they will also use comprehension skills to gather information from sources.

This strand also includes awareness of the writing process (i.e., *thinking, planning, drafting, writing, revising*). For the thinking stage, students benefit from explicit instruction for brainstorming strategies and skills for gathering information from written and multimedia sources, such as note taking. They also need to learn planning strategies for organizing their thoughts, including the use of prewriting graphic organizers. Students need to be metacognitive and purposeful about working recursively through the stages of the writing process, and they benefit from explicit instruction in revising and editing strategies.

Syntax Efficient processing of sentence structure is necessary for listening and reading comprehension, as well as for communicating information and ideas in writing. Syntax is the study and understanding of grammar—the system and arrangement of words, phrases, and clauses that make up a sentence. Students develop syntactic awareness as they learn the correct use of words in sentences. Students benefit from explicit instruction focused on building sentence skills, including activities such as sentence elaboration and sentence combining, addressed in Chapter 5, "Teaching Text Structure."

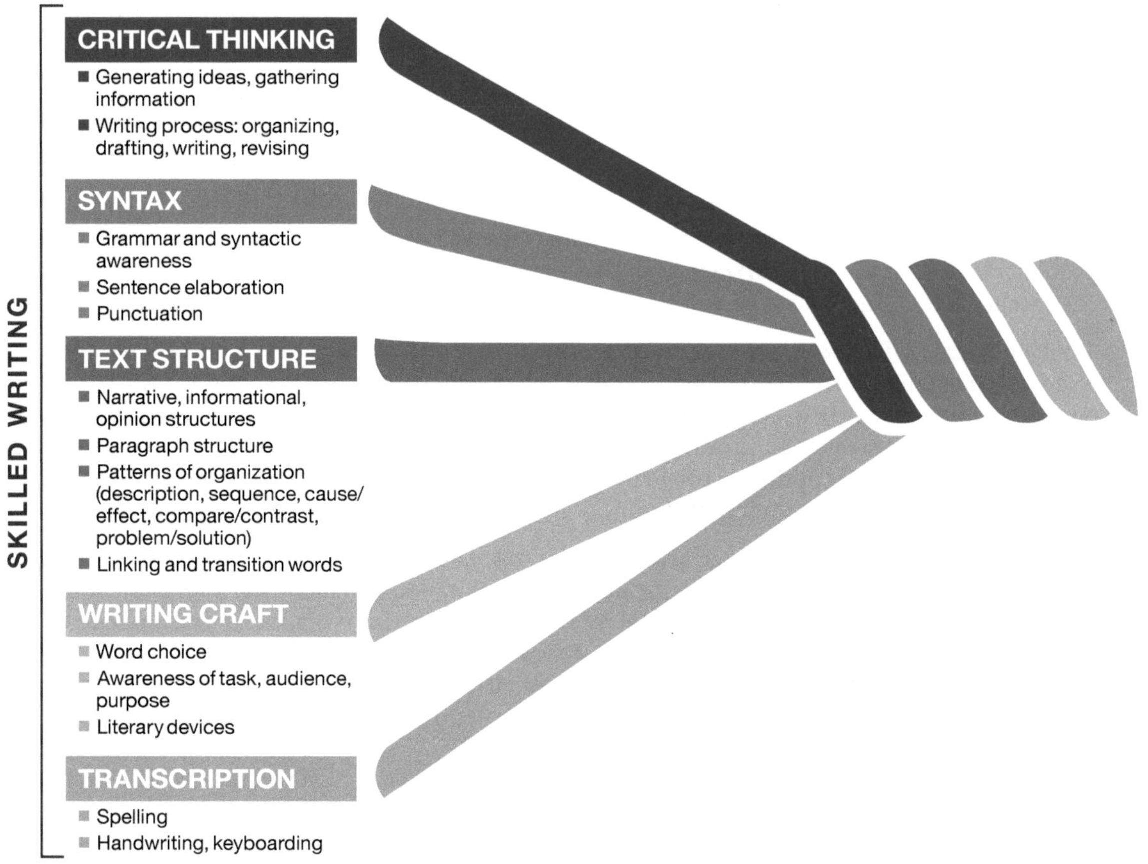

Figure 6.3. The Writing Rope®. *Full-color version available on the Brookes Download Hub.* (*From The Writing Rope®: The strands that are woven into skilled writing* [online article]. Keys to Literacy; reprinted by permission. © 2019 by Joan Sedita. All rights reserved.)

Text Structure Text structure is unique to written language, and awareness of several levels of text structure supports both writing and reading comprehension. Students benefit from explicit instruction for the following types of text structure:

- Informational, argument, and narrative text structure: Knowledge of the different organization structures for these three types of writing, including the use of introductions, body development, and conclusions
- Paragraph structure: Understanding that written paragraphs are used to chunk text into manageable units that are organized around a main idea and supporting details
- Patterns of organization: Understanding that sentences and paragraphs can be organized to convey a specific purpose, including description/explanation, sequence, cause and effect, compare and contrast, problem and solution
- Transition words and phrases: Ability to use words or phrases to link sentences, paragraphs, or sections of text, including use of transitions associated with specific patterns of organization

Suggestions for teaching text structure were provided in Chapter 5, "Teaching Text Structure."

Writing Craft This strand addresses skills and strategies often referred to as *writer's craft* or *writer's moves*. This includes a number of techniques that writers employ that affect writing style, text structure, and choice of words. Students benefit from explicit instruction in the following:

- Word choice: Purposeful use of specific vocabulary, word placement, and dialogue to convey meaning and create an effect on the reader

- Writer's voice: The techniques and style of writing an author uses to show emotion, personality, or point of view
- Literary devices: Understanding and use of common literary elements (e.g., plot, setting, narrative, characters, theme) and literary techniques (e.g., imagery, personification, figurative language, alliteration, allegory, irony)

This strand also addresses the importance of being mindful of the task, audience, and purpose when writing. Awareness of these elements influences a student's decisions about word choice, tone, length and style of a writing piece.

Transcription This strand addresses spelling and handwriting/keyboarding skills. They are basic skills that are needed to transcribe the words a writer wants to put into writing. Once students become automatic and fluent with spelling and handwriting/keyboarding, they can focus their attention on composing. If students in Grades 5–12 have not developed fluency with these skills, this will put a constraint on their writing development.

The Not-So-Simple View of Writing

The Not-So-Simple View is a developmental model for writing that highlights several processes and skills that support writing (Berninger & Winn, 2006). In addition to transcription skills and composing (text generation), students must have sufficient executive function abilities to write. These include the ability to attend and stay focused, set goals and plan before writing, revise writing, and self-regulate behavior. Working memory, the ability to hold onto ideas and information, is at the center of the model.

Students who have limited attention and difficulties with executive function processes may have difficulty planning what to put in their writing pieces. They may have difficulty attending to spelling, handwriting or keyboarding, and composing their ideas at the same time. They may also have difficulty maintaining their focus on their writing goals or sustaining attention for a writing task over a longer period of time. Executive functions and working memory are cognitive processes that cannot be taught. However, scaffolds that are the hallmark of explicit writing instruction (e.g., graphic organizers, writing templates, step-by-step directions, and revision checklists) provide support to students who have weaknesses in these processes.

CONTENT WRITING: USING WRITING TO LEARN

As noted in Chapter 1, writing is an effective tool for enhancing students' learning of content material for all subject areas (Graham & Perin, 2007; Graham et al., 2015). Students engage in critical thinking as they use writing to communicate ideas and information, especially when that writing is based on sources. Writing helps them organize, clarify, and understand what they are reading. It also helps them engage with the information by extending their thinking and building relationships between the information and their background knowledge.

Students' comprehension of content-area texts is improved when they write about what they read, including writing personal reactions to texts, analyzing and interpreting the text, writing summaries and notes, and answering and creating questions about text in writing (Graham & Hebert, 2010).

The Role of Content Teachers

Writing is a difficult task, and students will only demonstrate improvement if they are required to write often, throughout the school day, and in all subjects. As with other aspects of literacy, teaching students to write is often considered the job of English language arts and writing teachers during class time dedicated to writing instruction. However, the truth is they cannot do it alone—content teachers are needed to support adolescents in learning to write, and to teach them how to use writing to learn in different disciplines.

Writing-to-learn tasks can be based on reading, classroom discussion, teacher presentation, media such as video, or hands-on activities (Sedita, 2020d). For older students, these tasks may be discipline-specific; they also vary in length and formality.

Teach Discipline-Specific Writing Content teachers can help students learn to use many general content writing skills and strategies such as note taking, summarizing, answering an essay question, writing introductions and conclusions for informational and argument writing, and using knowledge of text structure. Content teachers are also needed to teach students what is unique about disciplinary writing in specific subjects, such as these examples:

- Science: experimental lab report, field notes
- History: political speech, analysis of a historical event
- Mathematics: algebraic proof, description of the steps used to solve a problem
- English: literary analysis, poetry, playwriting

Use Different Types of Content Writing Assignments Content writing in any subject can be sorted into three types of tasks, shown in Table 6.1. (A full-size, reproducible version of this chart is included with the downloads for this chapter.) *Quick Writes* are very short writing tasks teachers can integrate frequently into classroom instruction (i.e., at least two or three times per week). *Content learning tasks,* which require a bit more time and effort, are tasks that should be assigned on a regular basis to support content learning (e.g., at least once every 2 weeks). Because *formal writing tasks* take a significant amount of time and effort on the part of students and teachers, teachers will most likely use these kinds of writing assignments more infrequently (i.e., once or twice per semester).

A Closer Look at Quick Writes Quick Writes are short, informal writing tasks that are limited to 10 minutes of class time or assigned as brief, out-of-class assignments. Quick Writes help the writer remember, organize, and manage information, and they can be used at any point in a classroom lesson to help students communicate their thoughts, experiences, and reactions to what they are reading and learning. They can also be used as a formative assessment to determine how well students have learned content. Quick Writes are sometimes called *low-stakes* writing tasks because students focus on getting ideas on the page without the worry of spelling, multiple drafts, or grades. The first part of Figure 6.4 lists types of Quick Write tasks. The second part lists classroom examples by subject area.

In addition to the three types of writing tasks described previously, students in middle and high school need experience responding to narratives and responding to writing prompts.

Responding to Narrative Text One of the recommendations from the *Writing to Read* research guide is to ask students to respond in writing to narrative text, such as writing a personal response to material read or writing about a personal experience related to it (Graham & Hebert, 2010). The report suggests that this might take the form of a response journal, for which the teacher asks students to write their feelings, reactions, and questions during or after reading a story or other form of narrative text, such as a biography. Personal responses to narrative text help students clarify and organize what they are reading and become aware of their reactions to the text. A list of questions is provided in Figure 6.5 that can guide students as they write reflections to narrative text; a full-size, reproducible copy is included with the chapter downloads. The teacher should pose just a few of these questions for any given writing assignment to avoid overwhelming students.

Teacher-Generated Prompts Frequent informational and argument writing in response to teacher-generated writing prompts helps students interact more deeply with content and provides the writing practice that is essential to improving writing ability. Responses to prompts about classroom content and text also provide practice for similar writing tasks often found on high-stakes state assessments. A collective responsibility for developing students' writing skills is met when teachers of all subjects incorporate source-writing based on prompts on a regular basis. Figure 6.6 includes several examples of writing prompts across Grades 5–12 for informational and argument writing as well as literary analysis.

Table 6.1 Types of Content Writing Tasks

Types of Content Writing Tasks

Task type and frequency	Characteristics	Examples
Quick Writes Assigned at least twice per week	• Task takes less than 10 minutes to complete. • Task is related to content learning. • Objective is to help students process and reflect on content learning. • Task can be used to informally assess content learning. • Writing is typically not revised. • Task is typically not graded.	• Admit or exit tickets • Drawing, labeling, or explaining pictures or graphics • One- to three-sentence reflections or responses to a question • Free writing for a specified short amount of time
Content learning tasks Assigned at least once every 2 weeks	• Task takes one to three classroom or homework sessions to complete. • Task is related to content learning. • Length is up to one or two pages. • Objective is to deepen understanding and reflection. • Task can be used to informally assess content learning. • Writing may be revised. • Task may be informally evaluated or may be graded.	• Summary of reading or a lecture • Multiparagraph response to a question • Personal response to narrative text • Subject-specific writing task
Formal writing tasks Assigned once per semester	• Task is completed over multiple days or weeks. • Task is related to content learning. • Length is one or more pages. • Objective is to learn and explore content more deeply, and to practice advanced writing skills. • Task can be used to formally assess content learning and writing skills. • Writing should be revised, possibly multiple times. • Task is formally evaluated and graded.	• Research report • Multipage literary analysis

From Sedita, J. (2020d). *Keys to content writing.* Keys to Literacy; reprinted by permission.

USING MENTOR TEXTS AS MODELS FOR WRITING

Most people learn to write by emulating others, similar to learning other new skills such as playing a sport or a musical instrument. Mentor texts (written exemplars) are used to demonstrate high-quality writing for students so they can imitate style, language, and structure in their own writing. Mentor models can be used to show how authors use writing techniques, also called *writing moves.* Portalupi and Fletcher (2001) explain that students need to "apprentice themselves" to good writers as they learn to write their own informational or argument texts.

The *Writing Next* research report (Graham & Perin, 2007) identified studying models as one of the 11 effective instructional practices for students in Grades 3–12. This includes providing opportunities for students to read, analyze, and emulate the critical elements, patterns, and forms of the writing process.

Examples of Quick Write Tasks

- Admit and exit tickets
- Informal notes, margin notes while reading
- Lists of facts, ideas, or reactions related to something learned
- Set of instructions or directions
- Filling in a graphic organizer
- Free writing for a specified short amount of time
- One-paragraph description or summary
- Generating questions or short responses to questions
- K-W-L chart (what I know, what I want to know, what I learned)
- Definitions in the student's words
- Drawing, labeling, or explaining graphics, pictures, diagrams
- Sentence combining using sentences related to subject-area content

Examples of Classroom Quick Write Tasks

Science

- Write out the definition of *weathering* and *erosion*, then explain an example of each.
- In 10 sentences or less, list the five stages of human development.
- Make a list of the materials needed to complete this week's experiment.
- Work with a partner. You have 8 minutes to describe the Big Bang Theory.
- Admit ticket: in less than 3 minutes, list as many facts you can remember about the star Polaris.
- Identify which elements in the periodic table belong to the group that includes the most active metals. Write down the name, symbol, and periodic number for each of these elements.

Social Studies/History

- Pick the two most challenging vocabulary terms related to the different forms of government, and complete a Frayer template for each word.
- In 10 minutes or less, briefly describe the three major social reforms of the late Roman republic.
- Describe three reasons why people migrate.
- Based on the primary source letter, list three to five details that show how the mills provided opportunity for the workers.
- List what you think are the three most important tools for an archaeologist. Then, pick one and write a paragraph about why you chose that tool.
- Historical landmarks: List two possible locations for your curating project. Then write a pro and con statement for choosing each one for the project.

English Language Arts

- Admit ticket: Describe the character trait you learned about the main character in your reading last night.
- Exit ticket: Write out your personal writing goal for the collaborative writing assignment.
- Explain what the literary term *conflict* means. Then, write a few sentences describing a conflict you have faced in your own life.
- List the seven major stages of an epic.
- Organize the 15 detail sentences into three paragraphs. Then, write a topic sentence for each paragraph.
- Describe how the two settings in Chapter 3 are different and similar.

Mathematics

- Write out step-by-step instructions for calculating the volume of a box.
- Define the properties of a polygon.
- Identify and label each element in the sample coordinate system graph.
- Describe the strategy you used to solve the word problem about percentages.
- List and briefly describe the seven types of equations.
- Explain what a ratio shows, and describe one example.

Figure 6.4. Examples of Quick Writes. (*Source:* Sedita, 2020d.)

Graham and colleagues (2012) explain the value of emulating mentor text as follows:

> Students should be exposed to exemplary texts from a variety of sources, including published or professional texts, books, and textbooks, the teacher's own writing, and peer samples. Teachers should select texts that
>
> - support the instructional goals of the lesson,
> - are appropriate for students' reading levels and abilities,
> - and provide exemplary models of what students will write.
>
> Exemplary texts can illustrate multiple features, including text structure; use of graphs, charts and pictures; effective word choice; and varied sentence structure. Teachers should either read exemplary texts out loud or direct students to read and reread exemplary texts, paying close attention to the author's word choice, overall structure, or other style elements. Teachers should explain and students should discuss how each text demonstrates characteristics of effective writing in that genre. Students will then be prepared to emulate characteristics of exemplary texts at the word, sentence and/or text level, or they can use the text as a springboard for writing. (p. 22)

Responding to Narrative Text

Overall Personal Response

- Is there something that reminds you of yourself or people you know?
- Is there something that reminds you of something that happened in your life?
- Is there a confusing passage or part of the story?
- What do you agree or disagree with?
- Is there something you wonder about in the story?
- Is there something you wish had happened differently?
- Is there something that surprised you in the story?
- What is your overall opinion of this story? Would you recommend it to a friend?
- Does this story remind you of another story you have read?

Response to Theme

- What do you think is important in the story?
- What is the theme(s) in the story and what are your thoughts about it?
- Is there a lesson to be learned in the story?

Response to Characters

- What is your opinion of the characters?
- Did the main character change throughout the story?
- What was the main character's problem, and how did he or she solve that problem?
- Do you agree with the actions of the characters? Would your actions be similar or different?

Response to Setting

- What is your reaction to the setting(s) in the story (including time and place)?
- How does the setting fit into the story, and why is it important?

Response to the Author

- Why do you think the author wrote this story?
- What do you think about the author's choice for the title?
- Does the author make you feel that you are part of the story? How does the author do this?
- What did you like about the author's writing?
- Did you learn something you might try in your writing?

Source: Sedita (2023).

Figure 6.5. Responding to narrative text: Guiding questions. (*Source:* Sedita, 2023.)

Models of Discipline-Specific Text

Teachers can use examples of subject-specific classroom text that represent the aspects of writing that are unique to the discipline they teach. For example, teachers can closely read and analyze sentences from content classroom text with students, focusing on the way language is used in that subject, including the vocabulary and grammatical structure. This in turn helps students write longer, more complex sentences about that subject that include varied and precise vocabulary. In addition, teachers can help students analyze the techniques and text structures employed by authors of discipline-specific text, such as a science lab report, a comparison of two primary sources in history, an example of personification or use of dialogue in a literary work, or a mathematical proof. Teachers can then help students apply similar techniques and text structures to their own content-specific writing.

How to Use Mentor Text: Focus Areas and Process

Table 6.2 includes general suggestions for focus areas when using mentor text such as writing introductions and conclusions, word choice, using text features, and writing elements for informational, argument, and narrative writing. (A full-size, reproducible version of this chart is included with the downloads for this chapter.) Content teachers should identify focus areas specific to their discipline and provide written exemplars from text in their subject area.

Many students do not know what to look for when presented with a sample of mentor text. They need teachers to identify the writing strategy or technique and help them analyze how the author used it. The following procedure can be used:

1. First, the teacher models the analysis by using think-aloud. This means verbalizing thoughts and actions as they analyze a piece of text, including reading aloud portions of the text and

Examples of Classroom Writing Prompts

Grade 5 Informational	Based on information from both text sources, write an informational essay that explains three ways in which color is used by animals of the coral reef.
Grade 5 Opinion	Write an editorial for the school newspaper that makes a claim for or against banning the sale of sugary drinks in the school cafeteria and vending machines. Select editorials will be published in our school paper. Your claim should be supported by evidence from two sources provided by the teacher.
Grade 6 Informational	The population of the bullfrog in our state has declined since 1982. Write a short article that identifies and explains two possible reasons for this decline. Cite relevant and specific evidence from the text source.
Grade 6 Literary Analysis	In two to four paragraphs, explain the similarities and differences between what kept the character Brian (*Hatchet*) and the character Grayson (*Boy, Nine, Survives Wilderness*) alive during their experiences. Base your answer on information from both texts.
Grade 6 Argument	Write an argument that supports the use of vaccinations. Use evidence to support your argument found in the article, video, and infographic.
Grade 7 Informational	Write a three- to five-paragraph composition that explains the impact of globalization on everyday life in the United States. Be sure to first define globalization and include at least three impacts using information from our textbook chapter.
Grade 7 Informational	Based on the two articles about human sleep requirements, write a response that answers this question: What are the benefits of napping?
Grade 8 Literary analysis	Think carefully about the experiences of both Louie Zamperini in *Unbroken* and Jeanne Wakatsuki in *Farewell to Manzanar*. Write an informational essay that is between 400 and 600 words. First, describe how the characters survived their wartime experiences. Then explain the similarities and differences between their experiences. Use information and quotes from the two books.
Grade 8 Informational	Write a two-page informational piece based on the excerpt from the novel *The Great Fire*, the article *The Losses by the Fire*, and the *Chicago Tribune* video. Your writing should focus on the role the city government played in protecting people during the disaster. Be sure to include information from all three sources.
High school Informational	Write a multiparagraph informational essay on the relationship between clothing styles and developments in clothing creation. Your essay must be based on ideas, concepts, and information from the two articles.
High school Informational	In the period before 600 BCE, the adoption of agriculture had significant social, economic, and demographic effects. Explain how the adoption of agriculture in this time period affected the development of human societies. Use historical evidence from the sources.
High school Argument	Take a position in an argument piece that answers this question: Did working in the textile mills of New England improve the lives of 19th-century women, or were these workers mistreated and exploited by the factories that employed them? Use information from our textbook and the two primary sources to support your position.
High school Informational literary analysis	Read Jaques' soliloquy from Shakespeare's *As You Like It*. In an essay, analyze how Shakespeare ends his soliloquy on a sad or tragic note and explain whether the rest of the soliloquy either reflects this sadness or lessens it. Be sure your essay includes a thesis statement that answers the question, and use the rest of your essay to establish a clear position and defend it with enough details to convince the reader you are correct.

Figure 6.6. Examples of classroom writing prompts. (*Source:* Sedita, 2020d.)

Table 6.2. Focus Areas for Using Mentor Text

Focus Areas for Using Mentor Text

Focus area	Specific focus areas
General: All types of writing	• Writing introductions • Writing leads • Writing conclusions • Incorporating transition words and phrases • Organizing the body • Developing and explaining ideas • Using relevant details and specific descriptions • Word choice and incorporating content-related vocabulary • Creating a voice (i.e., a distinct personality, style, or point of view) • Writing in the first, second or third person • Using capitalization and punctuation • Writing elaborated sentences
Text features	• Writing titles • Incorporating graphics, charts, maps, and other visuals • Generating headings and subheadings
Informational and argument writing	• Using specific patterns of organization • Using examples • Using quotes and dialogue • Using anecdotes • Stating a claim • Explaining how evidence supports a reason • Explaining how a reason supports a claim
Narrative writing	• Developing a story line: beginning, middle, end, and plot sequence • Using techniques such as flashback, foreshadow, backstory • Creating, developing, describing characters • Using dialogue • Developing, describing settings • Using simile, metaphor, personification, alliteration, imagery • Writing a personal narrative • Writing a biography or autobiography

Sedita, J. (2020d). *Keys to content writing.* Keys to Literacy; reprinted by permission.

stopping to ask how and why the author chose to use certain words, sentences, text structure, or other techniques.

2. Next, the teacher gives students the opportunity to collaborate with a peer to emulate the strategy or technique in their own writing.
3. Once they are able, students incorporate the strategy or technique consistently in their own writing.

An example of how mentor text might be used to teach students about nonfiction leads in an introduction is shown in Figure 6.7. A nonfiction lead is a technique writers use to entice a reader to continue reading, such as posing a question, starting with a quote, providing an anecdote, or presenting a series of facts. The example in Figure 6.7 includes two samples of introductions from articles about high

Examples of Nonfiction Leads

Example 1: Quote
Sara White is an all too typical student in Philadelphia—she stopped going to school last year, and was on her way to becoming one more dropout. "The teachers didn't care, the students didn't care," White said. "Nobody cared, so why should I?" (Whitaker, 2010).

Example 2: Series of Facts
Since 2020, U.S. high school graduation rates have shown resilience and gradual improvement. In the 2021–22 school year, the national adjusted graduation rate for public high school students reached 87%, up from 80% in 2011–12. This increase reflects an upward trend, with annual gains of 0.5 to 1.4 percentage points, except for a slight dip in 2020–21 due to the COVID-19 pandemic (NCES, 2024).

Figure 6.7. Examples of nonfiction leads in introductions.

school dropouts. The first example uses a quote as a lead and the second example uses a series of facts. Following the steps outlined previously, the teacher would ask students to identify the type of lead used in each example. Next, the teacher would ask students to work collaboratively with a peer to incorporate one of the two types of leads in their writing pieces. Eventually, the teacher would require students to independently incorporate different types of leads when writing introductions.

TEACHING AWARENESS OF TASK, AUDIENCE, AND PURPOSE

Skilled writers learn that it is important to be aware of the *task, audience,* and *purpose* (TAP) for a piece of writing because these elements should influence decisions a writer makes, including the following:

- Tone of the piece (e.g., objective, critical, apathetic, sincere, skeptical)
- Language and word choice
- Type of information and level of detail to include in the piece
- How to arrange and present information

This awareness comes naturally to some students, but others, especially those who have difficulty writing, benefit from explicit instruction about these elements. Graham and colleagues (2012) offer the following recommendations about teaching audience and purpose:

> Writing for different purposes often means writing for different audiences. To help students understand the role of audience in writing, it is important to design writing activities that naturally lend themselves to different audiences. Otherwise, students may view writing in school as writing only for their teacher. When discussing writing purposes, teachers and students can generate a list of potential audiences for a given writing assignment. Students then can choose the audience that best fits their writing topic. For example, when writing persuasive letters, students could write for parents, friends, companies, or newspapers, depending on their chosen topic.
>
> Students should learn to adjust their tone and word choice to better convey their meaning and suit their audience. To develop this skill, students might write about the same topic for different audiences. For example, students could write a description of their favorite video game for a friend who also plays the game. Then, they could write a description for an adult, such as the school principal, who is unfamiliar with the game. Allowing students to write for a range of audiences enables them to think of writing as an authentic means of communication to accomplish a variety of goals. (p. 21)

The questions in Figure 6.8 can be shared with students to help them consider the task, audience, and purpose before they write. A full-size, reproducible copy of the questions is included with the downloads for this chapter.

TEACHING THE STAGES OF THE WRITING PROCESS

Beginning in the 1960s, Hayes and Flower researched the steps that successful writers follow when they write to better understand how to teach writing. They developed a model of the writing process with three stages: *planning, translating,* and *reviewing.* Over the years, the model was informed by new research and modified to include four stages (Hayes, 1996, 2004; Hayes & Flower, 1980):

1. Prewriting: reflection, selecting a topic, planning what to say
2. Text Production: writing a draft
3. Revising: reflection, making changes to improve the writing
4. Editing: proofreading

Graham and colleagues (2012) explain the writing process as follows:

> The writing process is the means through which a writer composes text. Writing is not a linear process, like following a recipe to bake a cake. It is flexible; writers should learn to move easily back and forth between components of the writing process, often alternating their plans and revising their text along the way. Components of the writing process include planning, drafting, sharing, evaluating, revising, and editing. (p. 14)

TAP Questions

Task

- What is your assignment?
- What are you being asked to do?
- What form will your writing take?

Audience

- Who is the audience for the writing piece?
- Is it your teacher or classmates, or is there another, more authentic audience?
- Who will read your piece?

Purpose

- What is the purpose for this writing piece?
- Is it to inform, convince, or tell a story?
- How might the audience determine the purpose?

From Sedita, J. (2020d). *Keys to content writing* (4th ed.). Keys to Literacy; reprinted by permission.

Figure 6.8. TAP Questions. (From Sedita, J. [2020d]. *Keys to content writing* [4th ed.]. Keys to Literacy; reprinted by permission.)

Think, Plan, Write, Revise

Sedita (2020d) developed a model for teaching the writing process that includes four stages: *Think, Plan, Write,* and *Revise.* This model separates the prewriting stage proposed by Hayes and Flower into two stages (*Think, Plan*) and combines the revising and editing stages into a single stage (*Revise*). The title of this model, *The Process Writing Routine,* is designed to help students recall the stages of the writing process by linking the four stages to the first letters of the words in the title. Details for the stages are provided in Figure 6.9; a full-size, reproducible copy is included with the downloads for this chapter. The arrow is added to remind students that the writing process is dynamic and recursive—writers repeat and revisit the stages as they develop a piece of writing.

Many students assume that the focus of their attention should be on writing the first draft and they do not spend sufficient time at the *Think* and *Plan* stages, or they skip them altogether. The amount of time spent on each stage will vary depending on the writing task, but a common recommendation is to spend 40% of the time reading, gathering ideas and information, and taking notes prior to writing (*Think* and *Plan*), 20% of the time writing a draft (*Write*), and 40% of the time rewriting and revising, including editing for conventions (*Revise*). *Writing Next,* the research guide based on Graham and Perin's (2007) meta-analysis of writing instruction research, identified prewriting at the *Think* and *Plan* stages as highly effective for helping students in Grades 5–12 learn to write well and use writing as a tool for learning. The guide notes the following:

> Pre-writing engages students in activities designed to help them generate or organize ideas for their composition. Engaging adolescents in such activities before they write a first draft improves the quality of their writing. Pre-writing activities include gathering possible information for a paper through reading or developing a visual representation of their ideas before sitting down to write. (p. 18)

Students need to learn that, in most cases, spending more time at the *Think, Plan,* and *Revise* stages will produce better writing.

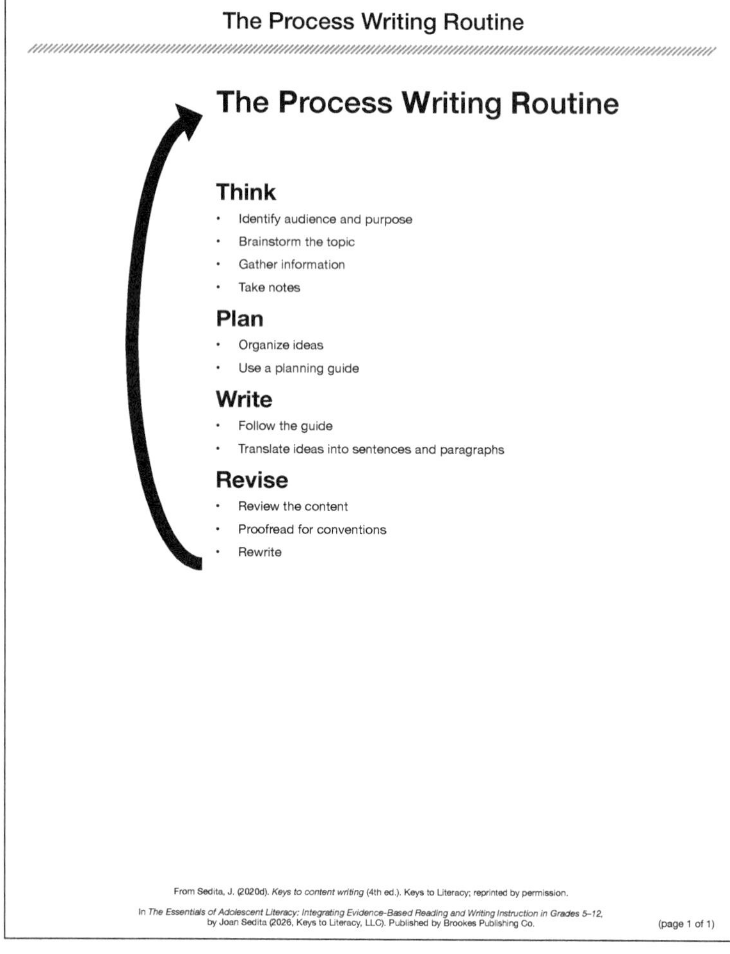

The Process Writing Routine

The Process Writing Routine

Think

- Identify audience and purpose
- Brainstorm the topic
- Gather information
- Take notes

Plan

- Organize ideas
- Use a planning guide

Write

- Follow the guide
- Translate ideas into sentences and paragraphs

Revise

- Review the content
- Proofread for conventions
- Rewrite

From Sedita, J. (2020d). *Keys to content writing* (4th ed.). Keys to Literacy; reprinted by permission.

(page 1 of 1)

Figure 6.9. The Process Writing Routine. (From Sedita, J. [2020d]. *Keys to content writing* [4th ed.]. Keys to Literacy; reprinted by permission.)

Teaching Suggestions Keep these suggestions in mind for teaching the writing process.

- Design a lesson plan that introduces the stages of the process with examples of products from each stage (e.g., prewriting notes and graphic organizers, writing drafts with editing annotations, final drafts).
- Emphasize with students the importance of using all stages of the process when they write. This includes providing grades for work completed at each stage, such as prewriting notes, graphic organizers, first drafts, and final drafts.
- Share examples with students of how you follow the stages of the writing process to complete professional or personal writing tasks.
- Identify opportune moments during classroom instruction to remind students to focus on the *Think, Plan,* and *Revise* stages.

Peer Collaboration Research has determined collaborative arrangements in which students work together at any stage of the writing process to be a highly effective and motivating instructional practice (Boscolo & Gelati, 2007; Graham & Perin, 2007; Graham et al., 2015; Pritchard & Honeycutt, 2007). Consider the following ways students can collaborate:

- During the *Think* stage, students work together to brainstorm ideas about a topic, gather information from sources, and take notes.
- During the *Plan* stage, students work together to use a graphic organizer to develop a plan for organizing the writing piece.
- During the *Write* stage, students work together to follow the plan and translate wording from notes into sentences and paragraphs.
- During the *Revise* stage, students work together to review the writing and make suggestions for improving the content and organization, make sure there is an introduction and conclusion, and edit for conventions (spelling, punctuation, capitalization, etc.).

Strategy Instruction for Each Writing Stage Research consistently confirms that teaching strategies to students for gathering information and ideas before writing, planning the organization of a writing piece, and revising writing can have a dramatic effect on the quality of their writing (Graham & Perin, 2007; Graham et al., 2016). Strategies include generic processes, such as how to participate in peer collaboration or use a revision checklist. Teachers can also teach strategies for accomplishing specific kinds of content writing tasks, such as writing a summary or a compare-and-contrast essay. They can also teach strategies for discipline-specific writing tasks such as data analysis in science, an interpretation of historical events, or a specific form of poetry.

Suggestions for strategies used at all four stages of the writing process are shared in the following sections, including several that are also addressed in other chapters.

Think Stage

Once the teacher assigns a writing task, the first step for students is to determine the audience and purpose for the writing piece. Students need to use critical thinking skills to identify what they will write about and use note taking to gather ideas and information. For some writing tasks, such as a personal narrative, the student will draw from their existing knowledge and experience. For writing tasks that involve writing from sources, the student will gather information from one or more text or multimedia sources. Graham and Hebert (2010, p. 16) note that the act of taking notes about text materials enhances comprehension, and explain the following:

> Taking notes involves sifting through a text to determine what is most relevant and transforming and reducing the substance of these ideas into written phrases or key words. Intentionally, or unintentionally, note takers organize the abstracted material in some way, connecting one idea to another, while blending new information with their own knowledge, resulting in new understandings of texts.

Students can use Two-Column Notes to gather and save information that will be included in a writing piece. This format was introduced in Chapter 4, "Comprehension Instruction." Teachers can share the following questions with students to support the *Think* stage of the writing process.

Identify Audience and Purpose

- What is the writing task, the purpose, and the audience for the writing piece?
- Which type of writing should I use: informational, narrative, opinion/argument, or a combination?

Brainstorm the Topic

- What do I already know about this topic?
- What sources might I use to learn more about this topic?
- What kinds of information do I need to gather about this topic?

Gather Information, Take Notes

- What strategies should I use to understand the sources?
- How should I set up notes to gather information?
- What ideas and information do I want to include in my writing piece?
    - *For informational writing:* What are the topics and subtopics?
    - *For opinion/argument:* What is my position? What are the reasons and evidence supporting my position? What is a possible counterclaim and my rebuttal?
    - *For narrative writing:* Who are the characters? What is the setting(s)? Is there a problem and solution? What are the events?

These questions, along with questions to support the *Plan, Write,* and *Revise* stages, are provided in the handout "Questions to Support Each Writing Process Stage" within the chapter downloads.

Plan Stage

At the *Plan* stage, students plan how they will organize and present the information they have gathered in notes at the *Think* stage. Research supports the use of a graphic organizer as a prewriting planning tool for this purpose (Graham et al., 2016). Graham and Harris (2007) note:

> Creating a written plan in advance of writing can be especially advantageous because it provides an external memory where ideas can be stored without the risk of losing them. Planning in advance can

> reduce the need to plan while writing, freeing needed resources to engage in other processes that demand attention, such as turning ideas into well-crafted sentences. (p. 120)

Teachers can share the following questions with students to support the *Plan* stage.

Organize Ideas

- How long should the writing piece be?
- What is the best structure for the writing piece?

Use a Planning Guide

- How should I set up a graphic organizer to plan the structure?
    - Have I included an introduction and conclusion?
    - How should I organize the body of the writing piece?

As discussed in Chapter 5, students need to address several text structure elements when planning the structure of a writing piece: introductions, conclusions, body development (including organizing sentences into paragraphs based on main ideas), and using transition words and phrases to link sentences, paragraphs, and sections of text. Students can use a Top-Down Topic Web for this purpose. Recall from Chapter 4 that this graphic organizer helps students organize the topics and subtopics from text. A topic web can be modified for students to use as a planning tool before writing. The examples in Figures 6.10, 6.11, and 6.12 are basic examples for relatively short writing pieces. The number of items and details in a topic web can be expanded for longer writing pieces. As you review the following examples, keep in mind that the number of ideas in some sections will vary depending on the content and length of the writing piece.

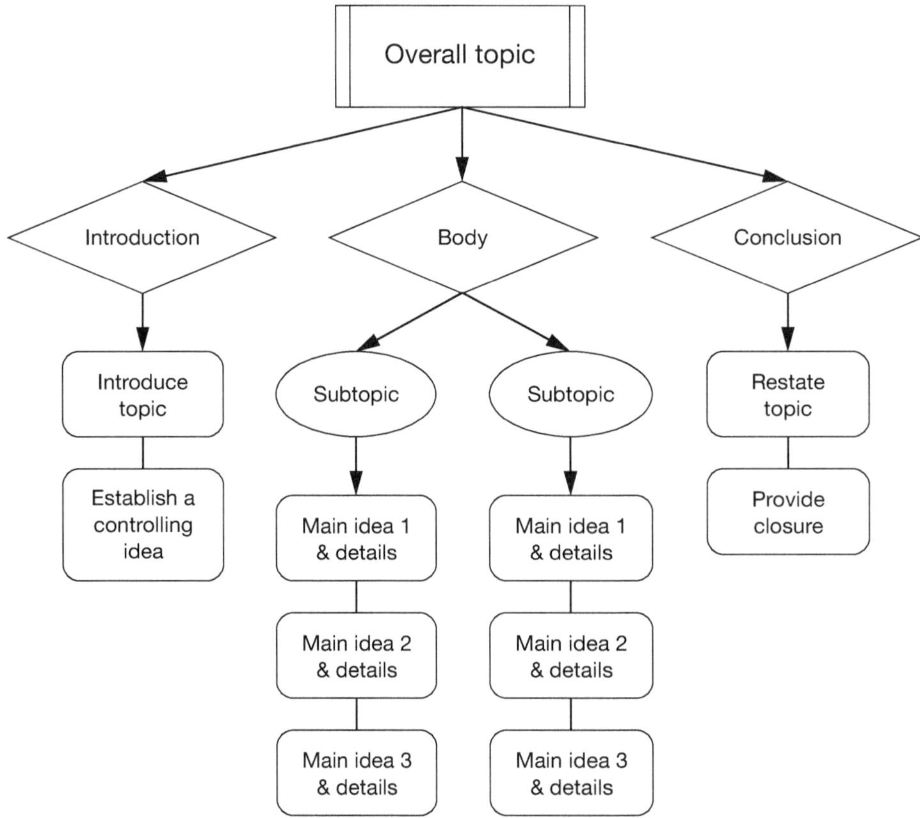

Figure 6.10. Basic topic web for informational writing. (From Sedita, J. [2023]. *The writing rope: A framework for explicit writing instruction in all subjects.* Paul H. Brookes Publishing Co.; reprinted by permission.)

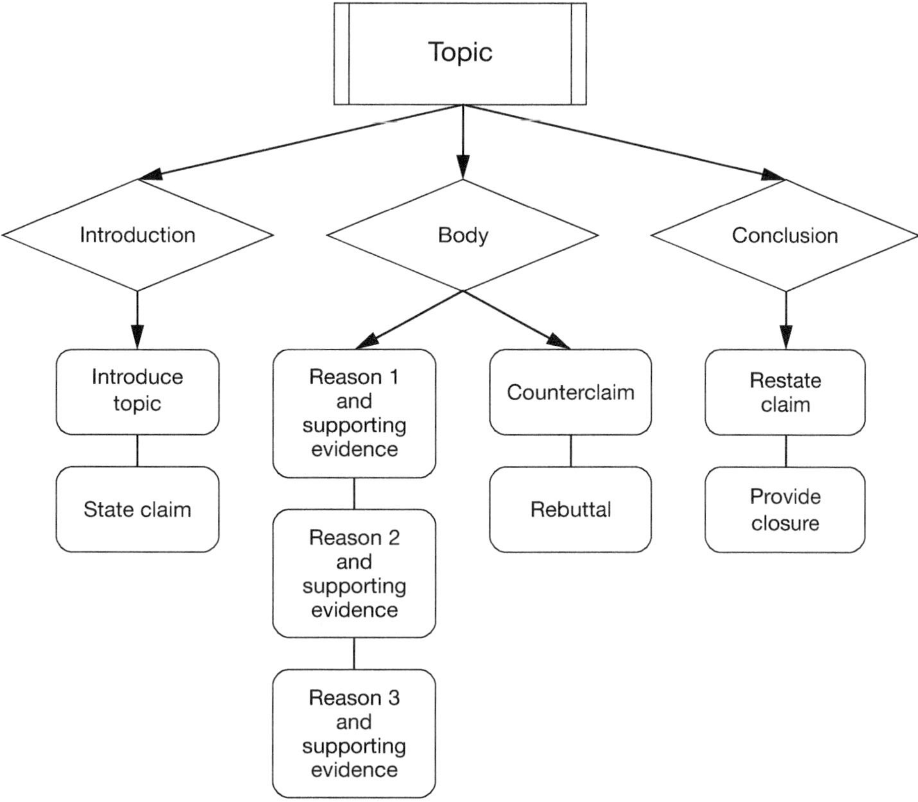

Figure 6.11. Basic topic web for argument writing. (From Sedita, J. [2023]. *The writing rope: A framework for explicit writing instruction in all subjects.* Paul H. Brookes Publishing Co.; reprinted by permission.)

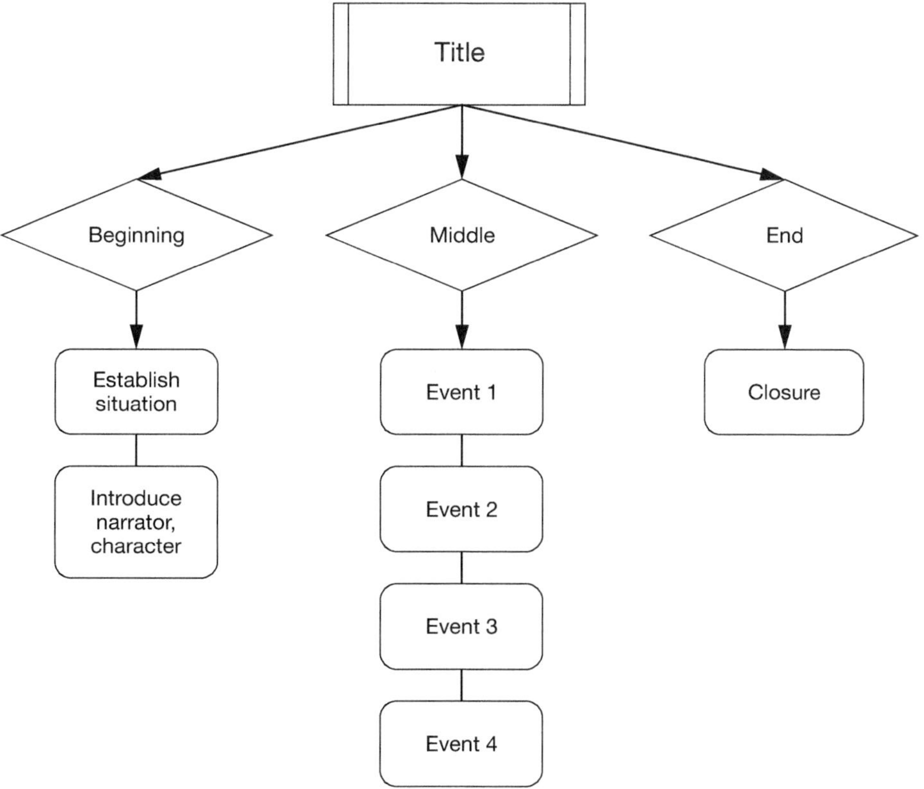

Figure 6.12. Basic topic web for narrative writing. (From Sedita, J. [2023]. *The writing rope: A framework for explicit writing instruction in all subjects.* Paul H. Brookes Publishing Co.; reprinted by permission.)

Informational Writing Figure 6.10 shows an example of a basic topic web for informational writing that begins with the overall topic of the writing piece at the top of the graphic, and three sections representing the *introduction, body,* and *conclusion.* The body is organized by topics and main ideas that support each topic. In the example, six main ideas are grouped into sections. (The number of topics and main ideas will vary.) When students write a draft, they start with an introduction, develop the body by turning main ideas into paragraphs that are organized by sections, and end with a conclusion.

Argument Writing Figure 6.11 shows an example of a basic topic web for argument writing that also begins with the overall topic at the top followed by three sections representing the *introduction, body,* and *conclusion.* An argument is organized by the components described in Chapter 5: claim, reasons, evidence, counterclaim, rebuttal. When students write a draft, they start with an introduction that includes a statement of their claim; write the body by developing reasons that support the claim with evidence, and include a counterclaim and rebuttal; then, end with a conclusion. (The number of reasons will vary.)

Narrative Writing Figure 6.12 shows an example of a basic topic web for narrative writing, which typically is organized around events. Students should orient the reader by establishing a situation and/or introducing a narrator or characters at the beginning of a narrative piece. Students organize events in the body of the piece (the middle) and end by providing a sense of closure. (The number of events will vary.)

Write Stage

Students move into the *Write* stage after they have planned what they want to write. To convey what they want to say, they make decisions about the best words to use in their sentences, how to combine sentences into paragraphs, and how to combine paragraphs into sections of writing. See Chapter 5 for instructional suggestions for writing sentences and paragraphs; these suggestions are designed to develop basic writing skills that students can automatically incorporate as they compose.

Students also make decisions about whether a particular pattern of organization and related transition words and phrases should be used (i.e., description/explanation, sequence/chronology, cause and effect, compare and contrast, problem and solution). Teachers can share the following questions with students to support the *Write* stage.

Follow the Guide

- Have I followed the plan from my graphic organizer?

Translate Into Sentences and Paragraphs

- Have I written clear, concise, and complete sentences?
- Have I included key vocabulary?
- Have I organized my paragraphs around main ideas and sentences with supporting detail?
- Have I included transition words and phrases to connect ideas between my sentences and paragraphs?

These questions, along with questions to support the *Think, Plan,* and *Revise* stages, are provided in the handout "Questions to Support Each Writing Process Stage" found in the chapter downloads.

A Closer Look at Introductions The purpose for an introduction varies for the three types of writing: informational, argument, or narrative. At the most basic level, the introduction for informational writing needs to introduce the topic and establish a controlling idea. For argument writing, it needs to introduce the topic and state a position (claim). For narrative writing, the introduction needs to orient the reader by establishing a situation and/or introducing a narrator or characters.

Introductions can include other common elements such as a lead, background information about the topic, or a preview of content to come. A lead captures the reader's interest and is sometimes referred to as a *hook* that draws the reader in, such as starting with a quote, posing a question, providing an anecdote, presenting a series of facts, or describing a memorable image. The length of an introduction can vary from one sentence to multiple paragraphs or pages, depending on the overall length of the writing piece and which elements are included.

A Closer Look at Conclusions A conclusion creates closure and holds a writing piece together by referring back to what has been said. For informational and argument writing, a conclusion enables the writer to have a final say on the topics or issues in a writing piece. It also provides a last chance to make an impression on the reader. A conclusion for informational writing can include a restatement of the topic, a summary of the main ideas, and an interesting comment or final impression. For argument, it can include a restatement of the topic and claim, a summary of the reasons, and a call to action. The length of a conclusion can vary from one sentence to multiple paragraphs or pages, depending on the overall length of the piece.

Revise Stage

During revision, students analyze and evaluate a piece of writing that is their own or a peer's. They apply critical thinking skills to make decisions about adding, deleting, moving, or changing ideas, words, phrases, sentences, and paragraphs. At the *Revise* stage, they also need to proofread for conventions such as spelling, capitalization, punctuation, and grammar. Keep in mind that not every piece of student writing has to be revised; revision can focus on just part of a writing piece. For example, teachers may have students narrow their revision focus by rewriting just the introduction or the topic sentences in paragraphs. Teachers can share the following questions with students to support the *Revise* stage.

Review the Content

- Are the introduction and conclusion clear and do they serve their purpose?
- Is the body of my writing piece organized?
- Should I add headings?
- Have I met the requirements of the writing task?
- Is there something I should add or delete?
- Do I need to go back to the *Think* stage to gather more information?

Proofread for Conventions

- Have I included correct capitalization and punctuation?
- Have I checked my spelling?

Rewrite

- Can I just make some changes to the first draft, or do I need to rewrite this piece?

Many students spend minimal time revising their work, or they skip it all together because they do not know how to modify and improve their writing. They also mistakenly assume that revision is simply correcting spelling, punctuation, or grammar. Unfortunately, when students focus revision on mechanical errors instead of the content and organization of their writing pieces, this can lead to a lack of motivation to write. Students benefit from revising in two parts—revising for content and organization, and editing for conventions (spelling, punctuation).

Revising for Content and Organization For this round, the focus is on revision to clarify and reshape the writing to effectively communicate the student's message, addressing these areas:

- Content and organization of the writing piece
- Quality of the sentences
- Use of transition words and phrases

First, students look at the overall content and organization of a writing piece, using the guiding questions for reviewing the content. Next, they determine how to improve the writing by reading sentence by sentence. The following questions can help them with this step:
Can I improve my writing piece by

- Adding more details?
- Deleting unnecessary wording or information?
- Elaborating or combining sentences?
- Rearranging sentences or paragraphs for more clarity?
- Writing better topic sentences for paragraphs?

Next, students consider how transition words and phrases might be used to improve the writing. Some students will integrate transitions as they write their first draft. Others, especially students who struggle with writing and some English learners, will need to add them during revision.

Revising for Conventions The second round of revision should focus on editing a writing piece for conventions: grammar, spelling, punctuation, and capitalization. It is easier for students to identify grammatical errors if they read their sentences slowly, out loud.

Using Teacher and Peer Feedback

The feedback students receive about their writing matters as much as the writing instruction they receive. Feedback lets students know if their writing is clear and conveys the ideas and information they want to communicate. Without the opportunity to revise based on teacher or peer feedback, students cannot learn how to improve their writing. It is therefore essential for teachers to devote homework and class time for students to rewrite at least portions of their writing based on feedback from others.

Teachers should consider the following research-based guidelines when giving feedback to students (Bangert-Downs et al., 1991; Walberg, 1999; Wiggins, 1993, 2012):

- Provide feedback about the final product and the process.
- Provide user-friendly feedback that is specific, concrete, and manageable. Feedback is not of much value if the student cannot understand it or is overwhelmed by it.
- The sooner feedback can be provided, the better. The longer students have to wait for feedback, the weaker the connection to their effort becomes and the less likely they are to benefit.
- Provide opportunities for students to give feedback to their peers and to provide their own feedback by monitoring their work against established criteria.
- Make the feedback actionable by providing opportunities for students to revise their writing.

Research also suggests that effective feedback incorporates criterion-referenced feedback tools such as checklists and rubrics. Rubrics are scoring tools used to assess writing and expectations for writing assignments. They list criteria and typically describe levels of proficiency for meeting each criterion along a scale of three or more levels. Writing rubrics are often used to assess student writing skills for district or state writing assessments. As such, they are tools better suited for teacher use for grading student writing. On the other hand, feedback checklists provide feedback to students in a more user-friendly format.

A set of generic feedback checklists for informational and argument writing are provided in Figures 6.13 and 6.14 that can be used with most writing assignments. Ideally, teachers should customize these examples by deleting or adding items that are specific to a particular content-based writing assignment. (Full-size, reproducible versions of these checklists are included with the downloads for this chapter.)

Getting the Most from Peer Feedback Students' writing skills improve when they have opportunities to receive and give feedback to their peers that is specific and when criterion-referenced tools are provided (Trupiano, 2006). Research finds the following:

- When editing a partner's writing, students should share both positive and constructive feedback about a set of notes or a writing draft. Students in the same class make especially good peer editors because they are familiar with the parameters of an assignment and face the same tasks and concerns (Murray, 2004).
- Studies show that peer feedback helps the student giving the feedback as well as the student receiving it (Trupiano, 2006). Evaluating another person's writing makes students more adept at identifying writing strengths and weaknesses, and therefore better at revising their own writing. Students who receive comments and suggestions from peers become more critical of their own work.
- To get the most value from peer revision, teachers should provide instruction on evaluation criteria and guidelines for revising. Without this instruction, students may be reluctant to give constructive criticism, or they may be unable to provide feedback because they lack strong evaluation and revision skills (MacArthur, 2007).

Figure 6.15 is an example of a feedback checklist students can use to assess their own writing or to provide feedback to a peer. The checklist begins by asking if the writing piece meets the requirements for task, audience, and purpose. It then requires the reviewer to engage with the writing piece by offering wording and using annotations to provide specific feedback. This is a generic example; teachers can add items based on the writing assignment. A full-size, reproducible version of this checklist is included with the downloads for this chapter.

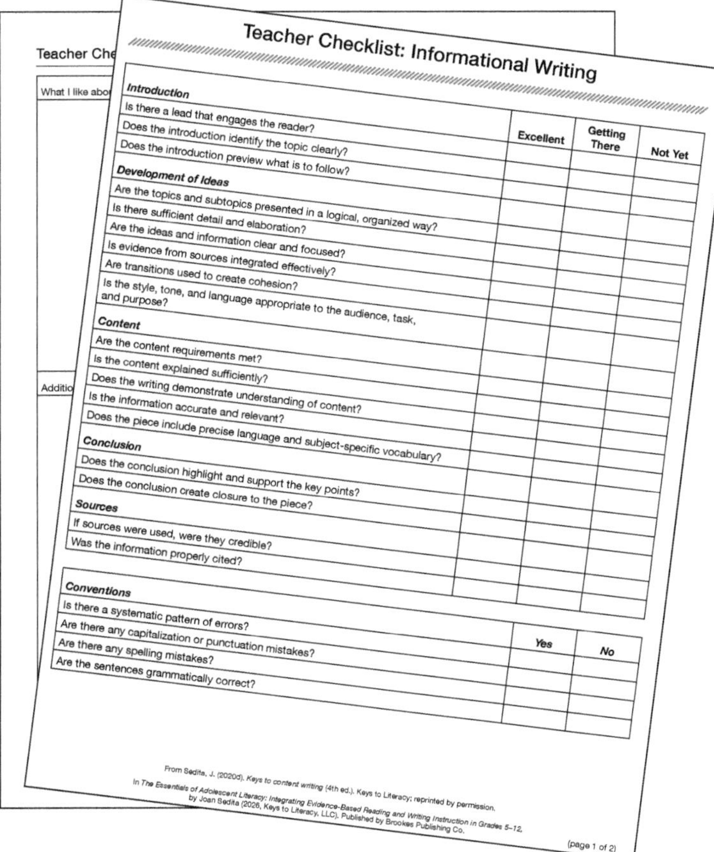

Teacher Checklist: Informational Writing

	Excellent	Getting There	Not Yet
Introduction			
Is there a lead that engages the reader?			
Does the introduction identify the topic clearly?			
Does the introduction preview what is to follow?			
Development of Ideas			
Are the topics and subtopics presented in a logical, organized way?			
Is there sufficient detail and elaboration?			
Are the ideas and information clear and focused?			
Is evidence from sources integrated effectively?			
Are transitions used to create cohesion?			
Is the style, tone, and language appropriate to the audience, task, and purpose?			
Content			
Are the content requirements met?			
Is the content explained sufficiently?			
Does the writing demonstrate understanding of content?			
Is the information accurate and relevant?			
Does the piece include precise language and subject-specific vocabulary?			
Conclusion			
Does the conclusion highlight and support the key points?			
Does the conclusion create closure to the piece?			
Sources			
If sources were used, were they credible?			
Was the information properly cited?			

Conventions	Yes	No
Is there a systematic pattern of errors?		
Are there any capitalization or punctuation mistakes?		
Are there any spelling mistakes?		
Are the sentences grammatically correct?		

From Sedita, J. (2020d). *Keys to content writing* (4th ed.). Keys to Literacy; reprinted by permission.
In *The Essentials of Adolescent Literacy: Integrating Evidence-Based Reading and Writing Instruction in Grades 5–12*, by Joan Sedita (2026, Keys to Literacy, LLC). Published by Brookes Publishing Co.

(page 1 of 2)

Figure 6.13. Teacher feedback checklist for generic informational writing. (Sedita, J. [2020d]. *Keys to content writing* (4th ed.) Keys to Literacy; reprinted by permission.)

Teacher Checklist: Argument Writing

	Excellent	Getting There	Not Yet
Introduction			
Is there a lead that engages the reader?			
Does the introduction identify the claim?			
Does the introduction acknowledge alternate or opposing claims?			
Does the introduction preview what is to follow?			
Development of Ideas			
Is the claim supported with logical reasons and relevant evidence?			
Are the reasons and evidence presented in an organized way?			
Is evidence from sources integrated effectively?			
Is the counterclaim presented clearly?			
Is the rebuttal supported with logical reasons and evidence?			
Are transitions used to link and to create cohesion among claim(s), reasons, and evidence?			
Is precise language (words, phrases, and clauses) used to clarify the relationships among claims, reasons, and evidence?			
Is there a formal style and an objective tone established and maintained throughout the piece?			
Content			
Are the content requirements met?			
Are the reasons and evidence clear and focused?			
Is the content explained sufficiently?			
Does the writing demonstrate understanding of content?			
Is the information presented accurate and relevant?			
Does the piece include precise and subject-specific vocabulary?			
Conclusion			
Does the conclusion highlight and support the claim?			
Does the concluding statement or section follow from and support the argument presented?			
Does the conclusion bring closure to the piece?			
Sources			
If sources were used, were they credible?			
Was the information properly cited?			

From Sedita, J. (2020d). *Keys to content writing* (4th ed.). Keys to Literacy; reprinted by permission.
In *The Essentials of Adolescent Literacy: Integrating Evidence-Based Reading and Writing Instruction in Grades 5–12*, by Joan Sedita (2026, Keys to Literacy, LLC). Published by Brookes Publishing Co.

(page 1 of 2)

Figure 6.14. Teacher feedback checklist for generic argument writing. (Sedita, J. [2020d]. *Keys to content writing* (4th ed.). Keys to Literacy; reprinted by permission.)

THE IMPORTANCE OF TEACHER PLANNING

If teachers do not provide specific directions for writing assignments and requirements are ambiguous, students can be uncertain of the expectations for the task. One recommendation in the *Writing Next* research report (Graham & Perin, 2007) is for teachers to provide specific product goals:

> Setting product goals involves assigning students specific, reachable goals for the writing they are to complete. It includes identifying the purpose of the assignment (e.g., to persuade) as well as characteristics of the final product. Specific goals in the studies reviewed included adding more ideas to a paper when revising, or establishing a goal to write a specific kind of paper, and assigning goals for specific structural elements in a composition. Compared with instances in which students were simply given a general overall goal, these relatively simple procedures resulted in a positive effect size, and the average effect was strong. Overall, assigning students goals for their written product had a strong impact on writing quality. (p. 17)

Planning Steps for Writing Assignments

To help students successfully complete writing tasks, follow these steps when planning a writing assignment:

1. *Determine the writing objective.* For example, is the objective to have students process their content knowledge, deepen their understanding, and reflect on what they have learned, or to assess students' content learning?

Self or Peer Feedback Checklist

Overall, does the writing piece meet the task, audience, and purpose requirements?

____

____

____

	YES	NO
Does the introduction introduce the topic and establish a controlling idea?		
Are the ideas in the writing clear? Are any parts confusing?		***Underline*** *parts that are confusing.*
Are the topics, ideas, and information presented in a logical, organized way?	*Provide a specific, positive comment about how the piece was organized.*	*Put the* ***letter O*** *in places that are disorganized and make suggestions.*
Is sufficient information and detail provided?		*Write* ***INFO*** *in spots that need more and make suggestions.*
Does the piece include precise and varied vocabulary?	*Put a ** ***star*** *next to good examples.*	*Add suggestions for vocabulary in places where the word choice could be improved.*
Were transitions used to connect sentences, paragraphs, and sections of text?	***Circle*** *transition words or phrases that were used effectively.*	*Add transitions in places where they would be helpful.*
Is there a conclusion that effectively provides closure to the writing piece?		
If sources were used, were they cited properly?		*Circle any sources that need improved citation*
Other:		

Additional Comments or Suggestions

____

____

____

From Sedita, J. (2020d). *Keys to content writing* (4th ed.). Keys to Literacy; reprinted by permission.

Figure 6.15. Self or Peer Feedback Checklist. (From Sedita, J. [2020d]. *Keys to content writing* [4th ed.]. Keys to Literacy; reprinted by permission.)

2. *Generate an appropriate writing task,* choosing the best type of writing for the task—informational, argument, or narrative.
3. *Set clear goals.* Identify the TAP (task, audience, purpose). Clearly state your expectations for the length of the piece, the form, and any other requirements.
4. *Provide scaffolds* such as models of sample text to emulate, lists of transition words and phrases, graphic organizers, and writing templates. These scaffolds can be provided to all students or just those who need support.
5. *Plan to include opportunities for student collaboration* at the *Think, Plan, Write,* or *Revise* stages of the writing process.
6. *Determine how feedback and revision will be addressed,* including feedback checklists used by the teacher or for peer feedback.

Using the Writing Assignment Guide

Teachers can use a *Writing Assignment Guide* (WAG; Sedita, 2020d) as they plan writing assignments, such as written summaries, responses to subject-area prompts, personal reflections to narrative text, writing tasks that support content learning, and discipline-specific writing tasks. The information in a WAG is shared with students so they know the requirements for a writing assignment and the support that will be provided. A WAG template, shown in Figure 6.16, is organized into the following sections:

- *Writing task:* The teacher describes the writing task, including the type of writing (informational, argument, narrative, or a combination).
- *Audience:* The teacher identifies the audience for the writing piece. This might be the teacher, peer students, or an authentic audience.
- *Purpose:* The teacher identifies the purpose for writing the piece, such as to reinforce content learning, to develop writing skills, or for a more specific purpose.
- *Length:* The teacher shares requirements for the length of the writing piece by identifying a range in number of words, sentences, paragraphs, or pages.
- *Directions and requirements:* The teacher presents directions for the writing task and shares specific requirements for the content or text structure. If there are requirements for source citations, these are included, as well as information about grading.
- *Writing supports:* The teacher identifies scaffolds and supports that are provided for some or all of the students.

Writing Assignment Guide (WAG) Template

Writing Task:	
Audience:	Purpose:
Length: Directions & Requirements: Writing Supports:	

From Sedita, J. (2020d). *Keys to content writing* (4th ed.). Keys to Literacy; reprinted by permission.

Figure 6.16. Writing Assignment Guide (WAG) Template. (From Sedita, J. [2020d]. *Keys to content writing* [4th ed.]. Keys to Literacy; reprinted by permission.)

A blank copy of a WAG template is included with the downloadable resources for this chapter. Figure 6.17 includes a list of guiding questions for teachers to consider when developing a WAG. Figure 6.18 includes several classroom examples of WAGs from different content areas. Teachers should share the information with students so they understand the requirements for a writing task and the support the teacher will provide. They can share a copy of the WAG, or they can modify the information into a more student-friendly layout.

Guiding Questions for a Writing Assessment Guide (WAG)

Writing Task

- What content topic are you covering?
- What type of writing task would be best to support the learning of this content?

Audience

- Does the assignment lend itself to an authentic audience (i.e., in addition to the teacher and student peers)?
- Consider these options: members of the community, organizations or their members, businesses, politicians, younger or older students, family members, peers, blogs, student publications.

Purpose

- What do you want the writing piece to do as it relates to the topic?
- What is the student's personal goal for writing this piece?
- If there is an authentic audience, what is the reason for communicating with this audience through this piece?

Length

- Suggest a range in number of words, sentences, paragraphs, or pages.

Directions and Requirements

- What content information must students address, including related vocabulary?
- Are there any requirements related to sources?
- Is there a particular format you want students to follow?
- Are there any specific requirements for the introduction, body development, use of transitions, or conclusion?
- What opportunities will be provided for peer collaboration?
- Will the student receive feedback from peers or the teacher?
- Will there be an opportunity for students to revise some or all of the writing piece?
- Will the piece be graded? If yes, how?

Writing Supports

- What scaffolds will you provide all or some of the students? Examples: mentor model samples, Two-Column Notes, graphic organizer, writing templates, checklists, or rubrics

Figure 6.17. Guiding questions for a Writing Assignment Guide (WAG). (From Sedita, J. [2020d]. *Keys to content writing* [4th ed.]. Keys to Literacy; reprinted by permission.)

SUMMARY

This chapter presents research-based principles and practices for effective writing instruction, along with an overview of The Writing Rope (Sedita, 2019) and the Not-So-Simple View of Writing (Berninger & Winn, 2006) models. It discusses the benefits of using writing as a tool for learning across all subject areas and highlights the value of sharing mentor texts that students can emulate. The chapter also offers instructional suggestions for each stage of the writing process—*Think, Plan, Write,* and *Revise.* It concludes with guidance on completing a WAG to support the planning of writing tasks.

Classroom Examples of Writing Assignment Guides (WAGs)

<table>
<tr><td colspan="2">English Language Arts
Writing Task:
In Chapter 5 of The Outsiders, Ponyboy recites Robert Frost's poem "Nothing Gold Can Stay." Write a short essay that identifies a theme that is present in both the poem and the novel.</td></tr>
<tr><td>Audience:
Teacher, your peers</td><td>Purpose:
To further develop your understanding of themes in literature</td></tr>
<tr><td colspan="2">Length:
400–600 words
Directions & Requirements:
• Include titles and authors of book and poem.
• Briefly describe the characters and setting for the chapter.
• State a common theme.
• Provide at least two quotes from the chapter and two quotes from the poem that are related to the theme.
• Include these terms: author's purpose, interpretation, significance.
Writing Supports:
• Refer to class notes about theme and to the "Short Essay Guidelines" handout.</td></tr>
</table>

<table>
<tr><td colspan="2">European History
Writing Task:
Write a cover letter in the voice of Napolean Bonaparte to the people of France reapplying for the job of leader before his return to France from Elba.</td></tr>
<tr><td>Audience:
Imaginary citizens, your peers</td><td>Purpose:
To recognize and remember Napoleon's achievements</td></tr>
<tr><td colspan="2">Length:
Half to full page, letter format
Directions & Requirements:
• Opening paragraph: Explain why Napoleon wants this position. Include information about France's needs and Napoleon's beliefs related to those needs.
• Middle paragraphs: Summarize Napoleon's experience and successes as a leader.
• Closing paragraph: Explain why Napoleon is a good fit for the job.
Writing Supports:
• Refer to model sample of letter format</td></tr>
</table>

Figure 6.18. Classroom examples of Writing Assignment Guides (WAGs). (From Sedita, J. [2020d]. *Keys to content writing* [4th ed.]. Keys to Literacy; adapted by permission.)

Science **Writing Task:** Write a short lab report.	
Audience: Your peers, the teacher	**Purpose:** To list materials and procedures, and identify the hypothesis, results, and your conclusion
Length: 3–5 paragraphs **Directions & Requirements:** • Provide appropriate details for these components of a lab report: - Hypothesis statement (introductory sentence to the report) - Materials used; step-by-step procedures followed (1–2 paragraphs) - Results (1 paragraph) - Conclusion (1 paragraph) • For the results, describe the kind of data that was collected and summarize your observations. • For the conclusion, state whether you accept or reject the hypothesis, then explain why. • Include at least two transitions. • This writing piece will be graded based on the checklist provided by the teacher. **Writing Supports:** • Refer to the two-column notes taken during the lab. • Refer to the list of transitions.	

Mathematics **Writing Task:** Write a description of the graph and interpret the data.	
Audience: Your peers, the teacher	**Purpose:** To understand the graph, to practice writing about graphs
Length: 2–4 paragraphs **Directions & Requirements:** • Provide an introduction that presents the main purpose of the graph. Include key words found in the title of the graph. • Develop body paragraphs that describe the two main trends indicated in the graph. Include key figures from the data as part of your description. • Provide a conclusion that paraphrases the main findings. • Include at least three transitions. **Writing Supports:** • Refer to the sample models of graph descriptions. • Refer to the handout: Set of Steps: Graph Description. • Use the writing template as a support. • Refer to the list of transitions.	

Figure 6.18. *(continued)*

REFLECTION QUESTIONS

1. Select at least one of the writing teaching principles that you already use with students, and at least one that you would like to use more often.
2. Briefly describe the skills and strategies represented in each component of The Writing Rope. Why are they represented as strands in a rope?
3. Create at least one Quick Write task you can assign your students that will support their content learning.
4. Generate a writing prompt that requires students to gather relevant information from texts or multimedia sources in order to construct a well-developed written response.
5. Define mentor text and how it can be used to help students learn writing skills.
6. What are the four stages of the writing process? What teaching suggestions related to this process resonate the most with you?
7. Why is it beneficial to find opportunities for students to work collaboratively with the teacher or peers to complete writing tasks?
8. Do you think the Writing Assignment Guide (WAG) shared in the chapter might help you plan writing tasks? Explain why or why not.

Focus Areas for Using Mentor Text

Focus area	Specific focus areas
General: All types of writing	• Writing introductions • Writing leads • Writing conclusions • Incorporating transition words and phrases • Organizing the body • Developing and explaining ideas • Using relevant details and specific descriptions • Word choice and incorporating content-related vocabulary • Creating a voice (i.e., a distinct personality, style, or point of view) • Writing in the first, second or third person • Using capitalization and punctuation • Writing elaborated sentences
Text features	• Writing titles • Incorporating graphics, charts, maps, and other visuals • Generating headings and subheadings
Informational and argument writing	• Using specific patterns of organization • Using examples • Using quotes and dialogue • Using anecdotes • Stating a claim • Explaining how evidence supports a reason • Explaining how a reason supports a claim
Narrative writing	• Developing a story line: beginning, middle, end, and plot sequence • Using techniques such as flashback, foreshadow, backstory • Creating, developing, describing characters • Using dialogue • Developing, describing settings • Using simile, metaphor, personification, alliteration, imagery • Writing a personal narrative • Writing a biography or autobiography

From Sedita, J. (2020d). *Keys to content writing* (4th ed.). Keys to Literacy; reprinted by permission.

Questions to Support Each Writing Process Stage

1. Questions to Support the Think Stage

Identify Audience and Purpose

- What is the writing task, the purpose, and the audience for the writing piece?
- Which type of writing should I use: informational, narrative, opinion/argument, or a combination?

Brainstorm the Topic

- What do I already know about this topic?
- What sources might I use to learn more about this topic?
- What kinds of information do I need to gather about this topic?

Gather Information, Take Notes

- What strategies should I use to understand the sources?
- How should I set up notes to gather information?
- What ideas and information do I want to include in my writing piece?
  - *For informational writing*: What are the topics and subtopics?
  - *For opinion/argument:* What is my position? What are the reasons and evidence supporting my position? What is a possible counterclaim and my rebuttal?
  - *For narrative writing:* Who are the characters? What is the setting(s)? Is there a problem and solution? What are the events?

2. Questions to Support the Plan Stage

Organize Ideas

- How long should the writing piece be?
- What is the best structure for the writing piece?

Use a Planning Guide

- How should I set up a graphic organizer to plan the structure?
  - Have I included an introduction and conclusion?
  - How should I organize the body of the writing piece?

3. Questions to Support the Write Stage

Follow the Guide

- Have I followed the plan from my graphic organizer?

Translate Into Sentences and Paragraphs

- Have I written clear, concise, and complete sentences?
- Have I included key vocabulary?
- Have I organized my paragraphs around main ideas and sentences with supporting detail?
- Have I included transition words and phrases to connect ideas between by sentences and paragraphs?

From Sedita, J. (2020d). *Keys to content writing* (4th ed.). Keys to Literacy; adapted by permission.

4. Questions to Support the Revise Stage

Review the Content

- Are the introduction and conclusion clear and do they serve their purpose?
- Is the body of my writing piece organized?
- Should I add headings?
- Have I met the requirements of the writing task?
- Is there something I should add or delete?
- Do I need to go back to the Think stage to gather more information?

Proofread for Conventions

- Have I included correct capitalization and punctuation?
- Have I checked my spelling?

Rewrite

- Can I just make some changes to the first draft, or do I need to rewrite this piece?

From Sedita, J. (2020d). *Keys to content writing* (4th ed.). Keys to Literacy; adapted by permission.

Responding to Narrative Text

Overall Personal Response

- Is there something that reminds you of yourself or people you know?
- Is there something that reminds you of something that happened in your life?
- Is there a confusing passage or part of the story?
- What do you agree or disagree with?
- Is there something you wonder about in the story?
- Is there something you wish had happened differently?
- Is there something that surprised you in the story?
- What is your overall opinion of this story? Would you recommend it to a friend?
- Does this story remind you of another story you have read?

Response to Theme

- What do you think is important in the story?
- What is the theme(s) in the story and what are your thoughts about it?
- Is there a lesson to be learned in the story?

Response to Characters

- What is your opinion of the characters?
- Did the main character change throughout the story?
- What was the main character's problem, and how did he or she solve that problem?
- Do you agree with the actions of the characters? Would your actions be similar or different?

Response to Setting

- What is your reaction to the setting(s) in the story (including time and place)?
- How does the setting fit into the story, and why is it important?

Response to the Author

- Why do you think the author wrote this story?
- What do you think about the author's choice for the title?
- Does the author make you feel that you are part of the story? How does the author do this?
- What did you like about the author's writing?
- Did you learn something you might try in your writing?

Source: Sedita (2023).

Self or Peer Feedback Checklist

Overall, does the writing piece meet the task, audience, and purpose requirements?

____

____

____

	YES	NO
Does the introduction introduce the topic and establish a controlling idea?		
Are the ideas in the writing clear? Are any parts confusing?		***Underline*** *parts that are confusing.*
Are the topics, ideas, and information presented in a logical, organized way?	*Provide a specific, positive comment about how the piece was organized.*	*Put the* ***letter O*** *in places that are disorganized and make suggestions.*
Is sufficient information and detail provided?		*Write* ***INFO*** *in spots that need more and make suggestions.*
Does the piece include precise and varied vocabulary?	*Put a ** ***star*** *next to good examples.*	*Add suggestions for vocabulary in places where the word choice could be improved.*
Were transitions used to connect sentences, paragraphs, and sections of text?	***Circle*** *transition words or phrases that were used effectively.*	*Add transitions in places where they would be helpful.*
Is there a conclusion that effectively provides closure to the writing piece?		
If sources were used, were they cited properly?		*Circle any sources that need improved citation*
Other:		

Additional Comments or Suggestions

____

____

____

TAP Questions

Task

- What is your assignment?
- What are you being asked to do?
- What form will your writing take?

Audience

- Who is the audience for the writing piece?
- Is it your teacher or classmates, or is there another, more authentic audience?
- Who will read your piece?

Purpose

- What is the purpose for this writing piece?
- Is it to inform, convince, or tell a story?
- How might the audience determine the purpose?

Teacher Checklist: Argument Writing

Introduction	**Excellent**	**Getting There**	**Not Yet**
Is there a lead that engages the reader?			
Does the introduction identify the claim?			
Does the introduction acknowledge alternate or opposing claims?			
Does the introduction preview what is to follow?			
Development of Ideas			
Is the claim supported with logical reasons and relevant evidence?			
Are the reasons and evidence presented in an organized way?			
Is evidence from sources integrated effectively?			
Is the counterclaim presented clearly?			
Is the rebuttal supported with logical reasons and evidence?			
Are transitions used to link and to create cohesion among claim(s), reasons, and evidence?			
Is precise language (words, phrases, and clauses) used to clarify the relationships among claims, reasons, and evidence?			
Is there a formal style and an objective tone established and maintained throughout the piece?			
Content			
Are the content requirements met?			
Are the reasons and evidence clear and focused?			
Is the content explained sufficiently?			
Does the writing demonstrate understanding of content?			
Is the information presented accurate and relevant?			
Does the piece include precise and subject-specific vocabulary?			
Conclusion			
Does the conclusion highlight and support the claim?			
Does the concluding statement or section follow from and support the argument presented?			
Does the conclusion bring closure to the piece?			
Sources			
If sources were used, were they credible?			
Was the information properly cited?			

From Sedita, J. (2020d). *Keys to content writing* (4th ed.). Keys to Literacy; reprinted by permission.

Teacher Checklist: Argument Writing *(continued)*

Conventions	**Yes**	**No**
Is there a systematic pattern of errors?		
Are there any capitalization or punctuation mistakes?		
Are there any spelling mistakes?		
Are the sentences grammatically correct?		

What I like about this writing piece:

____

____

____

____

____

____

____

____

Additional comments or suggestions:

____

____

____

____

____

____

____

____

Teacher Checklist: Informational Writing

Introduction	**Excellent**	**Getting There**	**Not Yet**
Is there a lead that engages the reader?			
Does the introduction identify the topic clearly?			
Does the introduction preview what is to follow?			
Development of Ideas			
Are the topics and subtopics presented in a logical, organized way?			
Is there sufficient detail and elaboration?			
Are the ideas and information clear and focused?			
Is evidence from sources integrated effectively?			
Are transitions used to create cohesion?			
Is the style, tone, and language appropriate to the audience, task, and purpose?			
Content			
Are the content requirements met?			
Is the content explained sufficiently?			
Does the writing demonstrate understanding of content?			
Is the information accurate and relevant?			
Does the piece include precise language and subject-specific vocabulary?			
Conclusion			
Does the conclusion highlight and support the key points?			
Does the conclusion create closure to the piece?			
Sources			
If sources were used, were they credible?			
Was the information properly cited?			

Conventions	***Yes***	***No***
Is there a systematic pattern of errors?		
Are there any capitalization or punctuation mistakes?		
Are there any spelling mistakes?		
Are the sentences grammatically correct?		

From Sedita, J. (2020d). *Keys to content writing* (4th ed.). Keys to Literacy; reprinted by permission.

Teacher Checklist: Informational Writing *(continued)*

What I like about this writing piece:

Additional comments or suggestions:

Teaching Principles for Writing

Gradual release of responsibility	This model of instruction is also referred to as an I do it, We do it, You do it approach to teaching. It includes explicit instruction using a direct approach to introduce and teach a new writing skill and gradually releasing support with a goal of independent use by students (Pearson & Gallagher, 1983).
Explicit instruction of writing strategies	Explicit instruction involves using structured and sequenced steps to teach a specific skill. It includes the teacher explaining a skill and modeling how it is applied using think-aloud and providing guided practice with feedback. Teaching students strategies for planning, revising, and editing their compositions has shown a dramatic effect on the quality of students' writing. Strategy instruction may involve teaching more generic processes, such as brainstorming or collaboration for peer revising, or it may involve strategies for accomplishing a specific type of writing task, such as writing an opinion or argument piece (Graham & Perin, 2007).
Differentiated instruction	Differentiated instruction calls for designing instruction to suit individual student needs rather than using a standardized approach to instruction that assumes all students learn to write the same way.
Scaffolding	Scaffolding is assistance offered by a teacher or a peer to support learning a writing skill that a student is initially unable to grasp independently, and then removal of the assistance once the skill is learned. This is not the same as doing the work for the student. Scaffolding is a hallmark of differentiated instruction. Examples of writing scaffolds include graphic organizers, writing templates, and lists of words such as transitions.
Opportunities for collaboration	Writing is a social activity and is best learned in a community. Collaborative writing has been found to have a significant effect on improving student writing and engagement in writing (Graham & Perin, 2007). It involves instructional arrangements whereby students work together to plan, draft, revise, and edit their writing pieces.
Mentor text as models for writing	Writing models, also referred to as mentor text, should be used to show students what high-quality writing looks like so they can emulate the style, language, and structure of the text.
Increasing the amount students write in all subjects	Adequate time for students to write is essential to the development of writing skills, and that time can occur during content instruction (Graham et al., 2012). Writing is one of the major strategies to extend critical thinking about a subject-area topic. Many state writing standards call for students to write routinely in all subject areas, including short- and long-term writing tasks.

Sources: Graham and Perin (2007), Graham et al. (2012), and Pearson and Gallagher (1983).

The Process Writing Routine

Think

- Identify audience and purpose
- Brainstorm the topic
- Gather information
- Take notes

Plan

- Organize ideas
- Use a planning guide

Write

- Follow the guide
- Translate ideas into sentences and paragraphs

Revise

- Review the content
- Proofread for conventions
- Rewrite

The Writing Rope

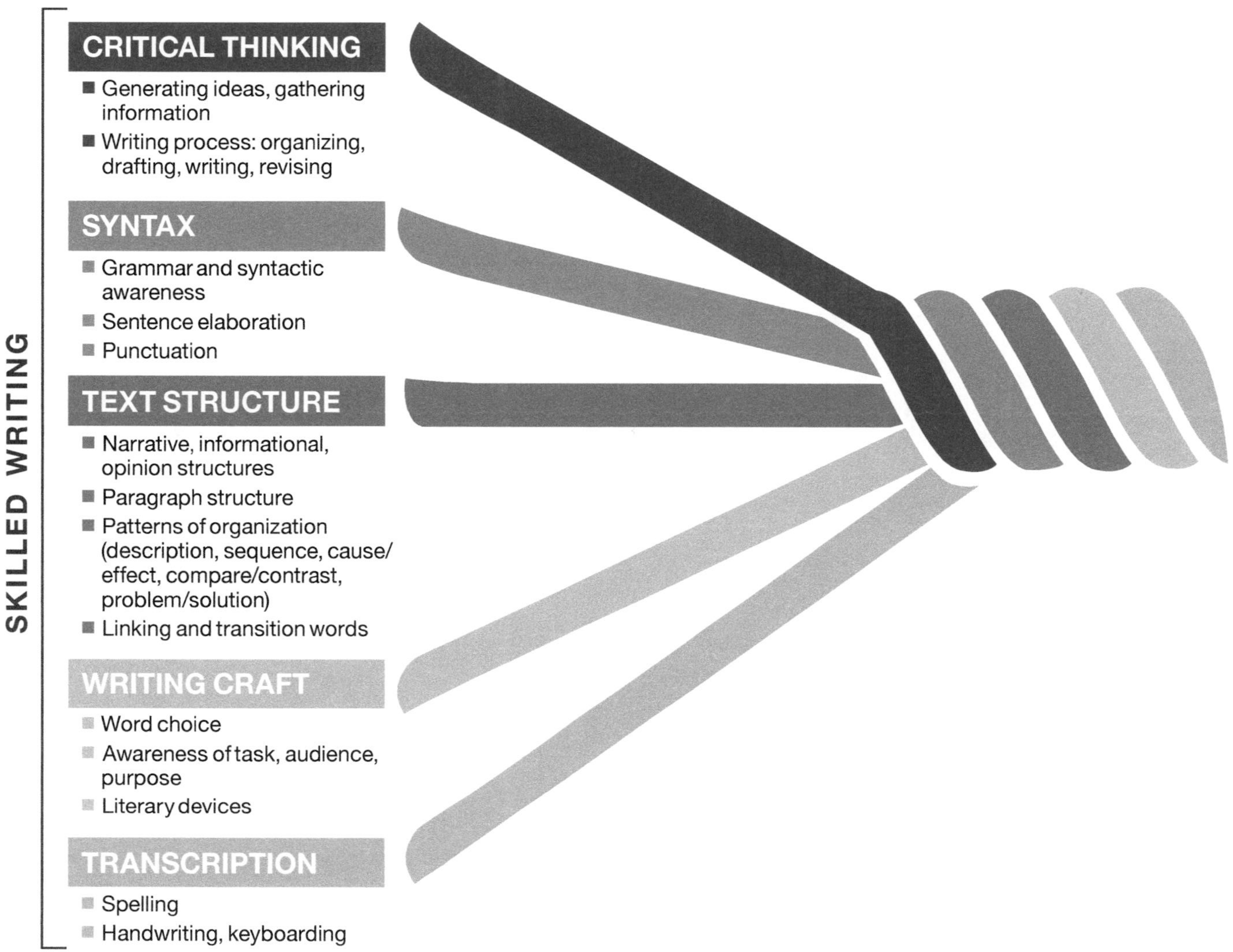

SKILLED WRITING

CRITICAL THINKING
- Generating ideas, gathering information
- Writing process: organizing, drafting, writing, revising

SYNTAX
- Grammar and syntactic awareness
- Sentence elaboration
- Punctuation

TEXT STRUCTURE
- Narrative, informational, opinion structures
- Paragraph structure
- Patterns of organization (description, sequence, cause/effect, compare/contrast, problem/solution)
- Linking and transition words

WRITING CRAFT
- Word choice
- Awareness of task, audience, purpose
- Literary devices

TRANSCRIPTION
- Spelling
- Handwriting, keyboarding

Types of Content Writing Tasks

Task type and frequency	Characteristics	Examples
Quick Writes Assigned at least twice per week	• Task takes less than 10 minutes to complete. • Task is related to content learning. • Objective is to help students process and reflect on content learning. • Task can be used to informally assess content learning. • Writing is typically not revised. • Task is typically not graded.	• Admit or exit tickets • Drawing, labeling, or explaining pictures or graphics • One- to three-sentence reflections or responses to a question • Free writing for a specified short amount of time
Content learning tasks Assigned at least once every 2 weeks	• Task takes one to three classroom or homework sessions to complete. • Task is related to content learning. • Length is up to one or two pages. • Objective is to deepen understanding and reflection. • Task can be used to informally assess content learning. • Writing may be revised. • Task may be informally evaluated or may be graded.	• Summary of reading or a lecture • Multiparagraph response to a question • Personal response to narrative text • Subject-specific writing task
Formal writing tasks Assigned once per semester	• Task is completed over multiple days or weeks. • Task is related to content learning. • Length is one or more pages. • Objective is to learn and explore content more deeply, and to practice advanced writing skills. • Task can be used to formally assess content learning and writing skills. • Writing should be revised, possibly multiple times. • Task is formally evaluated and graded.	• Research report • Multipage literary analysis

Writing Assignment Guide (WAG) Template

Writing Task:	
Audience:	Purpose:
Length: Directions & Requirements: Writing Supports:	

From Sedita, J. (2020d). *Keys to content writing* (4th ed.). Keys to Literacy; reprinted by permission.

7

Supporting Learning Through Discussion

Discussion supports learning in all subjects because it helps students think deeply and process information instead of just receiving it. Discussion-based learning is an alternative to having students memorize and recite information presented by the teacher or found in text. The guide *Improving Literacy in Secondary Schools* (Evidence for Learning, 2020) explains, "Talk is a powerful tool for learning and literacy. It can improve reading and writing outcomes, enhance communication skills, and increase students' understanding across the curriculum" (p. 24).

This chapter describes what effective text-based discussions look like in Grades 5–12 classrooms, delving into the research supporting discussion. In-depth guidance is provided about discussion formats and how to ensure discussions are collaborative, fair, and productive. In addition to general recommendations for discussion, 11 specific activities teachers can use are described in detail.

WHAT GOOD TEXT-BASED DISCUSSION LOOKS LIKE

Although discussion is associated with all-around learning success and can support learning from anything that is read, said, or done in the classroom, much of the research about discussion and related instructional recommendations is focused on discussion about text and its role in supporting reading comprehension. Discussion provides another way to help students comprehend and learn from text in addition to independently using reading comprehension strategies, such as making predictions, summarizing, and taking notes. The guide *Evidence-Based Reading Instruction for Adolescents in Grades 6–12* (Patrick & Acosta, 2024) points out:

> Class discussions, when thoughtfully conducted, are an important tool to enhance reading comprehension, foster critical thinking, and prepare students for college and their careers. Discussions can take place in all content classes and are excellent vehicles to increase the participation of students with disabilities. Recent research suggests that engaging students in effective in-depth discussions in combination with a close reading of a text is one of the most significant ways to improve comprehension for older readers (Pearson et al., 2020) including for English learners . . . for English learners, small group discussions with sentence starters and frames can support students in engaging in in-depth discussions (Proctor et al., 2020). (pp. 42–43)

A text-based discussion is an open-ended, collaborative exchange of ideas among teachers and students that provides opportunities for students to become more critical thinkers as they engage deeply with the text and construct meaning along with others. In a discussion about text, participants present and defend individual interpretations and points of view, reflect on and respond to the ideas of others, and use text content, background knowledge, and reasoning to support interpretations and conclusions to build their knowledge and understanding of the text (Kamil et al., 2008; Wilkinson & Nelson, 2020).

Text-based discussions are supported and driven by open-ended questions. Teachers identify some aspect of the text as a focus and use thought-provoking questions or prompts to guide student conversations about that focus.

Decades of research have demonstrated that high-quality discussion that incorporates different perspectives and background knowledge related to the content in text is effective for supporting text comprehension and learning. Further, discussion has direct and positive influence on students across a wide range of subjects (Kamil et al., 2008; Murphy et al., 2009, 2016; Resnick et al., 2015).

Research indicates that discussions are especially productive when students are asked to argue constructively about the content in text, explaining, elaborating, and defending their positions while considering the perspectives of others (Reznitskaya et al., 2015; Wilkinson & Nelson, 2020).

One of the recommendations in the research guide *Improving Adolescent Literacy: Effective Classroom and Intervention Practices* (Kamil et al., 2008) is for teachers to provide opportunities for extended discussion of text meaning and interpretation in various content areas. The report explains:

> Arguably the most important goal for literacy instruction with adolescents is to increase their ability to comprehend complex text. Further, the goal is not simply to enable students to obtain facts or literal meaning from text (although that is clearly desirable), but to also make deeper interpretations, generalizations, and conclusions. Students can, and will, internalize thinking processes experienced repeatedly during discussions. In high-quality discussions students have the opportunity to express their own interpretations of text and to have those positions challenged by others. They also have the opportunity to defend their positions and to listen as others defend their positions. (pp. 21–22)

One important research finding is that the quality of talk is more important for supporting reading comprehension than the quantity of talk (Wilkinson & Nelson, 2020). That is, increases in the amount students talk do not increase student comprehension. Rather, talk that is structured and focused, yet not dominated by the teacher, is necessary to support comprehension. This includes students discussing texts using open-ended questions for extended periods of time, prompted by the teacher or other students. It also includes the teacher or students incorporating others' ideas into their questions and building on each other's ideas.

Another finding is that whereas all students benefit from classroom discussion activities, discussion appears to be particularly beneficial for students with lower reading ability, possibly because students with higher reading ability already possess the skills needed to comprehend text (Wilkinson & Nelson, 2020). Based on research findings related to discussion-based interventions, Swanson and colleagues (2019) suggest asking questions and using text-based discussion as a method for engaging students who struggle to read and understand text.

DISCUSSION FORMATS

Many types of discussion activities can be used in the classroom (see examples later in this chapter) and the format can be whole-class, small-group, or partner discussion. Teachers should choose activities and a format that aligns with their discussion goals and will engage students. Resnick and colleagues (2018) provide the following descriptions of three common discussion formats:

1. *Teacher-Led Classroom Discussion:* The teacher guides discussion in which all students are invited to participate. This includes allocating turns. The teacher guides the content of the discussion by probing students' answers, commenting, adding information, clarifying, verifying, and encouraging participation by all. Everyone is together and benefits from access to the thinking of the whole group. The advantage of this format is that the teacher guides students through the content and knowledge, orchestrating the social interaction. The disadvantage is that only one person can speak at a time, which may lead to low participation rates.

2. *Small-Group, Student-Led Discussions:* The teacher divides students into groups of three to six to discuss an assigned topic. Typically, the teacher makes rounds to monitor each group's progress and, when needed, to offer support. Compared to teacher-led classroom dialogue, small-group peer discussions have more student-generated explanations and reasoning and more student participation overall. Some students may be more comfortable sharing to a small group of peers

rather than the whole class. Also, small-group discussion prior to a whole-class discussion can provide an opportunity for students to think through beforehand what they will contribute to the larger discussion. However, if students are still developing their discussion and collaboration competencies, and the teacher is not present for all discussions, the quality of the dialogue may not be as high, and a few students may dominate the discussion.

3. *Partner Talk:* The teacher poses a question and asks students to discuss for a few minutes with a partner. After that, the teacher asks single members of the pairs to share what they discussed. The advantage of this format is that it combines teacher-led classroom dialogue with episodes in which all students—not just a few—can think about, generate solutions, and engage in discussion. This is especially helpful for students who are not comfortable participating in large-group discussions. Partner talk can serve as an opportunity to practice what students might say in a whole-group discussion. The disadvantage is that partner talk typically is brief. (p. 29)

PLANNING FOR DISCUSSION

Kamil and colleagues (2008) offer evidence-based suggestions for engaging students in high-quality discussions of text. They note that it is important to establish a non-threatening and supportive environment that includes the teacher emphasizing and modeling acceptance of diverse viewpoints and discouraging criticism and negative feedback on ideas. They also suggest teachers help students participate by calling on students who may not otherwise contribute while asking questions they know these students can answer. Figure 7.1 lists additional suggestions.

To plan productive discussions, teachers should begin by identifying discussion goals, preparing questions in advance, and building in opportunities for students to debrief afterward.

Suggestions for High-Quality Discussions

1. Carefully prepare for the discussion.

Teachers should select texts that are engaging for students, provide opportunities for discussion, and allow for multiple interpretations. They should also develop questions that can stimulate students to think reflectively about the text and make high-level connections or inferences. These are questions that engage a reader to wonder and explore ideas, rather than questions designed simply to determine what students have learned from the text.

2. Ask follow-up questions that help provide continuity and extend the discussion.

Follow-up questions should sustain the discussion and help students consider a different interpretation, an explanation of reasoning, or an identification of content from the text that supports the student's position.

3. Provide a task, or a discussion format, that students can follow when they discuss text together in small groups.

Use a format where students take turns playing various roles, such as leading the discussion, predicting what the section might be about, identifying words that are confusing, and summarizing.

4. Develop and practice the use of a specific discussion protocol.

Identify a specific set of steps for participation in discussion, such as the *Accountable Talk* framework.

Figure 7.1. Suggestions for high-quality discussions. (Adapted from Kamil, M. L., Borman, G. D., Dole, J., Kral, C. C., Salinger, T., & Torgesen, J. [2008]. *Improving adolescent literacy: Effective classroom and intervention practices: A Practice Guide* [NCEE #2008-4027] [pp. 23–25]. National Center for Education Evaluation and Regional Assistance, Institute of Education Sciences, U.S. Department of Education. http://ies.ed.gov/ncee/wwc)

Identify Goals

Besides identifying the content and text that will be the focus of a discussion, the teacher should develop goals for the discussion and explain them to students. This includes considering what the students should be able to do during the discussion, such as explain what they learned from the text, critique the text, make a connection to another text, or agree/disagree with the author's position in an argumentative text.

Questions for teachers to consider include the following:

- What are the main ideas and essential concepts I want my students to learn?
- What are my goals for the discussion?
- Which discussion format(s) and activities will best support my goals?
- What are the best initial and follow-up questions to drive an effective discussion?
- What can I plan ahead of time to ensure that all students participate and stay engaged throughout the discussion?
- What tasks should I have students complete before the discussion that will prepare and enable them to participate in the discussion?

Prepare Questions

Questions are an important part of high-quality discussions. They are used to begin and sustain a discussion and will help the teacher anticipate and prepare for how a discussion may evolve. Productive discussions typically revolve around a series of well-thought-out, open-ended questions (sometimes called *interpretive questions*) that push students to think more critically. These kinds of questions have no pre-specified answers and are not simply answered with yes or no. Rather, they are designed to spark multiple positions and perspectives among students. Productive discussions include questions that "prompt the students to make connections to their own lives or feelings (*affective* response questions), to other texts or media (*intertextual* response questions), and to knowledge or understanding established by the group (*shared-knowledge* response questions)" (Wilkinson et al., 2015, p. 37). Patrick and Acosta (2024) suggest the following:

> Providing students with one or two overarching big idea questions related to themes from a reading that are engaging and thought-provoking can promote more in-depth discussion, allowing students to have opportunities to share their interpretations of a text using evidence from the text and their reasoning skills (Pearson et al., 2020; Proctor et al., 2020). There is also some evidence that providing one or two thought-provoking questions increases adolescent motivation and engagement with the reading thereby potentially increasing comprehension (Pearson et al., 2020). (pp. 42–43)

When developing questions, consider the value of teacher flexibility, the use of follow-up questions, and the use of authentic questions that do not have a single correct answer. Keep in mind the need to be flexible about the order in which you pose planned questions; not all questions may be used depending on how the discussion unfolds. Once students share responses to an initial question, ask follow-up questions, building on those responses with questions that incorporate what students said (called *uptake*). The initial and follow-up questions should afford students control over the flow of the discussion with you acting as facilitator (Wilkinson et al., 2015). Finally, questions that lead to good discussions are frequently described as *authentic* in that they ask a real question that may be open to multiple points of view, such as "Did the way ____ treated ____ in this story seem fair to you?" or "What is the author trying to say here?" or "How does that information connect with what the author wrote before?" (Kamil et al., 2008). These kinds of questions provide an opportunity for exploration and discussion and are very different from questions primarily used to test students' knowledge.

Plan After-Discussion Questions

Students benefit from the opportunity to debrief after a discussion. The following questions can help students continue to build on what they learned during a discussion and reflect on how to improve their participation in future discussions.

- What are the most important ideas or concepts we addressed during our discussion?
- Do we have any questions about these ideas or concepts?

- How can we summarize our discussion?
- How do we feel the discussion went?
- What was the most effective part of our discussion?

Establish Collaboration Norms

Engaging students in effective discussion begins with embedding the spirit of collaboration versus competition in the classroom. Students need to learn that classroom talk should combine supporting peers as well as holding each other accountable by helping clarify, restate, and challenge ideas. Participation in discussions with peers must also be fair and equitable. It is not just for the most academically able students. This means everyone has a chance to ask questions, make statements, and express their ideas.

Students may not participate in discussions if they feel their comments are not valued or are ignored, so teachers should establish discussion norms to support safe spaces for students to participate in discussions. Provide time to talk about the importance of norms with students and review the norms before each discussion. Michaels and O'Connor (2012) note the following about discussion norms:

> Students have to feel a sense of trust that their ideas will be taken seriously and that disagreements will be handled respectfully, so that ideas—not individuals—are challenged. Students have to speak loudly enough so that everyone can hear, and all students have to be on notice that if they cannot hear or understand what someone has said, they have to speak up and ask for clarification. Students need to understand that this kind of talk is expected of everyone, and everyone will have a chance to participate and express their ideas, perhaps not in every discussion, but certainly over the course of several days. (p. 2)

Figure 7.2 is an example of discussion norms that can be used across grades and subjects.

Sample Set of Discussion Norms

- **Come Prepared:** Complete any pre-reading or assigned tasks to enhance your ability to participate effectively in the discussion.
- **Respectful Listening:** Listen attentively to others without interrupting. Give your full attention when someone is speaking.
- **One Speaker at a Time:** Raise your hand or signal when you want to contribute and wait for the speaker to finish before responding.
- **Respect Other Viewpoints:** Appreciate and respect different viewpoints, even if they differ from your own. Everyone's ideas are important.
- **Stay on Topic:** Keep the conversation focused on the discussion topic. If you have a new point, relate it back to the subject at hand.
- **Encourage Participation:** Help create an inclusive environment by encouraging everyone to participate. Offer opportunities for quieter classmates to share their thoughts.
- **Support Your Ideas:** When sharing your opinion, provide reasons or evidence to explain your point of view. Use examples when possible.
- **Be Open to Constructive Feedback:** Accept and give feedback respectfully, without taking it personally. Critique ideas, not people.

Figure 7.2. Sample set of discussion norms.

MAKING DISCUSSIONS ACADEMICALLY PRODUCTIVE

Simply getting students to talk out loud or talk to one another does not necessarily lead to learning. Effective, academic talk and classroom discussions should be *productive,* meaning students share their own thinking and reasoning and listen with a purpose to other people's thinking. Productive discussion is sometimes called *dialogic teaching, dialogic pedagogy, argumentation, accountable talk,* and *respectful discussion.* It is more than just answering questions by teachers that have a single answer.

Focus on Academically Productive Talk

High-quality, productive discussions require critical thinking, are structured, are deliberative and reciprocal, and include academic language and vocabulary. Effective discussions are prepared in advance and are purposely led by the teacher. They include sustained talk with students defending their statements by referring to text or citing valid information. The classroom features of academically productive talk include students *explaining* what they are thinking, *relating* their own ideas or experiences to the focal issue, *reacting* to what other students have said, and students *reasoning* together (Michaels et al., 2013; Resnick et al., 2015; Strategic Education Research Partnership, n.d.-a, n.d.-b; Wilkinson & Nelson, 2020).

Resnick and colleagues (2015) explain high-quality, productive talk as follows:

> This kind of talk begins with students thinking out loud about a domain concept: noticing something about a problem, puzzling through a surprising finding, or articulating, explaining, and reflecting upon their own reasoning. Students do not simply report facts they already know for the teacher to evaluate. Instead, with teacher guidance, they make public their half-formed ideas, questions, and nascent explanations. Other students take up their classmates' statements: challenging or clarifying a claim or an alternate explanation. This form of talk is orchestrated by a teacher. It may be conducted in whole groups, smaller collaborative groups, or with pairs of students. The key component is the learning power generated by two or more minds working on the same problem together. (p. 6)

Michaels and O'Connor (2012) suggest that a teacher focus on one or more of these generic goals during a productive discussion:

Goal 1: Help individual students share, expand, and clarify their own thinking.

Goal 2: Help students listen carefully to one another.

Goal 3: Help students deepen their reasoning.

Goal 4: Help students think with others. (p. 9)

In addition, Michaels and O'Connor (2012) identify several ways that productive talk in the classroom promotes learning in school:

- Productive talk helps make thinking visible and serves as a window into student understanding and learning. It enables teachers and students to recognize what they do and do not understand.
- Productive talk supports robust learning by boosting memory. Talking and listening help students remember concepts and information.
- Productive talk supports language development. Through classroom talk, students are exposed to academic terminology and develop their ability to use and understand subject-area words and phrases.
- Productive talk helps students develop their ability to reason well, using evidence. By sharing their thinking and using evidence to support their ideas, students develop the kind of reasoning and explaining that is valued in school and later in life.
- Productive talk prepares students to learn in the disciplines. When students participate in discussions in all subject areas, they learn the norms of evidence that are unique to each subject.
- Productive talk has social benefits. Students learn to listen carefully to their peers, take their ideas seriously, and challenge ideas respectfully and constructively. They also learn to take risks and go public with their ideas, even if they are not sure that they are correct.

Use the Accountable Talk Framework

Accountable Talk is a framework for supporting academically productive talk developed by researchers at the University of Pittsburgh, Institute for Learning (Michaels et al., 2013; O'Connor, 2012). It can be used in a variety of ways to support discussion in the classroom. With this approach to discussion, students explain their thinking with evidence and listen and respond constructively to others' ideas.

Guided by teachers who provide scaffolds such as discussion sentence starters, Accountable Talk promotes learning and can be used for discussions about text (Michaels & O'Connor, 2012; Michaels et al., 2013). For this kind of talk to promote learning, it must be accountable to three levels (Michaels et al., 2013; O'Connor, 2012; Resnick et al., 2018):

1. **Accountable to Accurate Knowledge:** Students recognize that their contributions must be based on evidence and facts. This involves offering well-considered comments that include specific information and references to readings and research, rather than sharing thoughts that come to mind without support.
2. **Accountable to Standards of Reasoning:** Students engage in logical, critical, and reflective thinking. They are prepared to explain and justify their ideas and reasoning, as well as challenge and ask questions that promote deeper thought.
3. **Accountable to the Learning Community:** Students are responsible for making sure their contributions are relevant to the discussion and are aligned with the goals of the learning community and are respectful of others' ideas. Each student's comments should help advance understanding and respond to others in a meaningful way. This means that each student's comments should help.

Incorporate Teacher and Student "Talk Moves"

Talk Moves is a set of strategic moves developed as part of the Accountable Talk framework that help support productive, accountable discussions. They include actions teachers take to facilitate and support discussions, and statements students make that are driven by discussion sentence starters (Michaels & O'Connor, 2012; Michaels et al., 2013; O'Connor, 2012). Michaels and O'Connor (2012) describe Talk Moves as follows:

> Research over the past 20 years and documentation of teachers who facilitate productive discussions has led to the identification of a small number of general talk moves that are remarkably helpful tools for making discussions work. These talk moves can be used at any point in a discussion, in any subject domain, and are especially helpful in classroom settings. They strategically set students up to think, reason, and collaborate in academically productive ways. (p. 10)

Teacher Discussion Moves Eight strategies teachers can use as tools to support productive discussions are described in Figure 7.3. (A full-size, reproducible version of these strategies is included with the downloads for this chapter.)

Talk Moves: Student Sentence Starters Figure 7.4 lists sentence starters (Talk Moves) organized into nine categories that students can use to contribute their own ideas and respond to others during a discussion, ensuring productive, accountable talk (Michaels et al., 2008, 2013). (A full-size, reproducible version of these starters is included with the downloads for this chapter.) Teachers should introduce students to each set of sentence starters based on the grade and skill level of students, beginning with just

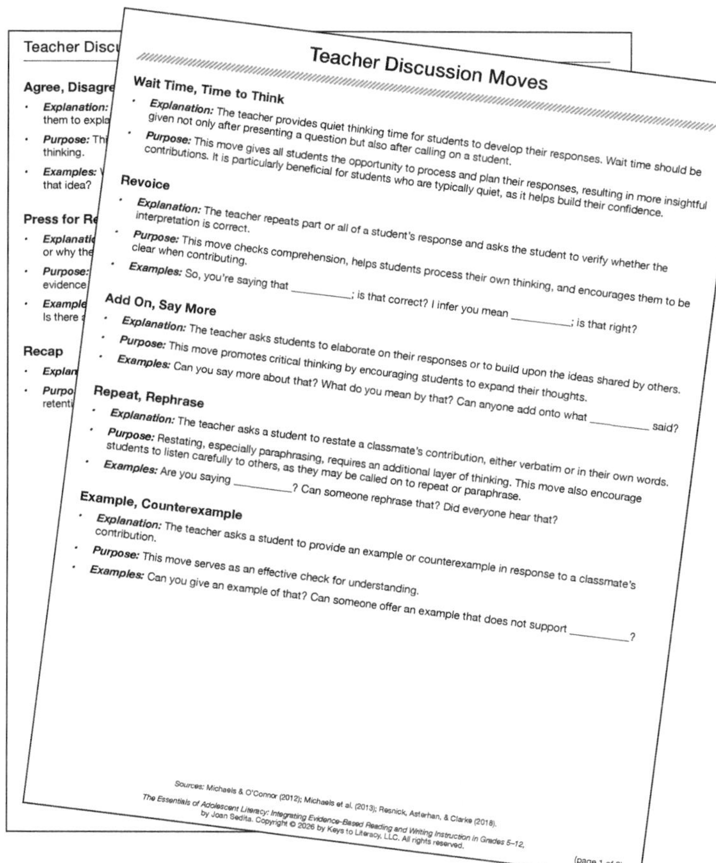

Teacher Discussion Moves

Wait Time, Time to Think

- ***Explanation:*** The teacher provides quiet thinking time for students to develop their responses. Wait time should be given not only after presenting a question but also after calling on a student.
- ***Purpose:*** This move gives all students the opportunity to process and plan their responses, resulting in more insightful contributions. It is particularly beneficial for students who are typically quiet, as it helps build their confidence.

Revoice

- ***Explanation:*** The teacher repeats part or all of a student's response and asks the student to verify whether the interpretation is correct.
- ***Purpose:*** This move checks comprehension, helps students process their own thinking, and encourages them to be clear when contributing.
- ***Examples:*** So, you're saying that ________; is that correct? I infer you mean ________; is that right?

Add On, Say More

- ***Explanation:*** The teacher asks students to elaborate on their responses or to build upon the ideas shared by others.
- ***Purpose:*** This move promotes critical thinking by encouraging students to expand their thoughts.
- ***Examples:*** Can you say more about that? What do you mean by that? Can anyone add onto what ________ said?

Repeat, Rephrase

- ***Explanation:*** The teacher asks a student to restate a classmate's contribution, either verbatim or in their own words.
- ***Purpose:*** Restating, especially paraphrasing, requires an additional layer of thinking. This move also encourage students to listen carefully to others, as they may be called on to repeat or paraphrase.
- ***Examples:*** Are you saying ________? Can someone rephrase that? Did everyone hear that?

Example, Counterexample

- ***Explanation:*** The teacher asks a student to provide an example or counterexample in response to a classmate's contribution.
- ***Purpose:*** This move serves as an effective check for understanding.
- ***Examples:*** Can you give an example of that? Can someone offer an example that does not support ________?

Sources: Michaels & O'Connor (2012); Michaels et al. (2013); Resnick, Asterhan, & Clarke (2018).

(page 1 of 2)

Figure 7.3. Teacher Discussion Moves. (*Sources:* Michaels & O'Connor, 2012; Michaels et al., 2013; Resnick, Asterhan, & Clarke, 2018.)

one or two for younger students. It is helpful to make a list of the sentence starters available on a classroom chart or on laminated cards that students can keep at their desks.

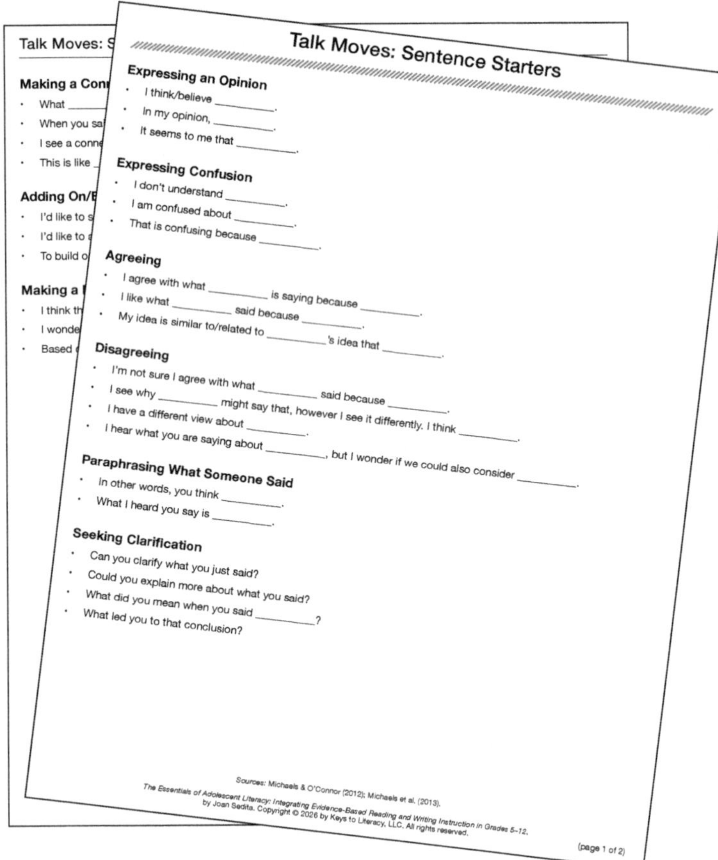

Talk Moves: Sentence Starters

Expressing an Opinion

- I think/believe __________.
- In my opinion, __________.
- It seems to me that __________.

Expressing Confusion

- I don't understand __________.
- I am confused about __________.
- That is confusing because __________.

Agreeing

- I agree with what __________ is saying because __________.
- I like what __________ said because __________.
- My idea is similar to/related to __________'s idea that __________.

Disagreeing

- I'm not sure I agree with what __________ said because __________.
- I see why __________ might say that, however I see it differently. I think __________.
- I have a different view about __________.
- I hear what you are saying about __________, but I wonder if we could also consider __________.

Paraphrasing What Someone Said

- In other words, you think __________.
- What I heard you say is __________.

Seeking Clarification

- Can you clarify what you just said?
- Could you explain more about what you said?
- What did you mean when you said __________?
- What led you to that conclusion?

Sources: Michaels & O'Connor (2012); Michaels et al. (2013).

(page 1 of 2)

Figure 7.4. Talk Moves: Sentence starters. (*Sources:* Michaels & O'Connor, 2012; Michaels et al., 2013.)

FACILITATING DISCUSSION

Facilitating a high-quality discussion is not the same as lecturing or more traditional forms of classroom discourse where the teacher poses questions that students answer. It is important to remember that rather than being the one who does most of the talking, the teacher as facilitator is there to guide a discussion where the students do most of the talking. Teachers should emphasize that all participants have something to contribute to a discussion. They can do this by asking questions that prompt students to consider the comments of others, revoicing students' ideas to give others the opportunity to reflect on and refine what was said, and acknowledging that sometimes students may share faulty or incomplete understandings and comments (Resnick et al., 2018).

One way to provide a more structured discussion during which all students have an opportunity to talk without being interrupted is to use a *talking object*—an item that can be passed easily from one student to another, such as a ball. The student holding the talking object is the only person speaking while others are actively listening. When the student is done speaking, they pass it along to another student who indicates they would like to speak. The sections that follow provide additional general suggestions for teachers and students to follow.

Suggestions for Teachers

Teachers should consider the following suggestions for supporting discussion (adapted from Cashin, 2011):

- Allow for wait time, pauses, and silences. Students need time to think, prepare what they want to say, and process what others are saying.
- Make sure everyone listens to whomever is speaking.
- Encourage and recognize students' contributions.
- Observe who is participating and provide opportunities for those who are not to contribute to the discussion. This includes controlling excessive talkers.
- Be sensitive to students' feelings and emotional reactions, especially students who may be fearful of being critiqued.
- Deal with conflicts; help clarify disagreements and misunderstandings.
- Provide summaries periodically during the discussion and at the end.
- Help students reflect and think about what took place during the discussion, including what worked well and what might be done differently.

Suggestions for Students

Teachers should make sure students know the following about high-quality discussions (adapted from Cashin, 2011):

- Students must come prepared, having read and thought about the text ahead of time. Teachers might ask students to complete some type of writing task prior to the start of the discussion, such as annotating the text, writing a list of key points from the text, or answering a few basic questions.
- Students must be active participants in discussions, ready to explain their ideas clearly. This includes being a good listener by maintaining eye contact and using body language that lets the speaker know the student is listening and participating in revoicing of others' statements.
- Students' focus during the discussion should be on more complex thinking rather than recalling facts. This includes supporting what they have to say with evidence from the text.

COMMON DISCUSSION ACTIVITIES

Teachers have many options for discussion formats and for activities that incorporate discussion, several of which are shared in the following sections. Teachers should aim for high-quality, productive talk when using any activity. They should teach and review norms ahead of a discussion. This includes students coming prepared for a discussion, being active participants, using accurate knowledge and evidence to support statements, participating in collaborative reasoning, and being respectful of others.

The following activities that integrate and support classroom discussion are shared here: Think, Pair, Share; Jigsaw; Fishbowl; Roundtable Brainstorming; Conversation Roundtable; Gallery Walk and Chat Stations; Concentric Circles; Converstations; Save the Last Word; Student-Directed Conversation; and Socratic Seminar. Any of the instructional suggestions from this chapter can be used with these activities, including pre-discussion planning, preparing questions, establishing discussion norms, and using the teacher and student Talk Moves that are part of the Accountable Talk framework.

Think, Pair, Share

Think, Pair, Share is a simple and widely used discussion strategy that uses a partner talk format.

Directions:

- The teacher poses a question and gives students 1–2 minutes to think about their responses.
- Students then have 2–4 minutes to discuss their responses with a partner.
- The teacher facilitates a whole class discussion based on the paired responses.

Jigsaw

Jigsaw is a collaborative small-group activity used to discuss sections of a text.

Directions:

- Students begin in a "home" group of four. Each member will later join a "task" group.
- The teacher assigns a reading task that can be divided into four sections. Each home group member is assigned one section.
- Students then join their task group, which is composed of students from other home groups who were assigned the same section. These groups read and discuss their section, taking notes on key ideas to report back.
- Students return to their home group to share what they learned and engage in a group discussion about the full text.

Fishbowl

Fishbowl is a structured discussion format in which a small group discusses a topic while others observe.

Directions:

- A small group of four to five students sits in a circle at the center of the room; the rest of the class forms a circle around them.
- The inner circle discusses a teacher-provided question or prompt. Only these students may speak.
- The outer circle remains silent, observing and taking notes on both content and process.
- After the discussion, the outer group shares their observations.
- Students rotate in and out of the fishbowl throughout the activity.

Roundtable Brainstorming

Roundtable is an activity that encourages students to collaboratively brainstorm responses to a prompt.

Directions:

- Students work in small groups of three to five.
- The teacher poses a question or prompt with multiple possible responses.
- Each group uses one sheet of paper. Students take turns adding written responses.
- Brainstorming continues until ideas are exhausted.
- During brainstorming, students may not evaluate, explain, or question ideas.
- Afterward, the group discusses, reviews, and clarifies the responses.
- Each group then shares its ideas with the class.

Conversation Roundtable

This is a discussion activity centered on a short text.

Directions:

- Students work in groups of four, each with a sheet of paper divided into four quadrants.
- Students silently read the text, then write one key point in the upper-left quadrant.
- They take turns sharing and discussing their key points, recording peers' responses in the remaining quadrants.
- At the end, students flip the paper over and write a summary or generate questions based on the discussion.

Gallery Walk and Chat Stations

This is a movement-based activity to promote discussion around content.

Directions:

- The teacher sets up posters around the room, each with a different question or prompt.

- Students work in small groups and rotate from station to station.
- At each station, they discuss the prompt and write a group response.
- Groups may respond to the original prompt or add comments to previous groups' contributions.

Concentric Circles

Concentric Circles is an interactive discussion strategy that involves rotating partners.

Directions:

- Students form two concentric circles, facing each other.
- Each pair (one inside, one outside) discusses a teacher-provided question.
- One circle rotates to form new pairs.
- Repeat as needed for additional rounds of discussion.

Converstations

This is a dynamic discussion strategy involving shifting group members.

Directions:

- Students begin in groups of four to six and discuss the teacher's prompt.
- One or two students from each group rotate to a new group.
- The new group continues the discussion with a related question.
- With each rotation, different students move, allowing the conversation to evolve.

Save the Last Word

This activity encourages deep discussion of a text through focused turn-taking.

Directions:

- Students work in groups of three to four.
- Each student reads the same text and selects two to three phrases or sentences that stood out.
    - o **Step 1:** The first student reads their selected quote without commenting.
    - o **Step 2:** Each of the other students has 1 minute to respond to the quote.
    - o **Step 3:** The first student then responds, explaining why they chose the quote. This is the "last word."
- Repeat for each group member.

Student-Directed Conversation

This is an open-ended discussion in which students guide the conversation.

Directions:

- Before the discussion, students prepare one critical-thinking question based on the assigned reading.
- Students form groups of three to four.

- Each student shares their question, and the group discusses it.
- After all questions are discussed, the group selects one to present to the teacher for classwide discussion. (Adapted from Center for Teaching Excellence [n.d.]).

Socratic Seminar

Socratic Seminar (also known as Socratic Circles) is a structured discussion strategy that encourages students to engage with one another around a carefully studied text, with the teacher serving as a guide and facilitator. This approach uses thought-provoking questions to drive the conversation and is based on the Socratic Method, developed by the Greek philosopher Socrates, who believed in teaching through dialogue and inquiry (Copeland, 2005; Schneider, 2013).

A Socratic Seminar is a formal discussion centered on a text, during which the leader poses open-ended questions. Students actively listen to one another, think critically, and respond thoughtfully to the ideas shared. They collaborate respectfully, asking questions and building on each other's contributions. Socratic Seminars can be conducted in either whole-class or small-group formats.

Directions are provided in Figure 7.5. A set of Socratic Seminar Questions is provided in Figure 7.6.

Socratic Seminar Directions

Directions for the Teacher

- Select a text that lends itself to analysis, interpretation, and discussion.
- Plan a thought-provoking, open-ended question to launch the discussion, such as the following:
  - What is the significance of ____?
  - What is the main idea, theme, or message of the text?
  - What stood out most to you about this text?
  - Are any assumptions made in this text?
  - What is the author's point of view?
  - Are there any contradictions in the text?
  - What is the most striking or surprising element in the text?
- Develop follow-up questions that guide the conversation. These should focus on essential information and concepts and support the discussion's goals.
- Ask students to read the text beforehand with a specific purpose in mind, aligned to the discussion goals. Encourage them to annotate the text and write down questions or reactions. Students should bring both the text and their notes to the discussion.
- Arrange chairs in a circle to ensure all participants can see and hear each other.
- Present the opening question to start the discussion.
- Students should take turns responding to the question and posing additional questions of their own.
- Use your follow-up questions as needed to keep the discussion active and focused.
- Monitor participation, encouraging contributions from as many students as possible.
- Conclude the session with a brief debrief to reflect on the discussion.

Student Guidelines

- Follow the class norms for participating in discussions.
- Use the text as a reference. Support your comments with specific evidence from the text.
- Take turns contributing ideas and asking questions. Try to build on others' comments before sharing your own.
- Use questions to help continue and deepen the discussion. You may refer to the sample questions provided by the teacher.
- While you are not expected to respond to every question or opportunity to contribute, active participation is required.
- Ask for clarification if you do not understand something about the text or a classmate's comment.

Figure 7.5. Socratic Seminar directions. (*Sources:* Copeland, 2005; Schneider, 2013.)

Socratic Seminar Questions

Questions About the Opening Question

- Is this question clear, and do we understand it?
- How difficult is this question to answer?
- Why is this question important?

Clarification

- What do you mean by ____?
- What do you think is the main idea(s)?
- Why do you say that?
- Do you mean ____, and are you saying ____?
- Can you explain/say more about ____?
- Can you say that another way?

Assumption

- What assumption are you or is ____ making?
- You seem to be assuming ____.
- Why might someone make this assumption?
- Can a different assumption be made?

Reasons and Evidence

- Explain the reasoning behind your position, belief, or conclusion.
- What led you to this viewpoint?
- Can you give an example or evidence for ____?
- What other information might we need?

Origin, Source

- Is your idea or position your own, or did it come from another source?
- What led you to feel this way or reach this conclusion?
- Have you always held this position?

Implications and Consequences

- What are you or is ____ implying?
- How does that affect ____?
- What are the potential consequences of this implication?
- If that is true, then what would happen as a result?

Viewpoint

- What is an alternative viewpoint?
- Who holds a different opinion, interpretation, or conclusion?
- What might someone who believed ____ think?
- ____ has expressed a different opinion. Are there others?
- How are ___'s and ____'s viewpoints the same and/or different?

Figure 7.6. Socratic Seminar questions. (*Sources:* Copeland, 2005; Schneider, 2013.)

SUMMARY

This chapter explores the value of classroom discussion in enhancing reading comprehension and supporting content learning across subject areas. It identifies three key discussion formats: teacher-led discussions, small-group student-led discussions, and partner talk. The chapter offers practical suggestions to help teachers prepare for effective discussions, including setting clear goals, developing purposeful questions, and establishing norms for collaborative dialogue. Emphasis is placed on academically productive talk, featuring "Talk Moves" for both teachers and students drawn from the Accountable Talk framework. The chapter concludes with step-by-step guidance for implementing 11 discussion-based activities.

REFLECTION QUESTIONS

1. Based on the information in this chapter, what are some advantages of using text-based classroom discussion?
2. Describe the differences between teacher-led classroom discussion, small-group student-led discussions, and partner talk.
3. What are the most important takeaways about planning for classroom discussions?
4. Define academically productive talk and explain the benefits of productive talk.
5. List four or more suggestions for facilitating discussions shared in the chapter.
6. What is the difference between Teacher Discussion Moves and Student Talk Moves?
7. Which of the suggested discussion activities would you like to incorporate in your instruction?

Talk Moves: Sentence Starters

Expressing an Opinion

- I think/believe __________.
- In my opinion, __________.
- It seems to me that __________.

Expressing Confusion

- I don't understand __________.
- I am confused about __________.
- That is confusing because __________.

Agreeing

- I agree with what __________ is saying because __________.
- I like what __________ said because __________.
- My idea is similar to/related to __________'s idea that __________.

Disagreeing

- I'm not sure I agree with what __________ said because __________.
- I see why __________ might say that, however I see it differently. I think __________.
- I have a different view about __________.
- I hear what you are saying about __________, but I wonder if we could also consider __________.

Paraphrasing What Someone Said

- In other words, you think __________.
- What I heard you say is __________.

Seeking Clarification

- Can you clarify what you just said?
- Could you explain more about what you said?
- What did you mean when you said __________?
- What led you to that conclusion?

Sources: Michaels & O'Connor (2012); Michaels et al. (2013).

Talk Moves: Sentence Starters *(continued)*

Making a Connection

- What __________ said reminds me of __________.
- When you said __________ I thought __________.
- I see a connection between what __________ said and what __________ said because __________.
- This is like __________, but it's different because __________.

Adding On/Extending

- I'd like to say more about what __________ said about __________.
- I'd like to add __________.
- To build on what __________ said, __________.

Making a Prediction

- I think that __________ will happen because __________.
- I wonder if __________.
- Based on __________, I infer that __________.

Sources: Michaels & O'Connor (2012); Michaels et al. (2013).

Teacher Discussion Moves

Wait Time, Time to Think

- ***Explanation:*** The teacher provides quiet thinking time for students to develop their responses. Wait time should be given not only after presenting a question but also after calling on a student.
- ***Purpose:*** This move gives all students the opportunity to process and plan their responses, resulting in more insightful contributions. It is particularly beneficial for students who are typically quiet, as it helps build their confidence.

Revoice

- ***Explanation:*** The teacher repeats part or all of a student's response and asks the student to verify whether the interpretation is correct.
- ***Purpose:*** This move checks comprehension, helps students process their own thinking, and encourages them to be clear when contributing.
- ***Examples:*** So, you're saying that __________; is that correct? I infer you mean __________; is that right?

Add On, Say More

- ***Explanation:*** The teacher asks students to elaborate on their responses or to build upon the ideas shared by others.
- ***Purpose:*** This move promotes critical thinking by encouraging students to expand their thoughts.
- ***Examples:*** Can you say more about that? What do you mean by that? Can anyone add onto what __________ said?

Repeat, Rephrase

- ***Explanation:*** The teacher asks a student to restate a classmate's contribution, either verbatim or in their own words.
- ***Purpose:*** Restating, especially paraphrasing, requires an additional layer of thinking. This move also encourage students to listen carefully to others, as they may be called on to repeat or paraphrase.
- ***Examples:*** Are you saying __________? Can someone rephrase that? Did everyone hear that?

Example, Counterexample

- ***Explanation:*** The teacher asks a student to provide an example or counterexample in response to a classmate's contribution.
- ***Purpose:*** This move serves as an effective check for understanding.
- ***Examples:*** Can you give an example of that? Can someone offer an example that does not support __________?

Sources: Michaels & O'Connor (2012); Michaels et al. (2013); Resnick, Asterhan, & Clarke (2018).

Agree, Disagree

- ***Explanation:*** The teacher asks students whether they agree or disagree with another student's comment and asks them to explain why.
- ***Purpose:*** This move encourages students to pay close attention to others' contributions and promotes critical thinking.
- ***Examples:*** Who agrees or disagrees, and why? Does anyone have a different view? Does anyone want to respond to that idea?

Press for Reasoning

- ***Explanation:*** The teacher asks students to support their statements with evidence or reasoning and to explain how or why they came to their conclusion.
- ***Purpose:*** This move emphasizes the importance of presenting evidence to support a claim, including citing text evidence.
- ***Examples:*** Can you explain why you think that? Can you explain your reasoning to us? What is your evidence? Is there any evidence in the text that supports that?

Recap

- ***Explanation:*** The teacher summarizes the ideas that evolved during the discussion.
- ***Purpose:*** Recapping helps ensure a shared understanding of the topic being discussed and aids in students' retention of key information.

Sources: Michaels & O'Connor (2012); Michaels et al. (2013); Resnick, Asterhan, & Clarke (2018).

8

Advanced Word Study and Fluency

Phonics and fluency are two of the five components of reading identified by the National Reading Panel (2000). Consider the three students described here. Do you work with students who have similar profiles?

- **Thomas** is a sixth grader who is able to read and comprehend grade-level texts. When asked to read aloud, he reads at an appropriate pace with proper phrasing and pauses at commas and periods. When he encounters an unfamiliar multisyllabic word composed of commonly recognized prefixes, suffixes, and syllables, he can readily decode and pronounce it (e.g., *inconsistent, disenchanted*). However, when he comes across unfamiliar words of Latin or Greek origin with more advanced spellings, he has difficulty decoding them (e.g., *psychologist, hypothesis, indigenous*).
- **Maria** is a ninth grader who has difficulty reading and understanding grade-level texts. When reading aloud, she is hesitant and often skips over multisyllabic words or guesses their pronunciation, sometimes recognizing the initial letters but guessing the remainder of the word (e.g., reading *conventional* as *conversation, equilibrium* as *equality,* or *metabolism* as *metal*). She reads slowly and does not consistently attend to phrasing or punctuation. However, when texts are presented audibly—either read aloud by someone else or accessed through text-to-speech software—she shows evidence of understanding the concepts and information. In addition, when asked to spell multisyllabic words, she often guesses, leaving out parts of the word and using only common graphemes to represent the sounds (e.g., spelling *clinician* as *klinsun,* or *emphasize* as *emfusiz*).
- **Luis** is an 11th-grade student enrolled in several Advanced Placement courses. He has developed strong disciplinary literacy skills, allowing him to read and understand most content-area texts. However, he occasionally struggles with pronouncing and spelling unfamiliar words.

All three of these students benefit from instruction for advanced phonics and word study skills, but for different reasons and at different levels. Thomas and Luis are proficient readers who benefit from grade-appropriate instruction, which will differ based on their respective grade levels. In contrast, Maria struggles with reading and requires intervention-focused instruction that addresses phonics, advanced word study, and fluency.

This chapter will review how word study skills progress across grade levels and what challenges might arise for adolescent readers who have word-reading difficulty. The chapter then addresses specific areas where additional teaching or intervention may be needed and provides recommendations for doing so.

A PROGRESSION OF SKILLS ACROSS GRADE LEVELS

Advanced word reading skills develop across grade levels as follows.

Upper Elementary Grades: Formal Instruction and Initial Learning

By Grade 4, proficient readers typically have solid foundational phonics skills and can read and spell most two-syllable words with common letter-sound correspondences (e.g., *public, radish, expect*). In Grades 4 and 5, students benefit from explicit instruction in advanced phonics and word study. This includes learning to apply knowledge of syllable types, meaningful word parts (common prefixes, suffixes, and roots), and word analysis procedures to decode unfamiliar multisyllabic words derived from Latin and Greek (e.g., *disagreement, convention, alphabetic*). Instruction also focuses on applying advanced spelling strategies to correctly spell these words. Regular practice across subjects enhances their ability to read and spell such words, contributing to improved fluency.

Middle Grades: Guided Practice and Refinement

Proficient readers in the middle grades automatically apply their phonics and word study skills along with word analysis to read and spell increasingly complex multisyllabic words (e.g., *microscopic, longitudinal, carnivorous, belligerent*). These students benefit from guided practice across content areas, with all teachers using a consistent word analysis routine. As their ability to read complex words becomes more automatic, their fluency continues to improve. Regular exposure to increasingly complex texts, both in and outside of school, further enhances their fluency.

High School Grades: Ongoing and Advanced Use

Proficient readers in high school typically possess the word analysis skills and fluency needed to independently decode and spell most new academic vocabulary encountered in content-area texts. However, they still benefit from teacher support in correctly pronouncing and spelling highly advanced or irregular words (e.g., *malapropism, facsimile, acquiesce, querulous*).

Adolescent Learners With Word Reading Difficulty

The Simple View of Reading (Gough & Tunmer, 1986), introduced in Chapter 1, emphasizes that reading comprehension cannot occur unless both fluent word recognition (decoding) and language comprehension (vocabulary knowledge and syntactic awareness) are strong. Advanced word-reading skills are critical because many of the multisyllabic words students encounter after Grade 4 are essential for reading comprehension and learning content in subject-area classrooms. Inadequate ability with the fluent word recognition side of the Simple View is one reason why some older students have difficulty with reading (Catts et al., 2012; Kamil et al., 2008; Patrick & Acosta, 2024; Vaughn et al., 2022). Vaughn and colleagues (2022) explain:

> When confronted with unfamiliar and complex multisyllabic words, students with reading difficulties often read words incorrectly. Students may, for example, recognize the beginning letters and guess the rest of the word, rather than sounding out the entire word. A student might see *ambi-* in the word *ambiguous* and read *ambitious* or see *disapp-* in the word *disappoint* and read *disappear*. Students need to learn how to tackle the difficult task of reading an unfamiliar word. Successfully tackling difficult words will improve students' ability to read and understand texts, build students' confidence in reading grade-level texts, and improve students' interest and motivation in reading. (p. 4)

For students in Grades 5–12, instruction in advanced word study and fluency may include explicit instruction to address any of the following: 1) the alphabetic principle and phonics, and automaticity in word reading; 2) how to decode multisyllabic words; 3) morphemes (base words, roots, affixes), syllable types, and syllable division; 4) spelling; and 5) fluency. These topics are addressed in the sections that follow.

THE ALPHABETIC PRINCIPLE AND PHONICS INSTRUCTION

The *alphabetic principle* is the understanding that letters and letter patterns represent the sounds of spoken language. Students must grasp this principle to decode and spell words effectively, as written English is based on an alphabetic system. The graphic in Figure 8.1 illustrates the layers of language that inform reading and spelling instruction, progressing from basic letter-sound correspondences to multisyllabic words derived from Latin and Greek (Moats, n.d.-b.).

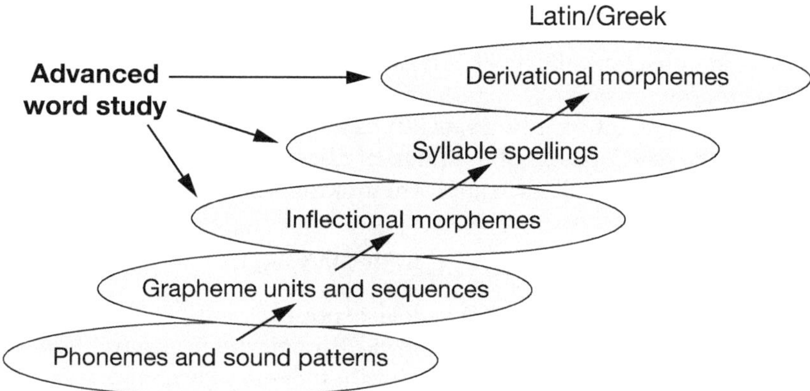

Figure 8.1. Layers of language. (From Moats, L. C. [n.d.-b]. *Teaching spelling using a structured literacy approach* [PowerPoint presentation, sponsored by CORE [Consortium for Reaching Excellence in Education].)

Moving From Basic to Advanced Instruction

Basic phonics instruction typically occurs in the early elementary grades. Students learn how the 26 individual letters and letter combinations (graphemes) represent the 44 sounds (phonemes) in English. Understanding the predictable relationships between sounds and letters enables students to decode both familiar and unfamiliar words and begin reading with fluency.

Young students apply phonemic awareness and phonics knowledge to read and spell one-syllable words such as *bat, sip, splash,* and *stick,* as well as high-frequency words like *the, her,* and *was,* which helps them begin reading phrases and sentences. By Grades 2 and 3, students are introduced to more complex phonics concepts and syllable types, allowing them to read two- and three-syllable words such as *tiptop, hotel, stumble, inside, fantastic,* and *potato.*

As noted previously, proficient readers in Grades 4 and 5 begin to develop advanced word study skills to read and spell multisyllabic words. A focus on morphemes also supports vocabulary development by helping students determine the meanings of unfamiliar words.

Providing Explicit Instruction

"Should I give explicit or incidental phonics instruction?" teachers may wonder. There is a significant body of research that finds an explicit, structured literacy approach to be the most effective type of phonics instruction (i.e., direct, systematic, cumulative, and diagnostic), especially for students who have reading difficulties (Adams, 1990; Chall, 1996; Cowen, 2016b; Lyon, 1998; National Reading Panel, 2000). Explicit instruction follows a sequential and planned set of phonics elements that gradually builds from base elements to more subtle and complex structures. A phonics scope and sequence, and additional teaching suggestions, are provided in Chapter 9, "Adolescent Learners With Literacy Difficulties."

An incidental approach to teaching phonics is quite different. With this approach, the teacher finds opportunities to point out phonics patterns as they appear in text rather than directly teaching phonics and word study skills. An explicit approach to phonics is preferable for two reasons. First, although some students discover the alphabetic principle and intuit how the phonics system works, there is no evidence that suggests exposure to an explicit, systematic instructional approach will impede their progress. Second, research does not support an incidental approach for students who have difficulty learning to read (Kilpatrick, 2015).

Building Automaticity

The goal of phonics and advanced word study instruction is to help students develop such automaticity in word decoding that they can focus their attention on making meaning. Automaticity is a key component of reading fluency; it allows students to recognize and process words accurately, quickly, and effortlessly, without conscious effort. This is critical because it frees up cognitive resources for higher-level reading comprehension.

Elementary teachers—and intervention specialists who work with older students struggling with word reading—support the development of automaticity by providing explicit instruction in phonics concepts, along with ample opportunities to apply these skills when reading text.

MULTISYLLABIC WORDS

The ability to decode longer words is critical for adolescents, especially as up to 90% of the words they encounter in texts are multisyllabic (Baayen et al., 1995). Proficient decoding of these words is essential in middle and high school, where academic texts contain increasingly complex vocabulary necessary for comprehension (Vaughn et al., 2022).

Latin-based words make up the majority of the academic words in English found in upper-grade texts, and Greek-based words form about 10% of the words typically found in science and math textbooks (Carlisle, 2007; Kearns, 2015; National Institute for Literacy, 2007). The Latin-based words typically combine a word root along with a prefix and/or suffix, such as *informing, conventional,* and *disrupted.* The Greek-based words tend to consist of a combination of roots that are connected to make a word, such as *chromosome, telescope,* and *atmosphere.*

Reading Multisyllabic Words

When proficient readers encounter an unfamiliar multisyllabic word, they automatically apply word analysis skills to recognize common letter patterns, syllables, and morphemes (meaningful word parts) in order to read and spell the word. Starting in the intermediate grades, students need to learn and practice these word analysis strategies to develop automaticity. Once these skills are internalized, students benefit from ongoing practice as they encounter increasingly complex multisyllabic words throughout middle and high school.

Proficient readers integrate three key word analysis strategies when reading unfamiliar multisyllabic words: analyzing meaningful units, breaking down syllables, and flexing vowel sounds. They combine these strategies to decode each part of a word and then blend those parts together to pronounce the whole word.

Word Analysis: Meaningful Units Students analyze words through recognition of prefixes, suffixes, and roots. These units are called morphemes. Examples: *pre-heat-ed, dis-agree-ment, trans-mis-sion, manu-script, hypo-therm-ia.*

Word Analysis: Syllables A syllable is a unit of pronunciation that contains one vowel sound. A syllable can make up an entire word or be just part of a word (***to, to****gether*). Students learn to break words into syllables in elementary grades by identifying the vowel sounds that represent spoken syllables. They pronounce each syllable and then blend them to read the whole word. This strategy is especially effective for decoding basic words (e.g., *fan-tas-tic, pen-man-ship*). Students can also identify syllables within a morpheme, such as *a-gree* in *disagreement* or *man-u* in *manuscript.*

Word Analysis: Flexing Vowel Sounds Vowels and vowel combinations can be pronounced in different ways—long, short, or as the schwa (a muffled sound, often like a short *u*). Once students break a word into syllables or morphemes, they may need to experiment with different vowel pronunciations to find the one that makes a recognizable word. This strategy is known as "flexing" the vowel sound. Students flex vowel sounds until they produce a familiar, real word. However, if they are unfamiliar with the word, this strategy may have limitations.

Teaching a Routine for Multisyllabic Words

Explicit routines that support word analysis have been shown to be effective in promoting word knowledge growth (Jones et al., 2019). One of the key recommendations in the research guide *Providing Reading Interventions for Students in Grades 4–9* (Vaughn et al., 2022) is to teach students a consistent routine for decoding multisyllabic words. The authors suggest selecting a single routine that outlines clear steps for breaking words into parts and blending those parts together to read the word accurately. The word parts include morphemes and syllables.

Review the example in Figure 8.2 of a word analysis routine (adapted from the Pennsylvania Training and Technical Assistance Network, 2021 and Regional Educational Laboratory at Florida State University, 2016). (A copy of this routine is included with the downloadable resources for this chapter.) For academic vocabulary derived from Latin and Greek (typically found in middle and high school), instruction should focus on identifying recognizable morphemes rather than simply breaking words into syllables. However, dividing roots into syllables may be helpful in some instances. Students should also be taught to "flex the vowel" to support word recognition. This step is especially important because English vowel spellings and pronunciations are often irregular in multisyllabic words.

Word Analysis Routine

1. Identify the word parts.
   a. Circle prefixes and box suffixes you recognize.
   b. Underline the vowels that represent syllables in the remaining parts of the word.
2. Say each part of the word by pronouncing prefixes, syllables, and suffixes.
3. Blend the parts together to make a whole word.
   a. Flex the vowel sound(s) if necessary to make the word sound like a word you know.

Sources: Pennsylvania Training and Technical Assistance Network (2021) & Regional Educational Laboratory at Florida State University (2016).

Figure 8.2. Word analysis routine. (*Sources*: Pennsylvania Training and Technical Assistance Network [2021] & Regional Educational Laboratory at Florida State University [2016].)

Additional Teaching Suggestions

Students in Grades 5–8 benefit from frequent practice applying word analysis strategies to read and spell multisyllabic words they encounter throughout the school day. These words often appear in content-area classrooms and include new vocabulary terms targeted during previewing and explicit vocabulary instruction.

Review the instructional suggestions that follow for implementing a word analysis routine with all students in upper elementary and middle grades, as well as for students in high school who have difficulty reading multisyllabic words (Vaughn et al., 2022).

- Teachers who work with the same group of students across a grade level should consistently use the same routine. This routine can be applied flexibly to multisyllabic words across various content areas.
- Explicitly teach the routine by demonstrating how it can be used to sound out words. Guide students through the steps of the routine and discuss how they would apply them to an unfamiliar word.

- Provide visual reminders of the steps in the routine by posting them on a classroom poster.
- Connect decoding to meaning by briefly explaining the definition or using the word in a sentence. This helps students remember that words they read carry meaning.
- Guide students through applying the routine to several words before asking them to practice applying the routine on their own.
- Provide multiple opportunities for students to apply the routine to build automaticity for reading multisyllabic words.

Previewing Challenging Academic Words

As students progress through middle and high school, they encounter an increasing number of academic multisyllabic words with unusual or complex spellings that do not easily conform to basic word analysis strategies. Consider the examples that follow. What makes these words difficult to read and spell for students who are not already familiar with them?

amoeba, archaeologist, buoyancy, bureaucracy, camouflage, champagne, coiffeur, conquistadors, crustacean, diaphragm, eukaryotic, fluorescence, kaleidoscope, lieutenant, meringue, nuisance, pterodactyl

Previewing new multisyllabic words that will appear in a unit of study or related text helps students read, spell, and understand them. This is especially important for challenging words such as those listed previously. During previewing, be sure to provide the correct pronunciation (repeated by students), the spelling, and the word's meaning—including multiple meanings and the specific one used in context.

Teaching Older Students With Reading Difficulties

As noted previously, many older students who struggle with reading have difficulty decoding multisyllabic words. Although they may have acquired basic phonics skills for reading one- and two-syllable words, they have not yet developed automaticity with longer words, hindering their ability to access and comprehend grade-level texts.

Research supports explicit instruction in word analysis, including morphological awareness and syllabication strategies, as an effective intervention—particularly for English learners and students with learning disabilities (Thomas, n.d.). Chapter 9 provides additional suggestions for phonics intervention instruction.

MORPHEMES AND MORPHOLOGICAL AWARENESS

Morphological awareness and knowledge are essential tools for older students as they learn new words—they are critical for both decoding and comprehending academic language. In addition to using structural analysis to read and spell words, you learned in Chapter 3 that structural analysis focused on morphemes—when combined with context—can help students determine the meaning of unfamiliar words. That chapter included suggestions for teaching students how to break words into meaningful parts and use word families to support vocabulary development.

Understanding Morphology

Morphemes are the smallest units of meaning in a word. *Morphology* is the study of these meaningful word parts and how they are combined to form words. *Morphological awareness* refers to the ability to recognize the presence of morphemes within words. This typically includes knowledge of prefixes, suffixes (collectively known as affixes), and word roots or base words (Foorman et al., 2016).

For example, the word *transportable* can be broken into *trans-port-able:*

- *trans-* (prefix) means *across* or *to the other side of*

- *port* (root) means *to carry*
- *-able* (suffix) means *capable of being*

Teaching Morphemes

There are numerous prefixes and suffixes, and thousands of word roots and base words, so how should they be taught? Aside from the 20 most common prefixes (see Table 8.1), it is generally more effective for teachers to point out word parts as they naturally appear in multisyllabic words in context, rather than

Table 8.1. Twenty most common prefixes

Twenty Most Common Prefixes

Prefix	Common meaning	Examples	No. of words	Percentage
un-	• not • opposite of, contrary to	• unhappy • unrest	782	26.4%
re-	• again, anew • backward, back	• rebuild • react	401	13.6%
in-, im-, ir-, il-	• not	• inactive, immobile, irrational, illegal	313	10.6%
dis-	• not • opposite of • remove	• dissimilar • disfavor • discolor	216	7.3%
en-, em-	• put or go into or onto • to cause to be	• engage, embed • endear, emblaze	132	4.5%
non-	• not	• nonhuman	126	4.3%
in-, im-	• into, inside, within	• inbound, immerge	105	3.5%
over-	• above, too much	• overuse	98	3.3%
mis-	• bad, wrong • failure, lack	• misconduct • misfire	83	2.8%
sub-	• below, under • secondary • less than complete	• subsoil • subplot • subhuman	80	2.7%
pre-	• before, in front of	• prehistoric	79	2.7%
inter-	• between, among	• international	77	2.6%
fore-	• before, in front of	• forerunner	76	2.5%
de-	• make opposite of • remove • reduce	• decriminalize • dethrone • declass	71	2.4%
trans-	• across, beyond • change • through	• transatlantic • transcribe • transfer	47	1.6%
super-	• above, over • superior • excessive	• superimpose • superfine • supercharge	43	1.5%
semi-	• half • partial	• semicircle • semiconscious	39	1.3%

From White, T. G., Sowell, J., & Yanagihara, A. (1989). Teaching elementary students to use word-part clues. *The Reading Teacher, 42*; adapted by permission.

teaching long lists in isolation. The report *What Content-Area Teachers Should Know About Adolescent Literacy* (National Institute for Literacy, 2007) provides several recommendations for content-area teachers:

- Adolescent learners benefit from learning the differences between Anglo-Saxon base words and Latin and Greek morphemes. Anglo-Saxon words are common, everyday words typically taught in early elementary grades (e.g., *house, friend, laugh*), whereas Latin and Greek words make up the majority of the academic vocabulary found in upper-grade texts.
- Classroom instruction should support the development of morphological awareness by helping students analyze the structural components of words, including syllable types, syllable division, and structural analysis of morphemes.
- Content-area teachers should focus on teaching word parts that connect directly to new vocabulary introduced in the curriculum, rather than teaching morphological skills in isolation.

Prefixes Prefixes appear before a base word or root and affect its meaning. White and colleagues (1989) found that 20 prefixes account for nearly 97% of the 2,959 prefixed words that most frequently appear in school reading materials. Just four of those prefixes (*un-, re-, in-,* and *dis-*) account for 58% of all occurrences. Given how often these prefixes appear, it makes sense to teach their meanings and usage. In addition to these high-frequency prefixes, some numeric prefixes (especially relevant in science and math) are also useful to teach (Ebbers, 2006). By the time students leave Grade 6, they should be familiar with these prefixes, although some older struggling readers may need intervention instruction focused on basic prefixes.

A list of the 20 most common prefixes is shown in Table 8.1, and a list of common numerical prefixes is shown in Table 8.2. Table 8.3 provides a list of additional common prefixes that may appear in academic vocabulary; however, teachers should not attempt to explicitly teach all of them. (Full-size, reproducible versions of the prefix lists in Tables 8.1 and 8.3 are included with the downloads for this chapter.)

Suggestions for teaching prefixes include:

- Provide explicit instruction on what prefixes are and how they change word meaning. Provide multiple examples in familiar words.
- Avoid focusing on memorization. Instead, point out prefixes as they naturally appear in context and help students analyze their effect on meaning.

Table 8.2. Common numerical prefixes

Meaning	Greek	Latin	Example
one	mono-	uni-	monotone, unicorn
two	di-	bi-, du-, duo-	dioxide, binoculars, duet
three	tri-	tri-	triangle, triplicate
four	tetra-	quad- (quart-)	tetrahedron, quadruplets, quarter
five	penta-	quint-	pentagon, quintet
six	hexa-	sext-	hexagon, sextuplets
eight	octo-	octo-	octopus, octagon
ten	deca-	deci-	decathlon, decimal
hundred	–	cent-	century
thousand	kilo-	mille-	kilometer, millennium
part, half	hemi-	semi-	hemisphere, semicolon
many	poly-	multi-	polygon, multifaceted

From Ebbers, S. M. (2006). *Linking the language: A cross-disciplinary vocabulary approach* [Self-published]; adapted by permission.

Table 8.3. Additional prefixes

Additional Prefixes

Prefix	Common meaning	Examples
a-, an-	not, without	atheist, anesthetic
ab-	away from	abdicate, abstract
ad-	toward	advance, adhere
ambi-	both	ambidextrous, ambivalent
ante-	before, preceding	antecedent, anteroom
bene-	good, well	benefit, benefactor
com-, co-, col-, con-, cor-	with jointly, completely	combat, collude, confide, corrode
contra	against, opposite	contraband
dia-	through, across	diagonal
dys-	ill, difficult, bad	dysfunctional, dyslexia
ecto-	on the inside	ectoderm
endo-	within, inside	endoscopic
ex-	out, from	expel, export
hyper-	beyond, more than	hyperactive, hypersonic
infra-	below	infrared, infrastructure
inter-	between, among	interact, interchange
macro-	large	macrocosm, macroeconomics
mal-	bad, wrong	malfunction, malady
meta-	beyond	metaphysical
neo-	new, recent	neoclassic, neonatology
ob-	against	obstruct, object
para-	false	paramilitary, paralegal
peri-	round, about	perimeter
poly-	many, much	polygon, polysyllabic
post-	after in time or order	postpone
pro-	favoring, in support of, motion forwards or away	pro-American, proconsul, propulsion
pseudo-	false	pseudonym, pseudoscience
retro-	back	retroactive, retrospect
tele-	distant, far off	telephone, telegram
ultra-	beyond, extreme	ultraviolet, ultrasonic, ultramicroscope
uni-	single, one	unicycle, unilateral

- Explain that some prefixes have more than one meaning, and the meaning is not always literal. In many instances, the common meaning provides just a clue to the full meaning of a word.
- Encourage students to brainstorm other words they know with the same prefix to build associations.
- Clarify that *in-, im-, ir-,* and *il-* (meaning *not*) are variations of the same prefix. The spelling changes based on the initial letter of the root word (e.g., *innumerable, immovable, irregular, illogical*).

- Take advantage of opportunities to point out prefixes in classroom reading.

Suffixes Suffixes appear after a base word or root. Inflectional suffixes (e.g., *-ed, -ing, -s, -er, -est*) are taught in the early grades. Derivational suffixes, which change a word's meaning or part of speech (e.g., *fearless, election, biology*), are more complex. A single word may contain several suffixes (e.g., *environmentalist: environ + ment + al + ist*).

Unlike prefixes, there is less consensus about which suffixes are worth teaching (Lehr et al., 2004; Stahl, 1999). Many suffixes are vague or have unstable meanings. However, a few suffixes (e.g., *-able/-ible, -cian, -ful, -ish, -logy/-ology*) have more consistent meanings and are useful for students to know. Most students learn these suffixes before they enter middle school, although some older struggling readers may need intervention instruction focused on common suffixes.

Teachers should not dedicate significant time to direct instruction of suffixes. Instead, they should take advantage of authentic reading moments when useful suffixes appear in context.

A list of common suffixes is provided in Table 8.4; a full-size, reproducible version of this list is included with the downloads for this chapter.

Table 8.4. Common suffixes

Common Suffixes

Suffix	Meaning	Example
-able, -ible	capable of	believable, collectible
-al, ial	pertaining to	personal
-ance	state or condition	performance
-ant	one who (occupation), a condition	consultant, compliant
-ate	quality of, to act upon	literate, calculate
-cian	one who	musician
-ee, -eer	one who	employee, volunteer
-er, -or	one who, that which	pitcher, inspector
-ful	full of	joyful
-ion, -tion, -sion	a thing, noun, condition of	companion, intuition, invasion
-ish	pertaining to, being	brownish
-ism	belief system, doctrine, practice	communism
-ity	state, quality of	abnormality
-ize	to cause to be or make	dramatize
-less	without	childless
-logy, -ology	study of	biology
-ly	resembling, having the quality of	happily
-ness	quality or state of	softness
-ous, -ious, -cious	full of, having	joyous, curious, delicious

Base Words and Roots A base word or root is the part of a word that holds the core meaning. Free-standing base words are usually of Anglo-Saxon origin (e.g., *water, drink, father*), making them easier to decode when affixed (e.g., *underwater, drinkable, fatherless*). Roots, often of Latin or Greek origin, usually do not stand alone (e.g., *vis* in *visual, aqua* in *aquamarine*). Greek roots frequently appear in science and math texts.

Although students in Grades 5–12 encounter many words derived from familiar roots, there are several reasons not to focus on direct instruction of individual roots (Graves, 2006):

- The sheer number of roots makes comprehensive instruction impractical.
- Spelling variations among Latin roots make recognition challenging.
- The link between the original and current meaning of many roots is weak.
- Only a few common words may include any given root.

Suggestions for teaching roots:

- Teach students how prefixes, roots, and suffixes combine to form words. Offer limited, direct instruction in some high-utility roots and emphasize incidental instruction through reading.
- If teaching roots directly, begin with Greek roots. Their meanings tend to be clearer and more visibly combine with other morphemes (Edwards et al., 2004).

A list of common roots is provided in Table 8.5; a full-size, reproducible version of this list is included with the downloads for this chapter.

Table 8.5. Common Greek and Latin Roots

Common Greek and Latin Roots

Root	Origin	Meaning	Example
astro	Greek	star	astrology
auto	Greek	self	autobiography
biblio	Greek	book	bibliography
bio	Greek	life	biology
chron	Greek	time	chronology
geo	Greek	earth	geology
hydro	Greek	water, liquid	hydrogen
macro	Greek	large	macroeconomics
phon	Greek	sound	phonology
scope	Greek	instrument for observing	telescope
therm	Greek	heat	thermometer
aqua	Latin	water	aquatic
cred	Latin	believe	credible
dic, dict	Latin	say	diction
form	Latin	shape	formation
grat	Latin	pleasing	gratify
jud, jur, jus	Latin	law	judiciary, jury, justice
lumen	Latin	light	luminous
ped	Latin	foot	pedestrian
scrib, script	Latin	write	transcribe, inscription
struct	Latin	build, form	construct
vid, vis	Latin	see	video, visual

Practice With Morphemes: Building Words

Some students, especially those with reading difficulties, benefit from hands-on activities that provide practice combining morphemes. A word matrix (Bowers & Cook, 2012; Ramsden, 2013) is a graphic that can be used as an activity to build words. A root is at the center of a word matrix. Prefixes are listed to the left and suffixes to the right that can be combined with the root to build words. If there are multiple prefixes that can be combined before and after a word, these are placed together.

There are two examples in Figure 8.3. The following words can be formed from the first example using the Latin root *spect: specter, inspect, inspects, inspected, inspecting, inspector, inspection, inspectable, respect, respects, respected, respecting, respectable, respective, suspect, suspects, suspected,* and *suspecting.* The following words can be formed from the second example using the Greek root *phon, phone: phoneme, phonic, geophone, gramophone, gramophonic, hydrophone, microphone, microphonic, telephone,* and *telephonic.*

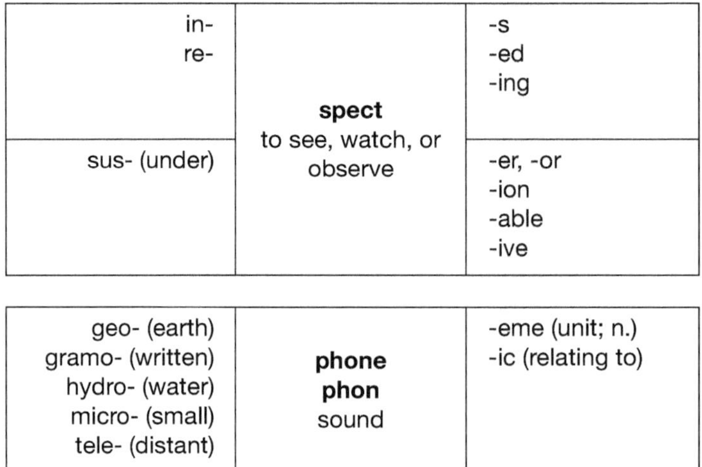

Figure 8.3. Building words: Word matrix. (*Key:* n., noun.) (*Source:* Ramsden, 2013.)

Word Families

A word family is a group of words that share the same root or base word. For example, the following word family shares the root *bio* which means *life: biology, biological, biography, biographer, bioautographic, biologist, bioclimatic, biopsy, biodegradable, biodiversity, bioengineer, bioluminescence, biomarkers, biowarfare, biometrics, biohazard, biotech, biosphere, antibiotic, microbiology, neurobiological, probiotic,* and *symbiotic.* The following word family shares the root *port,* which means *to carry: porter, portable, portability, portfolio, import, importer, importing, important, importance, deport, deportable, deportation, deportee, deportment, report, reportable, reporter, export, exporter, transport, transportable,* and *transportation.*

Teachers can begin building a word family by introducing a word that appears in classroom texts and then presenting one or two related words from the same family. As additional words from the same family are encountered in later texts, they can be added to the group. For example, the initial word "dictation" introduces the root *dic/dict,* meaning "speak" or "say." The teacher might then add the words "dictionary" and "predict" to form a word family, highlighting their shared root. Later, words such as "dictator," "indication," and "dedicate" can be included in the word family as they appear in subsequent texts.

A CLOSER LOOK AT SYLLABLES AND THE SCHWA VOWEL SOUND

Previously, you learned how the focus of instruction for advanced word study shifts across the grades:

- In Grade 5, proficient readers benefit from explicit instruction in advanced word study, including recognition of syllable types and word analysis procedures that emphasize both syllables and morphemes.

- In middle school, proficient readers benefit from guided practice and continued refinement of word analysis skills, with a focus on morphemes.
- By high school, proficient readers typically use word analysis skills independently and automatically to decode and spell most multisyllabic words. They can recognize morphemes and syllables within words with little to no conscious effort. However, they may still benefit from teacher support when encountering highly advanced or irregular words.

In contrast, adolescent learners across all grade levels who struggle with word reading and fluency often require explicit, intervention-based instruction in phonics and advanced word study, including instruction on syllables and the schwa vowel sound.

Syllable Instruction

A syllable is a unit of pronunciation that contains one vowel sound. All words contain at least one syllable. A syllable can make up an entire word (e.g., *so, pat, strength*) or be just part of a word (***so***journ, ***pat***io, ***strength***en).

Students are typically introduced to different syllable types and basic syllable division rules in Grades 2 and 3. However, this type of instruction has been shown to be beneficial to any students who struggle with reading (Bhattacharya & Ehri, 2004; Knight-McKenna, 2008).

When teaching syllables, it is important to focus on the vowel *sounds* rather than the letters used to spell the syllables. Because the mouth opens to produce a vowel sound, a simple way to count syllables in a spoken word is to place a hand under the chin and feel how many times the mouth drops open. For example, when saying the words *eggplant, raspberries,* and *asparagus,* you will notice the mouth drops open twice, three times, and four times, respectively.

Teaching Syllable Types

There are six main types of syllables in English. Review the chart in Figure 8.4 for details about each syllable type. The third column in the chart shows the approximate percentage of English words in which each syllable type appears. Open and closed syllables are the most commonly occurring types.

Other Final Stable Syllables

The consonant-le syllable is classified as a final stable syllable. Other syllables that should be taught as recognizable final stable units include *-tion, -sion,* and *-ture,* as seen in words like *explosion, vacation,* and *manufacture.* These syllables also function as common suffixes and frequently appear in multisyllabic words derived from Latin or Greek.

It is important to note that these are not considered a seventh syllable type. They are similar to consonant-le syllables in that they form predictable, recognizable units at the end of words. In words containing these syllables, the accent typically falls on the syllable that comes before, as demonstrated in the previous examples.

Suggestions for Teaching

Adolescent students who have difficulty with word reading may need supplemental instruction about syllables that incorporates the following suggestions:

- Begin with practice reading lists that include one- or two-syllable words featuring the same syllable type.
- Once students can recognize all syllable types, move on to reading two-, three-, and four-syllable words that include mixed syllable types. Start with words that contain only open and closed syllables.
- At each step, have students spell both the individual syllables and the complete words.
- Provide practice reading these words within connected text.

Teaching Syllable Division: Word Analysis Focused on Syllables

Once adolescent learners with word-reading difficulties have developed knowledge of syllable types, teachers can introduce the principles of syllable division. Syllable division is based on the relationship between vowel and consonant sounds within words. How a word is divided determines how its syllables are pronounced, an essential part of decoding multisyllabic words.

Syllable Types

Types	*Description*	*Approx. % occurrence in English words*	*Examples*
Closed	• Have a single vowel followed by at least one consonant; the vowel is short • Usually taught first • Is the most commonly used syllable	40%	cat, men, up, pill, pond pic nic, fan tas tic
Open	• End with one vowel • The vowel is long in accented syllables. • Is the second most commonly used syllable	30%	be, go, my, hi, solo, halo, robot, bacon
Vowel-Consonant-e (silent *e*)	• End with one vowel, one consonant and a final *e* • Final *e* is silent and the vowel is long. • Found in many single syllable words, and also in multisyllable words	10%	bike, late, role, cute, flute, compose, rotate, valentine
Vowel team	• Have two adjacent vowels; each vowel pair syllable must be learned individually • Some teams have two vowels that represent the long vowel, often of the first vowel (*rain, boat*). • Some teams represent a *variant* sound (*boil, saw, toon, few, now*). • Sometimes *w* and *y* function as vowels.	10%	rain, boat, meat, seed, pay, toe head, chief boil, boy, toon, book, now, out, saw, haunt maintain, heyday, because, contain, about, rainbow, roadside
Vowel-r	• Have an *r* after the vowel • Vowels followed by *r* do not make their common long or short sound. • The vowel makes an unexpected sound.	10%	car, her, for, sir, turn, horn, smart, burner, former dollar, doctor, market, hornet, dirty, summer, turnip
Consonant-le (and other final stable syllables)	• Ends in a consonant-le combination • Accent usually falls on the syllable before the final syllable • Has a schwa vowel sound • Considered a *final stable syllable*	2%	turtle, little, bundle, cuddle, maple, topple, shuffle, bible, bubble, dazzle, pickle
	Examples of other final stable syllables that should be taught as recognizable units: *-tion, -sion, -ture*		explosion, conclusion, nation, vacation, adventure, rupture

Figure 8.4. Syllable types.

There are three basic syllable division rules that students will use most frequently, along with two more advanced rules that are used less often. Figure 8.5 describes the five rules and provides examples.

The goal of syllable division instruction is to help students move from consciously applying rules to automatically and accurately recognizing syllables in words, making word decoding more fluent. Keep the following guidelines in mind:

- Focus primarily on the three basic rules, because they are the most useful.
- Avoid overemphasizing the rules. They are just one tool to support decoding of multisyllabic words. Many academic words, in particular, present exceptions to these generalizations.
- Initially, practice syllabication with multisyllabic words that do not contain prefixes or suffixes (e.g., *constable, penmanship, maximum, fantastic*).

Principles of Syllable Division

Basic and most helpful rules because CVC and CV are the most common syllable types:

1. VCCV: Words with more than one consonant between the vowels

- This is the easiest principle and should be taught first. It can be introduced as soon as students have learned the closed syllable type.
- Words with two consonants between two vowels are usually divided between the consonants.
  - The first syllable will be *closed* (short vowel sound).

    Examples: *rab/bit, fen/der, hip/hop, ham/mer, fan/tas/tic*
  - Consonant blends stay together if there are three or more consonants in a row.

    Examples: *pump/kin, mon/ster, spec/trum*
  - Consonant digraphs stick together.

    Examples: *ath/lete, dol/phin*

2. VCV: Words with one consonant between the vowels

- This is the next easiest principle. It can be introduced as soon as students have learned the closed and open syllable types.
- Words with one consonant between two vowels are *usually* divided before the consonant.
- The first syllable will be *open* (long vowel sound).

  Examples: *mu/sic, ro/bot, si/lent, re/cess*
- Sometimes, the word is divided after the consonant. Try dividing before the consonant; if the word is not recognized, then divide after the consonant.

  Examples: *cab/in, riv/er, sec/ond, dis/ease*

3. Words ending in consonant-le

Teach after teaching the consonant-le syllable type.
The three letters stay together; always divide before the consonant-le.
Hint: Count back three letters.

Examples: *bub/ble, pur/ple, spin/dle, sta/ple, ri/fle*

Exception: For words ending in *-ckle,* the *ck* must be kept with the short vowel.

Examples: *tick/le, knuck/le, pick/le*

Additional rules:

4. V-V: Words that divide between two vowels

- Teach after teaching the vowel team syllable type.
- This is uncommon and only happens in a few words.

Divide two adjacent vowels that do not form a team (they have their own sounds).

Examples: *li/on, flu/id, or/e/o, qui/et*

5. Words ending in *-ed*

- If *-ed* is added to a word ending in *t* or *d*, the *ed* is pronounced, the *e* is heard, and it is set off as a separate syllable.

  Examples: *pant/ed, start/ed, mend/ed*
- If *-ed* is added to a word ending in another letter, it is spoken as either /t/ or /d/ and it is not a separate syllable.

  Examples: *jumped, smiled, buzzed, pitched, saved*

Figure 8.5. Syllable division rules. (*Key:* C, consonant; V, vowel.)

- When working with words that include prefixes or suffixes, students should use a flexible approach. In these cases, word analysis focused on meaningful word parts (morphemes) is more effective. However, if the root word itself is multisyllabic, applying syllabication principles to break down the root can still be helpful.

The Schwa Vowel Sound

As students begin reading multisyllabic words, it is important for them to understand the schwa vowel sound and its role in word analysis. Remember that the word analysis routine includes "flexing," or adjusting the pronunciation of vowel sounds when attempting to decode a word.

The schwa is the most common vowel sound in the English language, accounting for approximately 20% of all vowel sounds (Yule, 1996). It is often the cause of spelling errors. The schwa replaces a vowel sound in the *unstressed* syllables of multisyllabic words and is sometimes called the "lazy" vowel. The symbol for the schwa is an upside-down *e* (ə).

The schwa sound often sounds like a muffled version of the ***short u*** sound (e.g., *magazine, problem, bottom*) though it can also sound like a muffled ***short i*** (e.g., *human, blanket, voluntary*). Schwa can be represented by any vowel, although it is more commonly spelled with ***a, e, i,*** and ***o.*** Figure 8.6 includes lists of words with a schwa vowel, organized by the vowels used to spell the words. The vowel that is pronounced as schwa is underlined in the examples.

Examples: Words With Schwa Vowel Sounds

a	e	i	o	y
amount	item	pencil	command	analysis
adapt	enemy	decimal	phantom	syringe
pleasant	system	president	harmony	vinyl
alphabet	celebrate	carnivore	astronaut	oxygen
topography	algebra	investigation	topography	
fundamental	expedition	immigrant	democratic	
federalism	hypothesis	germination	economic	
infrastructure	consequential	skeptical	conglomerate	

Figure 8.6. Examples of words with schwa vowel sounds.

About Unaccented Syllables Every multisyllabic word has one primary stressed syllable. This syllable receives the most emphasis and has a clearly pronounced vowel sound, either short or long. The remaining syllables may have secondary stress or be unstressed. The vowel sound in unstressed syllables is typically a schwa. For example, in the word *emphasize,* the first syllable is stressed, the second syllable is unstressed and pronounced as a schwa, and the third syllable has secondary stress.

Additional points to know about schwa:

- Vowels in unstressed syllables are usually spoken more quickly and at a lower volume than those in stressed syllables.
- In some words, an unstressed syllable with a schwa may be omitted altogether, as in the words *chocolate, camera, interest,* and *several.*
- Schwa is challenging for spellers because its sound cannot be easily linked to a specific vowel letter.

Suggestions for Teaching Schwa

Follow these suggestions.

- Teach students to try the schwa sound when a long or short vowel doesn't sound right while reading a word.

  Example: "I am eating a *sal-ad.*" First pronounce both *a*'s as short *a,* then try using schwa /uh/ for the second *a.*

- To help students remember the spelling of words with schwa, encourage them to use a "spelling voice"—that is, to pronounce the unstressed syllable as if the vowel were stressed and clearly enunciated.

  Example: Say the *a* in *infrastructure* as a long *a* to reinforce its correct spelling.

- Have students connect schwa-containing words to their base or root forms, where the correct vowel sound is often more evident.

  Example: *definition* comes from *define,* where the *i* sound is clearly heard.

SPELLING

Adolescent students who do not have well-developed spelling skills are at a disadvantage as they move through upper grades, postsecondary education settings, and into the work force. Despite the availability of grammar and spell-check tools on most digital devices, difficulty with spelling can contribute to difficulty with reading and writing for many adolescent learners.

Spelling difficulties can negatively impact the quality of student writing. When students are preoccupied with how to spell words or constantly checking their spelling, they divert cognitive resources away from more important tasks such as organizing ideas and composing text. In addition, students may avoid using words they cannot spell, which can limit vocabulary and expression. When writing contains frequent spelling errors, it can also make comprehension difficult for readers (Graham et al., 2012).

Spelling and word reading rely on the same foundational knowledge. Research shows that spelling instruction can improve reading fluency and word recognition (Graham & Santangelo, 2014; Graham et al., 2012). It's important to note that spelling is generally more difficult than reading. Whereas reading only requires partial recognition of letters or word parts, spelling demands complete and accurate recall of a word's letter sequence (Moats, 2019).

The Challenge of English Spelling

Although many English words follow predictable letter-sound correspondences, English spelling is more complex than that of some other languages. It is considered an *opaque orthography* rather than a transparent one. A *transparent orthography* is one in which each sound is consistently represented by the same letter or combination of letters. Spanish, Italian, and Hawaiian are examples of languages with transparent orthographies. In contrast, an *opaque orthography* features inconsistent relationships between sounds and letters, often allowing for numerous exceptions. English, French, and Danish are examples of languages with opaque orthographies.

One major challenge in English spelling is that many of the 44 speech sounds can be represented in multiple ways, making it difficult to choose the correct spelling. For example, consider the different ways to spell the long *e* sound, /ē/. There are at least eight common spellings:

ee (feet), **y** (baby), **ea** (eat), **ie** (piece),

e_e (Pete), **ey** (monkey), **i** (ski), **ei** (receive)

Another difficulty is that a single letter can represent different sounds depending on the word. For instance, the letter *a* is pronounced differently in each of the following examples (International Literacy Association, 2019):

c**a**t, w**a**s, m**a**ny, sc**a**r, sc**a**re, w**a**ter, o**a**t, **a**ge, **a**ver**a**ge, pizz**a**

Vowel sounds are particularly challenging. They can be long, short, or take on an unexpected pronunciation when followed by an *r* or another vowel. In addition, many multisyllabic words contain a schwa vowel sound, which may be spelled with any of the vowel letters.

The chart in Figure 8.7 lists vowel sounds along with the multiple ways each can be spelled, including how frequently each spelling appears. When teaching vowel spellings, it is most effective to focus on the most commonly used patterns, which are listed in the middle column.

Vowel Spellings

/ā/	baby	a	45%	ai (pain), ay (hay), ea (great), eigh (sleigh), aigh (straight)
	lake	a_e	35%	
/ē/	secret	e	70%	ee (feet), y (baby), ea (eat), ie (piece), e_e
/ī/	tiger	i	37%	igh (high), y (fly), ie (pie), y_e (type)
	bite	I_e	37%	
/ō/	pony	o	73%	o_e (hope), ow (row), oa (boat), oe (toe)
/yo͞o/	use	u	69%	u_e (cute), ew (few), ue (value)
/ă/	at	a	96%	ai (plaid)
/ĕ/	fed	e	91%	ea (head)
/ĭ/	it	i	66%	y (gym)
/ŏ/	odd	o	79%	ough (cough)
/ŭ/	up	u	86%	ou (touch), o (front), oo (flood)
/oo/	food	oo	38%	u_e (flute), ew (flew), ue (blue), ou (soup), o (who)
	lunar	u	21%	
/oŏ/	put	u	54%	ou (could), o (wolf)
	book	oo	31%	
/oi/	coin	oi	62%	oy (boy)
/ou/	house	ou	56%	NA
	cow	ow	29%	
/aw/	paw	NA	NA	aw (paw), augh (caught), a (water), au (because), ough (bought)
/ar/	car	ar	89%	ear (heart)
/er/	her	er	40%	or (doctor), ar (vinegar)
	fur	ur	26%	
	sir	ir	13%	
/or/	port	NA	NA	or (port), ou (four), ore (more), oar (board)
ə (schwa)	lemon	o	27%	NA
	about	a	24%	
	pencil	i	22%	
	taken	e	13%	

Figure 8.7. Vowel spellings. Percent of the time: Based on the number of occurrences each sound-spelling appeared in the 17,000 most frequently used words, including multisyllabic words (Hanna et al., 1966). (*Key:* NA, not applicable.) (*Sources:* Blevins, 1998; Moats, 2000; Snowball & Bolton, 1999; Vaughn & Linan-Thompson, 2004.)

How English Spelling Is Somewhat Predictable

Although many people feel frustrated by the challenge of spelling—especially when it comes to academic, multisyllabic words—English spelling is more predictable than it might appear.

Many consonants are pronounced and spelled as expected. In fact, approximately 84% of English words are phonetically regular (Hanna et al., 1966), which is why it is useful to teach the most common sound–spelling relationships, emphasizing them in elementary phonics instruction.

Moreover, the spelling of most English words can be explained by considering orthographic conventions, morphemes, and word origins. Therefore, spelling instruction in Grade 5 and beyond should address more than just letter-sound correspondences.

The factors that contribute to English spelling are described in Figure 8.8 (International Literacy Association, 2019; Moats, 2019; Stollar, 2024). Given these factors, older students with spelling difficulties benefit from learning spelling rules for adding suffixes, understanding the schwa vowel sound in multisyllabic words, recognizing common spelling patterns associated with word origin, and reminders to retain consistent morpheme spelling, especially of roots, even when pronunciation changes.

Factors Contributing to English Spelling

1. **Phonemic spelling**

   Sounds (phonemes) are represented by a consistent set of letters. It is important for students to learn letter-sound correspondences.

   Examples: *pot, belt, splash, feet, carpet*

2. **Orthographic conventions and common patterns**

   Certain letter patterns are permissible in English spelling, and there are conventions that govern the order and position of letters in words. For example:

   - Words do not begin with the letters *ck* or end with *wh.*
   - FLOSS rule: In single-syllable words ending in *f, s, l,* or *z,* the final letter is doubled (e.g., *stuff, mess, tell, buzz*).
   - Common patterns: *-igh* (e.g., *high, sigh, light, fright*); *-old* (e.g., *cold, bold, sold*); *-dge* (e.g., *lodge, badge*)

3. **Orthographic conventions: Spelling rules for adding suffixes**

   Certain rules apply when adding a suffix to words, including:

   - *y to i* rule: *bunny → bunnies*
   - Silent *e* rule: *hope → hoping*
   - Doubling rule: *mad → maddest, admit → admitted, limit → limited*

4. **Morphology**

   English spelling is also morphophonemic, meaning it reflects both sound (phonemes) and meaning units (morphemes). Some morphemes retain their spelling even when their pronunciation changes, especially when suffixes are added to base or root words. For example:

   - *-ed* is pronounced differently in *shouted, camped, masked*
   - Plural *-s* is pronounced differently in *cats, dogs*
   - Morpheme retention: *know/knowledge, act/action, music/musician, please/pleasure, heal/healthy, sign/signature, house/housing*

5. **Word origin and spelling**

   English spelling also reflects the language of origin. For example:

   - The spelling *ch* represents different sounds: *chef* (French), *chemist* (Greek), *church* (Anglo-Saxon)
   - Greek origin:
     - *y* represents the short or long *i* sound (e.g., *gym, system, hyphen, hypothesis*)
     - *psy* appears in words like *psychic, psychology*
   - French origin:
     - *que* spells the /k/ sound (e.g., *mystique, boutique*)
     - *ge* spells the /j/ sound (e.g., *barrage, mirage, beige*)
   - Italian origin:
     - *i* spells the long *e* sound (e.g., *graffiti, pizza, zucchini*)

Figure 8.8. Factors contributing to English spelling. (*Sources:* International Literacy Association, 2019; Moats, 2019; Stollar, 2024.)

Spelling Rules for Adding Suffixes

Doubling rule (1-1-1)	If a one-syllable base word ends in one consonant with one short vowel before it, double the final consonant of the base word when adding a suffix that begins with a vowel. Do not double the final consonant if the suffix begins with a consonant. Examples: *mad + est = maddest, mad + ly = madly*
Doubling rule for two-syllable words	Two-syllable words double the final consonant before a suffix that begins with a vowel if the second syllable of the word is consonant-vowel-consonant, and if the stress (accent) falls on the second syllable. Examples: *admit + ed = admitted, refer + ing = referring, suffer + ing = suffering, limit + ed = limited*
Silent *e* rule	Words ending in silent *e* drop the *e* before a suffix beginning with a vowel, but do not drop the *e* before a suffix beginning with a consonant. Examples: *hope, hoping, hopeful*
y to *i* rule	Final *y* after a consonant changes to *i* before any suffix except one beginning with *i* (*-ing, -ist*) Examples: *copy/copies/copying/copyist*

 (page 1 of 1)

Figure 8.9. Spelling rules for adding suffixes.

Spelling Rules for Adding Suffixes

As students begin reading and spelling multisyllabic words that include suffixes, it is important to teach spelling rules such as the doubling rule, the silent *e* rule, and the *y to i* rule. The chart in Figure 8.9 provides details; a full-size, reproducible version of this chart is included with the downloads for this chapter. Students benefit from reading and spelling multiple examples that demonstrate how a given rule or generalization applies.

FLUENCY

Fluency, along with *phonemic awareness, phonics, vocabulary,* and *comprehension,* is one of the five essential components of reading identified by the National Reading Panel (2000). The panel found compelling evidence that instruction aimed at improving fluency is critical to both comprehension and overall reading success. For older students, fluency plays a key role in maintaining motivation to read.

The Components of Fluency

Fluency is the ability to read text—across varying levels of complexity—accurately, at an appropriate rate, and with automaticity. It also includes reading with *prosody,* or expressive reading that reflects phrasing, intonation, and emotion. Fluency is often described as the bridge between word recognition and comprehension.

What are these components, and how do they come together as fluent reading? *Rate* refers to how quickly students read text, often measured in WCPM (words correct per minute). Proficient middle and high school readers typically read grade-level text at a rate of at least 145–150 WCPM. However, speed alone is not enough; students must also read accurately and understand the meanings and structure of words and sentences. *Accuracy* is the ability to correctly read the words on the page. Comprehension suffers when students cannot accurately read at least 95% of the words in a given text. *Automaticity* is the ability to recognize words quickly and effortlessly, without consciously decoding them. Adequate rate and accuracy contribute to automaticity. When students read words automatically, they free up cognitive resources that would otherwise be spent on decoding, allowing more mental energy for understanding larger chunks of text. Because working memory has limited capacity, frequent pauses to decode can interfere with comprehension (Reed, 2022, citing Baddeley, 2012). *Prosody,* as noted previously, refers to expressive reading that reflects phrasing and intonation. Students demonstrate prosody by pausing between meaningful phrases and at the end of sentences, as well as incorporating appropriate tone, volume, emphasis on key words, and rhythm when reading aloud.

Fluency is best observed during oral reading. It is assessed by measuring rate and accuracy, as well as prosody, expressed through appropriate expression, intonation, and phrasing.

Fluency, Motivation, and Adolescent Readers

Fluency plays a role in helping older students stay motivated as readers. When students are fluent readers they read more, which helps them develop their vocabulary knowledge. This in turn leads to increased comprehension, which leads to greater motivation to read. On the other hand, students who lack fluency read fewer words and develop smaller vocabularies. This leads to less reading and a lack of motivation to read. A lack of reading fluency is a major reason why some older students have difficulty reading.

Teaching Adolescent Students With Grade-Level Fluency

The benchmark fluency rate for the end of Grades 5 and 6 is 146 WCPM (Hasbrouck & Tindal, 2017). Middle and high school students who can read at a rate of at least 145–150 WCPM with 95% or higher accuracy—and who comprehend grade-level text—typically do not need additional fluency instruction. Regular reading, both in and outside of school, will support continued growth in reading fluency and enable students to handle increasingly complex texts.

Teachers across all subject areas should ensure that students are regularly engaging with challenging, complex texts. Consistent exposure helps students maintain and develop fluency as reading demands increase each year.

Fluency Intervention for Students With Reading Difficulties

Lack of fluency is often a root cause of reading difficulties in adolescents and requires targeted intervention. Some students struggle because they have not yet developed automatic word recognition. Although they may possess adequate word analysis skills to decode multisyllabic words, this process remains laborious, slowing their reading rate and distracting them from comprehension. Other students may still lack sufficient phonics and word study skills, which makes decoding even more difficult.

The second recommendation in *Providing Reading Interventions for Students in Grades 4–9* (Vaughn et al., 2022) is to incorporate purposeful fluency-building activities to help students read with greater ease. This includes improving the accurate reading of multisyllabic words. Three fluency-building strategies are recommended:

1. Repeated reading with a specific purpose
2. Prosody instruction
3. Extended opportunities to read a wide variety of texts

Additional information on fluency intervention is provided in Chapter 9.

SUMMARY

This chapter addresses the varying needs of proficient and struggling readers in Grades 5–12 in the areas of phonics and advanced word study. It explains the alphabetic principle, phonics, and advanced word study concepts. A routine is provided for decoding unfamiliar multisyllabic words. The chapter includes instructional suggestions for teaching morphology, including prefixes, suffixes, word roots, and base words. It also offers guidance on teaching syllable types, syllable division patterns, and the schwa vowel sound to older students with decoding challenges. In addition, the chapter presents information about the English spelling system and emphasizes the importance of teaching the factors that influence spelling. It concludes with a definition of fluency, a discussion of its role in supporting reading comprehension, and recommendations for promoting wide reading to strengthen fluency among grade-level readers, along with targeted interventions for nonfluent readers.

REFLECTION QUESTIONS

1. What is the alphabetic principle, and how does basic phonics differ from advanced word study?
2. Why do some adolescent students have difficulty reading multisyllabic words?
3. Could your students benefit from using the routine for multisyllabic words suggested in this chapter?
4. Define the following terms: *morpheme, morphology, morphological awareness.*
5. What are the key instructional recommendations from this chapter for teaching prefixes, suffixes, and word roots?
6. How can you increase the amount of reading students do both in and outside of school to improve fluency?
7. Can you think of any students you work with who would benefit from fluency intervention?

Additional Prefixes

Prefix	Common meaning	Examples
a-, an-	not, without	atheist, anesthetic
ab-	away from	abdicate, abstract
ad-	toward	advance, adhere
ambi-	both	ambidextrous, ambivalent
ante-	before, preceding	antecedent, anteroom
bene-	good, well	benefit, benefactor
com-, co-, col-, con-, cor-	with jointly, completely	combat, collude, confide, corrode
contra	against, opposite	contraband
dia-	through, across	diagonal
dys-	ill, difficult, bad	dysfunctional, dyslexia
ecto-	on the inside	ectoderm
endo-	within, inside	endoscopic
ex-	out, from	expel, export
hyper-	beyond, more than	hyperactive, hypersonic
infra-	below	infrared, infrastructure
inter-	between, among	interact, interchange
macro-	large	macrocosm, macroeconomics
mal-	bad, wrong	malfunction, malady
meta-	beyond	metaphysical
neo-	new, recent	neoclassic, neonatology
ob-	against	obstruct, object
para-	false	paramilitary, paralegal
peri-	round, about	perimeter
poly-	many, much	polygon, polysyllabic
post-	after in time or order	postpone
pro-	favoring, in support of, motion forwards or away	pro-American, proconsul, propulsion
pseudo-	false	pseudonym, pseudoscience
retro-	back	retroactive, retrospect
tele-	distant, far off	telephone, telegram
ultra-	beyond, extreme	ultraviolet, ultrasonic, ultramicroscope
uni-	single, one	unicycle, unilateral

Common Greek and Latin Roots

Root	Origin	Meaning	Example
astro	Greek	star	astrology
auto	Greek	self	autobiography
biblio	Greek	book	bibliography
bio	Greek	life	biology
chron	Greek	time	chronology
geo	Greek	earth	geology
hydro	Greek	water, liquid	hydrogen
macro	Greek	large	macroeconomics
phon	Greek	sound	phonology
scope	Greek	instrument for observing	telescope
therm	Greek	heat	thermometer
aqua	Latin	water	aquatic
cred	Latin	believe	credible
dic, dict	Latin	say	diction
form	Latin	shape	formation
grat	Latin	pleasing	gratify
jud, jur, jus	Latin	law	judiciary, jury, justice
lumen	Latin	light	luminous
ped	Latin	foot	pedestrian
scrib, script	Latin	write	transcribe, inscription
struct	Latin	build, form	construct
vid, vis	Latin	see	video, visual

Common Suffixes

Suffix	Meaning	Example
-able, -ible	capable of	believable, collectible
-al, ial	pertaining to	personal
-ance	state or condition	performance
-ant	one who (occupation), a condition	consultant, compliant
-ate	quality of, to act upon	literate, calculate
-cian	one who	musician
-ee, -eer	one who	employee, volunteer
-er, -or	one who, that which	pitcher, inspector
-ful	full of	joyful
-ion, -tion, -sion	a thing, noun, condition of	companion, intuition, invasion
-ish	pertaining to, being	brownish
-ism	belief system, doctrine, practice	communism
-ity	state, quality of	abnormality
-ize	to cause to be or make	dramatize
-less	without	childless
-logy, -ology	study of	biology
-ly	resembling, having the quality of	happily
-ness	quality or state of	softness
-ous, -ious, -cious	full of, having	joyous, curious, delicious

Spelling Rules for Adding Suffixes

Doubling rule (1-1-1)	If a one-syllable base word ends in one consonant with one short vowel before it, double the final consonant of the base word when adding a suffix that begins with a vowel. Do not double the final consonant if the suffix begins with a consonant. Examples: *mad + est = maddest, mad + ly = madly*
Doubling rule for two-syllable words	Two-syllable words double the final consonant before a suffix that begins with a vowel if the second syllable of the word is consonant-vowel-consonant, and if the stress (accent) falls on the second syllable. Examples: *admit + ed = admitted, refer + ing = referring, suffer + ing = suffering, limit + ed = limited*
Silent *e* rule	Words ending in silent *e* drop the *e* before a suffix beginning with a vowel, but do not drop the *e* before a suffix beginning with a consonant. Examples: *hope, hoping, hopeful*
y to *i* rule	Final *y* after a consonant changes to *i* before any suffix except one beginning with *i* (*-ing, -ist*) Examples: *copy/copies/copying/copyist*

Twenty Most Common Prefixes

Prefix	Common meaning	Examples	No. of words	Percentage
un-	• not • opposite of, contrary to	• unhappy • unrest	782	26.4%
re-	• again, anew • backward, back	• rebuild • react	401	13.6%
in-, im-, ir-, il-	• not	• inactive, immobile, irrational, illegal	313	10.6%
dis-	• not • opposite of • remove	• dissimilar • disfavor • discolor	216	7.3%
en-, em-	• put or go into or onto • to cause to be	• engage, embed • endear, emblaze	132	4.5%
non-	• not	• nonhuman	126	4.3%
in-, im-	• into, inside, within	• inbound, immerge	105	3.5%
over-	• above, too much	• overuse	98	3.3%
mis-	• bad, wrong • failure, lack	• misconduct • misfire	83	2.8%
sub-	• below, under • secondary • less than complete	• subsoil • subplot • subhuman	80	2.7%
pre-	• before, in front of	• prehistoric	79	2.7%
inter-	• between, among	• international	77	2.6%
fore-	• before, in front of	• forerunner	76	2.5%
de-	• make opposite of • remove • reduce	• decriminalize • dethrone • declass	71	2.4%
trans-	• across, beyond • change • through	• transatlantic • transcribe • transfer	47	1.6%
super-	• above, over • superior • excessive	• superimpose • superfine • supercharge	43	1.5%
semi-	• half • partial	• semicircle • semiconscious	39	1.3%

From White, T. G., Sowell, J., & Yanagihara, A. (1989). Teaching elementary students to use word-part clues. *The Reading Teacher, 42*; adapted by permission.

Word Analysis Routine

1. Identify the word parts.
   a. Circle prefixes and box suffixes you recognize.
   b. Underline the vowels that represent syllables in the remaining parts of the word.
2. Say each part of the word by pronouncing prefixes, syllables, and suffixes.
3. Blend the parts together to make a whole word.
   a. Flex the vowel sound(s) if necessary to make the word sound like a word you know.

Sources: Pennsylvania Training and Technical Assistance Network (2021) & Regional Educational Laboratory at Florida State University (2016).

III

Supporting Adolescents With Literacy Difficulties

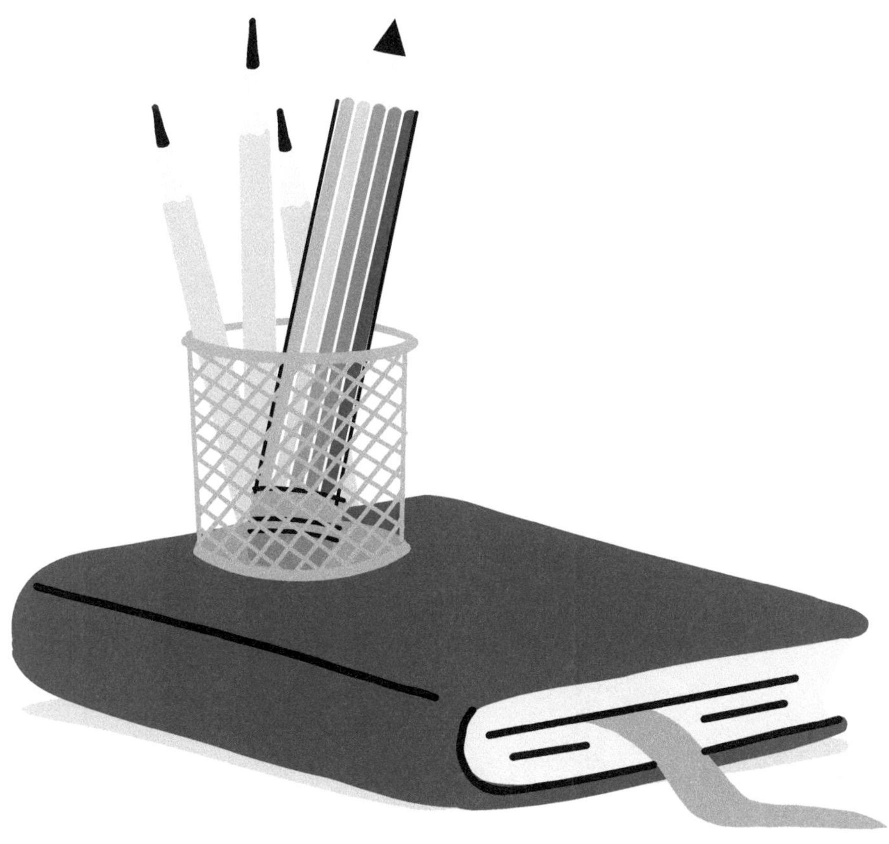

9

Adolescent Learners With Literacy Difficulties

By Grade 5, the emphasis starts to shift in schools from *learning to read* to *reading to learn,* and many teachers of adolescent learners assume they have sufficiently developed foundational skills to be able to read and make meaning from grade-level text. However, there are substantial numbers of students in Grades 5–12 who have not developed reading proficiency for their grade level. For example, the 2024 National Assessment of Educational Progress (NAEP) results for reading show that only 31% of Grade 4 students and 30% of Grade 8 students are at or above the proficient level.

Research has documented that reading difficulties can either persist in upper-elementary and later grades or, in some cases, begin in later grades. Literacy instruction that results in grade-level reading ability at the end of Grade 3 does not guarantee that students will not have literacy difficulties later on. Researchers have found that many third graders reading at grade level experience a drop in reading scores by fourth grade, referred to as the *fourth-grade slump* (Chall & Jacobs, 1983; Wanzek et al., 2013).

Regardless of when difficulties start to appear, students who do not have grade-level reading skills cannot engage with and gain information from complex texts, are at a disadvantage for academic achievement, and require intervention instruction (Vaughn et al., 2022; Wanzek et al., 2013). Boardman and colleagues explain (2008):

> Some struggling students lack the skills necessary to read new or unusual words or to figure out their meanings. Most fail to understand much of what they read. Older students who are tackling complex informational text face serious and growing challenges.... The ultimate goal of reading is understanding and learning from print; thus, reading programs must support students in reaching this goal. (p. 1)

This chapter identifies possible causes of reading and writing difficulties and offers suggestions for supporting older struggling readers and writers in the general education classroom. It outlines the elements of effective intervention instruction in specialized settings and provides specific recommendations for addressing multiple components of reading and writing through targeted instruction.

CAUSES OF LITERACY DIFFICULTY

There are many reasons why students struggle with reading and writing. Some causes are *environmental,* including limited exposure to language prior to entering school or a lack of exposure to effective literacy instruction (due to truancy, frequent moving, or teachers with limited knowledge of evidence-based practices). Some causes are *neurobiological,* including learning disabilities (LDs) such as dyslexia, dysgraphia, deficits in executive function processes (i.e., working memory, self-monitoring, planning and goal setting, cognitive flexibility), or limited cognitive ability. Many older English learners (ELs) face challenges developing literacy in English because they are learning English at the same time they have to speak, listen, read, and write in English to learn core content in multiple subjects.

Additional information about LDs, executive functions, and ELs is provided later in this chapter.

Individual Differences

There is a range in severity of reading and writing difficulties for students in Grades 5–12. Some students have just-below-grade-level skills and may only need some differentiation and scaffolding that is provided in general education classrooms where quality content literacy instruction is integrated into content teaching. Others may be significantly behind and require supplemental or intensive intervention instruction. Some students who have reading difficulty may be identified as having LDs, including dyslexia, whereas some may not.

A one-size-fits-all approach to intervention is ineffective. There is wide variation in which components of reading and writing require intervention support. Some students may benefit from intervention that targets one or two reading or writing components; others may need intervention that addresses all reading and writing across the board. It is essential to consider each student as an individual learner with unique needs, and assessment data should be used to inform instructional decisions.

Difficulty With Reading

In contrast to proficient readers, most struggling readers do not read strategically, and they typically do not have sufficient metacognitive awareness to use strategies to support comprehension of text. They begin reading without setting goals, and they often lack background knowledge about the topic of a text. Some struggling readers lack fluency and may have difficulty decoding words.

In Chapter 1, you were introduced to the Simple View of Reading (Gough & Tunmer, 1986) that suggests strong reading comprehension depends on proficiency in both word recognition (decoding, or translating letters into words) and language comprehension (understanding spoken language, including vocabulary and syntax).

You also learned in Chapter 1 that, in the elementary grades, a common type of nonproficient reader is a student who has strong language comprehension but weak word reading skills—especially students with dyslexia. For many of these students, intervention focused on phonics, word study, and fluency before Grade 5 is often sufficient to help them reach grade-level reading ability. However, students who do not receive adequate intervention are likely to experience broader reading difficulties that extend beyond word recognition.

Louisa Moats explains it this way:

> Therein lies the most challenging aspect of teaching older students: because reading is difficult for them, they do not like to read, and so they read (and write) very little. As a result, they are not familiar with the vocabulary, sentence structure, text organization, and concepts of academic “book” language. Over time, they fall further and further behind. Consequently, factual and experiential knowledge of the world may be very limited. Spelling and writing are poor. What begins as a core phonological and word recognition deficit—often associated with other language weaknesses—becomes a diffuse, debilitating problem with language, both spoken and written. (2015, p. 2)

Difficulty With Writing

Writing is a complex process that requires the coordination of multiple cognitive, language, and motor skills. For many students, especially those in upper elementary through high school, developing proficient writing skills presents a significant challenge. As discussed previously in this book, reading and writing are interconnected; they share a common foundation in oral language and cognitive processes. Therefore, it is not uncommon for students who struggle with reading to also have difficulty with writing.

In addition to a general lack of understanding about what good writing looks like or how to produce it, students may experience a range of common writing difficulties, including the following:

- Limited understanding of grammar concepts
- Difficulty planning and initiating writing tasks
- Infrequent use of graphic organizers or writing frameworks
- Limited use of precise or varied vocabulary
- Challenges with organizing ideas in a logical sequence
- Difficulty revising or editing written work

Similar to reading challenges, writing difficulties can arise from various causes, and the type of intervention needed can vary widely. Some students may require intensive support for foundational writing skills, such as constructing basic sentences and paragraphs. Others may need targeted instruction in more advanced writing tasks, such as note taking or summarizing.

Identifying the underlying causes of a student's writing difficulties is essential for providing effective, targeted support. This support may involve specialized interventions, differentiated instruction, or assistive technology. Common causes of writing challenges include the following:

- **Inadequate or ineffective instruction:** Some students struggle because they have not received explicit instruction in key writing skills, including text structure, the stages of the writing process, and foundational skills such as sentence construction and transcription (spelling, handwriting, and keyboarding).
- **Limited background knowledge or vocabulary:** Students who lack prior knowledge about a topic may struggle to generate ideas. Similarly, a limited vocabulary can make it difficult to express thoughts clearly and precisely.
- **Low motivation and writing anxiety:** Adolescent students who have experienced repeated writing failures may lack confidence in their abilities. This can lead to avoidance, minimal effort, rushed work, or overreliance on teacher support.
- **Language processing difficulties:** Writing is closely tied to language development. Students who struggle with expressive (speaking) or receptive (understanding) language—including ELs who are still developing academic English proficiency—often find written expression particularly challenging. Their writing may consist of simple sentences, limited vocabulary, and a lack of transitions to connect ideas.
- **Neurobiological factors, including LDs and executive function challenges:** Students with LDs such as dyslexia or dysgraphia often experience significant difficulty with writing. The Not-So-Simple View of Writing (Berninger & Winn, 2006), introduced in Chapter 6, "Writing Instruction," highlights how deficits in executive functions can affect students' ability to set goals and plan, attend, and self-regulate while writing.

SUPPORTING STRUGGLING READERS AND WRITERS IN THE GENERAL EDUCATION CLASSROOM

Although reading specialists and interventionists play a critical role in supporting adolescents who struggle with reading and writing, general education teachers—those who teach core subject areas like science, history, math, and English—also have a vital role in general education settings.

Intervention suggestions are provided later in this chapter, typically delivered in specialized instructional settings by reading, special education, and other intervention educators. However, even when pull-out instruction is available, most adolescent learners with reading and writing difficulties spend the majority of their day in general education classrooms. With the right strategies and support, content teachers can improve literacy outcomes for struggling readers and writers while ensuring access to rigorous, standards-based instruction.

Identify Students and Their Individual Needs

Content-area teachers should collaborate with literacy specialists, special educators, and instructional coaches to more effectively support struggling readers and writers. These teachers may not always have access to assessment data for all the students they teach, nor may they participate in data review meetings led by school counselors, intervention educators, or leadership teams. To ensure that students receive appropriate support, relevant information should be shared with content-area teachers so they can identify which students need additional help and better understand how each student's literacy difficulties impact their ability to access and learn content.

As noted previously, adolescent learners face varied challenges based on individual factors. It is important for content teachers to know whether students struggle with decoding and fluency, have limited academic vocabulary, lack background knowledge, demonstrate weak comprehension strategies, face foundational writing difficulties, or experience a combination of these challenges.

Create a Supportive Classroom Environment

Positive teacher–student relationships and a classroom culture that embraces diverse learners and normalizes support strategies can increase student motivation. When students feel safe and supported, they are more likely to participate in academic tasks and engage with challenging content. Teachers can do the following:

- Promote reading and writing as valuable tools for learning
- Praise effort and progress
- Model persistence in tackling difficult texts and writing tasks
- Create opportunities for success through scaffolded tasks

Employ Motivation and Engagement Suggestions

Adolescent struggling readers often lack motivation to read in school. They read less than their peers, which negatively impacts their fluency, vocabulary development, and exposure to important content knowledge, as well as the acquisition of effective reading strategies (Murray et al., 2010; Torgesen et al., 2007). Four research-based practices that have been shown to increase motivation among adolescent readers—especially those with reading difficulties—are listed here (Guthrie & Humenick, 2004; Kamil et al., 2008; Murray et al., 2010). These suggestions are explored further in Chapter 2, "What Is Adolescent Literacy?"

1. Provide content goals for reading.
2. Provide a range of choices in reading activities.
3. Provide students with interesting texts for reading instruction.
4. Increase collaborative reading.

Use Explicit Instruction and the Gradual Release of Responsibility Model

Struggling readers and writers benefit greatly from explicit instruction and the Gradual Release of Responsibility model, summarized here and introduced in Chapter 1, "Literacy Basics."

- *Explicit instruction* involves clearly explaining a skill, modeling its use through think-aloud demonstrations, and articulating what is being done and why.

- *Gradual Release of Responsibility* shifts learning from teacher-led instruction to independent student application (Pearson & Gallagher, 1983). This model includes three stages:
  - *I do it:* The teacher models the skill.
  - *We do it:* Students practice the skill in whole or small group with guidance and feedback from the teacher.
  - *You do it:* Students apply the skill independently.

The amount of practice and level of support vary for each student. Older students with literacy challenges often require more time in the *I do it* and *We do it* phases to build confidence and competence before students reach independent use.

Integrate Reading and Writing Into Content Instruction

Explicitly teaching the content-area reading skills and strategies presented in this book benefits all students—especially those with reading difficulties, who often lack effective comprehension strategies. Through explicit instruction in vocabulary, text structure, and comprehension strategies that support the understanding of complex texts, content-area teachers can help struggling readers develop essential reading skills while simultaneously building content knowledge. Literacy specialists, special educators, and instructional coaches can assist content teachers in adapting general reading strategies to fit subject-specific texts.

Struggling writers are not incapable; they simply need the right tools, scaffolded instruction, and timely assistance. These students often face a range of difficulties, including challenges with organizing ideas, generating content, applying grammar and syntax, and understanding genre-specific expectations.

Effective scaffolding strategies can help by breaking writing tasks into manageable steps, offering visual and linguistic supports, and gradually transferring responsibility to the student. The instructional suggestions and scaffolds presented in this book, especially in Chapter 6, "Writing Instruction," can be used to support struggling writers in the general education classroom. This includes setting clear goals for writing assignments, providing graphic organizers, sharing examples of mentor texts, providing sentence frames, and providing feedback and revision supports. Classroom teachers can also provide access to technology-based writing supports, such as speech-to-text tools, and word prediction and grammar support tools to assist with spelling, word choice, and sentence structure.

EFFECTIVE INTERVENTION INSTRUCTION

Louisa Moats (2015) emphasizes that older struggling readers can learn to read when several key conditions are met:

- They receive explicit instruction in the foundational skills they previously missed,
- They have ample opportunities to apply these skills by reading meaningful texts, and
- They learn in a supportive, age-appropriate environment that addresses their social, intellectual, and emotional needs. (p. 8)

Moats also highlights that effective intervention takes time:

> Intensive interventions can accelerate students' learning and narrow the achievement gap, but "intensive" may require more than one class period daily over more than one year. Providing remediation to groups of students in an alternative, credit-bearing English course is the best vehicle for ensuring that daily, concentrated instruction occurs. (2015, p. 7)

Reading Intervention Research

Several research guides and meta-analyses address effective interventions for older struggling readers.

The 2022 research guide *Providing Reading Interventions for Students in Grades 4–9* (Vaughn et al.) highlights recent findings showing that targeted interventions can successfully improve reading levels in students with reading difficulties in Grades 4–9. The guide presents four key recommendations for delivering effective reading intervention:

1. Build students' decoding skills so they can read complex multisyllabic words.
2. Provide purposeful fluency-building activities to help students read effortlessly.
3. Routinely use a set of comprehension-building practices to help students make sense of the text.
4. Provide students with opportunities to practice making sense of stretch text (i.e., challenging text) that will expose them to complex ideas and information.

Additional details from this guide are shared later in this chapter.

Scammacca and colleagues (2013) conducted a meta-analysis of research on reading interventions for students in Grades 4–12. Their findings indicate that adolescence is not too late for intervention. Older students benefit from instruction targeting both word-level and text-level skills, as well as from instruction that builds vocabulary and develops comprehension strategies. However, the research also shows that average gains in reading comprehension tend to be smaller than gains in other reading domains.

The research guide *Improving Adolescent Literacy: Effective Classroom and Intervention Practices* (Kamil et al., 2008), also based on a meta-analysis of adolescent literacy research, recommends providing intensive, individualized interventions for struggling readers, delivered by trained specialists. The report emphasizes that some students require more support than can be provided in general education classrooms. To accelerate literacy development and help students reach grade-level proficiency, interventions must be sufficiently intensive, tailored to individual needs based on assessment data, and delivered by educators with the expertise and experience to implement evidence-based practices effectively.

Tiered Instruction

A *multi-tiered system of support* (MTSS) is an instructional framework that promotes student reading achievement by providing instruction across different tiers. The MTSS model includes universal screening for all students, multiple tiers of instruction and support services, and an integrated data collection and assessment system to guide decisions at each tier of instruction.

The learning needs of students who struggle with reading are met across multiple tiers, depicted in Figure 9.1 and described here.

1. *Tier 1:* Universal, core reading instruction is provided in the classroom to all students using evidence-based practices and programs. Teachers incorporate differentiation and scaffolds during core instruction to support students who struggle.

   In middle and high school, Tier 1 instruction focuses primarily on grade-level vocabulary, comprehension, and writing. This instruction is integrated across all content areas.

2. *Tier 2:* Supplemental instruction is provided in addition to Tier 1 for students who do not yet demonstrate grade-level literacy skills. This targeted instruction is designed to meet individual student needs and may be delivered within the regular classroom or in a pull-out setting. The goal of Tier 2 instruction is to provide temporary, additional support to address skill gaps.

   In middle and high school, students who are 1–2 years below grade level in reading typically require Tier 2 support. These students benefit from explicit instruction and guided practice in vocabulary, comprehension, and strategies for reading multisyllabic words. If adequate progress is not made, they may require more intensive support through Tier 3 intervention.

3. *Tier 3:* More intensive intervention instruction is provided for students who have not responded sufficiently to Tier 2 instruction. Tier 3 instruction is typically longer in duration, more intensive, and individualized to meet each student's specific needs. It is usually delivered in a pull-out setting.

   In middle and high school, students who are two or more years behind in reading skills often require Tier 3 support. This instruction includes highly explicit teaching and guided practice and may focus on any component of reading—including phonics and fluency—based on the student's needs.

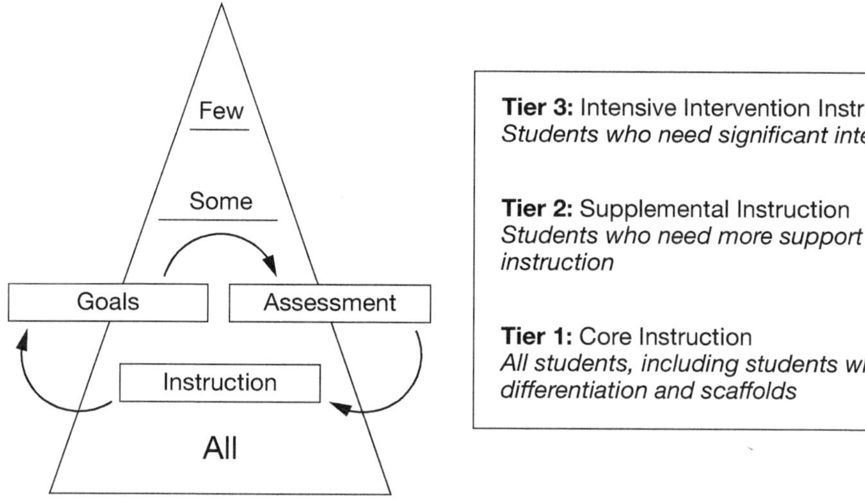

Figure 9.1. Multi-tiered system of support (MTSS).

Characteristics of Effective Interventions

In the research practice brief *Effective Instruction for Adolescent Struggling Readers* (2008), Boardman and colleagues note that effective intervention instruction almost always provides many more opportunities for re-teaching, review, and practice. They also note that targeted support is most effective when provided in well-planned, regular small-group sessions over a long period of time. For many middle and high school students who are significantly behind in reading skills, the intervention they receive is the last opportunity they may have to develop the skills they need to be college and career ready. Torgesen and colleagues (2007) explain:

> All struggling readers share a need for instruction that is sufficiently powerful to accelerate development. In fact, these students must grow in reading ability more rapidly than their grade-level peers if they are to become proficient in understanding and learning from grade-level text. Struggling readers must make more than one year's growth in reading for each year of instruction, rather than simply the expected annual yearly progress in reading. (p. 68)

In order to make this kind of progress, intensive intervention instruction for struggling readers must be provided that includes smaller group size, increased intervention time, individualized instruction, and intervention provided in a pull-out class (Kamil et al., 2008; Vaughn et al., 2012; Wanzek et al., 2013).

Smaller Instructional Group Size One of the most practical methods for intensifying intervention and improving outcomes for highly at-risk students is providing small-group instruction. Vaughn and colleagues (2012) make these points:

- Research has not found one ideal intervention group size that increases outcomes for all or most students. The literature suggests that small groups of two to four students or one-to-one instruction may provide the most intensive intervention, whereas some students make sufficient progress in larger groups. Because smaller group size can be expensive, if students can succeed in a larger instructional group, it makes sense to continue the intervention in that manner for cost considerations.
- In larger-group settings where student performance is clearly not improving, reducing group size might generate better results. Intervention educators need to carefully monitor students' progress when changing group size to determine whether the change increases student outcomes.
- When group size is decreased, intervention educators can divide their attention among fewer students and increase the potential for individualized instruction, more student response and practice, and timely teacher feedback.

Increased Intervention Time Another important way to intensify intervention is to increase learning time. Vaughn and colleagues (2012) describe several ways to do so:

- Increase the frequency of intervention. For example, an intervention provided 5 days a week may be more intensive than an intervention provided 3 days a week. Frequency can also be increased by providing more than one intervention session per day.
- Increase the length of instructional sessions. If a student currently receives 20 minutes of instruction per intervention session, providing 40 minutes may intensify the intervention if student engagement remains high.
- Increasing both the frequency of intervention and/or the length of the instructional sessions allows struggling students to receive additional, targeted instruction and increased opportunities for practice with feedback.
- Increase the duration of the intervention. Some students with learning difficulties may require additional weeks or months of an intervention, particularly when the goal is to increase cognitively complex tasks like reading comprehension that are not likely to be remedied quickly.
- Make decisions about learning time based on each student's circumstances:
    - How far the student's achievement level is below grade-level expectations
    - The length and frequency of previous interventions
    - The complexity of the learning tasks at hand

Individualized Intervention There is no "one-size-fits-all" for reading intervention. Given the variety of reading difficulties older students face, interventions will be most effective if they focus on the deficit skills that interfere with an individual student's ability to comprehend text. Some students will need a great deal of instruction to improve their reading accuracy and fluency, whereas others will need instruction for the use of comprehension strategies. Others will need broader, intensive intervention that integrates instruction across all reading components. If possible, students with similar needs should be grouped together for small-group instruction. This allows the teacher to target instruction to just those skills needed by the students in the group.

Intervention Provided in Pull-Out Class Although some interventions can be carried out in content classrooms (e.g., supporting vocabulary learning in science or history, practicing the application of comprehension strategies such as summarizing), many struggling readers need intensive instruction that is provided in a learning environment that is separate from the general classroom.

Additional Intervention Instruction Suggestions

In addition to intensifying intervention using the recommendations noted previously, teachers can apply several other instructional suggestions to support older struggling readers (Torgesen et al., 2007; Vaughn et al., 2012; Weingarten et al., 2018):

- Provide explicit and systematic instruction.
- Use precise, simple, consistent language.
- Provide opportunities for guided practice and teacher feedback.
- Use evidence-based practices and intervention programs.
- Provide access to curriculum content so students can keep up with peers.
- Extend intervention instruction into content classrooms.

These suggestions are further explained in Figure 9.2.

Instructional Supports for Adolescent Struggling Readers

Provide explicit and systematic instruction:
Research demonstrates that explicit and systematic instruction is associated with improved reading outcomes among struggling students. In an explicit instruction lesson, teachers overtly teach the steps or processes needed to understand and apply a reading skill. This includes clear and detailed explanation and teacher modeling. Systematic instruction is planned in a way that the skills presented in each lesson or activity build upon previously taught skills in a logical sequence. It includes breaking down complex skills into smaller, manageable chunks of learning that move from easier to more difficult. Scaffolds are provided as teachers gradually release responsibility for using a skill to students.

Use precise, simple, consistent language:
To support students who have difficulty processing the language used when teachers provide instruction, teachers use precise, simple language and ensure that their instructions and requests are clearly stated. Short, clear, and consistent phrasing helps students focus on key information and remember the steps involved in completing a task.

Provide opportunities for guided practice and teacher feedback:
Students benefit when teachers provide opportunities for guided practice that include teacher support as well as independent practice in which students work individually or in small groups. Increasing opportunities for students to practice a reading skill should provide a *double dose* of instruction in which a previously taught skill is retaught. Providing students with both positive feedback and error correction is essential to learning. Feedback prompts students to continue successful attempts during practice or to remedy errors before they become entrenched. Feedback should be provided during or immediately after a task is completed.

Use evidence-based practices and intervention programs:
Older struggling readers benefit from intervention instruction that is provided by specialists who are trained to deliver intervention instructional practices and programs that have been shown to improve reading skills.

Provide access to curriculum content so students can keep up with peers:
This can be accomplished by incorporating modifications and accommodations. For example, science or history text can be listened to using text-to-speech software or by having a peer student read the text aloud, and then a peer discussion can be used to support understanding of the content.

Extend intervention instruction into content classrooms:
Intervention specialists cannot do it alone! Many of the vocabulary and comprehension strategies that are taught during intervention instruction can be reinforced by content teachers. In addition to the explicit and intensive instruction provided by reading specialists, content teachers can explain and reinforce these strategies using subject-area textbooks and content texts.

Figure 9.2. Instructional supports for adolescent struggling readers. (*Sources:* Torgesen et al., 2007; Vaughn et al., 2012; Weingarten et al., 2018.)

The suggestions for effective intervention instruction can be used when teaching any components of reading or writing. Specific intervention suggestions for reading and writing are provided in the next sections of this chapter.

INTERVENTION FOR VOCABULARY, COMPREHENSION, PHONICS, AND FLUENCY

Whereas some adolescents who struggle with reading may require intervention that addresses phonics and fluency, most will require intervention that addresses vocabulary and comprehension. Students whose primary area of difficulty in the elementary grades is automatic word reading will eventually have difficulty with vocabulary and comprehension. These students typically do not have an opportunity to read a sufficient amount of high-quality, complex, and challenging text. Over time, this lack of exposure to text creates deficits in vocabulary, background knowledge, and awareness of advanced text structures, as well as an insufficient ability to use comprehension strategies. The next sections include intervention suggestions targeting vocabulary, comprehension, phonics, and fluency.

Intervention for Vocabulary

Figure 9.3 summarizes the differences between proficient readers and struggling readers related to developing vocabulary (Boardman et al., 2008; Murray et al., 2010). One of the recommendations in the research guide *Providing Reading Interventions for Students in Grades 4–9* (Vaughn et al., 2022) focuses on suggestions for teaching vocabulary: Build students' world and word knowledge so they can make sense of the text.

Read the recommendation and the related instructional suggestions that follow in Figure 9.4.

	Vocabulary
Adolescent Proficient Readers	• Enjoy reading and are motivated to engage with high-quality texts, resulting in frequent exposure to new words. • Understand at least 90% of the words they encounter in grade-level texts, which enhances comprehension. • Possess sufficient background knowledge on the topics in the texts they read, helping them understand how words are used in context. • Can make sense of unfamiliar words by using the context within the text and their knowledge of morphemes (prefixes, suffixes, and roots). • Exhibit word consciousness and a keen interest in learning new words.
Adolescent Struggling Readers	• Lack motivation and interest to read, leading to limited exposure to new words. • Struggle with comprehension due to unfamiliarity with more than 10% of the words in grade-level texts. • Often lack background knowledge related to the topics in the texts they read, hindering their understanding of how words are used in context. • Have difficulty using contextual clues and morpheme knowledge to make sense of unfamiliar words. • Exhibit limited word consciousness and show little interest in learning new words.

Figure 9.3. Proficient and struggling readers: Vocabulary. (*Sources:* Boardman et al., 2008; Murray et al., 2010.)

Intervention Recommendations: Vocabulary

Recommendation 3, Part A (Vaughn et al., 2022, pp. 22–46)
Build students' world and word knowledge so they can make sense of the text.

1. Develop world knowledge that is relevant for making sense of the passage.
2. Teach the meaning of a few words that are essential for understanding the passage.
3. Teach students how to derive meanings of unknown words using context.
4. Teach prefixes and suffixes to help students derive meanings of words.
5. Teach the meaning of Latin and Greek roots.

Vocabulary Instruction Suggestions (Boardman et al., 2008)

- Provide explicit instruction of specific words:
  - o Select the most useful words to teach in depth—that is, words that appear frequently in many contexts and essential content-specific words.
  - o Provide multiple, meaningful exposures to the words.
  - o Provide opportunities for students to use target words verbally in small- and large-group discussions.
- Actively engage students in vocabulary-learning tasks (e.g., creating definitions, drawing pictures, acting out words).
- Teach word-learning strategies and teach words in relation to other words:
  - o Use activities that connect new words to existing language.
  - o Show students how to break words into parts and how to use context clues, root words, prefixes, suffixes, and word families to identify their meaning.
  - o Develop word consciousness through activities such as talking about how authors use words, and word games.
- Use academic vocabulary instruction (focus on the meanings of words in a specific context and content area):
  - o Use content-area materials to identify important vocabulary; focus on their importance to understand new or difficult concepts.
  - o Provide multiple meanings of words and appropriate use of words within particular contexts.
  - o Use assessment procedures to identify target words students know and words students need to learn.
  - o Provide explicit instruction of the vocabulary needed to understand a specific text or content area by offering simple definitions prior to reading, generating examples, or creating semantic maps.

Figure 9.4. Intervention recommendations: Vocabulary. (Reprinted from Vaughn, S., Gersten, R., Dimino, J., Taylor, M. J., Newman-Gonchar, R., Krowka, S., Kieffer, M. J., McKeown, M., Reed, D., Sanchez, M., St. Martin, K., Wexler, J., Morgan, S., Yañez, A., & Jayanthi, M. [2022]. *Providing reading interventions for students in grades 4–9* [WWC 2022007]. National Center for Education Evaluation and Regional Assistance [NCEE], Institute of Education Sciences, U.S. Department of Education. https://whatworks.ed.gov/)

Intervention for Comprehension

Figure 9.5 summarizes the differences between proficient readers and struggling readers related to comprehension (Boardman et al., 2008; Murray et al., 2010). Several recommendations in the research guide *Providing Reading Interventions for Students in Grades 4–9* (Vaughn et al., 2022) focus on suggestions for comprehension. Read the recommendations and the related instructional suggestions that follow in Figure 9.6.

Comprehension	
Adolescent Proficient Readers	• Possess strong word decoding and fluency skills, which allow them to focus on comprehension while reading. • Set clear purposes for reading and maintain focus on these objectives throughout the text. • Have ample background knowledge and vocabulary to enhance comprehension and can connect new information to what they already know. • Understand how text features and structure contribute to comprehension. • Use background knowledge to make inferences while reading. • Are metacognitive, monitoring their understanding and recognizing when comprehension breaks down, applying strategies to repair understanding. • Employ a range of comprehension strategies before, during, and after reading and are able to apply them selectively.
Adolescent Struggling Readers	• May struggle with decoding and fluency, which impedes their ability to comprehend the text. • Often read without a clear purpose in mind. • Have limited vocabulary and background knowledge, hindering both comprehension and the ability to link new content to prior knowledge. • Have limited awareness of text structure. • Find it difficult to make inferences while reading. • Lack metacognitive awareness, struggle to monitor their understanding, and have insufficient strategies to address comprehension difficulties. • Have a limited set of comprehension strategies.

Figure 9.5. Proficient and struggling readers: Comprehension. (*Sources:* Boardman et al., 2008; Murray et al., 2010.)

Intervention for Phonics

Figure 9.7 summarizes the differences between proficient readers and struggling readers related to phonics (Boardman et al., 2008; Murray et al., 2010). The first recommendation in the research guide *Providing Reading Interventions for Students in Grades 4–9* (Vaughn et al., 2022) focuses on suggestions for decoding and spelling. The guide suggests addressing gaps in phonics knowledge, using a routine for multisyllabic words, and teaching spelling as part of phonics lessons. Additional details are provided in Figure 9.8.

The routine for decoding unfamiliar multisyllabic words, introduced in Chapter 8, "Advanced Word Study and Fluency," can be used for phonics intervention instruction. See Figure 8.2.

For students needing instruction in basic phonics, a diagnostic phonics assessment should be used to identify gaps in phonics concepts. A logically ordered scope and sequence of phonics concepts is useful for this purpose. Evidence-based phonics intervention programs for older students often provide a phonics scope and sequence, or the example in Figure 9.9 can be used (Sedita, 2020e).

Intervention for Fluency

Figure 9.10 summarizes the differences between proficient readers and struggling readers related to fluency (Boardman et al., 2008; Murray et al., 2010). The second recommendation in the research guide *Providing Reading Interventions for Students in Grades 4–9* (Vaughn et al., 2022) emphasizes the importance of purposeful, fluency-building activities to help students read more effortlessly. The report suggests strategies such as repeated reading of the same passage, providing a specific purpose for each reading, allocating instructional time to reading with prosody, and wide reading. Additional details are provided in Figure 9.11.

Intervention Recommendations: Comprehension

Recommendation 3, Part B (Vaughn et al., 2022, pp. 37–46)
Consistently provide students with opportunities to ask and answer questions to better understand the text they read.

1. Explicitly teach students how to find and justify answers to different types of questions.
2. Provide ample opportunities for students to collaboratively answer questions.
3. Teach students to ask questions about the text while reading.

Recommendation 3, Part C (Vaughn et al., 2022, pp. 47–58)
Teach students a routine for determining the gist (main idea) of a short section.

1. Model how to use a routine to generate gist statements.
2. Teach students how to use text structures to generate gist statements.
3. Work collaboratively with students to generate gist statements.

Recommendation 3, Part D (Vaughn et al., 2022, pp. 59–64)
Teach students to monitor their comprehension as they read.

1. Help students determine when they do not understand the text.
2. Teach students to ask themselves questions as they read to check their understanding and figure out what the text is about.
3. Provide opportunities for students to reflect on what they have learned.

Reading Comprehension Instruction Suggestions (Boardman et al., 2008)

- Teach comprehension strategies, such as:
  - o Strategies that activate prior knowledge (e.g., previewing headings or key concepts, making a prediction)
  - o Use of graphic organizers before, during, and after reading
  - o Comprehension monitoring strategies (e.g., awareness when understanding breaks down; asking questions before and during reading; active engagement when reading, such as taking notes)
  - o Summarizing (e.g., identify main ideas and topic sentences, use graphic organizers to write summaries)
  - o Ask and answer questions: Teach students to ask specific types of questions and to evaluate teacher-generated questions.
- Provide opportunities for students to practice strategies in meaningful contexts.
- Combine several comprehension strategies into a routine for reading.

Figure 9.6. Intervention recommendations: Comprehension. (Reprinted from Vaughn, S., Gersten, R., Dimino, J., Taylor, M. J., Newman-Gonchar, R., Krowka, S., Kieffer, M. J., McKeown, M., Reed, D., Sanchez, M., St. Martin, K., Wexler, J., Morgan, S., Yañez, A., & Jayanthi, M. [2022]. *Providing reading interventions for students in grades 4–9* [WWC 2022007]. National Center for Education Evaluation and Regional Assistance [NCEE], Institute of Education Sciences, U.S. Department of Education. https://whatworks.ed.gov/).

	Phonics
Adolescent Proficient Readers	• Automatically recognize letter-sound correspondences and apply this knowledge to decode and spell words. • Utilize an awareness of syllable types to decode words effectively. • Leverage their understanding of morphemes (prefixes, suffixes, and roots) to decode and spell words. • Employ a word analysis routine that integrates syllable and morpheme knowledge, along with flexing vowel sounds, to read unfamiliar multisyllabic words.
Adolescent Struggling Readers	• May have gaps in their knowledge of basic letter-sound correspondences. • May be able to read one-syllable words but lack knowledge of syllable types, making it difficult to decode multisyllabic words. • Often lack awareness of morphemes (prefixes, suffixes, and roots). • Usually do not use a word analysis routine when reading unfamiliar multisyllabic words, often relying on guessing the pronunciation based on the first few letters. • Are often hesitant to read aloud in front of their classmates.

Figure 9.7. Proficient and struggling readers: Phonics. (*Sources:* Boardman et al., 2008; Murray et al., 2010.)

Intervention Recommendations: Phonics

1. Address Gaps in Basic Phonics Knowledge

The first suggestion in the research guide *Providing Reading Interventions for Students in Grades 4–9* (Vaughn et al., 2022) is to assess students' word-reading skills and provide instruction on vowel and consonant letter-sounds and combinations where gaps exist. Students need a solid understanding of how letters represent sounds in order to read longer, multisyllabic words.

The authors offer the following guidance for addressing gaps in basic phonics knowledge:

- Some students will need intervention instruction to master common vowel and consonant letter-sounds and their combinations.
- For students who have already mastered basic sounds and combinations, instruction should focus on more advanced elements, such as **-dge** in *dodge* or vowel teams with three or four letters representing a single sound, like **-ough** in *thorough*.
- For students who can apply this knowledge to complex two-syllable words, instruction should advance to three-syllable words to broaden their skills.

2. A Routine for Multisyllabic Words

The second suggestion is to teach students a consistent routine for reading multisyllabic words. The guide recommends using the same routine across all classes, providing clear steps for breaking longer words into manageable parts and blending them together. Students with reading difficulties particularly benefit from modeling and guided practice with this routine until they can apply it independently.

3. Spelling

The third suggestion is to integrate spelling instruction into phonics lessons. Spelling reinforces students' learning of vowel and consonant letter-sounds and their combinations. Instruction should include practice with both monosyllabic and multisyllabic words. As students spell multisyllabic words, they should be encouraged to consider how many meaningful word parts (morphemes) and syllables are in each word.

Figure 9.8. Intervention recommendations: Phonics. (Adapted from Vaughn, S., Gersten, R., Dimino, J., Taylor, M. J., Newman-Gonchar, R., Krowka, S., Kieffer, M. J., McKeown, M., Reed, D., Sanchez, M., St. Martin, K., Wexler, J., Morgan, S., Yañez, A., & Jayanthi, M. [2022]. *Providing reading interventions for students in grades 4–9* [WWC 2022007]. National Center for Education Evaluation and Regional Assistance [NCEE], Institute of Education Sciences, U.S. Department of Education. https://whatworks.ed.gov/)

Phonics Scope and Sequence

Letter-sound correspondences (ordered from basic to more complex):

Consonants

- Start with the most common consonants (*b* /b/, *c* /k/, *d* /d/, *f* /f/, *g* /g/, *h* /h/, *k* /k/, *l* /l/, *m* /m/, *n* /n/, *p* /p/, *s* /s/, *t* /t/)
- Then, introduce the less common (*j* /j/, *r* /r/, *v* /v/, *w* /w/, *y* /y/, *z* /z/, *x* /ks/, *q* (with *u*) /kw/)

Short Vowels

- Begin teaching after a few common consonants
- Combine with consonants to decode CVC words (e.g., *bat, nip, hog*)

Basic Consonant Digraphs

A combination of consonants that represent one unique sound, unlike the sound made by any of the individual letters of the digraph

- *ch* /ch/, *sh* /sh/, *ck* /k/, *th* /th/ (voiced and unvoiced)
- Combine with short vowels and consonants to decode CVC words (e.g., *sick, thin, shop, wish*)

Consonant Blends

A blend is the combined sounds of two or three consonants. In consonant blends, each letter retains its common sound. Students learn how to blend the sounds together rather than learning one new sound.

- Examples of initial consonant blends: *bl-, br-, cl-, cr-, dr-, dw-, fl-, fr-, gl-, gr-, pl-, pr-, scr-, sl, spl-, sp-, spr-, squ-, st-, str-, sw-, thr-, tr-, tw-*
- Examples of final consonant blends: *-ct, -f, -ld, -lf, -lk, -lp, -lt, -mp, -nd, -pt, -rd, -rk, -rm, -rn, -rp, -rt, -sk, -sp, -st*
- Combine with short vowels to decode CCVC or CVCC words (e.g., *slip, frog, lift, camp*)

ng and nk

- Examples: *sang, king, long, hung,* and *sank, pink, honk, dunk*

"Floss" Rule

If a single-syllable short-vowel word ends in *f, l, s,* or *z,* double the last letter.

- Examples: ***stuff, cliff,*** *fill, bill, stall, moss, kiss, glass, jazz, buzz*
- There are some exceptions: If the final *s* makes the /z/ sound, the *s* is not doubled (e.g., *as, is, was, his*).

Figure 9.9. Phonics scope and sequence. (Adapted by permission from Sedita, J. [2020e]. *Systematic phonics scope and sequence.* Literacy Lines. Keys to Literacy. https://keystoliteracy.com/blog/systematic-phonics-scope-and-sequence/ and Sedita, J. [2024c]. *Keys to beginning reading.* Keys to Literacy.)

Long-Vowel Sounds in Open Syllables

- Examples: *he, me, hi, no, o-pen, a-pron, a-corn, i-vy, i-ris, si-lo, e-ven, be-hind, bo-nus, mu-sic, tu-lip*
- Including *y* at the end of a word

  Examples: *my, why, by* (long *i*), and *ivy, pony, envy* (long *e*)

Long-Vowel – Silent *e* (Vowel-Consonant-e)
Adding an e at the end of a CVC (or CCVC) word or syllable changes the vowel from a short sound to a long sound.

- Examples: *bake, brake, shame, bite, drive, shine, bone, slope, stroke, cube, crude, mute*

Other Long-Vowel Patterns

- Words with *-ild,- ind, -old, -ost*
- Examples: *mild, child, kind, blind, cold, hold, host, most*

Vowel Pairs
A vowel pair is two adjacent vowels in the same syllable that represent a single speech sound. The sound made by a vowel combination may vary.

- Basic Vowel Pairs With One Frequent Long-Vowel Sound
  - Examples: *ai* (*pain*), *ay* (*pay*), *ee* (*feet*), *ey* (*key*), *ie* (*chief*), *oa* (*boat*), *oe* (*toe*), *ue* (*blue*), *au* (*August*)
- Vowel Pairs With More Than One Frequent Sound
  - Examples: *ea* (*eat, head*), *oo* (*moon, book*), *ou* (*out, soup*), *ow* (*cow, snow*)
- *au* and *aw*

  Examples: *pause, August, saw, claw*
- Diphthongs: a sound formed by the combination of two vowels in a single syllable, in which the sound begins as one vowel and moves toward another
- Examples of *oi/oy: coin, boil, boy, toy*
- Examples of *ou/ow: mouse, loud, cow, brown*

Vowel-r (basic)

- /er/ spelled as *er* (*her, bother*); *ir* (*sir*), *ur* (*fur, turtle*), *or* (*work, doctor*), *ear* (*earth, search*)
- /or/ spelled as *or* (*fork, store, morning*), ore (*ore, store*), *oor* (*poor, door*), *our* (*pour, four*)
- /ar/ spelled as *ar* (*car, farm, yard*)

Silent Letters

- *kn* (*knight*), *mb* (*thumb*), *wr* (*wreck*)
- vowel combinations *igh* and *eigh* words (*fight, tight, sigh, eight, weight, sleigh*)

Hard and Soft Sound: *c* and *g*

- When the letters *c* or *g* are followed by the letters *i, e,* or *y,* it changes the sound from hard (*c* /k/, *g* /g/) to soft (*c* /s/, *g* /j/).
- Examples: *face, price, cent, pencil, city, icy, gist, gem, huge, gym*

k/ck, ch/tch, and ge/dge
For the sound /k/ spelled as *k* at the end of a short word:

- If there is only a short vowel before the /k/, add *c.*
  - Examples: *tuck, lock, deck*
- If there is another consonant sound after the vowel, only use *k.*
  - Examples: *milk, pink, bulk, task*

For the sound /ch/ spelled as *ch* at the end of a short word:

- If there is only a short vowel before the /ch/, add *t.*
  - Examples: *hitch, batch, Scotch*
- If there is another consonant sound after the vowel, only use *ch.*
  - Examples: *lunch, bench*

For the sound /j/ spelled as *ge* at the end of a short word:

- If there is only a short vowel before the /j/, add *d.*
  - Examples: *badge, lodge, judge*
- If there is another consonant sound after the vowel, only use *ge.*
  - Examples: *plunge, hinge*

Figure 9.9. *(continued)*

Vowel-r (advanced)

- /air/ spelled as *air* (*fair, stair*), *are* (*share, dare*)
- /ear/ spelled as *ear* (*hear, year*), *eer* (*deer, cheer*)

Advanced Digraphs

- *wh* for /w/ or /hw/ (*whale, which*)
- *ph* for /f/ (*phone, graph*)
- *gh* for /f/ (*laugh, cough*)

ti, ci for /sh/

- Examples: *action, motion, special, musician*

tu for /ch/

- Examples: *picture, mixture, nature*

Figure 9.9. *(continued)*

	Fluency
Adolescent Proficient Readers	• Can automatically decode words with at least 95% accuracy and self-correct when mispronunciations occur. • Typically read grade-level texts at a rate of at least 145 words correct per minute, adjusting their pace based on the text's difficulty. • Pay attention to punctuation and group words into meaningful phases when reading aloud. • Read aloud with appropriate prosodic expression and intonation. • Effectively combine fluency and comprehension skills during reading.
Adolescent Struggling Readers	• Read slowly and haltingly, often spending excessive time decoding words. • When encountering unfamiliar words, they may skip them, guess their pronunciation, or attempt to sound out individual letters. • Frequently mispronounce words. • Often read aloud in a flat, monotone voice, neglecting prosodic expression. • Typically read in a choppy, word-by-word manner, disregarding punctuation. • Have limited comprehension because their attentional focus is on word reading.

Figure 9.10. Proficient and struggling readers: Fluency. (*Sources:* Boardman et al., 2008; Murray et al., 2010.)

INTERVENTION FOR WRITING

To meet the increasing writing demands in middle and high school, both general content-area and discipline-specific writing instruction and practice must occur throughout the school day. However, adolescents who struggle with writing will also require targeted intervention to develop foundational writing skills they did not fully acquire during the elementary grades.

Intervention for Gaps in Writing Skills: The Writing Rope

Intervention teachers can support struggling writers by helping them identify the task, audience, and purpose for a writing assignment. They can also teach them skills and strategies they need at each stage of the writing process (*Think, Plan, Write, Revise*), addressed in Chapter 5, "Teaching Text Structure," and Chapter 6, "Writing Instruction." These skills and strategies are organized into the five components of writing represented as strands of a rope in *The Writing Rope* framework (Sedita, 2019, 2023), which was also introduced previously in this book. The strands include the following:

- **Critical thinking:** Generate ideas; gather information; apply the writing process.
- **Syntax:** Write sophisticated, elaborated sentences.
- **Text structure:** Apply knowledge of paragraph and longer text structures; incorporate patterns of organization and related transitions.

Intervention Recommendations: Fluency

Repeated Reading
Research strongly supports the use of repeated oral reading to help students—especially those with reading difficulties—develop fluency. Consider the following instructional strategies (Boardman et al., 2008; Hasbrouck & Hougen, 2012; Lee & Yoon, 2017; Stevens et al., 2019; Vaughn et al., 2022):

- Vaughn and colleagues (2022) note that repeated reading can be effective in building fluency, but caution that "if not structured well, it can be perceived as a dull and discouraging task" (p. 12). To avoid this, provide a clear purpose for each repeated reading instead of focusing just on increasing speed. For example, when rereading the same passage, students might answer questions for the first read, identify unfamiliar words for the second, or reflect on the text's meaning for a final read.
- Offer feedback and prompt students to focus on their accuracy and rate during reading.
- Emphasize accuracy and expression, not just speed.
- Reading alongside a model is more effective than independent silent reading. Use partner reading, where a more fluent reader models fluent reading for a less fluent peer. Partners can take turns reading aloud to support each other.
- Choral reading in small groups allows students to practice reading aloud with support before reading independently.
- Whenever possible, select texts for repeated reading that are connected to subject-area content students are currently studying.
- Encourage students to track their progress toward fluency goals and reflect on their growth.

Reading With Prosody
Prosody refers to expressive reading that reflects phrasing, intonation, and emotion. Pauses, tempo, and emphasis on different words help readers better understand what they are reading. Fluency interventions should draw students' attention to the features of prosody by modeling why it matters. Vaughn and colleagues (2022) suggest that teachers first read a short paragraph aloud without expression and without observing punctuation. Then, they should reread the same passage, this time demonstrating prosody. After both readings, teachers and students can discuss which version was easier to understand. During fluency practice, teachers should encourage students to pause at commas, stop at periods, raise or lower their voices for question marks, and express appropriate emotion while reading.

Wide Reading Practice
Teachers should allocate time each week in intervention classes for students to engage in wide reading (Vaughen et al., 2022). This involves reading a variety of texts on different topics and in different writing styles. These texts should be at the upper end of students' instructional reading level and aligned with grade-level content. Wide reading not only improves fluency but also exposes students to new vocabulary, content, and text structures. To increase engagement, choose high-interest topics relevant to older students, and when possible, allow students to select the texts they read aloud for fluency practice.

Low Accuracy Rate
For students whose accuracy rates are below 95%, this may indicate that they have not yet developed sufficient phonics knowledge to decode words effectively, particularly multisyllabic words. In addition to the suggestions described previously, these students may need targeted, explicit phonics instruction.

Figure 9.11. Intervention recommendations: Fluency. (Adapted from Vaughn, S., Gersten, R., Dimino, J., Taylor, M. J., Newman-Gonchar, R., Krowka, S., Kieffer, M. J., McKeown, M., Reed, D., Sanchez, M., St. Martin, K., Wexler, J., Morgan, S., Yañez, A., & Jayanthi, M. [2022]. *Providing reading interventions for students in Grades 4–9* [WWC 2022007]. National Center for Education Evaluation and Regional Assistance [NCEE], Institute of Education Sciences, U.S. Department of Education.)

- **Writing craft:** Consider the task, audience, and purpose; use craft techniques to enhance writing.
- **Transcription:** Spell accurately and write or type fluently and automatically.

As with reading, students vary widely in the writing components that require intervention. Some older students may struggle with writing basic sentences and paragraphs, may lack awareness of the stages of the writing process, or may have limited strategies for carrying out each stage. Others may need support with higher-level skills, such as understanding text structures or using note taking and summarizing strategies to support writing as a learning tool.

Analyze Student Writing Samples

Intervention educators can analyze student writing samples using the questions in Figure 9.12 to help determine which writing skills and strategies should be targeted for intervention instruction. (A reproducible copy of these questions is available with the downloads for this chapter.)

A CLOSER LOOK AT LEARNING DISABILITIES, EXECUTIVE FUNCTIONS, AND ENGLISH LEARNERS

This chapter began by noting that there are many reasons why students struggle with reading and writing, including environmental and neurobiological causes. The next section provides additional information about LDs, executive functions, and ELs.

Learning Disabilities

The federal Individuals with Disabilities Education Act (IDEA 2004) defines a specific LD as

> a disorder in one or more of the basic psychological processes involved in understanding or in using language, spoken or written, that may manifest itself in the imperfect ability to listen, think, speak, read, write, spell, or to do mathematical calculations, including conditions such as perceptual disabilities, brain injury, minimal brain dysfunction, dyslexia, and developmental aphasia. [34 CFR Section 300.8 (c)(10)]

It does not include visual, hearing, or motor disabilities; intellectual disability; emotional disturbance; or environmental, cultural, or economic disadvantage.

Questions to Analyze Student Writing

Overall

- Does this writing sample reflect grade-level writing ability?
- What positive feedback could you give the student about their writing?

Transcription Skills

- What do you notice about the student's spelling and handwriting?

Writing Craft

- Task, audience, purpose (TAP): Did the student complete the assigned task? Did they consider the audience and purpose when writing the piece?
- Word choice: Did the student use precise, varied, and engaging vocabulary?
- Literary devices: Did the student incorporate any literary devices such as figurative language, allusion, or hyperbole?

Text Structure

- Overall structure: Did the student include an introduction and conclusion? Are the ideas and information in the body organized logically?
- Paragraph structure: Are the paragraphs well-structured?
- Patterns of organization: Which pattern(s) of organization did the student use (description/explanation, sequence, cause and effect, compare and contrast, problem and solution)?
- Transitions: Did the student use grade-appropriate transition words and phrases?

Syntax

- What is the overall quality of the sentences?
- Are there any sentence fragments or run-on sentences?
- Is punctuation used correctly?

Critical Thinking

- Writing process: Is there evidence that the student engaged in prewriting or revision?
- Generating ideas, gathering information: To what extent did the student integrate information from text or other sources into the writing piece?

Figure 9.12. Questions to analyze student writing.

Dysgraphia is a common LD that affects writing. Dysgraphia may make it difficult to form letters or write within a defined space, cause difficulty with writing complete and grammatically correct sentences, and affect the ability to compose organized writing pieces.

Dyslexia is the most common LD causing difficulties with both reading and writing. Most experts agree that it affects between 10% and 15% of the population (Cowen, 2016a). It can be mild to severe, ranging from minor spelling challenges to a major impact on the ability to learn to read. In its more severe forms, dyslexia will qualify a student for special education, special accommodations, or extra support services.

In the early grades, dyslexia is characterized by difficulties with accurate and/or fluent word recognition and by poor spelling. However, over time, the secondary consequences of dyslexia often create difficulty with reading comprehension and limited growth in vocabulary and background knowledge if students do not read enough high-quality, challenging text. Over time, an additional consequence is less motivation to read. The older students with dyslexia become, the more ground they have to cover to catch up in critical reading skills, impacting the intensity and duration of necessary intervention.

Interventions for students with dyslexia and difficulty with word reading should address phonics instruction to support decoding and spelling of words, including explicit instruction for phonics concepts and practice using decodable text, syllable types and strategies for reading multisyllabic words, and morphology (prefixes, suffixes, roots). Intervention should also include fluency instruction and practice to develop automatic word reading ability (accuracy, rate, prosody). Older students with dyslexia who have not developed vocabulary and comprehension strategies will also need intervention in these areas.

Executive Functions

Executive functions are mental processes that students and adults use to manage tasks and achieve goals. As students move into the upper grades, their ability to successfully read and write becomes increasingly dependent on their ability to apply executive function processes (Cartwright, 2015; Meltzer, 2010). These processes can be described as follows:

- *Goal setting* includes setting a goal for a task, deciding what tasks are necessary to complete a goal, formulating actions in advance to approach a task in an organized and efficient manner, and planning the order in which tasks should be completed.
- *Organizing* includes the ability to impose order and create systems for managing information and objects, and to recognize successful use of such orders and systems.
- *Cognitive flexibility* includes the ability to consider multiple pieces of information, ideas, or tasks at one time and actively switch between them when engaging in a task. It requires attentional control to shift focus.
- *Working memory* is the capacity to hold information in mind while working with part of that information. It includes storing information while processing it.
- *Self-monitoring* includes the ability to step back and reflect on one's own thoughts, perspectives, and mental processes and assess their effectiveness. It refers to ways students edit and correct their behavior and schoolwork.
- *Attention and inhibition* include the ability to ignore and resist distraction and stay on task. It is sometimes referred to as impulse control.

Reading comprehension is often affected by executive function deficits. Intervention instruction should focus on equipping students with the cognitive skills and strategies that will help them regulate their learning while reading, including use of the comprehension strategies suggested in Chapter 4, "Comprehension Instruction" (Cartwright, 2015; Katzir et al., 2018; Meltzer, 2018; Sedita, 2024a). This includes reviewing vocabulary and background knowledge before reading, using graphic organizers, teaching awareness of text structure, and strategies such as note taking, summarizing, and question generation. Planning tools such as calendars and assignment books help students organize their time and school tasks.

Writing at every stage of the writing process is also affected by executive function deficits. Intervention instruction should focus on the suggestions for explicit instruction in Chapter 6, "Writing Instruction." This includes teaching students to follow every stage of the writing process (*Think, Plan, Write, Revise*) and to use prewriting strategies and graphic organizers to plan before writing. Writing templates and lists of words are helpful, as are user-friendly feedback and revision checklists to support revision. Students also benefit from clear, specific product goals and expectations for writing assignments, such as the details in a Writing Assignment Guide (WAG).

English Learners

Older ELs are held to the same accountability standards in content classrooms as their native English-speaking peers. They therefore must perform double the work as they learn to speak, listen, read, and write in English at the same time they are expected to use these literacy skills to learn content (Short & Fitzsimmons, 2007).

ELs benefit from the same instruction for the five components of reading that all students need: phonemic awareness, phonics, fluency, vocabulary, and comprehension, with adjustments that take into account their individual needs (August & Shanahan, 2006; Cárdenas-Hagan, 2020). This is true for reading intervention for older ELs who struggle with reading—interventions should focus on those components where students have gaps in skills, keeping in mind that there is no one-size-fits-all solution to the literacy challenges that confront some adolescent ELs.

Factors teachers should consider include students' level of proficiency in English and their native language, knowledge of academic subject matter, expectations of the school experience, level of English proficiency spoken in the home, and if a student is a newcomer or born in the United States. Students who can read and write fluently in their native language will learn English literacy skills more readily than ELs with limited literacy skills. Elsa Cárdenas-Hagan explains (2020):

> English learners bring with them prior knowledge, experiences and strengths related to language and learning that educators must find ways to identify and build upon. ELs enter school with varying literacy skills. Some may be able to read and write in their native language, whereas others may only have oral language skills in their native language. Likewise, some ELs enter school with basic reading and writing skills in English, whereas others present very limited English proficiency skills. (p. 41)

Providing Instruction to Support English Learners The research guide *Teaching Academic Content and Literacy to English Learners in Elementary and Middle School* (Baker et al., 2014) focuses on ELs with limited English proficiency in Grades 4–8 and the language and literacy skills they need to be successful in school. Baker and colleagues recommend that teachers do the following:

1. Teach a set of academic vocabulary words intensively across several days using a variety of instructional activities.
2. Integrate oral and written English language instruction into content-area teaching.
3. Provide regular, structured opportunities to develop written language skills.
4. Provide small-group instructional intervention to students struggling in areas of literacy and English language development.

Figure 9.13 provides additional details about these recommendations from the guide. Note that many of the instructional suggestions align with suggestions shared in multiple chapters in this book.

For Grades 6–12, the *Double the Work* report recommends the following nine instructional practices for developing literacy in adolescent ELs (Short & Fitzsimmons, 2007).

1. Integrate all four language skills into instruction from the start (listening, speaking, reading, writing).
2. Teach the components and processes of reading and writing.
3. Teach reading comprehension strategies.
4. Focus on vocabulary development.
5. Build and activate background knowledge.
6. Teach language through content and themes.
7. Use native language strategically.
8. Pair technology with existing interventions.
9. Motivate ELs through choice. (p. 1)

Making Content Available to English Learners While ELs are continuing to develop their English language ability, they also must keep up with content learning across the school day. Teachers should keep their academic and linguistic needs in mind (supporting the development of their language and literacy learning) when developing lessons. For example, in science class, the content objective might be studying how a saguaro cactus survives in the desert, whereas the language objective might be teaching cause-and-effect text structure and the transition words that signal this pattern. In history class, the content objective might be teaching students how to read and interpret a primary document, whereas the language objective might include providing explicit instruction for how to deconstruct complex sentences.

Sheltered Instruction Observation Protocol (SIOP) is an instructional model that emphasizes the integration of language and content instruction to make content easier to learn for ELs

(Echevarria et al., 2016). Components of the SIOP model include building background knowledge, providing comprehensible input, incorporating interaction, and incorporating practice and application. Descriptions of instructional suggestions for these components are provided in Figure 9.14. Note that although ELs benefit from these practices, they represent effective pedagogy for all students.

Recommendations for Teaching Literacy to English Learners

Recommendation 1: Teach a set of academic vocabulary words intensively across several days using a variety of instructional activities.

- Choose a brief, engaging piece of informational text that includes academic vocabulary as a platform for intensive academic vocabulary instruction.
- Choose a small set of academic vocabulary for in-depth instruction.
- Teach academic vocabulary in depth using multiple modalities (writing, speaking, listening). Use visuals or images as supports.
- Teach word-learning strategies to help students independently figure out the meaning of words.

Recommendation 2: Integrate oral and written English language instruction into content-area teaching.

- Strategically use instructional tools—such as short videos, visuals, and graphic organizers—to anchor instruction and help students make sense of content.
- Explicitly teach the content-specific academic vocabulary, as well as the general academic vocabulary that support it, during content-area instruction.
- Provide daily opportunities for students to talk about content in pairs or small groups.
- Provide writing opportunities to extend student learning and understanding of the content material.

Recommendation 3: Provide regular, structured opportunities to develop written language skills.

- Provide writing assignments that are anchored in content and focused on developing academic language as well as writing skills.
- For all writing assignments, provide language-based supports to facilitate students' entry into, and continued development of, writing.
- Use small groups or pairs to provide opportunities for students to work and talk together on varied aspects of writing.
- Assess students' writing periodically to identify instructional needs and provide positive, constructive feedback in response.

Recommendation 4: Provide small-group instructional intervention to students struggling in areas of literacy and English language development.

- Use available assessment information to identify students who demonstrate persistent struggles with aspects of language and literacy development. In addition to data from standardized assessments, teachers can assess students' academic language proficiency by providing authentic opportunities to demonstrate their language ability.
- Design the content of small-group instruction to target students' identified needs.
- Provide additional instruction in small groups consisting of three to five students to students struggling with language and literacy.
- For students who struggle with basic foundational reading skills, spend time not only on these skills but also on vocabulary development and listening and reading comprehension strategies.
- Provide scaffolded instruction that includes frequent opportunities for students to practice and review newly learned skills and concepts in various contexts over several lessons to ensure retention.

Figure 9.13. Recommendations for teaching literacy to English learners. (Adapted from Baker, S., Lesaux, N., Jayanthi, M., Dimino, J., Proctor, C. P., Morris, J., Gersten, R., Haymond, K., Kieffer, M. J., Linan-Thompson, S., & Newman-Gonchar, R. [2014]. *Teaching academic content and literacy to English learners in elementary and middle school* [NCEE 2014-4012]. National Center for Education Evaluation and Regional Assistance [NCEE], Institute of Education Sciences, U.S. Department of Education.)

SUMMARY

This chapter identifies several reasons why older students may struggle with reading and writing. Depending on individual student needs, one or more components of reading or writing may require intervention instruction. The chapter offers multiple suggestions for how general education teachers can support students with literacy difficulties in the classroom. It then provides an overview of intervention instruction, including related research, the MTSS framework, and the characteristics of effective interventions, such as smaller group sizes, increased instructional time, and individualized support. Specific intervention strategies are outlined for vocabulary, comprehension, phonics, fluency, and writing. The chapter concludes with a closer examination of LDs, executive functions, and the needs of ELs.

Components of the SIOP Model

Build Background Knowledge
Teachers focus on helping students connect new concepts with their existing knowledge. They do this by previewing vocabulary, using visuals, and providing context. As teachers tap into what students already know, they identify misinformation and fill in knowledge gaps.

Provide Comprehensible Input
Teachers present content in ways that students can understand. This includes providing visuals, graphic organizers and charts, hands-on demonstrations, modeling, role playing, and the use of gestures and pantomime to make concepts clear. It also includes presenting information through simplified language including restating, summarizing key points, and paraphrasing. The goal is to support students' understanding despite language barriers.

Incorporate Interaction
Teachers create opportunities for students to develop conversational and academic language through interactions with the teacher and peers about the content they are learning. This includes partner and small-group discussions along with collaborative reading and writing tasks. This provides opportunities for English learners to practice using new vocabulary and language structures, ask questions, and elaborate on their own or another's ideas.

Incorporate Practice and Application
Teachers use a variety of activities that help students practice and apply both the content and language skills they are learning. These activities can include group assignments and partner work with writing tasks, creative projects, and discussions.

Figure 9.14. Components of the SIOP model. (*Source:* Echevarria, Vogt, & Short, 2016.)

REFLECTION QUESTIONS

1. What is the difference between environmental and neurobiological causes of literacy difficulty?
2. How can the Simple View of Reading be used to explain why some older students struggle with reading?
3. How can The Writing Rope framework be applied to identify appropriate intervention instruction for students who struggle with writing?
4. What are the four characteristics of effective interventions discussed in the chapter?
5. What is your reaction to the differences between proficient readers and struggling readers in the areas of vocabulary, comprehension, phonics, and fluency? Do you observe these differences among the students you work with?
6. Identify at least two intervention suggestions for vocabulary, comprehension, phonics, or fluency that resonate most with you.
7. What information from the section on learning disabilities, such as dyslexia, will inform your instruction?
8. What information in the section about executive functions will inform your instruction?
9. The chapter notes that older ELs must do double the work, as they are learning to speak, listen, read, and write in English while simultaneously using these skills to learn academic content. What is your reaction to this point?

Questions to Analyze Student Writing

Overall

- Does this writing sample reflect grade-level writing ability?
- What positive feedback could you give the student about their writing?

Transcription Skills

- What do you notice about the student's spelling and handwriting?

Writing Craft

- Task, audience, purpose (TAP): Did the student complete the assigned task? Did they consider the audience and purpose when writing the piece?
- Word choice: Did the student use precise, varied, and engaging vocabulary?
- Literary devices: Did the student incorporate any literary devices such as figurative language, allusion, or hyperbole?

Text Structure

- Overall structure: Did the student include an introduction and conclusion? Are the ideas and information in the body organized logically?
- Paragraph structure: Are the paragraphs well-structured?
- Patterns of organization: Which pattern(s) of organization did the student use (description/explanation, sequence, cause and effect, compare and contrast, problem and solution)?
- Transitions: Did the student use grade-appropriate transition words and phrases?

Syntax

- What is the overall quality of the sentences?
- Are there any sentence fragments or run-on sentences?
- Is punctuation used correctly?

Critical Thinking

- Writing process: Is there evidence that the student engaged in prewriting or revision?
- Generating ideas, gathering information: To what extent did the student integrate information from text or other sources into the writing piece?

10

Data-Driven Reading Intervention

The use of ongoing formative and summative assessment of students and programs is essential to successful adolescent reading programs (Biancarosa & Snow, 2006). Assessment data is needed to guide instructional decisions, especially for intervention instruction. The guide *What Content-Area Teachers Need to Know About Adolescent Literacy* (National Institute for Literacy, 2007) explains it this way:

> Effective instruction depends on sound instructional decision-making, which, in turn, depends on reliable data regarding students' strengths and weaknesses, and progress in learning content and developing literacy. Adolescent reading difficulties may involve one or more literacy components. . . without assessments that are sensitive to the contributions of each component to overall reading ability, teachers will not be able to target their instruction to the skills and strategies most in need of improvement. (p. 27)

This chapter summarizes the role of assessment in guiding reading intervention instruction. It explains different types of assessments and the specific purpose they serve. Recommendations are provided for using assessment data to identify non-proficient readers and to inform decisions about appropriate intervention instruction. In addition, the chapter offers suggestions for analyzing assessment data through a problem-solving process at the student, class, and grade levels.

ASSESSMENT AND THE MULTI-TIERED SYSTEM OF SUPPORT FRAMEWORK

The multi-tiered system of support (MTSS) framework was introduced in Chapter 9, "Adolescent Learners With Literacy Difficulties." This framework promotes student reading achievement by providing instruction across three tiers. Tier 1 is core instruction delivered to all students, Tier 2 is supplemental instruction provided to students who do not demonstrate grade-level skills, and Tier 3 is more intensive intervention instruction for students who have not responded sufficiently to Tier 2 instruction.

The Role of Assessment

Research finds that using assessment data to inform reading instruction decisions leads to improved student outcomes (Hamilton et al., 2009; Wohlstetter et al., 2008). A repeating assessment cycle that supports intervention instruction is a hallmark of the MTSS framework. Assessment data are used to identify students who may need Tier 2 or Tier 3 instructional support and to determine instructional goals based on individual student needs. These goals may focus on one or more of the five components of reading. Once instruction is provided, reassessment in the form of progress monitoring is used to determine if the goals are being met through that instruction.

Multiple data sources are important because no single assessment provides all the information needed to make informed instructional decisions. There are multiple options for formal and informal reading assessments (Hamilton et al., 2009), including annual statewide assessments (typically tied to state literacy standards), commercially published assessments, and school- or district-developed assessments. This includes end-of-year assessments. Data from interim assessments that are administered during the school year allows teachers to measure changes in students' skills on an ongoing basis. Teachers can examine samples of student classwork along with assessment data to guide instructional decisions.

Making Instructional Decisions Through Data Analysis

The role of classroom teachers in analyzing assessment data differs between the elementary and secondary grades. In the elementary grades, classroom teachers typically work with 20–30 students and develop a close understanding of their needs. These teachers play a key role in administering assessments, analyzing results, and making instructional decisions for both core instruction for all students and interventions for students with reading difficulties. Phonics, fluency, and comprehension assessments are administered to all students in kindergarten (K) through Grade 3, and fluency and comprehension assessments are provided to all students in Grades 4 and 5. These assessments are typically administered three times during the school year: at the beginning, middle, and end.

In contrast, middle and high school classroom teachers are not positioned to play the same role as elementary teachers when it comes to assessment, primarily due to practical constraints. Secondary content-area teachers often instruct 125 or more students across multiple periods per day. With the exception of a universal screening assessment administered at the beginning of the year to identify students reading below grade level, most reading assessments in secondary schools are diagnostic or for progress monitoring. These are typically administrated and analyzed by intervention educators.

FOUR TYPES OF ASSESSMENTS

There are four main types of reading assessments. *Screening* and *diagnostic* assessments are used to identify students with reading difficulties and determine the focus for intervention instruction. *Progress monitoring* assessments determine effectiveness of instruction and are administered during the school year. *Summative* assessments measure overall gains or losses in student performance and are typically administered at the end of the school year.

Screening

Screening assessments are typically administered to all students at the beginning of the year to identify who might be at risk for reading difficulty. They provide an initial indication of which students might need extra instruction or intensive intervention if they are to reach grade-level reading standards by the end of the school year. The goal of these assessments is to identify students early before they start to fail. Sometimes information from the previous year's summative assessments can be used as part of the screening process. Screening assessments are not diagnostic—they do not provide detailed information about *why* a student is struggling. This type of assessment answers these questions: *Who is at risk? Which students need support?*

Diagnostic

Diagnostic assessments are used to provide information about individual students who have difficulty with reading. The results help teachers determine the cause of that difficulty and plan appropriate supplemental instruction or intensive intervention based on individual student needs. There are many kinds of diagnostic assessments that range from informal reading tasks to formal assessments used for psychoeducational testing. Formal assessments tend to be lengthy but provide in-depth, reliable assessment of essential reading skills. Torgesen (2006) notes that it is important to distinguish between diagnostic tests and diagnostic information:

> Diagnostic information is any knowledge about a child's skills and abilities that is useful in planning instruction. It can come from student work, teacher observations, or other tests, as well as diagnostic tests. Diagnostic tests are one important way to obtain diagnostic information that can help guide interventions for students who are experiencing difficulty learning to read. However, reliable and valid diagnostic information can come from sources other than formal diagnostic tests. (p. 6)

Diagnostic assessments should be administered only for adolescent students who are having difficulty learning to read. This type of assessment answers these questions: *Why is the problem(s) happening? What support is needed? What is the next step for instruction?*

Progress Monitoring

Progress monitoring assessments are sometimes called formative assessments and are given periodically to determine whether students are making adequate progress. The primary goal of these assessments is to determine if the instructional practices being used are enabling students to make sufficient progress related to the development of reading skills. The focus is on developing student learning. Progress monitoring is especially helpful to make sure that students at risk for reading difficulty are making adequate progress with the intervention instruction provided and to identify any students who may be falling behind. This type of assessment answers these questions: *Is the support working? Should instruction change or stay the same?*

Summative

Summative assessments are sometimes called outcome assessments. The most common are standardized tests that are group administered, typically at the end of the school year, and are used to give school leaders and teachers feedback about the overall effectiveness of a reading curriculum and program. The focus is on measuring student learning at a given point in time. The results help determine if the instruction provided by all the educators in the school was sufficient to help all students achieve grade-level reading standards by the end of each year. This type of assessment answers this question: *Did the instruction work?*

RELIABILITY, VALIDITY, AND OTHER ASSESSMENT TERMINOLOGY

Reliability refers to how consistently a test provides dependable, consistent measurement of a skill or ability. If a test is reliable, the same result should be achieved regardless of who administers the test. Personal judgment to determine a score should not be part of the process. Essential questions related to reliability include the following: *Can you trust the consistency of the scores? Are the test scores reliable between test administrators? Testing contexts? Test forms?*

A test is *valid* if it measures the skill or ability it says it is measuring. A test is only valid if it is being used for the target purposes for which it was designed. Essential questions related to validity include the following: *Does the test measure what it is supposed to measure? Are we using the test for the right purpose?*

The four categories discussed above include many types of assessments ranging from standardized tests to brief quizzes and other everyday classroom activities. Figure 10.1 defines additional terminology used to describe assessments—*norm-referenced, criterion-referenced, curriculum-based measurement (CBM), formative*—with examples of each.

A SECONDARY READING INSTRUCTION MODEL

Figure 10.2 illustrates common learning paths for proficient and non-proficient readers (Sedita, 2004b). The model uses assessment to determine students' needs and instruction paths. A reading screening assessment is given to all students at the beginning of the school year to identify students who are

Assessment Terminology

Norm-Referenced Assessments
These are formal, standardized assessments intended to compare a student's reading ability to other students in their peer group—typically, students in the same grade across the nation. Scores typically rank students from lowest to highest performing using percentile ranking or grade equivalent. A student's score can be used to gauge where the student is in relation to other students.
Example: If a student scores in the 90th percentile rank for reading comprehension, they are performing better than most of their peers. If the student scores in the 30th percentile rank, they are performing lower than most of their peers.

Criterion-Referenced Assessments
This type of assessment is designed to measure if a student has met a standard or criteria for learning a specific reading skill. It does not compare students; it only assesses how well a particular student knows the skill being tested. These can be formal or informal assessments that are often administered before and after instruction to measure growth in a particular skill. If the student falls short, additional instruction can be provided to help the student achieve proficiency with the skill. The criterion can be a certain percentage of items completed successfully or a state assessment benchmark.
Examples: A criterion-referenced assessment might measure how many letter-sound correspondences students have learned for basic phonics knowledge, or how many new words a student has learned in a content unit of study.

Curriculum Based Measurement
A curriculum-based measurement, often referred to as a CBM, is a criterion-referenced assessment used to find out how students are progressing in learning basic reading skills. The reading skill measures are tied to skills taught as part of a reading curriculum or program. CBM is a simple set of procedures that provide measurement of achievement, and administration time tends to be relatively short (1–5 minutes). These assessments are often used for progress monitoring, but they can also be used as screening and diagnostic assessments.
Examples: A CBM can be used to assess oral reading fluency by measuring how many words a student can read correctly in a 1-minute reading.

Formative Assessments
Formative assessments are used by teachers, inside classrooms, to determine whether students are learning what is taught. These assessments help teachers make instructional decisions.
Examples: End-of-chapter quizzes and tests, writing assignments such as summarizing, or responses to essay questions determine if students comprehended subject-area information when reading. One-to-one conferencing with teachers and participation in classroom discussion can also generate formative assessment data.

Figure 10.1. Assessment terminology. (From Sedita, J. [2024b]. *Keys to beginning reading.* Keys to Literacy; reprinted by permission.)

non-proficient readers. From that point, their paths diverge. Ideally, a standardized, norm-referenced assessment that measures reading comprehension should be used. If such an assessment is unavailable, results from English language arts state assessments may serve as an alternative.

Proficient Reader Path

Based on the screening assessment, students who demonstrate the ability to read and comprehend grade-level texts are identified as proficient readers. These readers need instruction to continue developing academic vocabulary, apply knowledge of text structure and comprehension strategies, and use writing to support learning. Tier 1 reading instruction for these students takes place in regular classrooms, delivered by subject-area teachers. This instruction needs to address increasingly more challenging information and texts as they move through middle and high school grades.

Non-Proficient Reader Paths

Students identified as non-proficient readers need additional, diagnostic reading assessment to determine the nature and severity of their reading difficulties, as well as the specific components of reading that need supplemental instruction. Based on diagnostic assessment, non-proficient readers will typically fall into two subcategories: *weak* and *struggling,* whose paths are slightly different, as explained in the following sections. The number of students who fall in the non-proficient reader category varies across schools, as does the number of students who fall in the weak and struggling subcategories.

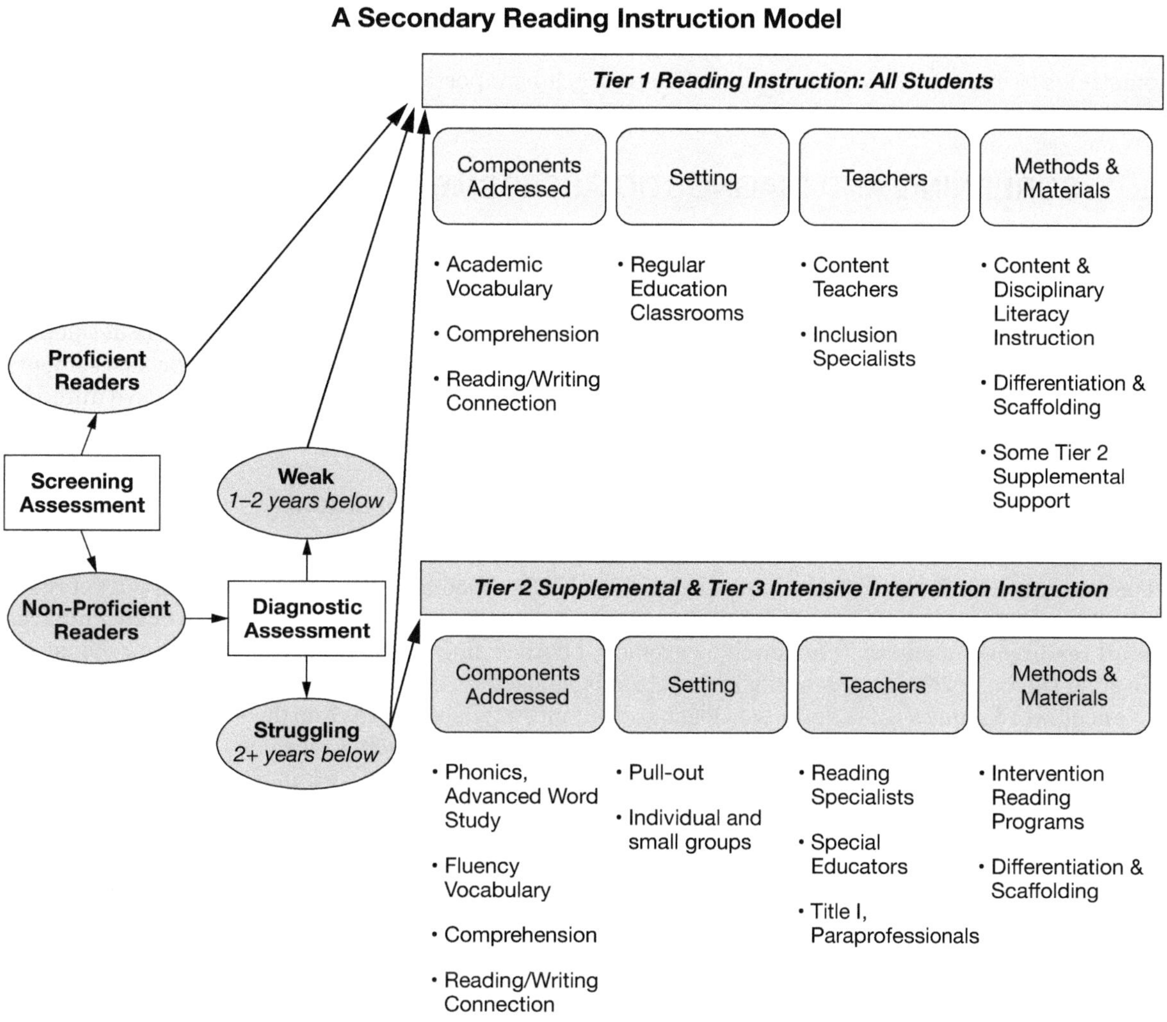

Figure 10.2. A secondary reading instruction model. (From Sedita, J. [2004b]. *Middle and high school reading achievement: A school-wide approach.* Keys to Literacy; reprinted by permission.)

Weak Reader Path These students have reading skills that are between 1 and 2 years below grade level and, typically, writing skills that are at least as low as their reading skills. Their difficulty with reading may be due to gaps in one or more reading components. Reading is challenging for these students, especially reading complex discipline-specific texts.

However, some are able to succeed in content classrooms, and if they are not given a screening assessment, their reading difficulties may go unnoticed. Given the potentially large number of non-proficient readers within a school, and given the limited resources available in most schools to provide intensive intervention in pull-out settings, there is a good chance that weak readers will only have access to Tier 2 supplemental support provided within regular classrooms in the form of differentiation and scaffolding.

Struggling Reader Path These students have reading skills that are 2 or more years below grade level. Their reading difficulty is typically due to gaps in two or more reading components. Reading and writing are very challenging for these students. Some have a history of reading difficulty identified in the elementary grades, some may be diagnosed as having a learning disability, and some may have individualized education programs (IEPs).

These students are the non-proficient readers most likely to have access to Tier 2 or Tier 3 intervention in pull-out settings. The amount of time spent with this kind of intervention is often limited, sometimes to one period or fewer per day. Therefore, it is important for teachers of all subjects to provide Tier 2 support in regular classrooms where these students spend most of the school day.

SCREENING AND DIAGNOSTIC ASSESSMENT FOR GRADES 5–12

A reliable method for identifying struggling readers should include "an initial screening test or a threshold score on a required reading test and subsequent use of a diagnostic reading test that must be administered, scored, and interpreted by a specialist" (Kamil et al., 2008, p. 34). Once teachers have identified the learning needs of non-proficient students through diagnostic assessments, they should develop an intervention instruction plan that targets each student's individual needs. If diagnostic assessments are not used, students may be assigned to an intervention class with students who may have different instructional needs.

How It Differs From Elementary Assessment

Screening and diagnostic assessment for adolescents is different from elementary assessment. In the elementary grades K–4, when students are learning skills associated with all five components of reading, screening assessments are given to determine if students have reached grade-level benchmarks for all reading components (phonemic awareness, phonics, fluency, vocabulary, and comprehension). Through the end of Grade 4, reading instruction is focused on expanding beginning phonics skills to advanced word study skills as students learn to read multisyllabic words and developing fluency levels to more than 130 words correct per minute (WCPM) with at least 95% accuracy. It is also focused on expanding vocabulary knowledge, as well as teaching students how to use knowledge of text structure and comprehension strategies to read and understand text. Therefore, elementary screening and progress monitoring during the school year should assess phonics, fluency, vocabulary, and comprehension, plus phonemic awareness in the primary grades.

Once students move into Grade 5 and are readily able to read and comprehend grade-level text, it can be assumed they have sufficient phonics and advanced word study skills, grade-level fluency, grade-level vocabulary knowledge, and comprehension strategies. A reading screening assessment should therefore focus on identifying which students can comprehend text and which cannot. Students who can comprehend grade-level text based on this assessment do not need any further assessment. Students who have difficulty with reading comprehension are given diagnostic assessments to identify which reading components may require intervention instruction.

A Screening and Diagnostic Assessment Plan

Sedita (2011, 2024d) developed the *Reading Assessment Plan for Grades 5–12,* which uses screening and diagnostic assessment to identify students who do not have grade-level reading skills and determine which components of reading might require instructional support for these students.

Figure 10.3 provides a graphic and description of the steps in this plan. (A full-size, reproducible copy of this plan is available with the downloads for this chapter.) Note that students at Step 1 who have grade-level reading comprehension skills do not require further assessment. As indicated by the arrow pointing to the first box on the left, these students benefit from Tier 1, high-quality instruction in all subject areas to continue growing their vocabulary and comprehension skills. Those students who are having difficulty with reading comprehension will follow the path on the right, proceeding through Steps 2–4 based on assessment findings at each step. A small set of students who have difficulty with all reading components will continue through all the steps.

ASSESSMENTS TO SUPPORT INTERVENTION INSTRUCTION

Reading assessment is essential for supporting effective intervention instruction for adolescents. The research guide *Using Student Achievement Data to Support Instructional Decision Making*

(Hamilton et al., 2009) describes the value of assessment data:

> Using data systematically to ask questions and obtain insight about student progress is a logical way to monitor continuous improvement and tailor instruction to the needs of each student. Armed with data and the means to harness the information data can provide, educators can make instructional changes aimed at improving student achievement, such as:
>
> - prioritizing instructional time;
> - targeting additional individual instruction for students who are struggling with particular topics;
> - more easily identifying individual students' strengths and instructional interventions that can help students continue to progress;
> - gauging the instructional effectiveness of classroom lessons;
> - refining instructional methods; and
> - examining schoolwide data to consider whether and how to adapt the curriculum based on information about students' strengths and weaknesses. (p. 5)

The remaining sections of this chapter describe how assessments can be used to support intervention instruction for students. These include monitoring progress across the school year, gathering and analyzing data to match students to interventions, and using data to problem-solve.

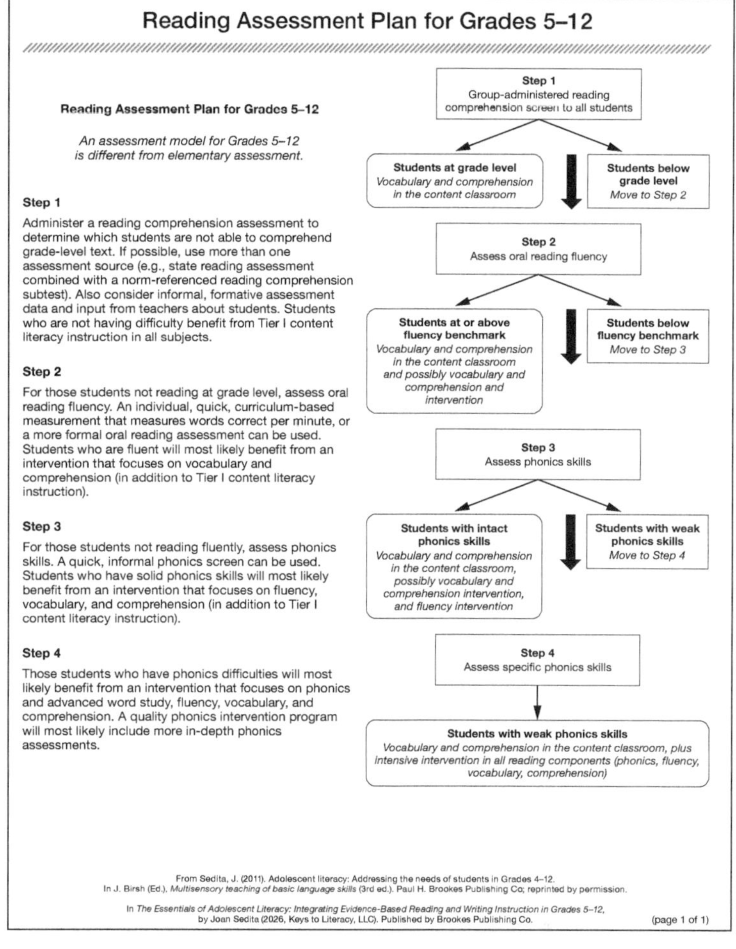
Reading Assessment Plan for Grades 5–12

Reading Assessment Plan for Grades 5–12

An assessment model for Grades 5–12 is different from elementary assessment.

Step 1

Administer a reading comprehension assessment to determine which students are not able to comprehend grade-level text. If possible, use more than one assessment source (e.g., state reading assessment combined with a norm-referenced reading comprehension subtest). Also consider informal, formative assessment data and input from teachers about students. Students who are not having difficulty benefit from Tier I content literacy instruction in all subjects.

Step 2

For those students not reading at grade level, assess oral reading fluency. An individual, quick, curriculum-based measurement that measures words correct per minute, or a more formal oral reading assessment can be used. Students who are fluent will most likely benefit from an intervention that focuses on vocabulary and comprehension (in addition to Tier I content literacy instruction).

Step 3

For those students not reading fluently, assess phonics skills. A quick, informal phonics screen can be used. Students who have solid phonics skills will most likely benefit from an intervention that focuses on fluency, vocabulary, and comprehension (in addition to Tier I content literacy instruction).

Step 4

Those students who have phonics difficulties will most likely benefit from an intervention that focuses on phonics and advanced word study, fluency, vocabulary, and comprehension. A quality phonics intervention program will most likely include more in-depth phonics assessments.

From Sedita, J. (2011). Adolescent literacy: Addressing the needs of students in Grades 4–12. In J. Birsh (Ed.), *Multisensory teaching of basic language skills* (3rd ed.). Paul H. Brookes Publishing Co; reprinted by permission.

Figure 10.3. Reading Assessment Plan for Grades 5–12. (Reprinted by permission from Sedita, J. [2011]. Adolescent literacy: Addressing the needs of students in grades 4–12. In J. Birsh [Ed.], *Multisensory teaching of basic language skills* (3rd ed.). Paul H. Brookes Publishing Co., and Sedita, J. [2024d]. *Reading assessment model, grades 5–12.* Keys to Literacy. https://keystoliteracy.com/blog/reading-assessment-model-grades-5-12/)

Monitoring Progress Across the School Year

As noted previously, reading assessment in Grades 5–12 for proficient readers should consist of screening assessment at the start of the year and summative assessment at the end. The assumption is that proficient readers will continue to develop grade-level reading ability as content teachers integrate vocabulary, comprehension, and writing instruction into content learning, providing practice using content-based text. If teachers suspect some students are not making sufficient gains in reading skills, they can use informal progress monitoring or another screening assessment to determine if these students might need some supplemental support.

The assessment plan for students who do not have grade-level reading skills is different. After a screening assessment identifies students who are not reading at grade level, a diagnostic assessment should follow to determine a plan for intervention instruction. Progress monitoring assessments should be administered by intervention educators on a frequent basis to monitor if that instruction is sufficient or if a different instructional support plan needs to be created.

A combination of CBMs (short, simple procedures that measures achievement of a specific skill) and informal formative assessments can be used to monitor progress in different reading skills, such as the following.

Phonics

Phonics CBM tasks ask students to read nonsense words that follow phonics patterns. The student can say the sounds or blend together the sounds in the nonsense word. Another option is to use phonics progress monitoring assessments that are built into intervention programs designed to teach phonics to older readers.

Passage Fluency

CBMs can be used with grade-level passages that students read out loud. WCPM and rate of accuracy are calculated.

Comprehension

A *maze* CBM measures silent reading comprehension. It consists of cloze passages in which every seventh word is deleted and replaced with a multiple-choice item consisting of the correct word and two distractors. Despite being a relatively short task, CBM maze tasks are highly correlated with reading comprehension ability. Formative assessments that ask students to read and answer questions about text can also be used.

Vocabulary

It is not easy to measure short-term gains in vocabulary growth. However, formative assessments that ask students to provide definitions or label visuals related to texts they are reading can be used to gauge if students are learning new words.

Students With Reading Difficulty:
Questions for Analyzing Assessment Data

1. *What is the student's reading comprehension (i.e., how far below grade level)?*

Language Comprehension

2. If a grade-level reading passage were read aloud to the student, how likely is it that the student would comprehend the passage?
3. Does a lack of grade-level vocabulary knowledge appear to be contributing to difficulty with reading comprehension? What is the basis for this assessment?
4. Does the complexity of the language used in the text (including sentence length and complexity) seem to contribute to difficulty with reading comprehension? What is the basis for this assessment?

Word Reading (Decoding) and Fluency

5. Does the student fluently read grade-level text? What is the basis for this assessment?
6. If the student has difficulty with fluent reading, would improving fluency and accuracy in word reading likely result in better comprehension?
7. If the student is not reading fluently, does the student require instruction to develop word reading skills? Should this instruction focus on advanced word study (e.g., reading multisyllabic words) or on a more basic phonics level? What is the basis for this assessment?
8. If the student has difficulty with basic word reading skills, is there evidence that instruction should include phonemic awareness? What is the basis for this opinion?

From Sedita, J. (2020a). *Adolescent reading intervention.* Keys to Literacy; reprinted by permission.

Figure 10.4. Questions to support data analysis. (From Sedita, J. [2020a]. *Adolescent reading intervention.* Keys to Literacy; reprinted by permission.)

Analyzing Assessment Data: Matching Students to Interventions

As noted previously, there is no "one-size-fits-all" intervention that works for all students. Assessment data needs to be analyzed to determine the unique needs of individual learners and the most appropriate intervention. The set of eight questions in Figure 10.4 can be used to guide the analysis of reading assessment data (Sedita, 2020a). (A full-size, reproducible copy of the questions is available with the downloads for this chapter.)

The first question focuses on assessing whether the student can read and comprehend grade-level text, and if not, how far below grade level the student is. Once the first question is answered, Questions 2–8 focus on both language comprehension and word reading (decoding) as identified in the Simple View of Reading (Gough & Tunmer,1986). Responses to these questions will help determine whether the student needs intervention focused primarily on reading comprehension, foundational skills, or both.

In addition, the following questions can be used to help shape recommendations for the student's intervention plan:

- Is additional diagnostic assessment needed to answer Questions 1–8?
- What additional information about this student would be helpful for developing an intervention plan?

- What is the student's reading profile (overview of strengths and areas of deficit)?
- What recommendations can be made for differentiation, scaffolds, and accommodations to benefit the student during Tier 1 classroom instruction?
- What recommendations are there for intervention instruction for this student? Should it be Tier 2 supplemental, or Tier 3 intensive intervention?
- What should be the focus of the intervention instruction, including recommended intervention programs?
- What is the recommended intensity and duration of instruction?

A student assessment and intervention profile such as the example in Figure 10.5 can be used to summarize individual student assessment results and recommendations for intervention, organized around the components of reading. (A full-size, reproducible copy of this profile form is available with the downloads for this chapter.)

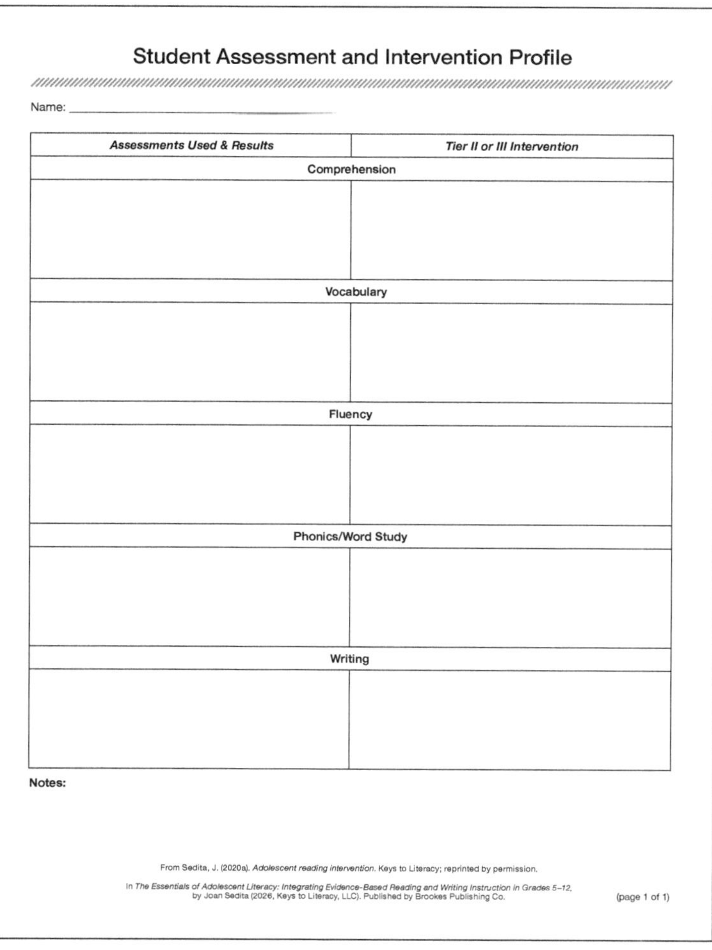

Student Assessment and Intervention Profile

Name: ______________________

Assessments Used & Results	*Tier II or III Intervention*
Comprehension	
Vocabulary	
Fluency	
Phonics/Word Study	
Writing	

Notes:

From Sedita, J. (2020a). *Adolescent reading intervention.* Keys to Literacy; reprinted by permission.

In *The Essentials of Adolescent Literacy: Integrating Evidence-Based Reading and Writing Instruction in Grades 5–12,* by Joan Sedita (2026, Keys to Literacy, LLC). Published by Brookes Publishing Co. (page 1 of 1)

Figure 10.5. Student Assessment and Intervention Profile. (From Sedita, J. [2020a]. *Adolescent reading intervention.* Keys to Literacy; reprinted by permission.)

Analyzing Data at the School, Grade, and Student Levels

To use assessment data effectively, schools need to develop a data-analysis framework. This includes identifying the screening, diagnostic, progress monitoring, and summative assessments that will be used; developing procedures for storing and sharing assessment data; and developing a data review and problem-solving protocol for analyzing data. Figure 10.6 includes questions to consider when developing a data-analysis framework.

Data analysis to determine which students need intervention and the type of intervention may be done by a school or grade-level problem-solving team, or by an individual intervention educator. View the different levels of data analysis in Table 10.1.

A Problem-Solving Process

A problem-solving process can be used when analyzing data at the student, classroom, or grade levels. The steps in this process, included in the graphic in Figure 10.7, are as follows:

Step 1, Problem Identification: *What is the problem?*

Step 2, Problem Analysis: *Why is the problem occurring?*

Step 3, Develop & Implement a Plan: *What instruction will we use?*

Step 4, Evaluate & Revise the Plan: *Is the instruction working?*

Problem-Solving at the Student Level

How can this problem-solving model be applied to instruction for a student having difficulty with reading? Screening and diagnostic reading assessments provide information for the first and

Data Analysis Framework Questions

Data Collection

- What screening, diagnostic, progress monitoring, and summative assessments will be used?
- Who will administer these assessments, and how often?
- Who will collect, tabulate, and enter data into a system so the data may be interpreted and used?

Data Interpretation and Recommendations

- Who will interpret assessment data and make instructional recommendations?
- Who will track results from progress monitoring assessments to determine if intervention instruction is working?

Data Use

- Who will make decisions about changes in instruction?
- Who will communicate information to parents and caregivers, teachers, and students?
- Who will address curricular and instructional changes?

Figure 10.6. Data analysis framework questions. (*Source:* Sedita, 2004b.)

Table 10.1. Levels of data analysis

Data level	Who	Role, purpose
District reading data	District team	• To establish and maintain an assessment data management system • To provide overall information needed to make district-based curriculum and professional development decisions
School, grade, or class reading data	School team, grade-level team	• To inform decisions about building-level curriculum and professional development • To inform core reading instruction decisions at the classroom level
Individual student data	Intervention educator, problem-solving team	• To determine if supplemental or intensive intervention instruction is needed • To inform decisions about modifying intervention instruction

From Sedita, J. (2024b). *Keys to beginning reading*. Keys to Literacy; reprinted by permission.

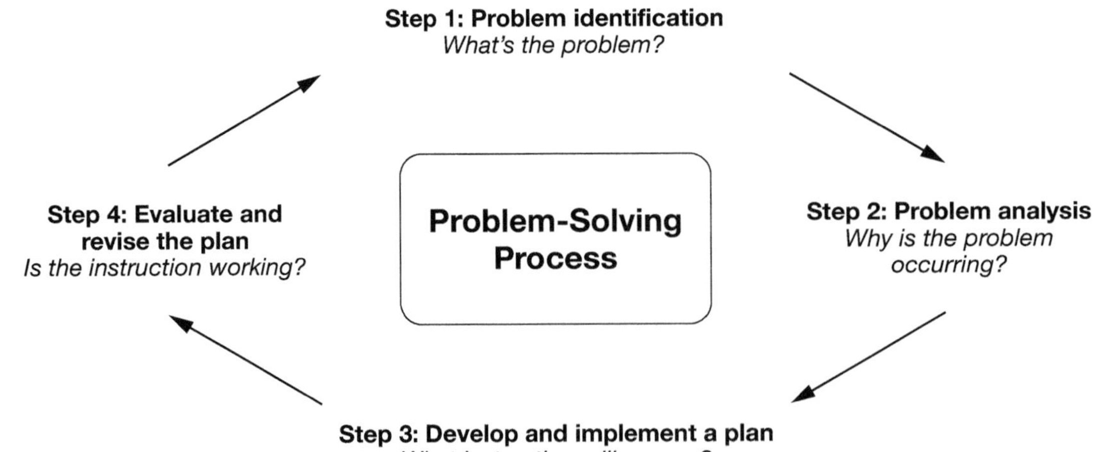

Figure 10.7. Steps in the problem-solving process.

second steps. For example, a screening assessment might identify that a student is not able to read and comprehend grade-level text, and further diagnostic assessment might determine that the problem has to do with insufficient word reading and fluency skills. At the third step, an instructional intervention plan might be developed that includes supplemental phonics and fluency instruction. After trying the intervention, progress monitoring assessment is used at the fourth step to evaluate the intervention plan, that is, is the intervention working? If it is, the intervention should continue. If it is not, the intervention plan should be modified. The cycle continues throughout the school year.

Problem Solving at the Grade or Classroom Level

How can this problem-solving model be applied to curriculum and instruction decisions at the grade or classroom level? Review the details of a problem-solving protocol that can be used by school or grade-level teams, shown in Figure 10.8 (North Carolina Department of Public Instruction, n.d.).

Grade- or Classroom-Level Problem-Solving Protocol

1. **Identify a Problem**
    1. The team uses screening results and other assessment data gathered for a grade level or a specific classroom.
    2. The team identifies the performance of students across a grade or in a specific classroom and notes how many students are below grade-level benchmark.
    3. The team determines if there are common or different deficits among students below benchmark.
    4. If there is not a single common deficit, the team sorts students into subgroups with similar problems.
2. **Develop a Hypothesis for a Subgroup**
    1. The team brainstorms reasons for the problem occurring in a subgroup.
    2. The team determines if the problem is caused by environmental or neurobiological factors affecting the students, the curriculum, and/or the instructional practices being used.
    3. The team finalizes one or more hypotheses about the cause of the problem.
3. **Develop an Action Plan**
    1. The team sets SMART goals that address the problem (Specific, Measurable, Attainable, Realistic, Timely).
    2. The team selects instructional strategies and curriculum materials that directly address the deficit areas of the subgroup.
    3. The teachers who are working with the subgroup agree to implement the instructional strategies.
4. **Evaluate and Revise the Action Plan**
    1. The team reviews progress on the instructional practices at regular intervals to determine if they are having the desired impact.
    2. Informal and formal progress monitoring assessments are used for this purpose.
    3. If sufficient progress is not being made, the team adjusts the action plan.

Figure 10.8. Grade- or classroom-level problem-solving protocol. (*Source:* North Carolina Department of Public Instruction, n.d.)

SUMMARY

This chapter addresses the role of assessment in guiding decisions about reading interventions. It describes four types of assessments—screening, diagnostic, progress monitoring, and summative—and explains the purpose of each. A secondary reading instruction model is presented, outlining the paths of both proficient and non-proficient readers. In addition, a screening and diagnostic assessment model is discussed for identifying non-proficient readers and determining which components of reading instruction should be the focus of intervention. The chapter also highlights the use of progress monitoring assessments to evaluate whether intervention instruction is effective. It concludes with recommendations for analyzing assessment data, including the application of a problem-solving model.

REFLECTION QUESTIONS

1. Summarize why assessment is essential for making intervention instruction decisions.
2. Briefly describe the purpose of each type of assessment: screening, diagnostic, progress monitoring, and summative.
3. Using the screening and diagnostic assessment plan for Grades 5–12 presented in the chapter, explain why there are fewer students being assessed at each stage.
4. What is the benefit of using progress monitoring assessment on a frequent basis for students receiving intervention instruction?
5. Briefly summarize the steps in a problem-solving process that can be used to analyze data at the student, classroom, or grade levels.

Student Assessment and Intervention Profile

Name: ______________________________

Assessments Used & Results	*Tier II or III Intervention*
Comprehension	
Vocabulary	
Fluency	
Phonics/Word Study	
Writing	

Notes:

From Sedita, J. (2020a). *Adolescent reading intervention*. Keys to Literacy; reprinted by permission.

Students With Reading Difficulty: Questions for Analyzing Assessment Data

1. *What is the student's reading comprehension (i.e., how far below grade level)?*

Language Comprehension

2. If a grade-level reading passage were read aloud to the student, how likely is it that the student would comprehend the passage?
3. Does a lack of grade-level vocabulary knowledge appear to be contributing to difficulty with reading comprehension? What is the basis for this assessment?
4. Does the complexity of the language used in the text (including sentence length and complexity) seem to contribute to difficulty with reading comprehension? What is the basis for this assessment?

Word Reading (Decoding) and Fluency

5. Does the student fluently read grade-level text? What is the basis for this assessment?
6. If the student has difficulty with fluent reading, would improving fluency and accuracy in word reading likely result in better comprehension?
7. If the student is not reading fluently, does the student require instruction to develop word reading skills? Should this instruction focus on advanced word study (e.g., reading multisyllabic words) or on a more basic phonics level? What is the basis for this assessment?
8. If the student has difficulty with basic word reading skills, is there evidence that instruction should include phonemic awareness? What is the basis for this opinion?

Reading Assessment Plan for Grades 5–12

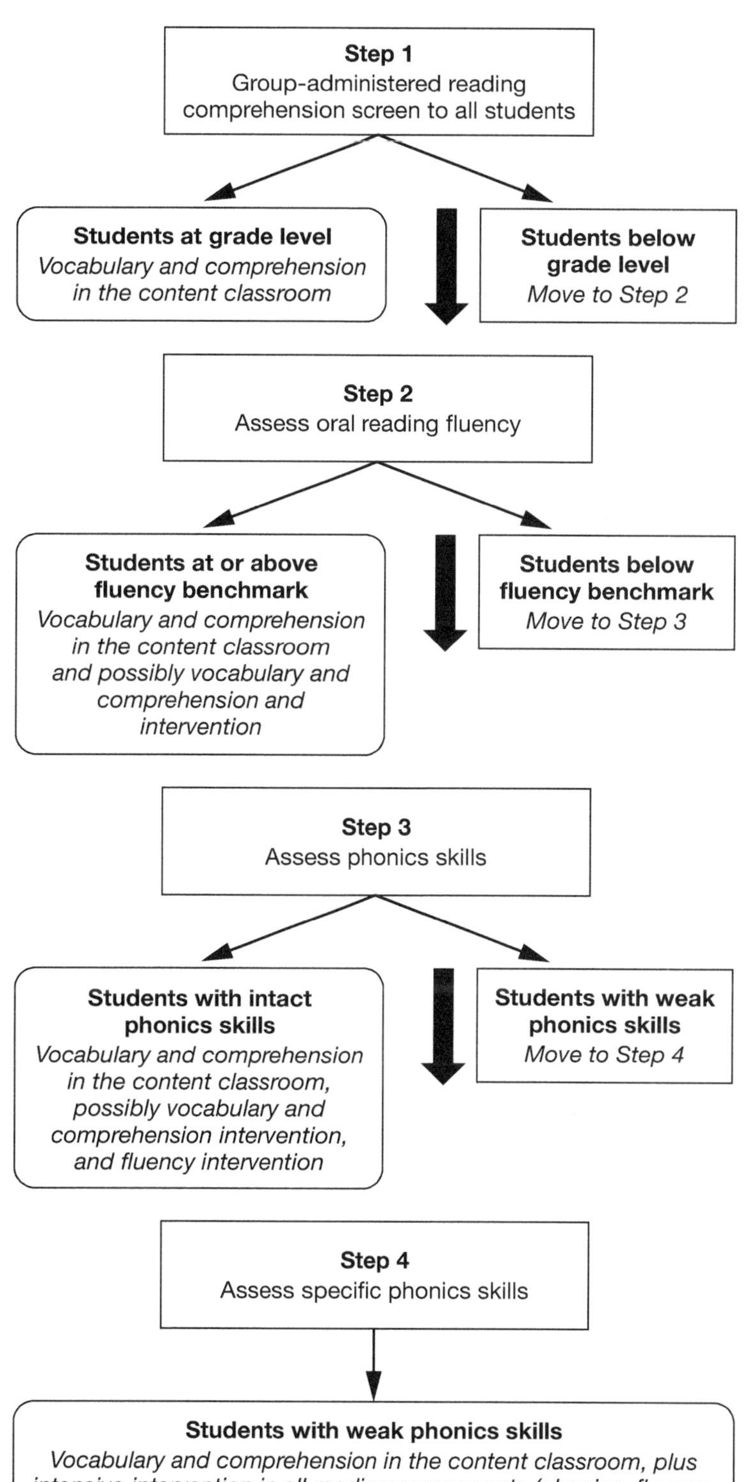

Reading Assessment Plan for Grades 5–12

An assessment model for Grades 5–12 is different from elementary assessment.

Step 1

Administer a reading comprehension assessment to determine which students are not able to comprehend grade-level text. If possible, use more than one assessment source (e.g., state reading assessment combined with a norm-referenced reading comprehension subtest). Also consider informal, formative assessment data and input from teachers about students. Students who are not having difficulty benefit from Tier I content literacy instruction in all subjects.

Step 2

For those students not reading at grade level, assess oral reading fluency. An individual, quick, curriculum-based measurement that measures words correct per minute, or a more formal oral reading assessment can be used. Students who are fluent will most likely benefit from an intervention that focuses on vocabulary and comprehension (in addition to Tier I content literacy instruction).

Step 3

For those students not reading fluently, assess phonics skills. A quick, informal phonics screen can be used. Students who have solid phonics skills will most likely benefit from an intervention that focuses on fluency, vocabulary, and comprehension (in addition to Tier I content literacy instruction).

Step 4

Those students who have phonics difficulties will most likely benefit from an intervention that focuses on phonics and advanced word study, fluency, vocabulary, and comprehension. A quality phonics intervention program will most likely include more in-depth phonics assessments.

Integrating Literacy Instruction in All Subjects

Students in middle and high school are expected to acquire, process, and retain content knowledge through reading, writing, and participating in discussions. Content-area teachers play an important role in teaching students how to apply both general content literacy skills and disciplinary-specific literacy strategies. Effective Tier 1 content literacy instruction should incorporate vocabulary development, comprehension strategies, writing tasks, and structured discussion activities across all subjects.

The following list of questions can guide the integration of literacy activities into unit plans and daily lessons in any subject. Classroom teachers can also refer to the list of content literacy activities in Figure A.1, organized by chapter, to identify vocabulary, comprehension, text structure, writing, and discussion activities that can be embedded into instruction.

- What is the topic for the unit of study?
- What texts and other sources will be used to support learning of this content?
- What literacy skills, knowledge, and abilities are unique to this discipline and should be emphasized with students?
- Are there any unique and particularly challenging aspects of the vocabulary, language, or structure of the text?
- Which instructional suggestions from this book can be integrated into the unit plan for:
    - Vocabulary
    - Comprehension
    - Text structure
    - Writing
    - Discussion
- What scaffolds can be provided to help students read and understand the text, complete writing tasks, or participate in discussions?

Content Literacy Activities

Vocabulary (Chapter 3)

- Previewing words
- Selecting and teaching targeted words in-depth
- Making connections among words: semantic mapping, categorizing, semantic feature analysis
- Using context and knowledge of meaningful word parts to determine the meaning of unfamiliar words
- Fostering word consciousness

Comprehension (Chapter 4)

- Activating and developing background knowledge before reading
- Using a Top-Down Topic Web
- Identifying main ideas
- Taking Two-Column Notes
- Summarizing
- Generating and answering questions

Text Structure (Chapter 5)

- Analyzing text types and structure
- Comprehending complex sentences

Writing (Chapter 6)

- Using Quick Writes to support content learning
- Analyzing informational and argument text in writing
- Responding to narrative text in writing
- Writing responses to prompts

Discussion (Chapter 7)

- Using classroom discussion to support learning

Figure A.1. Content literacy activities.

References

Adams, M. J. (1990). *Beginning to read: Thinking and learning about print.* MIT Press.

Adams, M. J. (2009). The challenge of advanced texts: The interdependence of reading and learning. In E. H. Hiebert (Ed.), *Reading more, reading better: Are American students reading enough of the right stuff?* (pp. 163–189). Guilford Press.

Akhondi, M., Malayeri, F. A., & Samad, A. A. (2011). How to teach expository text structure to facilitate reading comprehension. *The Reading Teacher, 64*(5).

Anderson, R. C., & Nagy, W. E. (1992). The vocabulary conundrum. *American Educator, 16*(4).

Anderson, V., & Hidi, S. (1988–1989). Teaching students to summarize. *Educational Leadership, 46,* 26–28.

Archer, A. L., & Hughes, C. A. (2010). *Explicit instruction: Effective and efficient teaching.* Guilford Press.

August, D., & Shanahan, T. (Eds.). (2006). *Developing literacy in second-language learners: Report of the National Literacy Panel on Language-Minority Children and Youth.* Lawrence Erlbaum Associates.

Baayen, R. H., Piepenbrock, R., & Gulikers, L. (1995). *The CELEX Lexical Database* [CD-ROM]. Linguistic Data Consortium, University of Pennsylvania.

Baddeley, A. D. (2012). Working memory: Theories, models, and controversies. *Annual Review of Psychology, 63.*

Baker, S., Lesaux, N., Jayanthi, M., Dimino, J., Proctor, C. P., Morris, J., Gersten, R., Haymond, K., Kieffer, M. J., Linan-Thompson, S., & Newman-Gonchar, R. (2014). *Teaching academic content and literacy to English learners in elementary and middle school* (NCEE 2014-4012). National Center for Education Evaluation and Regional Assistance (NCEE), Institute of Education Sciences, U.S. Department of Education.

Baldwin, R. S., Ford, J. C., & Readance, J. E. (1981). Teaching word connotations: An alternative strategy. *Reading World, 21,* 103–108.

Bangert-Downs, R. L., Kulik, C. C., Kulik, J. A., & Morgan, M. (1991). The instructional effects of feedback in test-like events. *Review of Educational Research, 61*(2), 213–238.

Barth, A. E., & Thomas, C. N. (2022). Scaffolding inference-making for adolescents with disabilities that impact reading. *Intervention in School and Clinic, 57*(4), 219–226. https://doi.org/10.1177/10534512211024929

Baumann, J. F., Kame'enui, E. J., & Ash, G. (2003). Research on vocabulary instruction: Voltaire redux. In J. Flood, D. Lapp, J. R. Squire, & J. Jenson (Eds.), *Handbook of research on teaching the English Language Arts* (2nd ed.; pp. 752–785). Lawrence Erlbaum Associates.

Baumann, J., Manyak, P., Blachowicz, C., Graves, M., Arner, J., Bates, A., Cieply, C., Davis, J., Peterson, H., & Olejnik, S. (2012, October 21). A multi-faceted, comprehensive vocabulary instruction program. *Vocabulogic.* http://vocablog-plc.blogspot.com/2012/10/mcvip-multi-faceted-comprehensive.html

Beck, I. L., & McKeown, M. G. (1991). Conditions of vocabulary acquisition. In R. Barr, M. Kamil, P. Mosenthal, & P. D. Pearson (Eds.), *Handbook of reading research* (Vol. 2, pp. 789–814). Longman.

Beck, I. L., McKeown, M. G., & Kucan, L. (2002). *Bringing words to life.* Guilford Press.

Beck, I. L., McKeown, M. G., & Kucan, L. (2008). *Creating robust vocabulary: Frequently asked questions and extended examples.* Guilford Press.

Berninger, V. W., & Winn, W. D. (2006). Implications of advancements in brain research and technology for writing development, writing instruction, and educational evolution. In C. A. MacArthur, S. Graham, & J. Fitzgerald (Eds.), *Handbook of writing research* (pp. 96–114). Guilford Press.

Bhattacharya, A., & Ehri, L. C. (2004). Graphosyllabic analysis helps struggling readers read and spell words. *Journal of Learning Disabilities, 37*(4), 331–348.

Biancarosa, C., & Snow, C. E. (2006). *Reading Next—A vision for action and research in middle and high school literacy: A report to Carnegie Corporation of New York* (2nd ed.). Alliance for Excellent Education.

Billmeyer, R., & Barton, M. L. (1998). *Teaching reading in the content areas: If not me then who?* Mid-continent Regional Educational Laboratory.

Blachowicz, C. L. Z., & Fisher, P. (2004). Keep the "fun" in fundamental. In J. F. Baumann & E. J. Kame'enui (Eds.), *Vocabulary instruction: Research to practice* (pp. 218–237). Guilford Press.

Blachowicz, C. L. Z., Fisher, P., Ogle, D., & Wats Taffe, S. (2013). *Teaching academic vocabulary K–8: Effective practices across the curriculum.* Guilford Press.

Blevins, W. (1998). *Phonics from A to Z.* Scholastic.

Bloom, B. (1956). *Taxonomy of educational objectives, Handbook 1: The cognitive domain.* David McKay.

Boardman, A. G., Roberts, G., Vaughn, S., Wexler, J., Murray, C. S., & Kosanovich, M. (2008). *Effective instruction for adolescent struggling readers: A practice brief.* RMC Research Corporation, Center on Instruction. https://files.eric.ed.gov/fulltext/ED521836.pdf

Boardman, A. G., Klingner, J. K., Buckley, P., Annamma, S., & Lasser, C. J. (2015). The efficacy of collaborative strategic reading in middle school science and social studies classes. *Reading and Writing: An Interdisciplinary Journal, 28*(9).

Boscolo, P., & Gelati, C. (2007). Best practices in promoting motivation for writing. In S. Graham, C. A. MacArthur, & J. Fitzgerald (Eds.), *Best practices in writing instruction* (pp. 202–221). Guilford Press.

Bower, G. H., & Morrow, D. G. (1990). Mental models in narrative comprehension. *Science, 247,* 44–48.

Bowers, P. N., & Cooke, G. (2012). Morphology and the Common Core: Building students' understanding of the written word. *Perspectives on Language and Literacy, 31,* 31–35.

Brozo, W. G., Moorman, G., Meyer, C., & Stewart, T. (2013). Content area reading and disciplinary literacy: A case for the radical center. *Journal of Adolescent & Adult Literacy, 56*(5).

Bruise, L. (2020). A study of the preparedness and efficacy of middle school teachers to teach literacy skills. *Doctor of Education Dissertations, 14.* https://digitalcommons.gardner-webb.edu/education-dissertations/14

Burke, P., & Kennedy, E. (2024). Why do you think that? Exploring disciplinary literacy in elementary science, history, and visual arts. *The Reading Teacher, 77*(5).

Burnford, S. (1961). *The incredible journey.* Hodder & Stoughton.

Butler, S., Urrutia, K., Buenger, A., Gonzalez, N., Hunt, M., & Eisenhart, C. (2010). *A review of the current research on vocabulary instruction.* National Reading Technical Assistance Center.

Cain, K. (2016). Reading comprehension development and difficulties: An overview. *Perspectives on Language and Literacy, 42*(2).

Cardenas-Hagan, E. (2020). *Literacy foundations for English learners: A comprehensive guide to evidence-based instruction.* Paul H. Brookes Publishing Co.

Carlisle, J. F. (2007). Fostering morphological processing, vocabulary development, and reading comprehension. In R. K. Wagner, A. E. Muse, & K. R. Tannenbaum (Eds.), *Vocabulary acquisition: Implications for reading comprehension* (pp. 78–103). Guilford Press.

Carnegie Council on Advancing Adolescent Literacy. (2010). *Time to act: An agenda for advancing adolescent literacy for college and career success.* Carnegie Corporation of New York. https://eric.ed.gov/?id=ED535318

Cartwright, K. B. (2015). *Executive skills and reading comprehension.* Guilford Press.

Cashin, W. E. (2011). *Effective classroom discussions.* The IDEA Center, Kansas State University. https://www.ideaedu.org/idea_papers/effective-classroom-discussions/

Catts, H. W. (2021–2022). Rethinking how to promote reading comprehension. *American Educator, Winter 2021–2022.*

Catts, H. W., Adlof, S. M., & Weismer, S. E. (2006). Language deficits in poor comprehenders: A case for the simple view of reading. *Journal of Speech, Language, and Hearing Research, 49*(2), 278–293. https://doi.org/10.1044/1092-4388(2006/022)

Catts, H. W., Compton, D., Tomblin, J. B., & Bridges, M. S. (2012). Prevalence and nature of late-emerging poor readers. *Journal of Educational Psychology, 104*(1), 166–181. https://psycnet.apa.org/doiLanding?doi=10.1037%2Fa0025323

CEEDAR Center. (n.d.). *Disciplinary literacy.* Professional development course offered by the University of Florida. https://ceedar.education.ufl.edu/cems/disciplinaryliteracy/#:~:text=Disciplinary%20literacy%20refers%20to%20the,Shanahan%20%26%20Shanahan%2C%202012

Center for Teaching Excellence. (n.d.). *Reading, writing & discussion.* The University of Kansas. https://cte.ku.edu/reading-writing-discussion

Cervetti, G., & Hiebert, E. H. (2019). Knowledge at the center of English language arts instruction. *The Reading Teacher, 72*(4).

Chall, J. S. (1983). *Stages of reading development.* McGraw-Hill.

Chall, J. S. (1996). *Learning to read: The great debate* (3rd ed.). Harcourt Brace College Publishers.

Chall, J. S., & Jacobs, V. A. (1983). Writing and reading in the elementary grades: Developmental trends among low SES children. *Language Arts, 60,* 617–626.

Chapman, M. (2006). Preschool through elementary writing. In P. Smagorinsky (Ed.), *Research on composition: Multiple perspectives on two decades of change* (pp. 15–47). Teachers College Press.

Coker, D. (2007). Writing instruction for young children. In S. Graham, C. A. MacArthur, & J. Fitzgerald (Eds.), *Best practices in writing instruction* (pp. 101–118). Guilford Press.

Copeland, M. (2005). *Socratic circles.* Stenhouse Publishers.

Cowen, C. (2016a). *How widespread is dyslexia?* International Dyslexia Association. https://dyslexiaida.org/how-widespread-is-dyslexia/

Cowen, C. (2016b). *What is structured literacy?* International Dyslexia Society. https://dyslexiaida.org/what-is-structured-literacy/

Donovan, C. A., & Smolkin, L. B. (2006). Children's understanding of genre and writing development. In C. A. MacArthur, S. Graham, & J. Fitzgerald (Eds.), *Handbook of writing research* (pp. 131–143). Guilford Press.

Duke, N. K., Ward, A. E., & Pearson, P. D. (2021). The science of reading comprehension. *The Reading Teacher, 74*(6), 574–586.

Ebbers, S. M. (2006). *Linking the language: A cross-disciplinary vocabulary approach* [Self-published].

Echevarria, J., Vogt, M. E., & Short, D. (2016). *Making content comprehensible for English learners: The SIOP model* (5th ed.). Pearson.

Edwards, C. E., Font, G., Baumann, J. F., & Boland, E. (2004). Unlocking word meanings: Strategies and guidelines for teaching morphemic and contextual analysis. In J. F. Baumann & E. J. Kame'enui (Eds.), *Vocabulary instruction: Research to practice* (pp. 159–176). Guilford Press.

Elbro, C., & Buch-Iversen, I. (2013). Activation of background knowledge for inference making: Effects on reading comprehension. *Scientific Studies of Reading, 17,* 435–452. https://psycnet.apa.org/record/2013-36328-005

Elleman, A. M. (2017). Examining the impact of inference instruction on the literal and inferential comprehension of skilled and less skilled readers: A meta-analytic review. *Journal of Educational Psychology, 109,* 761–781. https://psycnet.apa.org/record/2017-06326-001

Eslami, H. (2014). The effect of syntactic simplicity and complexity on the readability of the text. *Journal of Language Teaching and Research, 5*(5).

Evidence for Learning. (2020). *Improving literacy in secondary schools.* https://evidenceforlearning.org.au/education-evidence/guidance-reports/improving-literacy-in-secondary-schools

Faggella-Luby, M. N., Graner, P. S., Deshler, D. D., & Drew, S. V. (2012). Building a house on sand: Why disciplinary literacy is not sufficient to replace general strategies for adolescent learners who struggle. *Top Language Disorders, 32*(1), 69–84.

Fang, Z. (2012). Language correlates of disciplinary literacy. *Topics in Language Disorders, 32*(1), 19–34. https://doi.org/10.1097/tld.0b013e31824501de

Filderman, M. J., Austin, C. R., & Swanson, E. A. (2021). A meta-analysis of the effects of reading comprehension interventions on the reading comprehension outcomes of struggling readers in third through 12th grades. *Exceptional Children, 88*(2).

Fisher, D. B., & Frey, N. (2007). *Checking for understanding.* ASCD.

Foorman, B., Beyler, N., Borradaile, K., Coyne, M., Denton, C. A., Dimino, J., Furgeson, J., Hayes, L., Henke, J., Justice, L., Keating, B., Lewis, W., Sattar, S., Streke, A., Wagner, R., & Wissel, S. (2016). *Foundational skills to support reading for understanding in kindergarten through 3rd grade* (NCEE 2016-4008). National Center for Education Evaluation and Regional Assistance (NCEE), Institute of Education Sciences, U.S. Department of Education. http://whatworks.ed.gov

Frantz, R. S., Starr, L. E., & Bailey, A. L. (2015). Syntactic complexity as an aspect of text complexity. *Educational Researcher, 44*(7), 387–393.

Frayer, D. A., Frederick, W. D., & Klausmeier, H. J. (1969). *A schema for testing the level of concept mastery* (Technical Report No. 16). University of Wisconsin, Wisconsin Center for Education Research.

Gambrell, L. B., & Bales, R. J. (1986). Mental imagery and the comprehension monitoring performance of fourth and fifth grade poor readers. *Reading Research Quarterly, 21,* 454–464.

Goldenberg, C., & Cardenas-Hagan, E. (2023, January/February). Literacy research on English learners: Past, present, and future. *The Reading League Journal.*

Goldman, S., Britt, M., Brown, W., Cribb, G., George, M., Greenleaf, C., Lee, C., Shanahan, C., & Project READI. (2016). Disciplinary literacies and learning for understanding: A conceptual framework for disciplinary literacy. *Educational Psychology, 51*(2), 219–241.

Goodwin, A. P., & Ahn, S. (2013). A meta-analysis of morphological interventions in English: Effects on literacy outcomes for school-age children. *Scientific Studies of Reading, 17,* 257–285. https://doi.org/10.1080/10888438.2012.689791

Gough, P. B., & Tunmer, W. E. (1986). Decoding, reading, and reading disability. *Remedial and Special Education, 7*(1), 6–10.

Graham, S. (2019). Changing how writing is taught. *Review of Research in Education, 43.*

Graham, S. (2020). The sciences of reading and writing must become more fully integrated. *Reading Research Quarterly, 55*(Suppl. 1).

Graham, S., Bollinger, A., Booth Olson, C., D'Aoust, C., MacArthur, C., McCutchen, D., & Olinghouse, N. (2012). *Teaching elementary school students to be effective writers: A practice guide* (NCEE 2012-4058). National Center for Education Evaluation and Regional Assistance, Institute of Education Sciences, U.S. Department of Education.

Graham, S., Bruch, J., Fitzgerald, J., Friedrich, L., Furgeson, J., Greene, K., Kim, J., Lyskawa, J., Olson, C. B., & Smither Wulsin, C. (2016). *Teaching secondary students to write effectively* (NCEE 2017-4002). National Center for Education Evaluation and Regional Assistance (NCEE), Institute of Education Sciences, U.S. Department of Education.

Graham, S., & Harris, K. R. (2007). Best practices in teaching planning. In S. Graham, C. A. MacArthur, & J. Fitzgerald (Eds.), *Best practices in writing instruction* (pp. 119–140). Guilford Press.

Graham, S., Harris, K. R., & Santangelo, T. (2015). Research-based writing practices and the Common Core: Meta-analysis and meta-synthesis. *The Elementary School Journal, 115*(4), 498–522.

Graham, S., & Hebert, M. A. (2010). *Writing to read: Evidence for how writing can improve reading. A Carnegie Corporation Time to Act Report.* Alliance for Excellent Education.

Graham, S., Kim, Y. S., Cao, Y., Lee, W., Tae, T., Collins, P., Cho, M., Moon, Y., Chung, H. Q., & Olson, C. B. (2023). A meta-analysis of writing treatments for students in grades 6–12. *Journal of Educational Psychology, 115*(7). https://psycnet.apa.org/doiLanding?doi=10.1037%2Fedu0000819

Graham, S., & Perin, D. (2007). *Writing next: Effective strategies to improve the writing of adolescents in middle and high schools—A report to Carnegie Corporation of New York.* Alliance for Excellent Education.

Graham, S., & Santangelo, T. (2014). Does spelling instruction make students better speller, readers, and writers? A meta-analytic review. *Reading and Writing,* 1–41.

Graves, M. F. (2006). *The vocabulary book.* Teachers College Press.

Graves, M. F., Bauman, J. F., Blachowicz, C., & Manyak, P. C. (2014). *Words, words everywhere! But which ones do I teach? The Reading Teacher 67*(5).

Graves, M. F. (2016). *The vocabulary book: Learning and instruction* (2nd ed.). Teachers College Press.

Guthrie, J. T., & Davis, M. H. (2003). Motivating struggling readers in middle school through an engagement model of classroom practice. *Reading and Writing Quarterly, 19,* 59–85.

Guthrie, J. T., & Humenick, N. M. (2004). Motivating students to read: Evidence for classroom practices that increase reading motivation and achievement. In P. McCardle & V. Chhabra (Eds.), *The voice of evidence in reading research* (pp. 213–234). Paul H. Brookes Publishing Co.

Hall, C. S. (2016). Inference instruction for struggling readers: A synthesis of intervention research. *Educational Psychology Review, 28*(1), 1–22. https://doi.org/10.1007/s10648-014-9295-x

Hamilton, L., Halverson, R., Jackson, S., Mandinach, E., Supovitz, J., & Wayman, J. (2009). *Using student achievement data to support instructional decision making* (NCEE 2009-4067). National Center for Education Evaluation and Regional Assistance, Institute of Education Sciences, U.S. Department of Education. https://nces.ed.gov/pubsearch/pubsinfo.asp?pubid=20094067

Hanna, P. R., Hodges, P. R., Hanna, J. L., & Rudolph, E. H. (1966). *Phoneme-grapheme correspondences as cues to spelling improvement.* U.S. Office of Education. https://files.eric.ed.gov/fulltext/ED128835.pdf

Hasbrouck, J., & Hougen, M. C. (2012). Fluency instruction. In M. C. Hougen & S. M. Smartt (Eds.), *Fundamentals of literacy instruction and assessment, Pre-K–6* (pp. 147–172). Paul H. Brookes Publishing Co.

Hasbrouck, J., & Tindal, G. (2017). *An update to compiled ORF norms* (Technical Report No. 1702). Behavioral Research and Teaching, University of Oregon.

Hayes, J. R. (1996). A new framework for understanding cognition and affect in writing. In C. M. Levy & S. Ransdell (Eds.), *The science of writing: Theories, methods, individual differences and applications* (pp. 1–27). Lawrence Erlbaum Associates.

Hayes, J. R. (2004). What triggers revision? In L. Allal, L. Chanquoy, & P. Largy (Eds.), *Studies in writing: Vol. 13. Revision: Cognitive and instructional processes* (pp. 9–20). Kluwer.

Hayes, J. R., & Flower, L. (1980). Identifying the organization of writing processes. In L. W. Gregg & E. R. Steinberg (Eds.), *Cognitive processes in writing: An interdisciplinary approach* (pp. 3–30). Lawrence Erlbaum Associates.

Heimlich, J. E., & Pittelman, S. D. (1986). *Semantic mapping: Classroom applications.* International Reading Association.

Heller, R., & Greenleaf, C. L. (2007). *Literacy instruction in the content areas: Getting to the core of middle and high school improvement.* Alliance for Excellent Education. https://www.carnegie.org/publications/literacy-instruction-in-the-content-areas-getting-to-the-core-of-middle-and-high-school-improvement/

Hemingway, E. (1952). *The old man and the sea.* Charles Scribner's Sons.

Hidi, S., & Boscolo, P. (2006). Motivation and writing. In C. A. MacArthur, S. Graham, & J. Fitzgerald (Eds.), *Handbook of writing research* (pp. 144–157. Guilford Press.

Hirsch, E. D. (1996). The effects of weakness in oral language on reading comprehension growth. Cited in Torgesen, J. (2004). *Current issues in assessment and intervention for younger and older students.* Paper presented at the NASP workshop.

Hirsch, E. D. (2006). Building knowledge: The case for bringing content into the language arts block and for a knowledge-rich curriculum core for all children. *American Educator, 30*(1), 4–9. American Federation of Teachers.

History.com. (n.d.). *American women in World War II.* https://www.history.com/topics/world-war-ii/american-women-in-world-war-ii-1

Ho, A. H., & Guthrie, J. T. (2013). Patterns of association among multiple motivations and aspects of achievement in reading. *Reading Psychology, 34*(2). https://www.tandfonline.com/doi/abs/10.1080/02702711.2011.596255

Hollie, S. (2017). *Culturally and linguistically responsive teaching and learning: Classroom practices for student success, grades K–12.* Shell Education.

Houghton Mifflin Harcourt. (n.d.). *Ancient Greece.* https://athomemiddleschool.com/static/11.1_ancient_greece-dd46980066408f6435a44d73dd0d237a.pdf

Hwang, H., Cabell, S. Q., & Joyner, R. E. (2021). Effects of integrated literacy and content-area instruction on vocabulary and comprehension in the elementary years: A Meta-analysis. *Scientific Studies of Reading, 26*(3), 223–249. https://doi.org/10.1080/10888438.2021.1954005

Hwang, H., & Duke, N. K. (2020). Content counts and motivation matters: Reading comprehension in third-grade students who are English learners. *AERA Open, 6*(1).

IDEA. (1975). Individuals with Disabilities Education Act, Part B, Subpart A, Section 300.8 (c) (10). https://sites.ed.gov/idea/regs/b/a/300.8/c/10

Individuals with Disabilities Education Improvement Act (IDEA) of 2004, PL 108-446, 20 U.S.C. §§ 1400 *et seq.*

International Literacy Association. (2017). *Content area and disciplinary literacy: Strategies and frameworks* (Literacy leadership brief).

International Literacy Association. (2019). *Literacy leadership brief: Teaching and assessing spelling.* https://www.literacyworldwide.org/docs/default-source/where-we-stand/ila-teaching-and-assessing-spelling.pdf

Jennings, T., & Haynes, C. W. (2002). *From talking to writing: Strategies for scaffolding expository expression.* Landmark Outreach Program.

Jetton, T., & Shanahan, C. (2012). *Adolescent literacy in the academic disciplines: General principles and practical strategies.* Guilford Press.

Johnston, W. R. (2020). *Writing instruction in U.S. classrooms: Diverging perspectives for teachers across content areas.* RAND American Educator Panels. https://www.rand.org/pubs/research_reports/RR2575z14.html?utm_source=chatgpt.com

Jones, S. M., LaRusso, M., Kim, J., Yeon Kim, H., Selman, R., Uccelli, P., Barnes, S. P., Donovan, S., & Snow, C. (2019). Experimental effects of word generation on vocabulary, academic language, perspective taking, and reading comprehension in high-poverty schools. *Journal of Research on Educational Effectiveness, 12*(3), 448–483. https://doi.org/10.1080/19345747.2019.1615155

Kamil, M. L., Borman, G. D., Dole, J., Kral, C. C., Salinger, T., & Torgesen, J. (2008). *Improving adolescent literacy: Effective classroom and intervention practices: A Practice Guide* (NCEE #2008-4027). National Center for Education Evaluation and Regional Assistance, Institute of Education Sciences, U.S. Department of Education. http://ies.ed.gov/ncee/wwc

Katzir, T., Markovich, V., Tesler, E., & Shany, M. (2018). Self-regulation and reading comprehension: Self-perceptions, self-evaluations, and effective strategies for intervention. In L. Meltzer (Ed.), *Executive function in education: From theory to practice* (pp. 125–140). Guilford Press.

Kearns, D. M. (2015). How elementary-age children read polysyllabic polymorphemic words. *Journal of Educational Psychology, 107,* 364–390. https://psycnet.apa.org/record/2014-44659-001

Kilpatrick, D. A. (2015). *Assessing, preventing, and overcoming reading difficulties.* John Wiley & Sons.

Kintsch, W. (1998). *Comprehension: A paradigm for cognition.* Cambridge University Press.

Klingner, J. K., & Vaughn, S. (2004). Strategies for struggling second language learners. In T. L. Jetton & J. A. Dole (Eds.), *Adolescent literacy: Research to practice* (pp. 85–102). Guilford Press.

Klingner, J. K., Vaughn, S., Dimino, J., Schumm, J. S., & Bryant, D. (2001). *Collaborative strategic reading.* Sopris West.

Knight-McKenna, M. (2008). Syllable types: A strategy for reading multisyllabic words. *Teaching Exceptional Children, 40*(4), 32–37.

Kuhn, M. R., & Stahl, S. A. (1998). Teaching children to learn word meanings from context: A synthesis and some questions. *Journal of Literacy Research, 30*(2), 119–138.

Laflamme, J. G. (1997). The effect of the multiple exposure vocabulary method and the target reading/writing strategy on test scores. *Journal of Adolescent and Adult Literacy, 40*(5), 372–381.

Lee, C. D., & Spratley, A. (2010). *Reading in the disciplines: The challenges of adolescent literacy.* Carnegie Corporation of New York.

Lee, J., & Yoon, S.Y. (2017). The effects of repeated reading on reading fluency for students with reading disabilities. *Journal of Learning Disabilities, 50*(2). http://doi.org/10.1177/0022219415605194

Lehr, F., Osborn, J., & Hiebert, E. H. (2004). *A focus on vocabulary.* Pacific Resources for Education and Learning.

Lent, R. (2017). *Disciplinary literacy: A shift that makes sense.* ASCD Express, February 23, 2017. ASCD.

Lyon, R. G. (1998). Reading is not a natural process. *Educational Leadership, 55*(6), 14–18.

MacArthur, C. A. (2007). Best practices in teaching evaluation and revision. In S. Graham, C. A. MacArthur, & J. Fitzgerald (Eds.), *Best practices in writing instruction* (pp. 141–162). Guilford Press.

Manoli, P., & Papadopoulou, M. (2012). Graphic organizers as a reading strategy: Research findings and issues. *Creative Education, 3*(03). https://www.researchgate.net/publication/267842739_Graphic_Organizers_as_a_Reading_Strategy_Research_Findings_and_Issues

Maria, K. (1990). *Reading comprehension instruction: Issues and strategies.* York Press.

McKeown, M. G., & Beck, I. L. (2004). Direct and rich vocabulary instruction. In J. F. Baumann & E. J. Kame'enui (Eds.), *Vocabulary instruction: Research to practice* (pp. 13–27). Guilford Press.

The Meadows Center. (2016). *10 key reading practices for all middle and high schools with strong evidence of effectiveness from high-quality research.* The University of Texas at Austin, The Meadows Center for Preventing Educational Risk.

The Meadows Center for Preventing Risk. (2018). *Inference instruction to support reading comprehension for upper-elementary and middle grades students with learning disabilities.*

Meltzer, L. (2010). *Executive function in the classroom.* Guilford Press.

Meltzer, L. (2018). Creating strategic classrooms and schools: Embedding executive function strategies in the curriculum. In L. Meltzer (Ed.), *Executive function in education: From theory to practice* (pp. 193–206). Guilford Press.

Michaels, S., & O'Connor, C. (2012). *Talk Science primer.* Talk Science Project (TERC).

Michaels, S., O'Connor, C., Hall, M. W., & Resnick, L. B. (2013). *Accountable Talk source-book: For classroom conversation that works.* University of Pittsburgh Institute for Learning. https://www.fredhutch.org/content/dam/www/about-us/education/sep/2020/AT-Sourcebook.pdf

Michaels, S., O'Connor, C., & Resnick, L. B. (2008). Deliberative discourse idealized and realized: Accountable Talk in the classroom and in civic life. *Studies in Philosophy and Education, 27*(4), 283–297.

Moats, L. C. (n.d.-b). *Teaching spelling using a structured literacy approach* [PowerPoint presentation]. Sponsored by CORE (Consortium for Reaching Excellence in Education). https://www.corelearn.com/wp-content/uploads/2020/09/teaching-spelling-using-a-structured-literacy-approach-webinar.pdf

Moats, L. C. (2000). *Speech to print.* Paul H. Brookes Publishing Co.

Moats, L. C. (2015). *Teaching adolescents to read: It's not too late.* Voyager Sopris Learning. https://louisamoats.com/wp-content/uploads/2022/10/2022_Moats_Teaching_Adolescents_Article.pdf

Moats, L. (2019). *Teaching spelling: An opportunity to unveil the logic of language.* Resource Directory, Houston Branch of the International Dyslexia Association.

Moats, L. C., & Sedita, J. (2004). *Writing: A road to reading comprehension. LETRS (Language Essentials for Teachers of Reading and Spelling) Module 11.* Sopris West.

Moje, E. B. (2006). Motivating texts, motivating contexts, motivating adolescents: An examination of the role of motivation in adolescent literacy practices and development. *Perspectives, 32,* 10–14.

Moody, S., Hu, X., Kuo, L., Jouhar, M., Xu, Z., & Lee, S. (2018). Vocabulary instruction: A critical analysis of theories, research, and practice. *Education Sciences, 8,* 180. https://doi.org/10.3390/educsci8040180

Murphy, P. K., Wilkinson, I. A. G., Soter, A. O., & Firetto, C. M. (2016). Instruction based on discussion. In R. E. Mayer & P. A. Alexander (Eds.), *Handbook of research on learning and instruction* (2nd ed., pp. 432–459). Routledge.

Murphy, P. K., Wilkinson, I. A. G., Soter, A. O., Hennessey, M. N., & Alexander, J. F. (2009). Examining the effects of classroom discussion on students' high-level comprehension of text: A meta-analysis. *Journal of Educational Psychology, 101,* 740–764.

Murray, C. S., Wexler, J., Vaughn, S., Roberts, G., Klingler-Tackett, K., Boardman, A. G., Miller, D., & Kosanovich, M. (2010). *Effective instruction for adolescent struggling readers: Professional development module–Second Edition.* Center on Instruction. RMC Research Corporation.

Murray, D. (2004). *The craft of revision* (5th ed.). Heinle.

Nagy, W. E., & Anderson, R. C. (1984). How many words are there in printed school English? *Reading Research Quarterly, 19,* 304–330.

Nagy, W. E., & Scott, J. A. (2000). Vocabulary processes. In M. L. Kamil, P. Mosenthal, P. D. Pearson, & R. Barr (Eds.), *Handbook of reading research* (Vol. 3; pp. 269–284). Lawrence Erlbaum Associates.

Nagy, W. E., & Townsend, D. (2012). Words as tools: Learning academic vocabulary as language acquisition. *Reading Research Quarterly, 47*(1), 91–108.

National Assessment of Educational Progress. (2024). *NAEP reading assessment.* https://www.nationsreportcard.gov/highlights/reading/2024/

National Council for Social Studies. (2017). *College, Career, and Civic Life (C3) Framework for Social Studies State Standards: Guidance for enhancing the rigor of K–12 civics, economics, geography, and history.* https://www.socialstudies.org/standards/c3

National Geographic. (n.d.). *The science and art of meteorology.* https://education.nationalgeographic.org/resource/science-art-meteorology/

National Governors Association Center for Best Practices & Council of Chief State School Officers (NGA/CCSSO). (2010). *Common Core State Standards, Appendix A.*

National Institute for Literacy. (2001). *Put reading first: The research building blocks for teaching children to read.* National Institute for Literacy.

National Institute for Literacy. (2007). *What content-area teachers should know about adolescent literacy.* National Institute of Child Health and Human Development.

National Reading Panel. (2000). *Report of the National Reading Panel: Teaching children to read: An evidence-based assessment of the scientific research literature on reading and its implications for reading instruction* (NIH Publication No. 00-4769). U.S. Government Printing Office.

Next Generation Science Standards. (2013). *Appendix M: Connections to the Common Core Standards for Literacy in Science and Technical Subjects.* https://www.nextgenscience.org/sites/default/files/Appendix%20M%20Connections%20to%20the%20CCSS%20for%20Literacy_061213.pdf

Nice, M., Wijecumar, K., Lambright, K., & Stack, A. (2024). Promoting inference generation: Using questioning and strategy instruction to support upper elementary students. *The Reading Teacher, 78*(2).

North Carolina Department of Public Instruction. (n.d.). *Tier one data analysis, multi-tiered system of support.*

Oakhill, J., & Cain, K. (2016). Supporting reading comprehension development: From research to practice. *Perspectives on Language and Literacy, 42*(2).

Oakhill, J., Cain, K., & Elbro, C. (2015). *Understanding and teaching reading comprehension.* Routledge.

O'Connor, C. (2012, August 15). *Academically productive talk: Discussion within word generation* [PowerPoint presentation]. Baltimore Summer Institute.

Palinscar, A. S., & Brown, A. (1984). Reciprocal teaching of comprehension-fostering and comprehension-monitoring activities. *Cognition and Instruction, 1,* 117–175. https://doi.org/10.1207/s1532690xci0102_1

Paris, S. G., & Hamilton, E. E. (2009). The development of children's reading comprehension. In S. E. Israel & G. G. Duffy (Eds.), *Handbook of research on reading comprehension* (pp. 1–31). Routledge.

Patrick, D. J., & Acosta, K. (2024). *Evidence-based reading instruction for adolescents in grades 6–12* (Document No. IC-13b). University of Florida, Collaboration for Effective Educator, Development, Accountability, and Reform Center. http://ceedar.education.ufl.edu/tools/innovation-configurations/

Pauk, W. (1997). *How to study in college* (7th ed.). Houghton Mifflin.

Pearson, P. D., Palinscar, A. S., Biancarosa, G., & Bernman, A. I. (Eds.). (2020). *Reaping the rewards of the Reading for Understanding Initiative.* National Academy of Education. https://naeducation.org/reaping-the-rewards-of-reading-for-understanding-initiative/

Pearson, P. E., & Gallagher, M. C. (1983). The instruction of reading comprehension. *Contemporary Educational Psychology, 8,* 317–344. https://files.eric.ed.gov/fulltext/ED236565.pdf

Peng, P., Wang, W., Filderman, M. J., Zhang, W., & Lin, L. (2023, May 20). The active ingredient in reading comprehension strategy intervention for struggling readers: A Bayesian Network meta-analysis. *Review of Educational Research.* Advance online publication.

Pennsylvania Training and Technical Assistance Network (PATTAN). (2021). *Reading big words.* https://www.youtube.com/watch?v=7D-pKMT9WLY

Petscher, Y., Cabell, S. Q., Catts, H. W., Compton, D. L., Foorman, B. R., Hart, S. A., Lonigan, C. J., Phillips, B. M., Schatschneider, C., Steacy, L. M., Terry, N. P., & Wagner, R. K. (2020). How the science of reading informs 21st century education. *Reading Research Quarterly, 55*(Suppl. 1), S267–S282. https://doi.org/10.1002/rrq.352 3

Portalupi, J., & Fletcher, R. (2001). *Nonfiction craft lessons: Teaching informational writing K–8.* Stenhouse.

Pressley, M., Disney, L., & Anderson, K. (2007). Landmark vocabulary instructional research and the vocabulary instructional research that makes sense now. In R. K. Wagner, A. E. Muse, & K. R. Tannenbaum (Eds.), *Vocabulary acquisition: Implications for reading comprehension* (pp. 205–232). Guilford Press.

Pritchard, R. J., & Honeycutt, R. L. (2007). Best practices in implementing a process approach to teaching writing. In S. Graham, C. A. MacArthur, & J. Fitzgerald (Eds.), *Best practices in writing instruction* (pp. 28–49). Guilford Press.

Proctor, C. P., Silverman, R. D., Harring, J. R., Jones, R. L., & Hartranft, A. M. (2020). Teaching bilingual learners: Effects of a language-based reading intervention on academic language and reading comprehension in grades 4 and 5. *Reading Research Quarterly, 55*(1), 95–122. https://doi.org/10.1002/rrq.258

Ramsden, N. (2013). *Mini Matrix Maker.* http://www.neilramsden.co.uk/spelling/matrix/

Rankin, J., & Weise, C. (2022). *World History since 1500: An open and free textbook.* East Tennessee State University. https://dc.etsu.edu/etsu-oer/13/

Raphael, T. E., & Au, K. H. (2011). QAR: Enhancing comprehension and test taking across grades and content areas. *The Reading Teacher, 59,* 206–221. https://doi.org/10.1598/RT.59.3.5

The Reading League. (n.d.). *What is the science of reading?* https://www.thereadingleague.org/what-is-the-science-of-reading/

Reed, D. K. (2019). *Effective literacy lesson: Making and evaluating predictions to support comprehension.* Iowa Reading Research Center. https://irrc.education.uiowa.edu/blog/2019/09/effective-literacy-lesson-making-and-evaluating-predictions-support-comprehension

Reed, D. K. (2022). Fluency instruction for adolescents: Evidence from research to practice. *Learning Disabilities: A Contemporary Journal, 20*(2).

Regional Educational Laboratory at Florida State University. (2016). *Word analysis strategy.* Institute of Education Sciences. https://www.youtube.com/watch?v=RmKY3RFmajk&list=PLVHqsnePfULo3KA8dspX6558xwZxVr2rB&ubdex=30

Regional Educational Laboratory Northwest. (2024). *Montana ELA standards revision: Brief 5 disciplinary literacy processes and procedures.* Institute of Education Sciences. https://ies.ed.gov/ncee/rel/regions/northwest/pdf/RELNW_MT-OPI-ELA_Brief-5_Disciplinary-Literacy-Processes-and-Procedures.pdf

Resnick, L. B. C., Asterhan, C. S. C., & Clarke, S. N. (2015). Introduction: Talk, learning, and teaching. In: L. B. Resnick, C. S. C. Asterhan, & S. N. Clarke (Eds.), *Socializing intelligence through academic talk and dialogue* (pp. 1–12). AERA.

Resnick, L. B., Asterhan, C. S. C., & Clarke, S. N. (2018). Accountable Talk: Instructional dialogue that builds the mind. *Education Psychology, 29*(7).

Reznitskaya, A., Hsu, J. Y., & Anderson, R. C. (2015). Using inquiry dialogue to promote the development of argument skills: Possibilities, challenges, and new directions. In S. R. Parris & K. Headley (Eds.), *Comprehension instruction: Research-based best practices* (3rd ed., pp. 29–44). Guilford Press.

Saddler, B. (2005). Sentence combining: A sentence-level writing intervention. *The Reading Teacher 58*(5).

Saddler, B. (2012). *Teacher's guide to effective sentence writing.* Guilford Press.

Samuels, S. J. (2002). Reading fluency: Its development and assessment. In *Readings on fluency for "A focus on fluency forum."* Pacific Resources for Education and Learning.

Scammacca, N. K., Roberts, G., & Vaughn, S. (2013). A meta-analysis of interventions for struggling readers in grades 4–12: 1980–2011. *Journal of Learning Disabilities, 48*(4).

Scarborough, H. S. (2001). Connecting early language and literacy to later reading (dis)abilities: Evidence, theory, and practice. In S. Neuman & D. Dickinson (Eds.), *Handbook for research in early literacy* (pp. 97–110). Guilford Press.

Schneider, J. (2013). Remembrance of things past: A history of the Socratic method in the United States. *Curriculum Inquiry, 43*(5), 613–640. https://doi.org/10.1111/curi.12030

Schoenbach, R., & Greenleaf, C. (2009). Fostering adolescents' engaged academic literacy. In L. Christenbury, R. Bomer, & P. Smagorinsky (Eds.), *Handbook of adolescent literacy research* (pp.98–112). Guilford Press.

Scientific Advisory Committee. (2023). *Helping students access complex, knowledge-rich texts.* ASCD. https://ascd.org/blogs/helping-students-access-complex-knowledge-rich-texts

Scott, C. (2004). Syntactic contributions to literacy development. In C. Stone, E. Stillman, B. Ehren, & K. Apel (Eds.), *Handbook of language and literacy* (pp. 340–363). Guilford Press.

Sedita, J. (1989). *Study skills: A Landmark teaching guide.* Landmark Outreach Program.

Sedita, J. (2003). *The key three routine: Comprehension strategy instruction.* Sedita Learning Strategies.

Sedita, J. (2004a). *The comprehension-writing connection.* Sedita Learning Strategies.

Sedita, J. (2004b). *Middle and high school reading achievement: A school-wide approach.* Keys to Literacy.

Sedita, J. (2011). Adolescent literacy: Addressing the needs of students in grades 4–12. In J. Birsh (Ed.), *Multisensory teaching of basic language skills* (3rd ed., pp. 517–547). Paul H. Brookes Publishing Co.

Sedita, J. (2015). *The key comprehension routine.* Keys to Literacy.

Sedita, J. (2019). *The Writing Rope: The strands that are woven into skilled writing.* Keys to Literacy.

Sedita, J. (2020a). *Adolescent reading intervention.* Keys to Literacy.

Sedita, J. (2020b). *Creating a close reading lesson.* Keys to Literacy.

Sedita, J. (2020c). *Keys to adolescent literacy.* Keys to Literacy.

Sedita, J. (2020d). *Keys to content writing* (4th ed.). Keys to Literacy.

Sedita, J. (2020e). *Systematic phonics scope and sequence.* Literacy Lines. Keys to Literacy. https://keystoliteracy.com/blog/systematic-phonics-scope-and-sequence/

Sedita, J. (2023). *The Writing Rope: A framework for explicit writing instruction in all subjects.* Paul H. Brookes Publishing Co.

Sedita, J. (2024a, October 25). *Executive function in reading and writing instruction* [PowerPoint presentation]. International Dyslexia Association annual conference, Dallas, TX, United States.

Sedita, J. (2024b). *In support of main idea and comprehension strategy instruction.* Literacy Lines, Keys to Literacy. https://keystoliteracy.com/blog/in-support-of-main-idea-and-comprehension-strategy-instruction/

Sedita, J. (2024c). *Keys to beginning reading.* Keys to Literacy.

Sedita, J. (2024d). *Reading assessment model, grades 5–12.* Keys to Literacy. https://keystoliteracy.com/blog/reading-assessment-model-grades-5-12/

Sedita, J. (2025). *The key vocabulary routine.* Keys to Literacy

Seidenberg, M. S., Borkenhagen, M. C., & Kearns, D. M. (2020). Lost in translation? Challenges in connecting reading science and educational practice. *Reading Research Quarterly, 55*(Suppl. 1).

Shanahan, C. (2015). *Disciplinary literacy strategies in content area classes.* International Literacy Association. https://www.literacyworldwide.org/get-resources/ila-e-ssentials/8069

Shanahan, T. (2017). *Disciplinary literacy: The basics.* Shanahan on Literacy. https://www.shanahanonliteracy.com/blog/disciplinary-literacy-the-basics

Shanahan, T. (2023, July 22). *Knowledge or comprehension strategies: What should we teach?* Shanahan on Literacy. https://www.shanahanonliteracy.com/blog/knowledge-or-comprehension-strategies-what-should-we-teach

Shanahan, T., Callison, K., Carriere, C., Duke, N. K., Pearson, P. D., Schatschneider, C., & Torgesen, J. (2010). *Improving reading comprehension in kindergarten through 3rd grade: A practice guide* (NCEE 2010-4038). National Center for Education Evaluation and Regional Assistance, Institute of Education Sciences, U.S. Department of Education. https://whatworks.ed.gov/publications/practiceguides

Shanahan, T., Fisher, D., & Frey, N. (2012). The challenge of challenging text. *Educational Leadership, 69*(6).

Shanahan, T., & Shanahan, C. (2008). Teaching disciplinary literacy to adolescents: Rethinking content-area literacy. *Harvard Educational Review, 78*(1), 40–59.

Shanahan, T., & Shanahan, C. (2012). What is disciplinary literacy and why does it matter. *Topics in Language Disorders, 32*(1), 7–18.

Short, D., & Fitzsimmons, S. (2007). *Double the work: Challenges and solutions to acquiring language and academic literacy for adolescent English language learners—A report to Carnegie Corporation of New York.* Alliance for Excellent Education. https://www.carnegie.org/publications/double-the-work-challenges-and-solutions-to-acquiring-language-and-academic-literacy-for-adolescent-english-language-learners/

Snow, C. (2002). *Reading for understanding: Toward an R&D program in reading comprehension.* RAND Reading Study Group. RAND.

Snow, C. E., & Kim, Y. (2007). Large problem spaces: The challenge of vocabulary for English language learners. In R. K. Wagner, A. E. Muse, & K. R. Tannenbaum (Eds.), *Vocabulary acquisition: Implications for reading comprehension* (pp. 142–165). Guilford Press.

Snow, C. E., Scarborough, H. S., & Burns, M. S. (1999). What speech-language pathologists need to know about early reading. *Topics in Language Disorders, 20*(1), 48–59.

Snowball, D., & Bolton, F. (1999). *Spelling K–8.* Stenhouse.

Stahl, S. A. (1999). *Vocabulary development.* Brookline Books.

Stahl, S. A., Richek, M. A., & Vandevier, R. J. (1991). Learning meaning vocabulary through listening: A sixth grade replication. In J. Zutell & S. McCormick (Eds.), *Learner factors/teacher factors: Issues in literacy research instruction* (pp. 185–192). The Fortieth Yearbook of the National Reading Conference, Chicago, IL.

Steinbeck, J. (1939). *The grapes of wrath.* Viking Press.

Stevens, E. A., Park, S., & Vaughn, S. (2019). A review of summarizing and main idea interventions for struggling readers in grades 3 through 12: 1978–2016. *Remedial and Special Education, 40*(3).

Stollar, S. (2024, November 15). *Can you spell morphophonemic?* [Webinar]. Keys to Literacy Write Now Conference.

Strategic Education Partnership. (n.d.-a). *About academically productive talk.* SERP Institute. https://www.serpinstitute.org/wordgen-weekly/academically-productive-talk#:~:text=Cathy%20O'Connor%20explains%20that,evidence%20of%20this%20world%2Dwide

Strategic Education Partnership. (n.d.-b). *What do we mean by academically productive talk?* SERP Institute. https://www.academically-productive-talk.org/what-is-academically-productive-talk

Strong, W. (1986). *Creative approaches to sentence combining.* ERIC Clearinghouse on Reading and Communication Skills. National Council of Teachers of English.

Swanson, E., Stevens, E. A., & Wexler, J. (2019). Engaging students with disabilities in text-based discussions. *Teaching Exceptional Children, 51*(4).

Swanson, E., Vaughn, S., & Wexler, J. (2017). Enhancing adolescents' comprehension of text by building vocabulary knowledge. *Exceptional Children, 50(2).* https://files.eric.ed.gov/fulltext/EJ1163963.pdf

Tartaglione, M. (2023). *U.S. high school graduation rates remained stable in 2022–23, NCES reports.* K–12 Dive. https://www.k12dive.com/news/us-high-school-graduation-rates-2022-23-nces/736152/

Thomas, G. (n.d.). *Turning the page to secondary literacy: Tested practices for schools to identify gaps and implement interventions for secondary readers.* Marshall Street. https://www.marshall.org/initiative/marshall-colab/research-to-impact/literacy/

Torgesen, J. K. (2006). *A comprehensive K–3 reading assessment plan: Guidance for school leaders.* RMC Research Corporation, Center on Instruction.

Torgesen, J. K., Houston, D. D., Rissman, L. M., Decker, S. M., Roberts, G., Vaughn, S., Wexler, J., Francis, D. J., Rivera, M. O., & Lesaux, N. (2007). *Academic literacy instruction for adolescents: A guidance document from the Center on Instruction.* RMC Research Corporation, Center on Instruction.

Trupiano, C. (2006). Best classroom practices. In A. Horning & A. Becker (Eds.), *Revision: History, theory, and practices* (pp. 177–196). Parlor Press.

U.S. Department of Education. (2012). *Institute of Education Sciences, National Center for Education Statistics, National Assessment of Educational Progress (NAEP), 2011 writing Assessment.* https://nces.ed.gov/nationsreportcard/

U.S. Department of Education. (2025). *Institute of Education Sciences, National Center for Education Statistics, National Assessment of Educational Progress (NAEP), 2024 Reading Assessment.* https://nces.ed.gov/nationsreportcard/

U.S. Department of Education, National Center for Education Statistics, Common Core of Data (CCD). (2024, September). *State Nonfiscal Survey of Public Elementary/Secondary Education, 1986-87 through 2020-21; State Dropout and Completion Data File, 2005-06 through 2012-13, 2018-19, and 2022-23.*

Varela, K., Arman, H. D., & Yoshimoto, F. K. (2021). How can we make antimalarial medicine faster? *Physical Science Journal for Teens.* https://www.sciencejournalforkids.org/wp-content/uploads/2021/09/artemisinin-2_article.pdf

Vaughn, S., Gersten, R., Dimino, J., Taylor, M. J., Newman-Gonchar, R., Krowka, S., Kieffer, M. J., McKeown, M., Reed, D., Sanchez, M., St. Martin, K., Wexler, J., Morgan, S., Yañez, A., & Jayanthi, M. (2022). *Providing reading interventions for students in Grades 4–9* (WWC 2022007). National Center for Education Evaluation and Regional Assistance (NCEE), Institute of Education Sciences, U.S. Department of Education.

Vaughn, S., & Linan-Thompson, S. (2004). *Research-based methods of reading instruction: Grades K–3.* Association for Supervision and Curriculum Development.

Vaughn, S., Wanzek, J., Murray, C. S., & Roberts, G. (2012). *Intensive interventions for students struggling in reading and mathematics: A practice guide.* RMC Research Corporation, Center on Instruction.

Walberg, H. J. (1999). Productive teaching. In H. C. Waxman & H. J. Walberg (Eds.), *New directions for teaching practice and research* (pp. 75–104). McCutchin Publishing Corporation.

Wallace, T. (2010). *Beginning and intermediate algebra.* http://www.wallace.ccfaculty.org/book/Beginning_and_Intermediate_Algebra.pdf

Wanzek, J., Vaughn, S., Scammacca, N. K., Metz, K., Murrray, C. S., Roberts, G., & Danielson, L. (2013). Extensive reading interventions for students with reading difficulties after Grade 3. *Review of Educational Research, 82*(2).

Weingarten, Z., Bailey, T. R., & Peterson, A. (2018). *User guide for sample reading lessons.* National Center on Intensive Intervention at American Institutes for Research. https://intensiveintervention.org/sites/default/files/User_Guide_Sample_Reading_Lessons-508v2.pdf

Whitaker, B. (2010). *High school dropouts costly for American economy.* CBS Evening News. https://www.cbsnews.com/news/high-school-dropouts-costly-for-american-economy/

White, T. G., Sowell, J., & Yanagihara, A. (1989). Teaching elementary students to use word-part clues. *The Reading Teacher, 42.*

Wiggins, G. (1993). *Assessing student performance: Exploring the purpose and limits of testing.* Jossey-Bass.

Wiggins, G. (2012). Seven keys to effective feedback. *Educational Leadership, 70*(1), 10–16.

Wilkinson, A. G., & Nelson, K. (2020). Role of discussion in reading comprehension. In J. Hattie & E. M. Amderman (Eds.), *Visible learning guide to student achievement: Schools edition* (pp. 231–237). Routledge.

Wilkinson, I., Murphy, K., & Binici, S. (2015). Dialogue-intensive pedagogies for promoting reading comprehension: What we know, what we need to know. In L. Resnick, C. Asterhan, & S. Clarke (Eds.), *Socializing intelligence through academic talk and dialogue* (pp. 37–50). American Educational Research Association. https://www.researchgate.net/publication/292964051_Dialogue-Intensive_Pedagogies_for_Promoting_Reading_Comprehension_What_We_Know_What_We_Need_to_Know/link/56df3fe708aee77a15fcf83b/download?_tp=eyJjb250ZXh0Ijp7ImZpcnN0UGFnZSI6InB1YmxpY2F0aW9uIiwicGFnZSI6InB1YmxpY2F0aW9uIn19

Williams, J. (2017, March 21). Teaching text structures improves reading comprehension. *Psychology Today.* https://www.psychologytoday.com/us/blog/how-to-raise-your-child/201703/teaching-text-structures-improves-reading-comprehension

Willingham, D. T. (2017). *The reading mind: A cognitive approach to understanding how the mind reads.* Jossey-Bass.

Wohlstetter, P., Datnow, A., & Park, V. (2008). Creating a system for data-driven decision-making: Applying the principal-agent framework. *School Effectiveness and School Improvement, 19*(3), 239–259.

Young, C., Paige, D., & Rasinski, T. V. (2022). *Artfully teaching the science of reading.* Routledge.

Yule, G. (1996). *The study of language* (2nd ed.). Cambridge University Press.

Zipoli, R. (2016). Unraveling difficult sentences. *Intervention in School and Clinic, 52*(4), 218–227.

Zwaan, R. A. (2016). Situation models, mental simulations, and abstract concepts in discourse comprehension. *Psychonomic Bulletin & Review, 23*(4), 1028–1034. https://link.springer.com/article/10.3758/s13423-015-0864-x

Index

Bold page numbers indicate tables; *italic* page numbers indicate figures.